How to access your on-line resources

Kaplan Financial students will have a MyKaplan account and these extra resources will be available to you online. You do not need to register again, as this process was completed when you enrolled. If you are having problems accessing online materials, please ask your course administrator.

If you are not studying with Kaplan and did not purchase your book via a Kaplan website, to unlock your extra online resources please go to www.en-gage.co.uk (even if you have set up an account and registered books previously). You will then need to enter the ISBN number (on the title page and back cover) and the unique pass key number contained in the scratch panel below to gain access.

You will also be required to enter additional information during this process to set up or confirm your account details.

If you purchased through the Kaplan Publishing website you will automatically receive an e-mail invitation to register your details and gain access to your content. If you do not receive the e-mail or book content, please contact Kaplan Publishing.

Your code and information

This code can only be used once for the registration of one book online. This registration and your online content will expire when the final sittings for the examinations covered by this book have taken place. Please allow one hour from the time you submit your book details for us to process your request.

Please scratch the film to access your unique code.

Please be aware that this code is case-sensitive and you will need to include the dashes within the passcode, but not when entering the ISBN.

CIMA

Subject P1

Management Accounting

Study Text

Published by: Kaplan Publishing UK

Unit 2 The Business Centre, Molly Millars Lane, Wokingham, Berkshire RG41 2QZ

Acknowledgements

We are grateful to the CIMA for permission to reproduce past examination questions. The answers to CIMA Exams have been prepared by Kaplan Publishing, except in the case of the CIMA November 2010 and subsequent CIMA Exam answers where the official CIMA answers have been reproduced. Questions from past live assessments have been included by kind permission of CIMA,

Notice

British Library Cataloguing in Publication Data

A catalogue record for this book is available from the British Library.

ISBN: 978-1-78740-709-1

Printed and bound in Great Britain

Contents

Introduction

How to use the Materials

These official CIMA learning materials have been carefully designed to make your learning experience as easy as possible and to give you the best chances of success in your objective tests.

The product range contains a number of features to help you in the study process. They include:

- a detailed explanation of all syllabus areas

- extensive 'practical' materials

- generous question practice, together with full solutions.

This Study Text has been designed with the needs of home study and distance learning candidates in mind. Such students require very full coverage of the syllabus topics, and also the facility to undertake extensive question practice. However, the Study Text is also ideal for fully taught courses.

The main body of the text is divided into a number of chapters, each of which is organised on the following pattern:

- **Detailed learning outcomes.** These describe the knowledge expected after your studies of the chapter are complete. You should assimilate these before beginning detailed work on the chapter, so that you can appreciate where your studies are leading.

- **Step-by-step topic coverage.** This is the heart of each chapter, containing detailed explanatory text supported where appropriate by worked examples and exercises. You should work carefully through this section, ensuring that you understand the material being explained and can tackle the examples and exercises successfully. Remember that in many cases knowledge is cumulative: if you fail to digest earlier material thoroughly, you may struggle to understand later chapters.

- **Activities.** Some chapters are illustrated by more practical elements, such as comments and questions designed to stimulate discussion.

- **Question practice.** The text contains three styles of question:

    - Exam-style objective test questions (OTQs).

    - 'Integration' questions – these test your ability to understand topics within a wider context. This is particularly important with calculations where OTQs may focus on just one element but an integration question tackles the full calculation, just as you would be expected to do in the workplace.

- 'Case' style questions – these test your ability to analyse and discuss issues in greater depth, particularly focusing on scenarios that are less clear cut than in the objective tests, and thus provide excellent practice for developing the skills needed for success in the Management Level Case Study Examination.

- **Solutions.** Avoid the temptation merely to 'audit' the solutions provided. It is an illusion to think that this provides the same benefits as you would gain from a serious attempt of your own. However, if you are struggling to get started on a question you should read the introductory guidance provided at the beginning of the solution, where provided, and then make your own attempt before referring back to the full solution.

If you work conscientiously through this Official CIMA Study Text according to the guidelines above you will be giving yourself an excellent chance of success in your objective test. Good luck with your studies!

Quality and accuracy are of the utmost importance to us so if you spot an error in any of our products, please send an email to mykaplanreporting@kaplan.com with full details, or follow the link to the feedback form in MyKaplan.

Our Quality Co-ordinator will work with our technical team to verify the error and take action to ensure it is corrected in future editions.

Icon explanations

 Definition – These sections explain important areas of knowledge which must be understood and reproduced in an assessment environment.

 Key point – Identifies topics which are key to success and are often examined.

 Supplementary reading – These sections will help to provide a deeper understanding of core areas. The supplementary reading is **NOT** optional reading. It is vital to provide you with the breadth of knowledge you will need to address the wide range of topics within your syllabus that could feature in an assessment question. **Reference to this text is vital when self-studying.**

 Test your understanding – Following key points and definitions are exercises which give the opportunity to assess the understanding of these core areas.

 Illustration – To help develop an understanding of particular topics. The illustrative examples are useful in preparing for the Test your understanding exercises.

Exclamation mark – This symbol signifies a topic which can be more difficult to understand. When reviewing these areas, care should be taken.

 New – Identifies topics that are brand new in subjects that build on, and therefore also contain, learning covered in earlier subjects.

 Tutorial note – Included to explain some of the technical points in more detail.

Study technique

Passing exams is partly a matter of intellectual ability, but however accomplished you are in that respect you can improve your chances significantly by the use of appropriate study and revision techniques. In this section we briefly outline some tips for effective study during the earlier stages of your approach to the objective tests. We also mention some techniques that you will find useful at the revision stage.

Planning

To begin with, formal planning is essential to get the best return from the time you spend studying. Estimate how much time in total you are going to need for each subject you are studying. Remember that you need to allow time for revision as well as for initial study of the material.

With your study material before you, decide which chapters you are going to study in each week, and which weeks you will devote to revision and final question practice.

Prepare a written schedule summarising the above and stick to it!

It is essential to know your syllabus. As your studies progress you will become more familiar with how long it takes to cover topics in sufficient depth. Your timetable may need to be adapted to allocate enough time for the whole syllabus.

Students are advised to refer to the examination blueprints (see page P.13 for further information) and the CIMA website, www.cimaglobal.com, to ensure they are up-to-date.

The amount of space allocated to a topic in the Study Text is not a very good guide as to how long it will take you. The syllabus weighting is the better guide as to how long you should spend on a syllabus topic.

Tips for effective studying

(1) Aim to find a quiet and undisturbed location for your study, and plan as far as possible to use the same period of time each day. Getting into a routine helps to avoid wasting time. Make sure that you have all the materials you need before you begin so as to minimise interruptions.

(2) Store all your materials in one place, so that you do not waste time searching for items every time you want to begin studying. If you have to pack everything away after each study period, keep your study materials in a box, or even a suitcase, which will not be disturbed until the next time.

(3) Limit distractions. To make the most effective use of your study periods you should be able to apply total concentration, so turn off all entertainment equipment, set your phones to message mode, and put up your 'do not disturb' sign.

(4) Your timetable will tell you which topic to study. However, before diving in and becoming engrossed in the finer points, make sure you have an overall picture of all the areas that need to be covered by the end of that session. After an hour, allow yourself a short break and move away from your Study Text. With experience, you will learn to assess the pace you need to work at. Each study session should focus on component learning outcomes – the basis for all questions.

(5) Work carefully through a chapter, making notes as you go. When you have covered a suitable amount of material, vary the pattern by attempting a practice question. When you have finished your attempt, make notes of any mistakes you made, or any areas that you failed to cover or covered more briefly. Be aware that all component learning outcomes will be tested in each examination.

(6) Make notes as you study, and discover the techniques that work best for you. Your notes may be in the form of lists, bullet points, diagrams, summaries, 'mind maps', or the written word, but remember that you will need to refer back to them at a later date, so they must be intelligible. If you are on a taught course, make sure you highlight any issues you would like to follow up with your lecturer.

(7) Organise your notes. Make sure that all your notes, calculations etc. can be effectively filed and easily retrieved later.

Progression

There are two elements of progression that we can measure: how quickly students move through individual topics within a subject; and how quickly they move from one course to the next. We know that there is an optimum for both, but it can vary from subject to subject and from student to student. However, using data and our experience of student performance over many years, we can make some generalisations.

A fixed period of study set out at the start of a course with key milestones is important. This can be within a subject, for example 'I will finish this topic by 30 June', or for overall achievement, such as 'I want to be qualified by the end of next year'.

Your qualification is cumulative, as earlier papers provide a foundation for your subsequent studies, so do not allow there to be too big a gap between one subject and another. For example, P1 *Management accounting* builds on your knowledge of costing and decision making from BA2 *Fundamentals of management accounting* and lays the foundations for P2 *Advanced Management accounting* and all strategic papers.

We know that exams encourage techniques that lead to some degree of short term retention, the result being that you will simply forget much of what you have already learned unless it is refreshed (look up Ebbinghaus Forgetting Curve for more details on this). This makes it more difficult as you move from one subject to another: not only will you have to learn the new subject, you will also have to relearn all the underpinning knowledge as well. This is very inefficient and slows down your overall progression which makes it more likely you may not succeed at all.

Also, it is important to realise that the Operational Case Study (OCS) tests knowledge of all subjects within the Operational level. Please note that you will need to return to this P1 material when studying OCS as it forms a significant part of the OCS syllabus content.

In addition, delaying your studies slows your path to qualification which can have negative impacts on your career, postponing the opportunity to apply for higher level positions and therefore higher pay.

You can use the following diagram showing the whole structure of your qualification to help you keep track of your progress. Make sure you seek appropriate advice if you are unsure about your progression through the qualification.

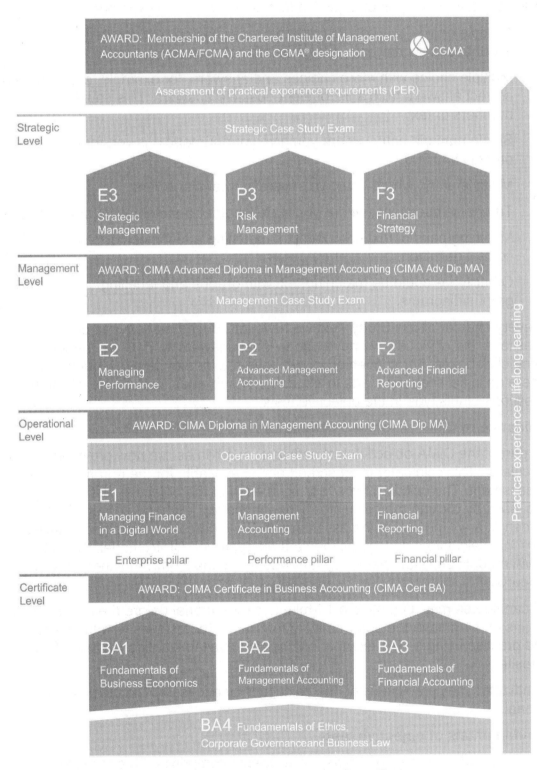

Objective test

Objective test questions require you to choose or provide a response to a question whose correct answer is predetermined.

The most common types of objective test question you will see are:

- Multiple choice, where you have to choose the correct answer(s) from a list of possible answers. This could either be numbers or text.

- Multiple choice with more choices and answers, for example, choosing two correct answers from a list of eight possible answers. This could either be numbers or text.

- Single numeric entry, where you give your numeric answer, for example, profit is $10,000.

- Multiple entry, where you give several numeric answers.

- True/false questions, where you state whether a statement is true or false.

- Matching pairs of text, for example, matching a technical term with the correct definition.

- Other types could be matching text with graphs and labelling graphs/diagrams.

In every chapter of this Study Text we have introduced these types of questions, but obviously we have had to label answers A, B, C etc. rather than using click boxes. For convenience, we have retained quite a few questions where an initial scenario leads to a number of sub-questions. There will be no questions of this type in the objective tests.

Guidance re CIMA on-screen calculator

As part of the CIMA objective test software, candidates are now provided with a calculator. This calculator is on-screen and is available for the duration of the assessment. The calculator is available in each of the objective tests and is accessed by clicking the calculator button in the top left hand corner of the screen at any time during the assessment. Candidates are permitted to utilise personal calculators as long as they are an approved CIMA model. Authorised CIMA models are listed here: https://www.cimaglobal.com/Studying/study-and-resources/.

All candidates must complete a 15-minute exam tutorial before the assessment begins and will have the opportunity to familiarise themselves with the calculator and practise using it. The exam tutorial is also available online via the CIMA website.

Candidates may practise using the calculator by accessing the online exam tutorial.

Fundamentals of objective tests

The objective tests are 90-minute assessments comprising 60 compulsory questions, with one or more parts. There will be no choice and all questions should be attempted. All elements of a question must be answered correctly for the question to be marked correctly. All questions are equally weighted.

CIMA syllabus 2019 – Structure of subjects and learning outcomes

Details regarding the content of the new CIMA syllabus can be located within the CIMA 2019 professional syllabus document.

Each subject within the syllabus is divided into a number of broad syllabus topics. The topics contain one or more lead learning outcomes, related component learning outcomes and indicative knowledge content.

A learning outcome has two main purposes:

(a) To define the skill or ability that a well prepared candidate should be able to exhibit in the examination.

(b) To demonstrate the approach likely to be taken in examination questions.

The learning outcomes are part of a hierarchy of learning objectives. The verbs used at the beginning of each learning outcome relate to a specific learning objective, e.g.

Calculate the break-even point, profit target, margin of safety and profit/volume ratio for a single product or service.

The verb '**calculate**' indicates a level three learning objective. The following tables list the verbs that appear in the syllabus learning outcomes and examination questions.

The examination blueprints and representative task statements

CIMA have also published examination blueprints giving learners clear expectations regarding what is expected of them.

The blueprint is structured as follows:

*   Exam content sections (reflecting the syllabus document)

*   Lead and component outcomes (reflecting the syllabus document)

*   Representative task statements.

A representative task statement is a plain English description of what a CIMA finance professional should know and be able to do.

The content and skill level determine the language and verbs used in the representative task.

CIMA will test up to the level of the task statement in the objective tests (an objective test question on a particular topic could be set at a lower level than the task statement in the blueprint).

The format of the objective test blueprints follows that of the published syllabus for the 2019 CIMA Professional Qualification.

Weightings for content sections are also included in the individual subject blueprints.

CIMA VERB HIERARCHY

CIMA place great importance on the definition of verbs in structuring objective tests. It is therefore crucial that you understand the verbs in order to appreciate the depth and breadth of a topic and the level of skill required. The objective tests will focus on levels one, two and three of the CIMA hierarchy of verbs. However, they will also test levels four and five, especially at the management and strategic levels.

Skill level	Verbs used	Definition
Level 5 **Evaluation** How you are expected to use your learning to evaluate, make decisions or recommendations	Advise	Counsel, inform or notify
	Assess	Evaluate or estimate the nature, ability or quality of
	Evaluate	Appraise or assess the value of
	Recommend	Propose a course of action
	Review	Assess and evaluate in order, to change if necessary
Level 4 **Analysis** How you are expected to analyse the detail of what you have learned	Align	Arrange in an orderly way
	Analyse	Examine in detail the structure of
	Communicate	Share or exchange information
	Compare and contrast	Show the similarities and/or differences between
	Develop	Grow and expand a concept
	Discuss	Examine in detail by argument
	Examine	Inspect thoroughly
	Interpret	Translate into intelligible or familiar terms
	Monitor	Observe and check the progress of
	Prioritise	Place in order of priority or sequence for action
	Produce	Create or bring into existence
Level 3 **Application** How you are expected to apply your knowledge	Apply	Put to practical use
	Calculate	Ascertain or reckon mathematically
	Conduct	Organise and carry out
	Demonstrate	Prove with certainty or exhibit by practical means
	Prepare	Make or get ready for use
	Reconcile	Make or prove consistent/compatible

Skill level	Verbs used	Definition
Level 2 **Comprehension** What you are expected to understand	Describe	Communicate the key features of
	Distinguish	Highlight the differences between
	Explain	Make clear or intelligible/state the meaning or purpose of
	Identify	Recognise, establish or select after consideration
	Illustrate	Use an example to describe or explain something
Level 1 **Knowledge** What you are expected to know	List	Make a list of
	State	Express, fully or clearly, the details/facts of
	Define	Give the exact meaning of
	Outline	Give a summary of

Information concerning formulae and tables will be provided via the CIMA website, www.cimaglobal.com.

SYLLABUS GRIDS

P1: Management Accounting

What the finance function does

Content weighting

Content area		Weighting
A	Cost accounting for decision and control	30%
B	Budgeting and budgetary control	25%
C	Short-term commercial decision-making	30%
D	Risk and uncertainty in the short term	15%
		100%

P1A: Cost accounting for decision and control

This section is about understanding why costing is done and what it is used for. It introduces candidates to the basic building blocks of costing and how to apply them in the costing methods and techniques organisations use. In a fast-changing digital world this understanding is critical and can enable candidates to develop their own ways of calculating costs when existing methods are no longer appropriate. Digital costing is introduced in this section.

Lead outcome	Component outcome	Topics to be covered	Explanatory notes	Study text chapter
1. Distinguish between the different rationales for costing.	a. Define costing b. Distinguish between the rationales for costing	• Inventory valuation • Profit reporting • Cost management and transformation • Decision-making	This seeks to address the following pertinent questions: What are reasons for calculating costs? What types of costs are appropriate for a particular purpose and why?	1 1
2. Apply the main costing concepts to organisations and cost objects.	a. Explain the main costing concepts b. Apply costing concepts to different organisations and cost objects	• Cost elements • Costs structure • Cost behaviour • Cost drivers • Costing applied to different types of organisations • Costing applied to digital cost objects	Examine the basic building blocks of costing and how they apply to different types of organisations and operating contexts (e.g., manufacturing and service sectors). How has the digital world affected the nature of these building blocks of costing?	1, 3 2, 3, 4
3. Apply costing methods to determine the costs for different purposes.	Apply the following: a. Cost accumulation, allocation, apportionment and absorption b. Standard costing c. Variance analysis (without mix and yield variance) d. Activity based costing e. Digital costing	• Trace, classify and allocate costs • Marginal costing • Absorption costing • Price and rate variances • Usage and efficiency variances • Interpretation of variances • Product and service costing using ABC • Advantages of ABC over other costing systems • Features of digital costing	Investigate how costs are traced, classified, accumulated, allocated, apportioned and absorbed to arrive at the costs of a product, service or other cost object. Calculate the costs of products or services using various costing methods. Determine which costing methods are appropriate and why?	2 5 5, 6 3 4

P1B: Budgeting and budgetary control

Taken together, budgeting and budgetary control is one way the finance function enables and shapes how organisations create and preserve value. This section examines the various reasons organisations prepare and use budgets, how the budgets are prepared, the types and sources of data, the technologies used to improve the quality of budgets, how budgets are implemented and the impact on the people who work with the organisation.

Lead outcome	Component outcome	Topics to be covered	Explanatory notes	Study text chapter
1. Distinguish between the different rationales for budgeting.	a. Explain the role of budgets. b. Distinguish between the different rationales for budgeting.	• Planning • Communication • Coordination • Motivation • Control	Why do organisations prepare budgets? In what ways are the different rationales for preparing budgets compatible with each other? How do organisations get the most out the budgeting process?	7 7
2. Prepare budgets.	a. Explain forecasting and its relationship with budgeting. b. Prepare master budgets. c. Conduct what-if analysis in budgeting. d. Describe the technologies available for improving budgeting.	• Time series and trend analysis to forecast sales volumes • Components of master budgets and their interaction with each other • Limiting factors • Stress testing budgets • Big data analytics and budgets • Alternative approaches to budgeting	What is the process by which budgets are prepared? What types of budgets are required by organisations? What data do they use and where do they get the data from? How are those budgets prepared and presented? What technologies are available for improving the quality of the budgets?	8 7 7 7
3. Discuss budgetary control.	Discuss: a. The concept of budgetary control b. Human dimensions of budgeting	• Feedback and feedforward control • Flexed budgets • Target setting and motivation • Controllable and uncontrollable outcomes • Dysfunctional behaviours in budgeting • Ethical considerations in budgeting	What is budgetary control? Describe and discuss how and why the budgetary control system provides feedback and feedforward to the organisation. What are the behavioural impacts of budgetary control and how are they managed?	9 9

P1C: Short-term commercial decision-making

Organisations cannot foresee every opportunity that might arise during their operations, so they need mechanisms by which to identify and take advantage of these opportunities as they arise. The primary objective of this section is to guide candidates in how to do this in the short term through effective decision-making. The finance function supports such decisions (e.g., pricing and product choice) using techniques such as relevant revenue and cost analysis and break- even analysis. Candidates are introduced to these techniques and the concepts that underpin the techniques. They are expected to be able to apply the techniques to support short-term decision-making.

Lead outcome	Component outcome	Topics to be covered	Explanatory notes	Study text chapter
1. Describe the main types of short-term decisions made by organisations.	a. Describe pricing and revenue maximising decisions. b. Describe product decisions.	• Marginal and full cost recovery for pricing decisions • Differences in pricing and revenue maximisation for the short term and long term • Product mix	Describe the types of short-term decisions organisations make and the circumstances that give rise to them. What do these short-term decisions seek to achieve? How important are they to performance of organisations? The emphasis is on both revenue and costs.	2, 10 10
2. Explain the underlying concepts used for short-term decision-making.	a. Explain the objectives of decision-making. b. Explain the underlying concepts of short-term decision-making.	• Implications of commercial decision-making in the short term • Relevant revenues • Relevant costs • Difference with profit reporting	What are the objectives and underlying concepts that are used to guide short-term decision-making and why? Distinguish between those concepts of revenue, costs and information from other concepts.	10 10
3. Apply appropriate techniques to support short-term decisions.	Apply the following to support short-term decision-making: a. Relevant cost analysis b. Break-even analysis c. Product mix decisions with constraints d. Data and technology	• Make or buy decisions • Discontinuation decisions • Multi-product break-even analysis • Use of data and technology to analyse product mix decisions • Ethical considerations in short-term decision-making	Use data (financial and non-financial) and the appropriate concepts and techniques to support decision-making to achieve organisational objectives of value creation and preservation.	10 11 4, 10, 12 12

P1D: Risk and uncertainty in the short term

Budgets and decisions focus on the future. This introduces uncertainties and risks that need to be identified, assessed and managed. The aim of this section is to help candidates identify, assess and manage the risks and uncertainties associated with the short term.

Lead outcome	Component outcome	Topics to be covered	Explanatory notes	Study text chapter
1. Apply basic risk management tools in the short term.	a. Explain nature of risk and uncertainty in short term. b. Apply basic sensitivity analysis to budgeting and short-term decision-making.	• Stress testing • Sensitivity and what-if analysis • Probability distributions • Decision trees	What types of risks and uncertainties do organisations face when preparing and implementing budgets and when making short-term decisions? How are those risks and uncertainties identified, assessed and managed?	13 7, 13

Rationales for costing

Chapter learning objectives

Lead outcome	Component outcome	
A1. Distinguish between the different rationales for costing	(a)	Define costing
	(b)	Distinguish between the rationales for costing
A2. Apply the main costing concepts to organisations and cost objects	(a)	Explain the main costing concepts

1　Chapter overview diagram

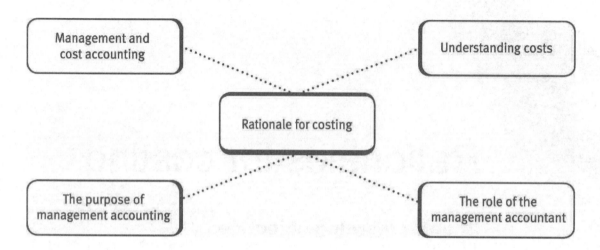

In this chapter we will introduce cost and management accounting. These will be defined and their purpose explained. It will be important that you understand the reasons for calculating costs and how management accounting can play a role in the operations of a business.

For students who have studied at the CIMA Certificate level much of this chapter will be familiar to you.

2　Management and cost accounting

Accountancy involves the measurement, analysing and reporting of financial and non-financial information to help managers, shareholders and other interested parties make decisions about organisations.

As a student of CIMA, a major focus of your studies will be on a part of accountancy called management accounting.

 The *CIMA Terminology* defines **management accounting** as 'the application of the principles of accounting and financial management to create, protect, preserve and increase value for the stakeholders of for-profit and not-for-profit enterprises in the public and private sectors.'

Cost accounting is a sub-set of management accounting. Cost accounting is focused more on calculating the costs of a product or service and extending this into potentially controlling and managing this cost. It means that the focus is often on short-term improvements and decisions.

 The *CIMA Terminology* defines **cost accounting** as 'the gathering of cost information and its attachment to cost objects, the establishment of budgets, standard costs and actual costs of operations, processes, activities or products; and the analysis of variances, profitability or the social use of funds.'

Cost accounting tends to be more useful for operational and tactical decisions.

Operational and tactical decisions

Operational decisions are decisions made mainly by low level managers which focus on day-to-day resource management. It will involve decisions such as where to employ staff, what type and how much staff to use, which machines to employ, what materials to use etc.

Tactical decisions are employed by middle-level managers and are more medium term in scope. It will involve decisions on areas such as staff training and recruitment, changing suppliers, purchasing new machines etc.

Management accounting will take a broader view of the business and take decisions that include a more strategic basis with a longer-term view.

Strategic decisions

Strategic decisions are made by the highest level of management in an organisation. These decisions will consider areas such as whether to launch a new product, whether to expand into new markets or whether to buy other organisations.

Cost accounting mainly focuses on quantitative data such as how much a piece of material costs or how long staff should spend on providing a particular service (i.e. quantitative data is data than can be measured, often in financial terms).

Management accounting will expand this by adding qualitative data such as the impact on customer satisfaction or employee motivation. Qualitative data is much more difficult to measure and quantify.

A comparison to financial accounting

Now that we are clear about the meaning of management accounting we can compare it with another branch of accounting, financial accounting, which you will study as part of your CIMA qualification.

The *CIMA Terminology* defines **financial accounting** as 'classification and recording of the monetary transactions of an entity in accordance with established concepts, principles, accounting standards and legal requirements and their presentation, by means of statements of profit or loss, statements of financial position and cash flow statements, during and at the end of an accounting period'.

Look back at the definition of management accounting and you will see that these two are very different.

Details on the differences

You can see from this that the role of the financial accountant is much more clearly defined and narrower than that of the management accountant. There is also a legal aspect to financial accounting. It is a legal requirement for organisations to produce financial statements which show a true and fair view of their financial position for each accounting period. There is no legal requirement to have management accounting.

Financial accounting is also governed by many rules and regulations whereas there are no rules covering how the management accountant provides information. They will provide whatever is required by their managers in whatever format suits the particular organisation.

Financial accountants deal with historical (past) financial information, while management accountants deal with all types of information (financial and non-financial) both historical and future.

The main role of financial accounting is to produce the statutory financial statements, whereas management accountants provide any information needed by management.

It is important from this to see that the audiences using management and financial accounting information are different. Management accountants provide information internally to managers. The statutory financial reports produced by the financial accountants are available to the public and to anyone who has an interest in the organisation.

The differences can be summarised as follows:

Financial accounting	Management accounting
For external use	For internal use
Statutory requirement	At the discretion of management
Concerned with the production of statutory accounts for an organisation	Concerned with the provision of information to management to aid decision making
Governed by many rules and regulations	Not governed by rules or regulations, can be provided in any format
Deals with historical financial information	Deals with historical and future financial and non-financial information

> **Example 1**
>
> Consider the following statements relating to management accounting:
>
> (i)   The main purpose of management accounting statements is to provide a true and fair view of the financial position of an organisation at the end of an accounting period.
>
> (ii)   Management information may be presented in any format deemed suitable by management.
>
> **Which of the above statements is/are true?**
>
> A   (i) and (ii)
>
> B   (i) only
>
> C   (ii) only
>
> D   neither

3   The purpose of management accounting

While providing information for decision making is clearly key to what management accountants do, their role is usually expanded to include **three** main elements:

- **Planning**
- **Control**
- **Decision making**.

These three purposes of management accounting (planning, control and decision making) form the basis of your Management Accounting subject. Each of these areas will be looked at in detail throughout this text book.

Planning

Planning involves establishing the objectives and goals of an organisation, i.e. what they are trying to achieve, and formulating relevant strategies (long-term actions to improve an organisation's position) that can be used to achieve those objectives and goals.

The management accountant will create **budgets** which explain the potential impacts of different courses of action. These budgets are financial plans of what will occur based on different assumptions.

Budgets are looked at in more detail in the budgeting chapters.

Control

Control is the process of monitoring, measuring, evaluating and correcting actual results to ensure that the organisation's plans are being achieved. Information relating to the actual results of an organisation must be gathered and can be compared to the budget. The differences between the actual and the budgeted results can be calculated and reported to management. These are known as **variances**. This type of information facilitates managers to determine whether the organisation is in or out of control and take corrective action if necessary. We will study variances in detail in later chapters.

Decision making

We have seen already that decision making involves considering information that has been provided and making informed decisions. In most situations, decision making involves making a choice between two or more alternatives. Managers need reliable information to compare the different courses of action available and understand what the consequences might be of choosing each of them.

Managers at different organisational levels will take different type of decisions (operational, tactical and strategic).

Illustration 1

XYZ is a successful pizza restaurant which currently operates a chain of four restaurants, all of which offer the same standard menu.

Consider the following decisions which XYZ may have to make and suggest at what levels of management these decisions would be made.

- Start producing frozen pizzas and selling these through supermarkets.

- Hire a new waiter in one of the restaurants.

- Decide on the pricing of the dishes on the standard menu.

- Open a new restaurant.

Solution

- Starting production and sales of frozen pizzas is a fundamental change to what the company currently do and involves entering a new market. This would therefore be a **strategic** decision.

- Hiring a new waiter would be an **operational** decision as it involves a day to day decision which should be able to be made at a lower level.

- Deciding on the pricing is likely to be a **tactical** decision. In general, the strategic decisions decide on which markets in which to operate and tactical decisions will decide on how to operate within these markets. Pricing would come under this remit.

- Opening a new restaurant is a more difficult one. In this case a decision to expand the number of restaurants would likely be a **strategic** decision. In some much larger organisations this type of decision would be made considered a tactical decision. However given that XYZ only has four restaurants, then the decision to open a fifth would likely be made by the senior managers.

4 The management accountant

At this point it is worth looking in more detail at the various roles management accountants play in organisations and how this has changed over the years.

The whole of the accountancy profession is changing, and this is especially true for the management accountant.

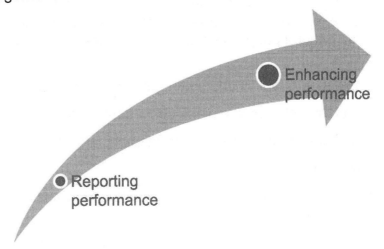

The traditional management accountant was largely involved in reporting business results to management, but this is no longer the case. Management accountants today are seen as **value-adding business partners** and are expected to not only forecast the future of the business, but to assist in delivering this future by identifying opportunities for enhancing organisational performance. The following table summarises the changing role of the management accountant:

In the past: reporting performance	In modern organisations: enhancing performance
Reporting business results to management	Translating business results into a variety of information to aid planning, control and decision making.
Working in isolation of other functions.	Working alongside business managers as mentors, advisors and drivers of performance.
Separate business function.	Integral part of the business, providing a variety of information to management.
Not part of the senior management team.	Management accountants often hold senior positions in the organisation.

CIMA's definition of the role of the management accountant

The work of the Chartered Management Accountant (produced by CIMA):

Chartered management accountants help organisations establish viable strategies and convert them into profit (in a commercial context) or into value for money (in a not-for-profit context). To achieve this, they work as an integral part of multi-skilled management teams in carrying out the:

- formulation of policy and setting of corporate objectives

- formulation of strategic plans derived from corporate objectives

- formulation of shorter-term operational plans

- acquisition and use of finance

- design of systems, recording of events and transactions and management of information systems

- generation, communication and interpretation of financial and operating information (such as product costs) for management and other stakeholders

- provision of specific information and analysis on which decisions (such as how many units to produce or what products to make) are based

- monitoring of outcomes against plans (such as budgets) and other benchmarks and the initiation of responsive action for performance improvement

- derivation of performance measures and benchmarks, financial and non-financial, quantitative and qualitative, for monitoring and control; and

- improvement of business systems and processes through risk management and internal audit review.

Through these forward-looking roles and by application of their expert skills management accountants help organisations improve their performance, security, growth and competitiveness in an ever more demanding environment.

We will start to look at some of these functions in the *Management Accounting* syllabus, and others will be studied in later subjects.

It can be seen from this that there is no one clear definition of the role of the management accountant. Their work, experience and responsibilities are extraordinarily varied and continue to change to reflect the changing needs of stakeholders.

5 The importance of understanding costs

 The word **'cost'** can be used in two contexts. It can be used as a noun, for example when we are referring to the cost of an item. Alternatively, it can be used as a verb, for example we can say that we are attempting to cost an activity, when we are undertaking the tasks necessary to determine the costs of carrying out the activity.

The understanding of costs is fundamental to your accounting studies.

In financial accounting all costs must be recorded so that profit can be calculated and the true and fair financial position can be presented in the financial statements.

In management accounting an understanding of costs is required in order to carry out the three main functions of planning, control and decision making. If we understand and calculate costs, we can use this information in a number of ways such as:

- Determining the cost to manufacture a product or provide a service can be used to record costs in the financial statements.

- The cost per unit can be used to value inventory in the statement of financial position.

- Cost information can inform decisions on our products or services. Product and service costs can be used to determine the selling price we should charge for our products or services. For example, if the cost per unit is $0.30, the business may decide to price the product at $0.50 per unit in order to make the required profit of $0.20 per unit.

- Knowing the profit (or, as we will see in a later chapter, the contribution of a product) can help determine the products and services we should supply and in what quantity.

- The cost can also act as a benchmark for future performance. Differences from the expected (or standard) cost can be calculated (known as variances) and evaluated.

The cost transformation model

As we have seen above, cost management is therefore a key component of a management accountant's role. In order to survive in today's global business environment, businesses need to continually look for opportunities to improve their cost structures while continuing to generate value for customers. The CGMA Cost Transformation Model has been developed to provide a framework to help businesses achieve and maintain their cost-competitiveness. The model has six suggested changes for organisations aimed at achieving this objective.

These changes are:

- Creating a cost conscious culture – the organisation should aim to be a cost leader so that its costs are lower than rivals and set a competitive benchmark. Everyone in the organisation should be motivated and enabled to reduce costs in whatever way possible. Technology can play a key role in reducing costs.

- Understanding cost drivers – this involves investigating costs to determine why they change and how different variables impact on the cost. Plans should be put in place to reduce the drivers of costs, and possibly even the costs themselves if they are not necessary or sustainably profitable in meeting customer's needs. This may involve critical evaluations of current systems and processes to ensure that they provide the necessary information to support effective decision making.

- Managing the risks that come from a cost conscious culture – careful consideration needs to be given to what might get in the way of the business achieving its cost transformation and management objectives. For example, whilst new technologies may enable a business to reduce cost, this may also result in reducing quality and customer satisfaction. These technologies may also lead to increased competition. The organisation should therefore have a clear risk management process in place to identify, assess and manage such risks.

- Ensuring products and services are profitable – it will be important that every product or service makes a positive contribution to overall organisational profits. This will involve understanding what drives costs for each individual product and allocating shared costs to products as accurately as possible.

- Maximising value from new products – the potential profitability of new products should be assessed before production begins. Also, as part of product design, the product or service should be made to be as flexible as possible so that it appeals to or can be adapted to satisfy as many customer segments as possible.

- Consider the environmental impact of products – negative impacts (such as creating unnecessary waste) can add costs as well as damaging reputation and sales.

The model suggests a number of tools and models which can be used in order to achieve these changes. Many of these tools will be employed across your CIMA studies, some of them in this text, such as Activity Based Costing which considers cost drivers and how these can be used to allocate shared costs to products.

Cost units, cost centres and cost objects

Costs can be attributed to cost units, cost centres or cost objects.

 The *CIMA Terminology* defines a **cost unit** as 'a unit of product or service in relation to which costs are ascertained'.

This means that a cost unit can be **anything for which it is possible to ascertain the cost**. The cost unit selected in each situation will depend on a number of factors, including the amount of information available and the purpose for which the cost unit will be used.

A cost unit can be anything which is measurable and useful for cost control purposes. For example, a company manufacturing a mobile phone might calculate the cost per mobile phone. Or perhaps if the phones are made and sold in very large quantities the cost per 1,000 phones might be used instead.

Not all cost units will be for tangible items. Intangible items cannot be seen and touched and do not have physical substance but they can be measured, for example the cost per chargeable hour of accounting service.

 A **cost centre** is a production or service location, a function, an activity or an item of equipment for which costs are accumulated.

A cost centre is one type of responsibility centre. Responsibility centres will be covered in the budgeting chapter. A cost centre is used as a 'collecting place' for costs.

The cost of operating the cost centre is determined for the period, and then this total cost is related to the cost units which have passed through the cost centre.

An example of a production cost centre could be the machine shop in a factory. The production cost for the machine shop might be $100,000 for the period. If 1,000 cost units have passed through this cost centre we might say that the production cost relating to the machine shop was $100 for each unit.

Other examples of a cost centre are a canteen department, a project management team or a subsidiary of a company. Costs could be collected for each of these cost centres. Every organisation will have its own cost centres for accumulating costs.

 The *CIMA Terminology* contains the following for **cost objects:** 'For example a product, service, centre, activity, customer or distribution channel in relation to which costs are ascertained.'

All of the cost units and cost centres we have described in this chapter are therefore types of cost object.

Classification of costs

In order to calculate costs we need to understand them. A key to this is understanding different ways in which costs can be classified.

There are three main ways to classify costs:

- by behaviour
- by element
- by nature

What follows is some revision on these different types of classification

Classification of costs according to their behaviour

Before calculating costs we need to understand how different costs behave.

In cost accounting we typically classify costs by three types of behaviour:

- Fixed costs – costs which don't change as the activity level changes
- Variable costs – costs which change in direct proportion to changes in the activity level
- Semi-variable costs – costs which have both fixed and variable elements.

Different cost behaviours

Many factors affect the level of costs incurred; for instance, inflation will cause costs to increase over a period of time. In management accounting, when we talk about cost behaviour we are referring to the way in which costs are affected by fluctuations in the level of activity. The level of activity can be measured in many different ways. For example, the number of units produced, miles travelled, hours worked, percentage of capacity utilised and so on.

An understanding of cost behaviour patterns is essential for many management tasks, particularly in the areas of planning, decision-making and control. It would be impossible for managers to forecast and control costs without at least a basic knowledge of the way in which costs behave in relation to the level of activity.

Fixed cost

The CIMA Terminology defines a fixed cost as 'a cost which is incurred for an accounting period that, within certain output or turnover limits, tends to be unaffected by fluctuations in the levels of activity (output or turnover)'.

Examples of fixed costs are rent, rates, insurance and executive salaries.

However, it is important to note that this is only true for the relevant range of activity. Consider, for example, the behaviour of the rent cost. Within the relevant range it is possible to expand activity without needing extra premises and therefore the rent cost remains constant. However, if activity is expanded to the critical point where further premises are required, then the rent cost will increase to a new, higher level. This cost behaviour pattern can be described as a stepped fixed cost. The cost is constant within the relevant range for each activity level but when a critical level of activity is reached, the total cost incurred increases to the next step.

This warning does not only apply to fixed costs: it is never wise to attempt to predict costs for activity levels outside the range for which cost behaviour patterns have been established.

Also, whilst the fixed cost total may stay the same within a relevant activity range, the fixed cost per unit reduces as the activity level is increased. This is because the same amount of fixed cost is being spread over an increasing number of units.

Variable cost

The CIMA Terminology defines a variable cost as a 'cost that varies with a measure of activity'.

Examples of variable costs are direct material, direct labour and variable overheads. In most examination situations, and very often in practice, variable costs are assumed to be linear.

Although many variable costs do approximate to a linear function, this assumption may not always be realistic. Non-linear variable costs are sometimes called curvilinear variable costs. There may be what are known as economies of scale whereby each successive unit of activity adds less to total variable cost than the previous unit. An example of a variable cost which follows this pattern could be the cost of direct material where quantity discounts are available.

On the other hand, there may be what are known as diseconomies of scale, which indicates that each successive unit of activity is adding more to the total variable cost than the previous unit. An example of a variable cost which follows this pattern could be the cost of direct labour where employees are paid an accelerating bonus for achieving higher levels of output.

The important point is that managers should be aware of any assumptions that have been made in estimating cost behaviour patterns. They can then use the information which is based on these assumptions with a full awareness of its possible limitations.

Semi-variable cost

A semi-variable cost is also referred to as a semi-fixed, hybrid, or mixed cost. The CIMA Terminology defines it as 'a cost containing both fixed and variable components and thus partly affected by a change in the level of activity'.

Examples of semi-variable costs are gas and electricity. Both of these expenditures consist of a fixed amount payable for the period, with a further variable amount which is related to the consumption of gas or electricity.

Alternatively, the cost might remain constant up to a certain level of activity and then increase as the variable cost element is incurred. An example of such a cost might be the rental cost of a photocopier where a fixed rental is paid and no extra charge is made for copies up to a certain number. Once this number of copies is exceeded, a constant charge is levied for each copy taken.

Example 2

Classify the following items of expenditure according to their behaviour i.e. as fixed, variable or semi-variable costs.

1   Monthly rent   *fixed*

2   Production line workers' wages   *Variable*

3   Electricity bill   *Semi-variable*

4   Raw materials   *Variable*

Example 3

Study the following graphs, where the vertical axis represents 'Total Costs' or 'Cost per unit'. Then answer the questions shown below.

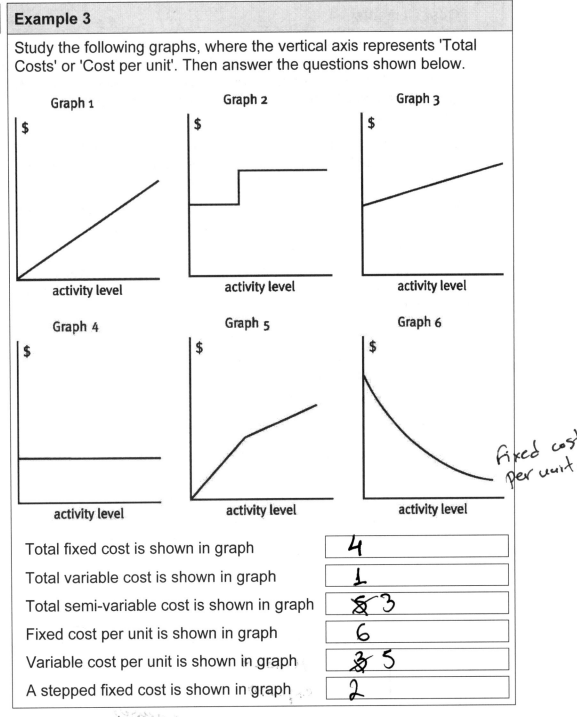

Total fixed cost is shown in graph	4
Total variable cost is shown in graph	1
Total semi-variable cost is shown in graph	~~5~~ 3
Fixed cost per unit is shown in graph	6
Variable cost per unit is shown in graph	~~3~~ 5
A stepped fixed cost is shown in graph	2

Classification of costs according to their element

As well as classifying costs by their behaviour, costs can also be classified according to their element.

Classifying costs according to their element means grouping costs according to whether they are **material, labour** or **expense** costs. These are the three main cost elements.

Cost elements

Materials are the components bought in by the company which are used in manufacturing the product. For example, the materials used by a food producer could be meat or vegetables. Material costs include the cost of obtaining the materials and receiving them within the organisation.

Labour costs are the costs of the people working for the organisation. These costs include wages and salaries, bonuses and overtime, together with related employment costs.

Expense costs are the regularly incurred costs of running the business such as rent, business rates, utility costs, insurance, postage, telephones and similar items.

Note: Within the cost classifications there can be subdivisions; for example, within the materials classification the subdivisions might include the following:

- Raw materials, that is, the basic raw material used in the manufacturing process.

- Components, that is, complete parts that are used in the manufacturing process.

- Consumables, that is, cleaning materials, etc.

- Maintenance materials, that is, spare parts for machines, lubricating oils, etc.

This list of subdivisions is not exhaustive, and there may even be further subdivisions of each of these groups. For example, the raw materials may be further divided according to the type of raw material, for example steel, plastic, glass, etc.

Example 4

Classify the following costs for a clothes retailer by element:

1   Designer skirts   *Material*

2   Heating costs   *expenses*

3   Depreciation of fixtures and fittings   *expenses*

4   Cashier staff salaries   *Labour*

Classification of costs according to their nature

When costs are classified having regard to their nature, the broadest classification of this type is to divide costs into **direct** costs and **indirect** costs.

- Direct costs – costs which can be directly traced to the cost object that we are trying to cost.

- Indirect costs – costs which cannot be directly traced to a single cost object.

Direct and indirect costs

Direct costs can be clearly identified with the cost object we are trying to cost. For example, suppose that a furniture maker is determining the cost of a wooden table. The manufacture of the table has involved the use of timber, screws and metal drawer handles. These items are classified as **direct materials**. The wages paid to the machine operator, assembler and finisher in actually making the table would be classified as **direct labour**. The designer of the table may be entitled to a royalty payment for each table made, and this would be classified as a **direct expense**.

The total of all direct costs is known as the **PRIME COST**.

Indirect costs cannot be directly attributed to a particular cost unit, although it is clear that they have been incurred in the production of the table. These indirect costs are often referred to as production **overheads**. Examples of indirect production costs are as follows:

Cost incurred	Cost classification
Lubricating oils and cleaning materials	Indirect material
Salaries of factory supervisors	Indirect labour
Factory rent and power	Indirect expense

It is important to realise that a particular cost may sometimes be a direct cost and sometimes an indirect cost. It depends on the cost object we are trying to cost.

For example, consider a member of a quality inspection department in a production factory. The salary for this employee will be a direct cost for the cost centre (the quality inspection department) if that is the object that we are trying to cost. But it would be an indirect cost for the units produced in the factory (the cost units) as it cannot be directly traced to one individual cost unit.

Another way of classifying costs by their nature is to classify a cost as a period or product cost.

- Product costs – costs which are only incurred if production takes place.

- Period costs – costs which are incurred due to the passage of time.

Product and period costs

Product costs would include direct material, direct labour and absorbed production overheads. Therefore if an organisation does not produce any items it will not incur any product costs.

Period costs include costs such as rent and rates, insurance, directors' salaries and depreciation. These costs accrue on daily, monthly or annual basis and will still accrue even if an organisation does not produce any items.

It will be vital for most of the chapters in this syllabus that you understand the behaviour, elements and nature of different types of cost.

Example 5

Camberwell runs a construction company. Classify the following costs by nature:

A   Bricks   *Direct*

B   Plant hire for long term contract   *Indirect · Direct*

C   Builder's wages   *Direct*

D   Accountant's wages   *Indirect*

6   Chapter summary

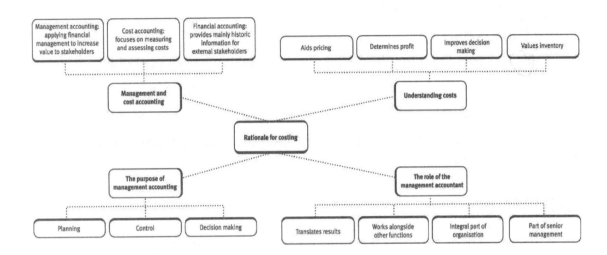

7 Practice questions

Test your understanding 1

Direct costs are:

(A) costs that can always be identified with a single cost object

B all costs that are expensed to the Income Statement

C costs that can be attributed to a single accounting period

D costs that change in direct proportion to the number of units produced.

Test your understanding 2

State which three of the following characteristics relate to financial accounting:

A For internal use

(B) Governed by rules and regulations

(C) Required by law

(D) Output is mainly used by external parties

E One of its main purposes is planning

Test your understanding 3

Identify the following statements as either true or false:

A Semi-variable costs have both a fixed and a variable element T

B Fixed costs change directly with changes in activity F

C Variable costs change directly with changes in activity T

Test your understanding 4

Classify the following costs for a supermarket chain by element:

A Tins of baked beans M

B Lighting costs E

C Depreciation of freezers E

D Checkout staff salaries L

E Flour used in in-store bakery M

Test your understanding 5

Aki and Aesha are the founding partners of an accountancy firm. They employ 20 accountants and have over 100 clients.

Classify the following costs by nature:

A   Travelling costs for when staff visit client sites   *D*

B   Rechargeable accountants' time   *D*

C   Office heating costs   *I*

D   Recruitment costs   ~~D~~ *I*

E   Accountants' time recorded as 'general admin' on time sheets   *I*

Test your understanding 6

The total of all direct costs of production is also known as:

A   Variable cost

B   Production cost

Ⓒ   Prime cost

D   Total cost

Test your understanding 7

A cost which is connected with production but does not vary directly with the level of output may also be known as:

A   Overhead

B   Direct cost

C   Semi-variable cost

Ⓓ   Indirect production cost

Example and test your understanding answers

Example 1

C

Statement (i) is incorrect as providing a true and fair view of the financial position of the organisation is only relevant to financial accounting.

Example 2

The expenditure would be analysed as follows:

1   Monthly rent – fixed. This would not change if the level of activity was to increase.

2   Production line workers' wages – variable. As activity increases, so too would the work required on the production line to complete the units being produced.

3   Electricity bill – semi-variable. This will include a fixed fee for the standing charge and then a variable amount depending on how much electricity is used in the period.

4   Raw materials – variable. This will increase in direct proportion to the level of production.

Example 3

Total fixed cost is shown in graph	4
Total variable cost is shown in graph	1
Total semi-variable cost is shown in graph	3
Fixed cost per unit is shown in graph	6
Variable cost per unit is shown in graph	4
A stepped fixed cost is shown in graph	2

Example 4

1   Designer skirts: materials

2   Heating costs: expenses

3   Depreciation of fixtures and fittings: expenses

4   Cashier staff salaries: labour

Example 5

A	Bricks: direct
B	Plant hire for long term contract: direct
C	Builder's wages: direct
D	Accountant's wages: indirect

Test your understanding 1

A

Direct costs are costs directly attributable to the item being costed, which can be a single unit or a batch of cost units. D may be true but is the definition of a variable cost. Direct costs will normally be charged to the Income Statement (option B), but not all costs that are charged to the Income Statement will be direct costs. Direct costs are attributed to units (or batches) not accounting periods.

Test your understanding 2

B, C and D

A and E relate to management accounting.

Management accounting is internally focused and one of its main purposes is planning.

Financial accounting is governed by rules and regulations, required by law and its output is mainly used by external parties.

Test your understanding 3

A	Semi-variable costs have both a fixed and a variable element - TRUE
B	Fixed costs change directly with changes in activity – FALSE. Fixed costs do not change with changes in activity, they remain constant.
C	Variable costs change directly with changes in activity – TRUE.

Test your understanding 4

A   Tins of baked beans: materials

B   Lighting costs: expenses

C   Depreciation of freezers: expenses

D   Checkout staff salaries: labour

E   Flour used in in-store bakery: materials

Test your understanding 5

A   Travelling costs for when staff visit client sites: direct

B   Rechargeable accountants' time: direct

C   Office heating costs: indirect

D   Recruitment costs: indirect

E   Accountants' time recorded as 'general admin' on time sheets: indirect

Test your understanding 6

Correct answer is C.

The **prime cost** is the total of all direct costs.

Test your understanding 7

Correct answer is D.

Indirect production costs cannot be directly attributed to a particular cost unit, although it is clear that they have been incurred in the production of the item.

Traditional costing

Chapter learning objectives

Lead outcome	Component outcome
A2. Apply the main costing concepts to organisations and cost objects	(b) Apply costing concepts to different organisations and cost objects
A3. Apply costing methods to determine the costs for different purposes	(a) Cost accumulation, allocation, apportionment and absorption
C1. Describe the main types of short-term decisions made by organisations	(a) Describe pricing and revenue maximisation decisions

1   Chapter overview diagram

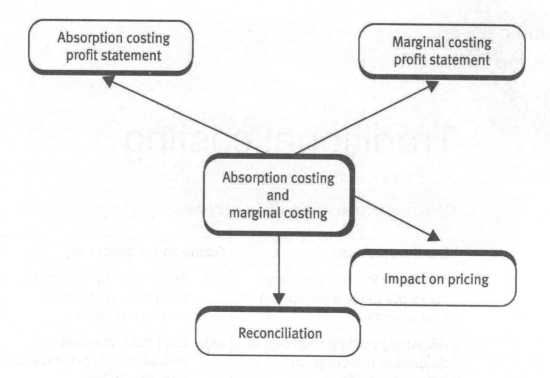

Having understood why it's so important for the business to determine the cost of its products or services, we now need to consider how we can calculate this cost.

The first two ways of doing this are examined in this chapter.

2   Absorption costing

The aim of traditional absorption costing is to determine the full production cost per unit.

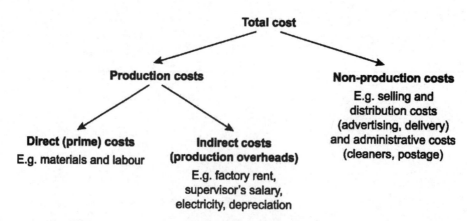

When we use absorption costing to determine the cost per unit, we focus on the production costs only.

We can summarise these costs into a cost card:

	$
Direct materials per unit	X
Direct labour per unit	X
Production overhead per unit (Note 1)	X
Full production cost per unit	X

Note 1:

All production overheads must be absorbed into units of production, using a suitable basis. There are many methods which may be used, but the most common are:

- units produced

- machine-hour rate

- labour-hour rate

It is quite likely that different production departments will measure their production in different ways. The objective is to use a measure which reflects the nature of the work involved.

The units produced method is, in theory, the simplest but it is only valid when all cost units produced in the period are identical.

The direct labour-hour rate would be most appropriate in labour-intensive cost centres. These are becoming rarer nowadays as a lot of production becomes automated and so this method is less widely used that it was in the past.

The machine-hour rate is most appropriate in cost centres where machine activity predominates and is therefore more widely used than the direct labour hour rate.

Production overheads are usually calculated at the beginning of an accounting period in order to determine how much overhead cost to assign to a unit before calculating a selling price.

The overhead absorption rate (OAR) is calculated as follows:

$$\frac{\text{Total budgeted overhead cost (allocated and apportioned)}}{\text{Budgeted quantity of absorption base}}$$

Illustration 1

SVP Ltd manufactures a number of different products, all of which pass through SVP's two production cost centres, Machining and Assembly. Budgeted information for the next period is as follows:

	Machining	Assembly	Total
Budgeted production overheads	$42,000	$48,000	$90,000
Machine hours	28,000	4,000	32,000
Labour hours	6,000	42,000	48,000

The OAR of the machining department is to be based on the number of machine hours, while the OAR of the assembly department is to be based on the number of direct labour hours. The reasons for this can be seen from the information in the table above. The machining department estimates to require 28,000 machine hours but only 6,000 labour hours, suggesting that production is predominantly automated. Whereas in the assembly department there are only 4,000 machine hours in comparison to 42,000 labour hours. Production in the assembly department would therefore appear to be labour-intensive.

Calculate the OAR for each department.

Machining department:

$$OAR = \frac{\$42,000}{28,000 \text{ machine hours}} = \$1.50 \text{ per machine hour}$$

Assembly department:

$$OAR = \frac{\$48,000}{42,000 \text{ labour hours}} = \$1.14 \text{ per labour hour}$$

Suppose that SVP Ltd now only produced a single product, with production levels budgeted at 45,000 units in the next period.

Calculate the most appropriate OAR for the period.

As only one product is now being manufactured, the most appropriate basis of absorption will be the 'unit' method. The OAR will be calculated as follows:

$$OAR = \frac{\$90,000}{45,000 \text{ units}} = \$2.00 \text{ per unit.}$$

Example 1

A company accountant has gathered together some cost information for her company's product as follows:

	Cost
Direct materials	$4 per kilogram (kg) used
Direct labour	$22 per hour worked
Variable overheads	$6 for each direct labour hour

She has also determined that fixed production overheads will be $400,000 in total. Overheads are absorbed on a per unit basis.

Investigation has shown that each unit of the product uses 3 kilograms of material and needs 2 hours of direct labour work.

Sales and production were budgeted at 20,000 units, but only 16,000 were actually produced and 14,000 actually sold.

There was no opening inventory.

Required:

Produce a standard cost card using absorption costing and value the company's closing inventory on that basis.

Example 2

A company produces three products, the cost of each being:

	A	B	C
Direct materials	$14.40	$25.60	$36.00
Direct labour:			
Machining @ $4.80 per hour	2 hours	1.5 hours	2 hours
Assembling @ $3.20 per hour	2 hours	2.5 hours	1 hour
Planned production is:			
Product A	10,000 units		
Product B	20,000 units		
Product C	40,000 units		

Production overheads for the forthcoming period are estimated at $120,000.

Required:

Using absorption costing with direct labour hours as the basis, produce a standard cost card for each product.

More on calculating absorption rates

It is relatively easy to estimate the cost per unit for direct materials and labour. In doing so we can complete the first two lines of the cost card. However, it is much more difficult to estimate the production overhead per unit. This is an indirect cost and so, by its very nature, we do not know how much is contained in each unit. Therefore, we need a method of attributing the production overheads to each unit.

Review of overhead absorption procedure

Accounting for overhead costs in an absorption costing system can be quite complex, and production overhead costs are first allocated, then apportioned and finally absorbed into product costs (or service costs).

- **Overhead allocation.** Indirect production costs are initially allocated to cost centres or departments. Allocation is the process of charging a cost directly and in full to the source of the expenditure. For example, the salary of a maintenance engineer would be allocated to the engineering maintenance department.

- **Overhead apportionment.** The overhead costs that have been allocated to cost centres and cost codes other than direct production departments must next be apportioned to direct production departments. Apportionment is the process of sharing on a fair basis. For example, factory rental costs might be apportioned between the production departments on the basis of the floor area occupied by each department. Similarly, the costs of the engineering maintenance department might be apportioned between production departments on the basis of the operating machine hours in each department. At the end of the apportionment process, all the production overheads have been allocated or apportioned to the direct production departments.

- **Overhead absorption**. An absorption rate is calculated for each production department. This is the rate at which production overheads will be added to the cost of production going through the department.

When the department produces a single product, production volume can be measured as the number of units produced, and the absorption rate would be a rate per unit produced.

More usually, organisations produce different products or carry out non-standard jobs for customers, and production volume is commonly measured as one of the following:

- direct labour hours worked in the department, and the absorption rate is a rate per direct labour hour worked

- machine hours worked in the department, and the absorption rate is a rate per machine hour operated

- sometimes the cost of direct labour might be used as a measure of production volume, and the absorption rate is then calculated as a percentage of direct labour cost.

This often results in a factory wide absorption rate. This is used when all products produced in the factory use the same type of labour or machines. Dividing total factory indirect costs by, say, total direct machine hours results in this absorption rate that can be charged to all products based on the number of machine hours used. So, for example, if all products are produced on the same machines and a factory wide absorption rate of $40 per machine hour has been determined, every product will be charged $40 worth of overheads for every machine hour that they use.

Predetermined absorption rates

Although it is possible to calculate absorption rates using actual overhead costs and actual production volume, this is not the usual practice. This is because:

- It is usually inconvenient to wait until the end of an accounting period to work out what the absorption rates should be. In absorption costing systems, overhead costs are added to the cost of production as it passes through each stage in the production process, and overhead costs are absorbed when the production happens

- A predetermined rate is required to enable a price to be estimated.

- Overhead costs may vary throughout the year. The overhead absorption rate smooths variations in overheads by applying an average overhead cost to each unit of product throughout the year.

The normal practice is therefore to absorb production overhead costs at a predetermined rate, based on budgeted overhead expenditure and budgeted production volume.

This however can lead to an over-or under-absorption of the overheads when compared to the actual overheads incurred.

This **over-or under-absorption** can be calculated as follows:

= (Budgeted overhead rate per unit × actual units) – Actual overheads incurred

Absorption advantages/disadvantages

Advantages of absorption costing

The arguments used in favour of absorption costing are as follows:

- Fixed production costs can be a large proportion of the total production costs incurred. Unless production overheads are absorbed into product costs, a large proportion of cost would be excluded from the measurement of product costs.

- Absorption costing follows the matching concept (accruals concept) by carrying forward a proportion of the production cost in the inventory valuation to be matched against the sales value when the items are sold.

- It is necessary to include fixed production overhead in inventory values for financial statements; absorption costing produces inventory values which include a share of fixed production overhead.

- Analysis of under-/over-absorbed overhead may be useful for identifying inefficient utilisation of production resources.

- There is an argument that in the longer term, all costs are variable, and it is appropriate to try to identify overhead costs with the products or services that cause them. This argument is used as a reason for activity-based costing (ABC). ABC is a form of absorption costing, and is described in a later chapter.

Disadvantages of absorption costing

There are serious disadvantages with using absorption costing to measure costs and profits.

- **The apportionment and absorption of overhead costs is arbitrary**

  The way in which overhead costs are apportioned between cost centres and absorbed into production costs is subjective and many methods of cost allocation may be deemed appropriate. Although the process attempts to be 'fair', it is arbitrary.

  For example, suppose that a factory rental cost is apportioned between production departments on the basis of the floor area for each department. This might seem a fair way of sharing out the costs, but it is still subjective. Why not apportion the costs on the basis of the number of employees in each department? Or why not allow for the fact that some of the accommodation might be more pleasant to work in than others? In a manufacturing environment, production overheads might be absorbed on the basis of either direct labour hours or machine hours. However, choosing one instead of the other can have a significant effect on job costs or product costs, and yet it still relies on a subjective choice.

It may be easier in some departments than others. If a department is labour intensive then allocations can be made on the basis of labour hours worked. Or if the department is machine intensive then allocations can be made on the basis of machine hours. But not every department will have this clear distinction.

- **Profits vary with changes in production volume**

  A second criticism of absorption costing is that profits can be increased or reduced by changes in inventory levels.

  For example, by increasing output, more fixed overhead is absorbed into production costs, and if the extra output is not sold, the fixed overhead costs are carried forward in the closing inventory value. This can encourage managers to over-produce in order to inflate profits.

3 Marginal costing

Marginal costing is a costing method which charges products or services with variable costs alone. No fixed overheads are included in the inventory valuation; they are treated as period costs and are written off in total against the contribution of the period.

The contribution concept lies at the heart of marginal costing. It is calculated as:

Contribution = Sales price – All variable costs

Marginal cost

Marginal cost is the extra cost arising as a result of producing one more unit, or the cost saved as a result of producing one less unit. It comprises:

- Direct material
- Direct labour
- Variable overheads

Example 3

Use the same data as that provided in Example 1.

Required:

Produce a standard cost card using marginal costing and value the company's closing inventory on that basis.

Marginal costing advantages/disadvantages

Advantages of marginal costing

- It is a simpler costing system, because there is no requirement to apportion and absorb overhead costs.

- Marginal costing reflects the behaviour of costs in relation to activity. When sales increase, the cost of sales rise only by the additional variable costs. Since most decision-making problems involve changes to activity, marginal costing information is more relevant and appropriate for short-run decision-making than absorption costing.

- Marginal costing avoids the disadvantages of absorption costing, described above.

Disadvantages of marginal costing

- When fixed costs are high relative to variable costs, and when overheads are high relative to direct costs, the marginal cost of production and sales is only a small proportion of total costs. A costing system that focuses on marginal cost and contribution might therefore provide insufficient and inadequate information about costs and product profitability. Marginal costing is useful for short-term decision-making, but not for measuring product costs and profitability over the longer term.

- It could also be argued that the treatment of direct labour costs as a variable cost item is often unrealistic. When direct labour employees are paid a fixed wage or salary, their cost is fixed, not variable.

4 Absorption and marginal costing profit statements

In order to be able to prepare a statement of profit or loss under absorption costing, you need to be able to complete the following proforma:

Absorption costing format

	$	$
Sales		X
Less: Cost of sales		
Opening inventory	X	
+ Production costs	X	
	―	
	X	
Less: Closing inventory	(X)	
	―	(X)
		―
		X
(Under)/over absorption		(X)/X
		―
Gross profit		X
Less: Selling, distribution and administration costs,		
Variable	X	
Fixed	X	
	―	
		(X)
		―
Net profit/(loss)		X
		―

- **Valuation of inventory** – opening and closing inventory are valued at full production cost.

- **(Under)/over absorbed overhead** – an adjustment for under or over absorbed overheads is necessary in absorption costing statements.

- Absorption costing statements are split into **production costs** in the cost of sales and **non-production costs** after gross profit.

In order to be able to prepare a statement of profit or loss under marginal costing, you need to be able to complete the following proforma:

Marginal costing format

	$	$
Sales		X
Less: *Variable* cost of sales		
Opening inventory	X	
+ Variable production costs	X	
	—	
	X	
Less: Closing inventory	(X)	
	—	(X)
		—
		X
Less: **Variable** selling, distribution and administration costs		(X)
		—
Contribution		X
Contribution		X
Less: Fixed costs		
Production	X	
Selling, distribution and admin.	X	
	—	
		(X)
		—
Net profit/(loss)		X
		—

- **Valuation of inventory** – opening and closing inventory are valued at marginal (variable) cost.

- The fixed costs **incurred** are deducted from the contribution earned in order to arrive at the net profit/ (loss) for the period.

- Marginal costing statements are split into all the **variable costs before contribution** and all the **fixed costs after contribution**.

- **Note:** only the production variable costs are included in the cost of sales and valuation of inventory. If there are variable non-production costs (i.e. selling costs) these would be deducted before contribution but not included in the cost of sales.

Illustration 2 – Impact of inventory on profit

A company commenced business on 1 March making one product only, the cost card of which is as follows:

	$
Direct labour	5
Direct material	8
Variable production overhead	2
Fixed production overhead	5
	—
Standard production cost	20

The fixed production overhead figure has been calculated on the basis of a budgeted normal output of 36,000 units per annum. The fixed production overhead actually incurred in March was $15,000.

Selling, distribution and administration expenses are:

Fixed	$10,000 per month
Variable	15% of the sales value

The selling price per unit is $50 and the number of units produced and sold were:

Production	2,000
Sales	1,500

Prepare the absorption costing and marginal costing statements of profit or loss for March.

Absorption costing statement of profit or loss – March

	$	$
Sales		75,000
Less Cost of sales: (full production cost)		
Opening inventory	–	
Variable cost of production (2,000 × $15)	30,000	
Fixed production overhead absorbed (2,000 × $5)	10,000	
Less Closing inventory **(W1)** (500 × $20)	(10,000)	
		(30,000)
(Under)/over-absorption **(W2)**		(5,000)
		———
Gross profit		40,000
Less Non-production costs **(W3)**		(21,250)
		———
Profit/loss		18,750
		———

Workings

(W1) Closing inventory = opening inventory + production – sales units

= 0 + 2,000 – 1,500 = 500 units

(W2)

	$
Overheads absorbed (2,000 × $5)	10,000
Overheads incurred	15,000
Under-absorption on overheads	5,000

(W3)

Fixed = $10,000

Variable = 15% × $75,000 = $11,250

Total = $(10,000 + 11,250) = $21,250

Marginal costing statement of profit or loss – March

	$	$
Sales		75,000
Less Cost of sales: (marginal production costs)		
Opening inventory	–	
Variable cost of production (2,000 × $15)	30,000	
Less Closing inventory (500 × $15)	(7,500)	
		(22,500)
		52,500
Less Other variable costs (15% × $75,000)		(11,250)
Contribution		41,250
Less Total fixed costs (actually incurred) $(15,000 + 10,000)		(25,000)
Profit/loss		16,250

Example 4

Perry Ltd makes and sells a single product with the following information:

	$/unit
Selling price	50
Direct material	15
Direct labour	10
Variable overhead	5

Fixed overheads are $5,000. Budgeted and actual output and sales are 1,000 units.

(a) Using absorption costing:

    (i) calculate the profit for the period

    (ii) calculate the profit per unit.

(b) Using marginal costing:

    (i) calculate the contribution per unit

    (ii) calculate the total contribution

    (iii) calculate the profit for the period.

5   Reconciling the profits

When inventory levels increase or decrease during a period then profits differ under absorption and marginal costing.

- If inventory levels increase, absorption costing gives the higher profit.

- If inventory levels decrease, marginal costing gives the higher profit.

- If inventory levels remain constant, both methods give the same profit.

The differences between the two profits can be reconciled as follows:

	$
Absorption costing profit	X
(Increase)/decrease in inventory × fixed overheads per unit	(X)X
Marginal costing profit	X

Justification

The profit differences are caused by the different valuations given to the closing inventories in each period. With absorption costing, an amount of fixed production overhead is carried forward in inventory to be charged against sales of later periods.

If inventories increase, then absorption costing profits will be higher than marginal costing profits. This is because some of the fixed overhead is carried forward in inventory instead of being written off against sales for the period.

If inventories reduce, then marginal costing profits will be higher than absorption costing profits. This is because the fixed overhead which had been carried forward in inventory with absorption costing is now being released to be charged against the sales for the period.

Marginal costing and absorption costing systems give the same profit when there is no change in inventories.

Profit differences in the long term

In the long term the total reported profit will be the same whichever method is used. This is because all of the costs incurred will eventually be charged against sales; it is merely the timing of the sales that causes the profit differences from period to period.

Illustration 3 – Reconciling profits

A company commenced business on 1 March making one product only, the cost card of which is as follows (details as per illustration 1).

	$
Direct labour	5
Direct material	8
Variable production overhead	2
Fixed production overhead	5
Full production cost	20

- Marginal cost of production = 5 + 8 + 2 = $15

- Absorption cost of production = 5 + 8 + 2 + 5 = $20

- Difference in cost of production = $5 which is the fixed production overhead element of the absorption cost of production.

- This means that each unit of opening and closing inventory will be valued at $5 more under absorption costing.

The number of units produced and sold was as follows.

	March (units)
Production	2,000
Sales	1,500

Closing inventory is 500 units (as calculated in illustration 1)

- Profit for March under absorption costing = $18,750 (as calculated in illustration 1).

- Profit for March under marginal costing = $16,250 (as calculated in illustration 1).

- Difference in profits = $18,750 – $16,250 = $2,500.

This difference can be analysed as follows

Absorption costing:

- There are zero opening inventories so no fixed production costs have been brought forward.

- $10,000 of fixed production costs have been charged to production (2,000 units × $5).

- $2,500 of this has then been deducted from the cost of sales as part of the closing inventory value (500 × $5).

- An adjustment for the under-absorption of $5,000 has been charged.

- Therefore **$12,500** of fixed costs has been charged in this month's statement of profit or loss ($10,000 – $2,500 + $5,000).

Marginal costing:

- The statement of profit or loss is charged with the full **$15,000** of fixed production overhead costs as none are included in the cost of sales.

Reconciliation:

- Inventory levels are increasing by 500 units (zero opening inventory and 500 units of closing inventory)

- $2,500 ($15,000 – $12,500) less cost is charged in the period using absorption costing principles when compared to marginal costing principles therefore the profit will be $2,500 higher under absorption costing principles.

Example 5

The details are exactly the same as for Example 3, except output is now 3,000 units and sales are now 2,700 units.

Calculate the profit for the period using both absorption and marginal costing.

Example 6

Z Limited manufactures a single product, the budgeted selling price and variable cost details of which are as follows

	$
Selling price	15.00
Variable costs per unit:	
Direct materials	3.50
Direct labour	4.00
Variable overhead	2.00

Budgeted fixed overhead costs are $60,000 per annum charged at a constant rate each month.

Budgeted production is 30,000 units per annum.

In a month when actual production was 2,400 units and exceeded sales by 180 units, identify the profit reported under absorption costing:

A $6,660

B $7,570

C $7,770

D $8,200

Profits from one period to the next can be reconciled in a similar way. For example, the difference between periods can be explained as the change in unit sales multiplied by the contribution per unit if using marginal costing.

Further explanation on reconciling profits between periods

Just like reconciling profits between the two accounting systems can be achieved via a proforma, similar proformas can be used for reconciling profits between one period and the next using the same accounting system as follows:

Marginal costing reconciliation

	$
Profit for period 1	X
Increase/(decrease) in sales × contribution per unit	(X)X
Profit for period 2	X

Absorption costing reconciliation

This is a little trickier as the reconciliation needs to be adjusted for any over/under-absorptions that may have occurred of fixed overheads.

	$
Profit for period 1	X
Increase/(decrease) in sales × profit per unit	X(X)
(Over–)/under-absorption in period 1	(X)/X
Over– /(under)-absorption in period 2	X/(X)
Profit for period 2	X

Note:

You must be careful with the direction of the absorption. For example, an over-absorption in period 1 makes profit for that month higher, therefore it must be deducted to arrive at period 2's profit. On the other hand, an over-absorption in period 2 makes period 2's profit higher than period 1's, therefore it must be added in the reconciliation.

6 Pricing strategies based on cost

We have now looked at marginal and absorption costing and how they are calculated. Both can be used when determining the selling price of a product. The way overheads are treated will have a big impact on the selling price calculated. Pricing decisions is an element of the decision making part of the syllabus which will be explored again in a later chapter when we look at how pricing should be set for one-off or short-term decisions. In any pricing decision there are four key factors to consider:

- Costs – the organisation needs to ensure that the price is sufficient to cover the cost of producing the product or providing the service.

- Competitors – organisations will often monitor the prices of competing products/services to ensure that the price set for their own product/service is in line with the organisation's competitive goals.

- Customers – the value placed on the product by customers will often determine how the product/service is priced. Organisations will consider how much the customer is willing to pay for the product/service.

- Corporate objectives – pricing will often have a link to the organisation's overall strategic objectives. If, for example, an organisation is trying to break into a market and gain market share it might set an initially low price in order to attract customers to the product/service. On the other hand, if the organisation wants to project an image of quality and difference then it might set a high price in order to do this.

The **cost** of the product or service is therefore one of the elements that can impact on the selling price of a product or service. For many organisations it will be **the key determinant of the selling price**. Often referred to as 'cost-plus pricing', this involves adding a mark-up to the cost of the product or service in order to arrive at the selling price.

Choosing the mark up percentage

A standard mark-up is used by some organisations, such as government contractors and some job costing companies, but the majority of companies vary the percentage to reflect differing market conditions for their products or services.

This mark-up may be influenced by factors such as:

- The amount that customers are willing to pay. For example, the product may have a high perceived value (if, say, it is in short supply) which would therefore encourage the organisation to use a higher mark up.

- The level of competition that the product will experience. If the product has many close competitors and substitutes then the organisation may be forced to use a lower mark up.

- The organisation's objectives. For example, when first trying to break into a market and gain market awareness and market share an organisation might use a lower mark-up percentage.

- Alternatively, the profit mark-up may be fixed so that the company makes a specific return on capital based on a particular capacity utilisation.

Under different circumstances there may be different interpretations of what gets included in the 'cost' element of cost plus pricing. In some circumstances full cost may be used (including absorbed overheads), in other circumstances it might be more appropriate to use marginal cost.

Full cost plus pricing

Using this method, the selling price for the product is determined as follows:

> **Selling price = Full cost per unit × (1 + mark-up percentage)**

So that, for example, if the full cost was $40 and the organisation was using a 15% mark-up percentage then the selling price would be set at $46 (i.e. $40 × 1.15).

Full cost can be interpreted in different ways. It will always include the full production cost, including all absorbed overheads. But some organisations may also interpret it to include sales, distribution and administration costs.

(**Note**: typically, the more costs that are included in the full cost then the lower that the mark up percentage used is likely to be).

Illustration 4 – Full cost-plus pricing

A company is replacing product A with an updated version, B, and must calculate a base cost, to which a mark-up will be added in order to arrive at a selling price. The following variable costs have been established by reference to the company's experience with product A, although they may be subject to an error margin of + or – 10 % under production conditions for B:

	$ per unit
Direct material	4
Direct labour (1/4 hr @ $16/hr)	4
Variable manufacturing overheads (1/4 hr of machine time @ $8/hr)	2
	___
Total variable cost per unit	**10**
	___

As the machine time for each B would be the same as for A, the company estimates that it will be able to produce the same total quantity of B as its current production of A, which is 20,000 units.

The production facilities currently use 50,000 hours of machine time for all of the company's products (including A) and this should be used as the basis for absorbing fixed costs. Current fixed costs are $240,000 for the production facilities, $200,000 for selling and distribution, and $180,000 for administration.

For costing purposes, the 20,000 units of B can be assumed to consume 10 per cent of the total selling, distribution and administration costs.

Alternative 1, using conventional absorption costing principles and building in the conservative error margin

	$
Variable production costs (as above)	10.0
Add: allowance for underestimate (10%)	1.0
Add: fixed production facilities cost 1/4 hour of machine time @ $4.80/hour ($240,000/50,000 hours)	1.2
Full cost	**12.2**

Alternative 2, as 1 but including administrative costs

	$
Base cost as under 1 above	12.2
Add: fixed administrative costs ($180,000 × 10% = $18,000/20,000 units)	0.9
Full cost	**13.1**

Alternative 3, as 2 but including selling and distribution costs

	$
Base cost as under 2 above	13.1
Add: fixed selling and distribution costs ($200,000 × 10% = $20,000/20,000 units)	1.0
Full cost	**14.1**

Depending on the analysis adopted, the full cost varies from $12.20 to $14.10. The full cost rises with each alternative, as an increasing proportion of the total costs is recovered. The profit mark-up built into the pricing formula is therefore likely to fall with each alternative from 1 to 3

Advantages and disadvantages of full cost plus pricing

A number of advantages are claimed for full cost-plus pricing:

(1) The required profit will be made if budgeted sales volumes are achieved.

(2) It is a particularly useful method in contract costing industries such as building, where a few large individual contracts can consume the majority of the annual fixed costs and the fixed costs are low in relation to the variable costs.

(3) Assuming the organisation knows its cost structures, full cost-plus is quick and cheap to employ. Its routine nature lends itself to delegation, thus saving management time.

(4) Full cost-plus pricing can be useful in justifying selling prices to customers; if costs can be shown to have increased, this strengthens the case for an increase in the selling price.

However, there are a number of **problems** with full cost-plus pricing:

(1) There will always be problems associated with the selection of a 'suitable' basis on which to charge fixed costs to individual products or services. Selling prices can show great variation, depending on the apportionment basis chosen. This can lead to over-or under-pricing relative to competitors causing the firm to either lose business or make sales at an unintentional loss.

(2) If prices are set on the basis of normal volume, and actual volume turns out to be considerably lower, overheads will not be fully recovered from sales and predicted profits may not be attainable.

(3) The mark up can be very arbitrary and may not properly account for factors such as competition levels, how much customers are willing to pay etc

Marginal cost-plus pricing

Using this method, the selling price for the product is determined as follows:

Selling price = Marginal cost per unit × (1 + mark-up percentage)

To the accountant, marginal cost is the same as variable cost. In setting the selling price using this method a larger mark-up percentage is added because both fixed costs and profit must be covered.

It is a particularly useful method when determining a minimum acceptable selling price (for example, for a one-off product order) and this is examined in more detail in a later chapter.

Benefits and problems when using marginal cost pricing

Some of the reasons for using marginal cost in preference to full cost are as follows:

(1)   It is just as accurate as total cost-plus pricing. A larger mark-up percentage is added because both fixed costs and profit must be covered, but the uncertainty over the fixed costs per unit remains in both pricing methods.

(2)   Knowledge of marginal cost gives management the option of pricing below total cost when times are bad, in order to fill capacity.

(3)   It is particularly useful in pricing specific one-off contracts because it only accounts for costs which are likely to change because of the new contract. This pricing decision is covered in more detail in a later chapter.

(4)   It also recognises the existence of scarce or limiting resources. Where these are used by competing products and services it must be reflected in the selling price if profit is to be maximised. If there is a scarce or bottleneck resource the aim must be to maximise the total contribution from the limiting factor. The contribution that each alternative product or service makes from each unit of the scarce resource must be calculated and a suitable profit margin added.

The main criticisms of marginal cost pricing are:

(1)   Like any cost based pricing method, it ignores other factors such as levels of competition, customer attitudes etc.

(2)   The mark-up becomes even more arbitrary than that used in full cost plus as now it must also include a subjective element which allows for the selling price to cover fixed costs. For this reason, many accountants argue that marginal cost plus pricing should only be used for marginal (short-term or one-off) decisions.

Target return on capital

As well as determining the selling price by adding a mark-up on cost, an organisation may also set the mark-up at a level that provides a target return on the investment that has been made in the product.

The mark-up is calculated as:

> **Profit mark-up = Targeted return on investment in the product/budgeted level of production**

The targeted return on investment is calculated as:

Targeted return on investment in the product = Total investment in the product × targeted rate of return

Example 7

This method involves determining the amount of capital invested to support a product. For example, some fixed or non-current assets and certain elements of working capital such as inventory and trade receivables can be attributed to individual products.

The selling price is then set to achieve a specified return on the capital invested on behalf of the product. The following example will demonstrate how the method works.

Direct material cost per unit	$62
Direct labour cost per unit	$14
Direct labour hours per unit	4 hours
Production overhead absorption rate	$16 per direct labour hour
Mark-up for non-production overhead costs	8% of total production cost

LG Ltd sells 1,000 units of product B each year. Product B requires an investment of $400,000 and the target rate of return on investment is 12% per annum.

Calculate the selling price for one unit of product B, to the nearest cent.

Target return on sales

An organisation can use a similar technique to determine a selling price which provides a target return on sales. This pricing method involves determining the full cost of a cost unit and then adding a mark-up that represents a specified percentage of the final selling price.

WP Ltd manufactures product A. Data for product A are as follows:

Direct material cost per unit	$7
Direct labour cost per unit	$18
Direct labour hours per unit	2 hours
Production overhead absorption rate	$6 per direct labour hour
Mark-up for non-production overhead costs	5% of total production cost

WP Ltd requires a 15% return on sales revenue from all products.

Calculate the selling price for product A, to the nearest cent.

Solution

	$ per unit
Direct material cost	7.00
Direct labour cost	18.00
Total direct cost	25.00
Production overhead absorbed (2 hours × $6)	12.00
Total production cost	37.00
Mark-up for non-production costs (5% × $37.00)	1.85
Full cost	38.85
Profit mark-up (15/85* × $38.85)	6.86
Selling price	45.71

*Always read the question data carefully. The 15% required return is expressed as a percentage of the sales revenue, not as a percentage of the cost. Sales revenue is therefore equal to 100%; the cost is equal to 85% and the profit is the remaining 15%.

Profit margin

As an alternative calculation, the examiner may provide a profit margin rather than a mark-up on cost. The selling price using a profit margin can be calculated as follows:

> **Selling price = Total cost ÷ (1 − required margin)**

The decision as to what gets included in the total cost (for example, whether that is the absorption or marginal cost) and the associated calculations required to get to the total cost will be the same as when using a mark-up on cost.

Example 8

A product has a total production cost of $60. Determine the selling price for the product if the company wants to achieve:

(a) a 25% mark-up on total production cost

(b) a 20% margin on total production cost

7   Chapter summary

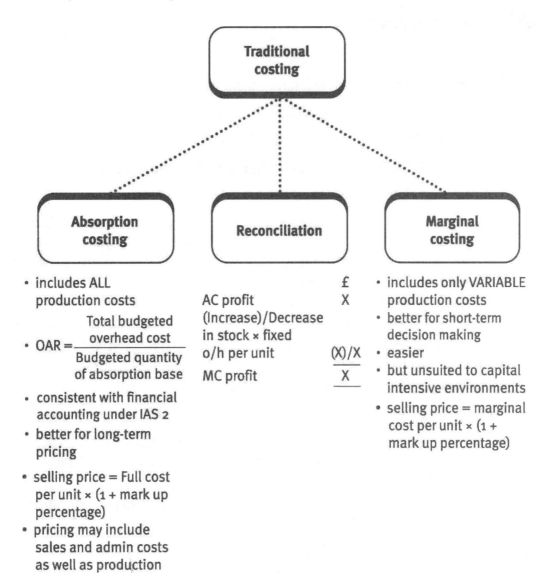

Traditional costing

Absorption costing

- includes ALL production costs
- OAR = $\dfrac{\text{Total budgeted overhead cost}}{\text{Budgeted quantity of absorption base}}$
- consistent with financial accounting under IAS 2
- better for long-term pricing
- selling price = Full cost per unit × (1 + mark up percentage)
- pricing may include sales and admin costs as well as production overheads

Reconciliation

	£
AC profit	X
(Increase)/Decrease in stock × fixed o/h per unit	(X)/X
MC profit	X

Marginal costing

- includes only VARIABLE production costs
- better for short-term decision making
- easier
- but unsuited to capital intensive environments
- selling price = marginal cost per unit × (1 + mark up percentage)

8   Practice questions

Test your understanding 1 ✓

Scenario

Saturn, a chocolate manufacturer, produces three products:

*   The Sky Bar, a bar of solid milk chocolate.

*   The Moon Egg, a fondant filled milk chocolate egg.

*   The Sun Bar, a biscuit and nougat based chocolate bar.

Information relating to each of the products is as follows:

	Sky Bar	Moon Egg	Sun Bar
Direct labour cost per unit ($)	0.07	0.14	0.12
Direct material cost per unit ($)	0.17	0.19	0.16
Actual production/sales (units)	500,000	150,000	250,000
Direct labour hours per unit	0.001	0.01	0.005
Direct machine hours per unit	0.01	0.04	0.02
Selling price per unit ($)	0.50	0.45	0.43

Annual production overhead = $80,000

Tasks

Using traditional absorption costing, calculate the full production cost per unit and the profit per unit for each product. Explain the implications of the figures calculated.

(Time allowed: 20 minutes)

Test your understanding 2 ✓

E plc operates a marginal costing system. For the forthcoming year, variable costs are budgeted to be 60% of sales value and fixed costs are budgeted to be 10% of sales value.

If E plc increases its selling prices by 10%, but if fixed costs, variable costs per unit and sales volume remain unchanged, identify the effect on E plc's contribution:

A   a decrease of 2%

B   an increase of 5%

C   an increase of 10%

D   an increase of 25%

Test your understanding 3

When comparing the profits reported under marginal and absorption costing during a period when the level of inventories increased, identify which of the following statements would be true:

A   absorption costing profits will be higher and closing inventory valuations lower than those under marginal costing

B   absorption costing profits will be higher and closing inventory valuations higher than those under marginal costing

C   marginal costing profits will be higher and closing inventory valuations lower than those under absorption costing

D   marginal costing profits will be lower and closing inventory valuations higher than those under absorption costing

Test your understanding 4

Exe Limited makes a single product whose total cost per unit is budgeted to be $45. This includes fixed cost of $8 per unit based on a volume of 10,000 units per period. In a period, sales volume was 9,000 units, and production volume was 11,500 units. The actual profit for the same period, calculated using absorption costing, was $42,000.

If the profit statement were prepared using marginal costing, identify the profit for the period:

A $10,000

B $22,000

C $50,000

D $62,000

Test your understanding 5

Scenario

Keats plc commenced business on 1 March making one product only, the standard cost of which is as follows:

	$
Direct labour	5
Direct material	8
Variable production overhead	2
Fixed production overhead	5
Standard production cost	20

The fixed production overhead figure has been calculated on the basis of a budgeted normal output of 36,000 units per annum.

You are to assume that actual fixed overheads were as expected and that all the budgeted fixed expenses are incurred evenly over the year. March and April are to be taken as equal period months.

Selling, distribution and administration expenses are:

Fixed	$120,000 per annum
Variable	15% of the sales value

The selling price per unit is $35 and the number of units produced and sold were:

	March (units)	April (units)
Production	2,000	3,200
Sales	1,500	3,000

Tasks

(a) prepare profit statements for each of the months of March and April using:

    (i)   absorption costing, and

    (ii)   marginal costing

(b) prepare a reconciliation of the profit or loss figures given in your answers to (a)(i) and (a)(ii) accompanied by a brief explanation.

(Time allowed: 20 minutes)

Test your understanding 6 √

If inventory levels have increased during the period, the profit calculated using marginal costing would be _lower_ (choose between 'higher' and 'lower') than the profit when compared with that calculated using absorption costing.

Test your understanding 7 √

Identify which of the following statements would be true: fixed production overheads will always be under-absorbed when:

A   actual output is lower than budgeted output

B   actual overheads incurred are lower than budgeted overheads

C   overheads absorbed are lower than those budgeted

D   overheads absorbed are lower than those incurred

Test your understanding 8 √

A company uses a standard absorption costing system. The fixed overhead absorption rate is based on labour hours.

Extracts from the company's records for last year were as follows:

	Budget	Actual
Fixed production overhead	$450,000	$475,000
Output	50,000 units	60,000 units
Labour hours	900,000	930,000

The _under_ (choose between 'over' and 'under') -absorbed fixed production overheads for the year were $ _10,000_ (fill in the value).

Test your understanding 9 √

GY Ltd budgets to produce and sell 3,800 units of product R in the forthcoming year. The amount of capital investment attributable to product R will be $600,000 and GY Ltd requires a rate of return of 15% on all capital invested.

Further details concerning product R are as follows:

Direct material cost per unit	$14
Direct labour cost per unit	$19
Variable overhead cost per unit	$3
Machine hours per unit	8

Fixed overhead is absorbed at a rate of $11 per machine hour.

Required:

Calculate all answers to the nearest cent.

(a)   The variable cost of product R is $ ~~124~~ 36 per unit.

(b)   The total (full) cost of product R is $ 124 per unit.

(c)   The selling price of product R which will achieve the specified return on investment is $ 147.68 per unit.

Test your understanding 10 √

A company manufactures a range of products one of which, product Y, incurs a total cost of $20 per unit. The company incurs a total cost of $600,000 each period and the directors wish to achieve a return of 18% on the total capital of $800,000 invested in the company.

Required:

Based on this information the cost-plus selling price of one unit of product Y should be $ 24.80

Test your understanding 11 √

Scenario

ML is an engineering company that specialises in providing engineering facilities to businesses that cannot justify operating their own facilities in-house. ML employs a number of engineers who are skilled in different engineering techniques that enable ML to provide a full range of engineering facilities to its customers.

Most of the work undertaken by ML is unique to each of its customers, often requiring the manufacture of spare parts for its customers' equipment, or the building of new equipment from customer drawings. As a result most of ML's work is short-term, with some jobs being completed within hours while others may take a few days.

To date, ML has adopted a cost plus approach to setting its prices. This is based upon an absorption costing system that uses machine hours as the basis of absorbing overhead costs into individual job costs. The Managing Director is concerned that, over recent months, ML has been unsuccessful when quoting for work with the consequence that there has been an increase in the level of unused capacity. It has been suggested that ML should adopt an alternative approach to its pricing based on marginal costing since 'any price that exceeds variable costs is better than no work'.

Tasks

With reference to the above scenario:

(a) briefly explain absorption and marginal cost approaches to pricing

(b) discuss the validity of the comment 'any price that exceeds variable costs is better than no work'.

(Time allowed: 20 minutes)

Test your understanding 12 ✓

A company has calculated its marginal cost of production for its bestselling product as $50 per unit and its full cost of production as $85 per unit.

Which two of the following statements are true?

A   If the company uses a mark-up of 20% on full cost, the selling price would be $106.25 per unit.

B   If the company uses a margin on sales of 25%, based on full cost, the selling price would be $113.33 per unit.

C   If the company uses a mark-up on marginal cost of 120%, the selling price will be $110 per unit.

D   If the company requires a margin on sales of 20%, the profit will be $17.00 per unit.

Test your understanding 13 ✓

FGH makes only one product, which has the following costs per unit:

	$
Direct materials	3
Direct labour	6
Variable production overhead	2
Fixed production overhead	4
Variable selling cost	5

The selling price of one unit is $21.

Budgeted fixed overheads are based on budgeted production of 5,000 units. Actual production and sales were 6,000 and actual fixed production overheads incurred were $25,000.

Which THREE of the following statements are true?

A   Overheads were under-absorbed by $1,000.

B   Overheads were over-absorbed by $5,000.

C   The contribution earned was $30,000.

D   The marginal costing profit was $5,000.

E   The marginal costing profit would be higher than the absorption costing profit.

Example and test your understanding answers

Example 1

Standard cost card

		$
Direct materials per unit	3 kgs × $4/kg	12
Direct labour per unit	2 hrs × $22/hr	44
Variable overheads	2 hrs × $6/hr	12
Production overhead per unit (note)		20
Full/absorption cost per unit		88

Note:

Production overhead per unit in the standard cost card should be based on budgeted production. Therefore in this example they will be ($400,000/20,000 units =) $20 per unit.

Inventory valuation

If 16,000 units were produced and 14,000 units sold then there will be 2,000 units in closing inventory.

Valuing that inventory at the absorption cost will give a value of

= 2,000 × $88

= $176,000

Example 2

	A	B	C
Direct materials	$14.40	$25.60	$36.00
Direct labour:			
Machining @ $4.80 per hour	$9.60	$7.20	$9.60
Assembling @ $3.20 per hour	$6.40	$8.00	$3.20
Prime cost	$30.40	$40.80	$48.80
Production overhead per unit (W1)	$2.00	$2.00	$1.50
Full production cost per unit	$32.40	$42.80	$50.30

(W1) OAR = $\dfrac{\$120,000}{240,000 \text{ labour hours (W2)}}$ = $0.50 per direct labour hour

Overheads product A: 4 labour hours × $0.50 = $2.00

Overheads product B: 4 labour hours × $0.50 = $2.00

Overheads product C: 3 labour hours × $0.50 = $1.50

(W2) Direct labour hours:

	A	B	C	Total
Production (units)	10,000	20,000	40,000	70,000
Production hours:				
Machining	20,000	30,000	80,000	130,000
Assembly	20,000	50,000	40,000	110,000
Total hours	40,000	80,000	120,000	240,000

Example 3

Standard cost card

		$
Direct materials per unit	3 kgs × $4/kg	12
Direct labour per unit	2 hrs × $22/hr	44
Variable overheads	2 hrs × $6/hr	12
Marginal cost per unit		68

Note:

Fixed production overhead is not included in a marginal costing standard cost card.

Inventory valuation

Valuing that inventory at the marginal cost will give a value of

= 2,000 × $68

= $136,000

Example 4

(a)　(i)

		$	$
Sales	1,000 units × $50		50,000
Direct materials	1,000 units × $15	15,000	
Direct labour	1,000 units × $10	10,000	
Variable overheads	1,000 units × $5	5,000	
Fixed overheads		5,000	
			35,000
Profit			15,000

(ii)

$$\text{Profit per unit} = \frac{\$15000}{1,000 \text{ units}} = 15/\text{unit}$$

(b)　(i)　Contribution per unit = $50 − ($15 + $10 + $5) = $20

(ii)　Total contribution = $20/unit × 1,000 units = $20,000

(iii)

	$
Contribution	
$20/unit × 1,000 units	20,000
Fixed cost	5,000
Profit	15,000

The two systems give the same profit provided there is no change in inventory.

Example 5

Marginal costing is illustrated first.

		$
Contribution		
$20/unit × 2,700 units		54,000
Fixed cost		5,000
		———
Profit		49,000
		———

Absorption costing:

		$	$
Sales	2,700 units × $50		135,000
Less Cost of sales:			
Direct materials	3,000 units × $15	45,000	
Direct labour	3,000 units × $10	30,000	
Variable overheads	3,000 units × $5	15,000	
Fixed overheads	3,000 units × $5	15,000	
Less closing inventory (300 **(W1)** units @ $35)		(10,500)	
		———	
			(94,500)
Over-absorption of fixed overheads **(W2)**			10,000
			———
			50,500
			———

(W1)

Closing inventory = opening inventory + output – sales

$$= 0 + 3,000 - 2,700 = 300$$

(W1)

Overheads absorbed (3,000 × $5)	$15,000
Overheads incurred	$5,000
Over-absorption of overheads	$10,000

It can be seen that inventory levels have increased by 300 units, therefore absorption costing profits will be higher than marginal costing profits. This is because of the fixed overhead that is carried forward to the next period in the closing inventory. The total of this is $5 × 300 units = $1,500.

Example 6

B

A common short-cut in multiple choice questions is to calculate the marginal costing profit and then use the reconciliation of profits to get to the absorption costing profit.

First of all – the profit under marginal costing:

Contribution per unit = $15 – (3.50 + 4.00 + 2.00) = $5.50

No of units sold = 2,400 – 180 = 2,220

	$
Contribution	
$5.50/unit × 2,220 units	12,210
Fixed cost	
$60,000 p.a./12 months	5,000
	———
	7,210
	———

As production is greater than sales, absorption costing will show the higher profit.

Difference in profit = change in inventory × fixed production overhead per unit.

Difference in profit = 180 units × $2/unit = $360.

Therefore, profit reported under absorption costing = $7,210 + 360 = $7,570.

The FOAR was worked out as = $\dfrac{\text{Budgeted overheads}}{\text{Budgeted level of activity}}$ =

$\dfrac{\$60,000}{30,000 \text{ units}}$ = $2 per unit

Example 7

The selling price is calculated as follows:

	$ per unit
Direct material cost	62.00
Direct labour cost	14.00
Total direct cost	76.00
Production overhead absorbed (4 hours × $16)	64.00
Total production cost	140.00
Mark-up for non-production costs (8% × $140)	11.20
Full cost	151.20
Profit mark-up (see working)	48.00
Selling price	199.20

Working:

Target return on investment in product B = $400,000 × 12% = $48,000

Target return per unit of product B = $48,000/1,000 units = $48

Example 8

Margin			**Mark up**		
	$	Ratio		$	Ratio
Sales	75	100%	Sales	75	125%
Cost of sales	(60)	80%	Cost of sales	(60)	100%
Gross profit	15	20%	Gross profit	15	25%

(a) With a profit mark-up, the cost is 100% and so the selling price is:

Selling price = total cost × (1 + 25%)

= $60 × 1.25 = $75

(b) With a profit margin, the selling price is equal to 100%, and will be:

Selling price = total cost / (1 – 20%)

= $60 / 0.8 = $75

We can see here that a profit margin of 20% is the same as a profit mark-up of 25%.

Test your understanding 1

As mentioned, it is relatively easy to complete the first two lines of the cost card. The difficult part is calculating the production overhead per unit, so let's start by considering this. We need to absorb the overheads into units of production. To do this, we will first need to calculate an overhead absorption rate (OAR):

$$OAR = \frac{\text{Production overhead}}{\text{Activity level}} = \frac{\text{(this is \$80,000, as per the question}}{\text{(this must be chosen)}}$$

The activity level must be appropriate for the business. Saturn must choose between three activity levels:

- Units of production – This would not be appropriate since Saturn produces more than one type of product. It would not be fair to absorb the same amount of overhead into each product.

- Machine hours or labour hours – It is fair to absorb production overheads into the products based on the labour or machine hours taken to produce each unit. We must decide if the most appropriate activity level is machine or labour hours. To do this we can look at the nature of the process. Production appears to be more machine intensive than labour intensive because each unit takes more machine hours to produce than it does labour hours. Therefore, the most appropriate activity level is machine hours.

Working – OAR

$$OAR = \frac{\$80,000 \text{ production overhead}}{(0.01 \times 500k) + (0.04 \times 150k) + (0.02 \times 250k) \text{ hours}}$$

$$= \frac{\$80,000}{16,000 \text{ hours}}$$

= $5 per machine hour

We can now absorb these into the units of production:

	Sky Bar	Moon Egg	Sun Bar
Production overheads ($) = machine hours per unit × $5	0.05	0.20	0.10

This is the difficult part done.

We can now quickly complete the cost card and answer the question:

	Sky Bar	Moon Egg	Sun Bar
Direct labour cost per unit	0.07	0.14	0.12
Direct material cost per unit	0.17	0.19	0.16
Production overhead per unit	0.05	0.20	0.10
Full production cost per unit	**0.29**	**0.53**	**0.38**
Selling price per unit	0.50	0.45	0.43
Profit/(loss) per unit	**0.21**	**(0.08)**	**0.05**

Outcome of absorption costing

Based on absorption costing, the Sky Bar and the Sun Bar are both profitable. However, the Moon Egg is loss making. Managers would need to consider the future of the Moon Egg. They may look at the possibility of increasing the selling price and/or reducing costs. If this is not possible, they may make the decision to stop selling the product. However, this may prove to be the wrong decision because absorption costing does not always result in an accurate calculation of the full production cost per unit. ABC can be a more accurate method of calculating the full production cost per unit and as a result should lead to better decisions. ABC is explored in the next chapter.

Test your understanding 2

D

The easiest way to answer this question is to make up a number for sales, say $1,000, then the relationships will be much easier to visualise.

If sales = $1,000, then:

Variable cost = 60% × $1,000 = $600

Current situation

	$
Sales	1,000
Variable cost	600
Contribution	400

New situation

	$
Sales (10% higher)	1,100
Variable cost	600
	———
Contribution	500
	———

Contribution increases by $100, which is an increase of 25% on its original value.

Fixed cost should be ignored as it does not affect contribution.

Test your understanding 3

B

Where inventories increase in the period, absorption costing profits will be higher than marginal costing profits. This is because some of the fixed overhead is carried forward in inventory instead of being written off against sales for the period. The value of closing inventory is higher with absorption costing as it includes the absorbed fixed overhead.

Test your understanding 4

B

Production is greater than sales, so absorption costing will have the higher profit.

Difference in profit = change in inventory × fixed production overhead per unit.

Difference in profit = 2,500 units × $8/unit = $20,000.

Therefore, profit reported under marginal costing = $42,000 − 20,000 = $22,000.

Test your understanding 5

(a)   (i)

	March		April	
	$	$	$	$
Sales		52,500		105,000
Cost of sales				
Opening stock (W1)	0		10,000	
Production costs (@$20/unit)	40,000		64,000	
	40,000		74,000	
Less closing inventory (@$20/unit) (W2)	10,000		14,000	
		30,000		60,000
		22,500		45,000
(Under)/over-absorption (W3)		(5,000)		1,000
Gross profit		17,500		46,000
Selling and other costs				
Fixed (W4)	10,000		10,000	
Variable	7,875		15,750	
		17,875		25,750
Net Profit/Loss		(375)		20,250

(ii)

	March		April	
	$	$	$	$
Sales		52,500		105,000
Variable cost of sales				
Opening inventory (W1)	0		7,500	
Variable production costs (@$15/unit)	30,000		48,000	
	30,000		55,500	
Less: closing inventory (@$15/unit) (W2)	7,500		10,500	
		22,500		45,000
		30,000		60,000
Variable selling and other costs		7,875		15,750
Contribution		22,125		44,250
Fixed costs				
Production	15,000		15,000	
Selling etc.	10,000		10,000	
		25,000		25,000
Profit/Loss		(2,875)		19,250

Workings

(W1) The closing inventory for March becomes the opening stock for April.

(W2)

	March Units	April Units
Opening inventory	0	500
Production	2,000	3,200
	2,000	3,700
Less sales	1,500	3,000
Closing inventory	500	700

(W3) Under-/over-absorption is the difference between overheads incurred and overheads absorbed.

"Overheads incurred" means actual overheads and we are told that the actual fixed overheads were as expected. Therefore the actual overheads incurred are the same as the budgeted fixed overheads.

Budgeted fixed overhead = $5 per unit × 36,000 units annum		= $180,000 per
This works out as		= $15,000 per month

March

Overheads incurred		15,000
Overheads absorbed	$5/unit × 2,000 units	10,000
Under-absorption		(5,000)

April

Overheads incurred		15,000
Overheads absorbed	$5/unit × 3,200 units	16,000
Over-absorption		1,000

(W4) Selling and other costs fixed overhead = $120,000/12 = $10,000 per month.

(b) If there is no change in inventory, the 2 systems give the same profit. If production is greater than sales then absorption costing shows the higher profit.

Difference in profit = change in inventory × fixed production overhead cost per unit

In both March and April, production is greater than sales and thus absorption costing will show the higher profit (the smaller loss in March).

	March	April
Marginal costing profit/loss	(2,875)	19,250
Difference in profit		
(2,000 – 1,500) × $5 per unit	2,500	
(3,200 – 3,000) × $5 per unit		1,000
Absorption costing profit/loss	(375)	20,250

This difference occurs because marginal costing writes off the entire fixed overhead in the period incurred, whereas absorption costing carries forward some fixed production overhead into the next period in the valuation of closing inventory.

Test your understanding 6

Missing word: lower

Marginal costing values inventory at a lower amount because it does not include fixed overheads in the valuation. Therefore as inventory levels increase the value of closing inventory under marginal costing will be lower. This will give a higher cost of sales and a lower profit.

Test your understanding 7

D

Under-absorption occurs when the amount absorbed is less than the actual overheads incurred.

Test your understanding 8

The **over**-absorbed fixed production overheads for the year were **$65,000**

$$\text{Absorption rate} = \frac{\$450,000}{900,000} = \$0.50/\text{hour}$$

Absorbed overheads	60,000 units × 18 hrs/unit × $0.50/hour	= $540,000
Actual overheads	=	$475,000
Over-absorption	=	$65,000

Test your understanding 9

(a) The variable cost per unit of product R is $36.00 per unit.

Direct material $14 + direct labour $19 + variable overhead $3 = **$36.**

(b) The total (full) cost of product R is $124.00 per unit.

Variable cost $36 + fixed overhead (8 hours × $11) = **$124.**

(c) The selling price of product R which will achieve the specified return on investment is $147.68 per unit.

Working:

Required return from investment in product R
= $600,000 × 15% = $90,000

Required return per unit sold = $90,000/3,800 units = $23.68

Required selling price = $124.00 full cost + $23.68 = **$147.68**

Test your understanding 10

The cost-plus selling price of one unit of product Y should be **$24.80.**

Required annual return = $800,000 × 18% = $144,000

Return as a percentage of total cost = 144,000/$600,000 = 24%

Required cost-plus selling price = $20 + (24% × $20) = **$24.80**

Test your understanding 11

[Make sure that you focus your answer on absorption and marginal cost approaches to pricing (not costing). A main issue is therefore how the level of mark-up is determined. Your answer should take a balanced view of the comment in the short and long term. While it may be true in the short term, under certain circumstances a price which does not generate a profit in the long term could not be acceptable.]

(a) An absorption cost approach to pricing involves adding a profit margin to the full cost of the product. The full cost is calculated by taking prime cost and adding a share of overhead which, in ML's case, is absorbed using machine hours.

A marginal cost approach to pricing takes the variable cost of the product and adds a mark-up to cover fixed cost and profit. Fixed overheads are not absorbed to product but are treated as a period cost in the accounts.

The mark-up added using a marginal costing approach would have to be greater than that under an absorption costing approach to ensure that the same profit level is achieved. Mark-ups may be varied depending on the market conditions. ML's work is unique to each of its customers and it may therefore be difficult to estimate a suitable mark-up.

(b) The comment 'any price that exceeds variable costs is better than no work' may have some validity in the short term. In the case of a company like ML, which has unused capacity, fixed costs will be incurred in the short term irrespective of workload, i.e. the fixed costs will not change as no extra capacity is required (for example, premises will not have to be expanded in order to accommodate the extra production), and they can therefore be ignored for decision making purposes. Any price that exceeds variable cost will provide some contribution and will reduce losses.

Care must be taken that special prices based on variable cost do not become the normal expectation or upset existing customers who are paying a price which generates a profit.

In the long run fixed cost must be covered and a profit made in accordance with company objectives. An absorption costing approach may not provide an accurate total product costs and an activity-based approach may improve the accuracy of total costs and enable ML to identify those products or customers which generate most profit.

If resources are scarce (i.e. they cannot easily be obtained at the prices or rates contained in the standard cost card) then this statement is not true, even in the short term, as scarce resources typically cost a premium and the marginal cost will increase. This concept will be explored in the decision making chapter later in the text.

Test your understanding 12

B and C are true.

A   If the company uses a mark-up of 20% on full cost, the selling price would be $106.25 per unit. This is false.

Using a mark-up of 20% on full cost of $85 per unit would give a selling price per unit of $85 × 1.2 = **$102 per unit**.

B   If the company uses a margin on sales of 25%, the selling price would be $113.33 per unit. This is true.

Selling price = $85 ÷ (1 − 0.25) = **$113.33 per unit**.

C   If the company uses a mark-up on marginal cost of 120%, the selling price will be $110 per unit. This is true.

Selling price = $50 + 120% = **$110 per unit**.

D   If the company requires a margin on sales of 20%, the profit will be $17 per unit. This is false.

Profit = $85 × (0.2 ÷ 0.8) = **$21.25 per unit**.

Test your understanding 13

A, C and D are true.

A	Fixed production overheads absorbed (6,000 × $4)	$24,000
	Fixed production overheads incurred	$25,000
	Under absorption	**$1,000**

B is incorrect as overheads are under absorbed by $1,000

C   Variable costs = 3 + 6 + 2 + 5 = $16
Unit contribution = $21 – $16 = $5
Total contribution = 6,000 × $5 = **$30,000**

D	Total contribution	$30,000
	Fixed cost	$25,000
	Profit	**$5,000**

E is incorrect. As there is no change in inventory levels, the profits under marginal and absorption costing would be the same.

Activity-based costing

Chapter learning objectives

Lead outcome	Component outcome
A2. Apply the main costing concepts to organisations and cost objects	(a) Explain the main costing concepts (b) Apply costing concepts to different organisations and cost objects
A3. Apply costing methods to determine the costs for different purposes	(d) Activity based costing

1 Chapter overview diagram

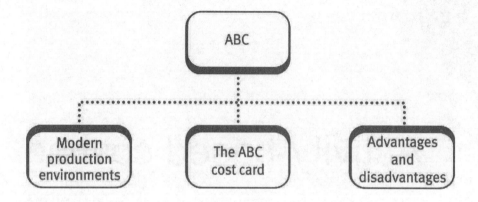

2 Modern production environments

Modern producers have changed the way that they produce so that they have:

- much more machinery and computerised manufacturing systems
- smaller batch sizes
- less use of 'direct' labour

This has had the following **impact on production costs:**

- more indirect overheads (for example, insurance and depreciation of the machines and computers)
- less direct labour costs

This means that the **traditional** methods of costing (marginal and absorption, as seen in the previous chapter) produce **standard cost cards that are less useful** due to inaccurate product costs:

- the largest cost of production is indirect overheads but these are categorised together in one figure that lacks detail and is not useful to management
- because management does not know what the components are of the largest production cost (indirect overheads) they cannot implement proper cost control
- the costs are often allocated between products on the basis of direct labour hours – despite the fact that direct labour is becoming a smaller proportion of product costs and does not fairly reflect the relationship between the products and the indirect overheads
- because costs are inappropriately or inaccurately shared between products it means that the total production cost can be wrong, which can lead to poor pricing and production decisions.

Activity based costing **(ABC) has been developed to solve the problems** that traditional costing methods create in these modern environments.

Traditional costing problems

Problems with traditional absorption costing

Traditional absorption costing charges overhead costs to products (or services) in an arbitrary way. In product costing, overheads are absorbed on the basis of the volume of production in each production department or centre. The basis for setting an absorption rate is volume-related, such as an overhead absorption rate per unit produced, a rate per direct labour hour or a rate per machine hour.

The assumption underlying this method of costing is that overhead expenditure is connected to the volume of production activity.

- This assumption was probably valid many years ago, when production systems were based on labour-intensive or machine-intensive mass production of fairly standard items. Overhead costs were also fairly small relative to direct materials and direct labour costs; therefore any inaccuracy in the charging of overheads to products costs was not significant.

- The assumption is not valid in a complex manufacturing environment where production is based on smaller, customised batches of products. In such environments, indirect costs are high in relation to direct costs, and a high proportion of overhead activities – such as production scheduling, order handling and quality control – are not related to production volume.

- For similar reasons, traditional absorption costing is not well-suited to the costing of many services.

The criticism of absorption costing is that it cannot calculate a 'true' product cost that has any valid meaning. Overheads are charged to departments and products in an arbitrary way, and the assumption that overhead expenditure is related to direct labour hours or machine hours in the production departments is no longer realistic.

Problems with marginal costing

There are also major problems with marginal costing, but for different reasons. In marginal costing, products or services are valued at their marginal cost, and profitability is assessed by calculating the contribution earned from each product or service. Fixed costs are assumed to be time-related and are charged against profits as a cost for the period. This can be a useful costing method when variable costs are a large proportion of total costs.

The main criticisms of marginal costing as a method of measuring product costs and profitability are that:

- variable costs might be small in relation to fixed costs

- 'fixed' costs might be fixed in relation to production volume, but they might vary with other activities that are not volume-related or even production-related.

In many manufacturing and service environments, it is therefore inappropriate to treat overhead costs as fixed period costs, and they should be charged to products or services in a more meaningful way.

3 Activity-based costing

Activity-based costing (ABC) is an alternative approach to product costing. It is a form of absorption costing, but, rather than absorbing overheads on a production volume basis, it firstly allocates them to **cost pools** before absorbing them into units using **cost drivers.**

- A **cost pool** is an activity that consumes resources and for which overhead costs are identified and allocated. For each cost pool, there should be a cost driver.

- A **cost driver** is a unit of activity that consumes resources. An alternative definition of a cost driver is a factor influencing the level of cost

Illustration 1

Imagine the machining department in a traditional absorption costing system. The OAR would be based on machine hours because many of the overheads in the machine department would relate to the machines, e.g. power, maintenance, machine depreciation, etc., so using a machine hour basis would seem fair. However, not only does the machine department have machine related costs, but also in an absorption costing system, it would also have picked up a share of rent and rates, heating, lighting, building depreciation, canteen costs, personnel cost, etc. These costs would also be absorbed on a machine hour basis, because everything in the machine department is absorbed on machine hours and whilst this is fair for power, maintenance and machine depreciation, it is inappropriate for the other costs.

ABC overcomes this problem by not using departments as gathering points for costs. It instead uses activities, and there would, for example, be a separate machine-related activity to which power, machine depreciation and machine maintenance would be charged. It would not pick up a share of personnel costs or rent or rates or indeed anything not machine related. ABC's flexibility thus reduces the incidence of arbitrary apportionments.

Identifying activities and drivers

If a business decides to adopt activity-based costing to measure the costs and profitability of its products or services, it must identify the key activities that consume resources and the cost driver for each of those activities.

- There might be a large number of different activities, but in an accounting system it is usually necessary to simplify the overhead cost analysis and select a fairly small number of activities. If a large number of activities are identified and used in ABC, the task of analysing costs becomes more complex and time-consuming, and the value of the additional accuracy might not justify the cost and effort.

- For any activity there might be just one cost driver or several different cost drivers. Where there are several cost drivers, it is necessary to select just one for the purpose of ABC analysis.

Identifying activities

The main activities that consume overhead resources differ from one type of business to another. A useful approach to identifying suitable activities within a business is to consider four different categories of activity or transaction:

- **Logistical transactions.** These are activities or transactions concerned with moving materials or people, and with tracking the progress of materials or work through the system.

- **Balancing transactions.** These are concerned with ensuring that the resources required for an operation are available. For example, the buying department has to make sure that raw materials are available to meet production requirements.

- **Quality transactions.** These are concerned with ensuring that output or service levels meet quality requirements and customer expectations. Inspections and handling customer complaints are both examples of quality transactions.

- **Change transactions.** These are activities required to respond to changes in customer demand, a change in design specifications, a scheduling change, a change in production or delivery methods, and so on.

For any business, there could be important resource-consuming activities in each of these categories.

Identifying cost drivers

For each selected activity, there should be a cost driver. The chosen cost driver must be:

- **Relevant.** In other words, there should be a connection between the cost driver and the consumption of resources for the activity.

- **Easy to measure.** Measuring the units of cost driver and identifying the products or services to which they relate needs to be a fairly easy and straightforward process.

Often, the cost driver is the number of transactions relating to the activity. For example:

- the cost of setting up machinery for a production run might be driven by the number of set-ups (jobs or batches produced)

- the cost of running machines might be driven by the number of machine hours for which the machines are running

- the cost of assembling the product may be based on the number of direct labour hours

- the cost of order processing might be related to the number of orders received

- the cost of dispatch might be related to the number of orders dispatched or to the weight of items dispatched

- the costs of purchasing might be related to the number of purchase orders made

- the costs of quality control might be related to the number of inspections carried out, or to the incidence of rejected items.

It is possible to identify three types of cost driver:

Transaction drivers

Here, the cost of an activity is affected by the number of times a particular action is undertaken. Examples would include number of set-ups, number of power drill operations, number of batches of material received, number of purchase orders, etc.

Duration drivers

In this case, the cost of the activity is not so much affected by the number of times the action is undertaken as by the length of time that it takes to perform the action, e.g. set-up costs may not be related to the number of set-ups so much as to the set-up time, because some products involve more complicated and time consuming set-ups than others.

Intensity drivers

In this case, efforts would be directed at determining what resources were used in the making of a product or service, e.g. rather than charging all purchase orders with the same cost per order, we might determine that overseas orders involve more work than home orders and apply a weighting to the overseas orders to reflect the extra work.

Calculating the full production cost per unit using ABC

There are five basic steps to calculating an activity based cost:

Step 1: **Group production overheads into activities, according to how they are driven.**
A cost pool is the grouping of costs relating to a particular activity which consumes resources and for which overhead costs are identified and allocated. For each cost pool, there should be a cost driver.

Step 2: **Identify cost drivers for each activity, i.e. what causes these activity costs to be incurred.**
A cost driver is a factor that influences (or drives) the level of cost.

Step 3: **Calculate a cost driver rate for each activity.**
The cost driver rate is calculated in the same way as the absorption costing OAR. However, a separate cost driver rate will be calculated for each activity, by taking the activity cost and dividing by the cost driver information.

Step 4: **Absorb the activity costs into the product.**
The activity costs should be absorbed by applying the cost driver rate into the individual products.

Step 5: **Calculate the full production cost and/or the profit or loss.**
Some questions ask for the production cost per unit and/ or the profit or loss per unit.
Other questions ask for the total production cost and/or the total profit or loss

Illustration 2 – ABC

Smart Company manufactures two different washing machines, the Standard model and the Deluxe model. In the past, overheads have been absorbed by direct labour hour. However, the Managing Director is now considering a move to ABC. Budgeted cost information for both models is provided below:

	$
Set-up costs	96,000
Material handling costs	116,000
Other overheads	68,000
Total production overhead	280,000

	Standard	Deluxe
	$	$
Sales price per unit	130	200
Direct material cost per unit ($4 per kg)	12	16
Direct labour cost per unit ($15 per hour)	90	120
Variable overhead per unit ($2 per direct labour hour)	12	16
Actual production/sales units	20,000	2,000
Number of set-ups	900	60
Components per unit	25	40

Required:

Using ABC, calculate the full production cost per unit and the profit per unit for each product.

Step-by-step approach

Step 1: Group production overheads into activities, according to how they are driven.

This has been done above. The $280,000 production overhead has been split into three different activities (cost pools).

Step 2: Identify cost drivers for each activity, i.e. what causes these activity costs to be incurred.

Activity	Cost driver
Set-up costs	Number of set-ups
Material handling costs	Number of components
Other overheads	Number of direct labour hours

Step 3: Calculate a cost-driver rate (OAR) for each activity

$$\text{OAR set-up costs} = \frac{\$96,000}{960 \text{ set-ups } (900+60)}$$

$$= \textbf{\$100 per set-up} \checkmark \checkmark$$

$$\text{OAR materials handling costs} = \frac{\$116,000}{580,000 \text{ components (W1)}}$$

$$= \textbf{\$0.20 per component} \checkmark$$

$$\text{OAR other overheads} = \frac{\$68,000}{136,000 \text{ labour hours (W2)}}$$

= $0.50 per direct labour hour

(W1) Number of components = (20,000 × 25) + (2,000 × 40) = 580,000

(W2) Number of labour hours = (20,000 × 6 hours) + (2,000 × 8 hours) = 136,000

Note: each unit of the Standard includes $90 of direct labour, which is paid at $15 per hour. This is therefore $90/$15 = 6 hours. Each unit of the Deluxe includes $120 of direct labour, which is $120/$15 = 8 hours.

Step 4: Absorb the activity costs into the product

	Standard $	Deluxe $
Set-up costs =	90,000	6,000
$100 × no. of set-ups (900 / 60)		
Material handling costs =	100,000	16,000
$0.20 × no. of components (500,000 / 80,000)		
Other overheads =	60,000	8,000
$0.50 × no. direct labour hours (120,000 / 16,000)		
Total production overhead	**250,000**	**30,000**
Units produced	20,000	2,000
Production overhead per unit	**12.50**	**15.00**

Step 5: Calculate the full production cost and the profit or loss, using Activity-Based Costing

	Standard $	Deluxe $
Direct material cost per unit	12.00	16.00
Direct labour cost per unit	90.00	120.00
Variable overhead per unit	12.00	16.00
Production overhead per unit	12.50	15.00
Full production cost per unit	**126.50**	**167.00**
Selling price per unit	130.00	200.00
Profit/(loss) per unit	**3.50**	**33.00**

Example 1

A manufacturing business makes a product in two models, model M1 and model M2. Details of the two products are as follows.

	Model M1	Model M2
Annual sales	8,000 units	8,000 units
Number of sales orders	60	250
Sales price per unit	$54	$73
Direct material cost per unit	$11	$21
Direct labour hours per unit	2.0 hours	2.5 hours
Direct labour rate per hour	$8	$8
Special parts per unit	2	8
Production batch size	2,000 units	100 units
Setups per batch	1	3

	$	Cost driver
Setup costs	97,600	Number of setups
Material handling costs	42,000	Number of batches
Special part handling costs	50,000	Number of special parts
Invoicing	31,000	Number of sales orders
Other overheads	108,000	Direct labour hours
Total overheads	328,600	

A customer has indicated an interest in placing a large order for either model M1 or M2, and the sales manager wished to try to sell the higher-priced model M2.

Required:

(a) Calculate the profit per unit for each model, using ABC.

(b) Using the information above identify which product the sales manager should try to sell on the basis of the information provided by your ABC analysis.

ABC in service industries

Activity based costing was originally developed for manufacturing industries. But it has now gained widespread use in many service organisations such as hospitals, accountancy practices, banks and insurance companies. It is just as important for these businesses to control costs, maximise the use of resources and improve pricing as it is in a manufacturing business.

Illustration

Boomer Jones is a firm of business advisors. It offers two services to its clients – tax advisory services (TAS) and business advisory services (BAS). Revenue from service is expected to be $3m. The cost for each service is budgeted as follows:

	TAS $	BAS $
Direct labour	300,000	400,000
Overheads (W1)	3,000,000	2,000,000
Total costs	3,300,000	2,400,000
Revenue	3,000,000	3,000,000
Profit/(loss)	(300,000)	600,000

Workings

(W1) Overhead recovery rate

Total budgeted overheads = $5m

Total budgeted direct labour hours = 25,000 hours (15,000 hours in TAS, 10,000 hours in BAS)

Recovery rate per hour of service provided = $200 per hour Budgeted overheads include material costs within the firm which are negligible.

Switch to ABC

As labour costs have become a lesser proportion of total costs and overheads have become more significant, Boomer Jones wants to examine a switch to activity based costing (ABC). The finance director has put together the following information on overheads:

	Cost ($)	Cost Driver	Drivers	
			TAS	BAS
Marketing	500,000	Number of client lunches	500	3,500
Client meetings	1,000,000	Number of clients	9,000	1,000
Data input	1,500,000	Computer hours	10,000	5,000
Analysis and research	1,500,000	Research hours	5,000	10,000
Training and development	500,000	Number of staff	1,000	1,000

This has allowed the finance director to re-allocate the overheads and create a new charge out rate for clients as follows:

	TAS $	BAS $
Direct labour	300,000	400,000
Overheads		
Marketing	62,500	437,500
Client meetings	900,000	100,000
Data input	1,000,000	500,000
Analysis of research	500,000	1,000,000
Training and development	250,000	250,000
Total costs	3,012,500	2,687,500
Revenue	3,000,000	3,000,000
Profit/(loss)	(12,500)	312,500

Boomer Jones now has a better understanding of its costs. TAS continues to make a loss but Boomer Jones now better understands the reasons behind it. It could, for example, seek out ways to reduce the amount of computer hours needed for client work by either training staff to use the computers more efficiently or seeking out more efficient software.

From this illustration it can be seen how service organisations can get great benefit from a switch to activity based costing.

4 When is ABC relevant?

ABC is a more expensive system to operate than traditional costing, so it should only be introduced when it is appropriate to do so. Activity-based costing could provide much more meaningful information about product costs and profits when:

- indirect costs are high relative to direct costs
- products or services are complex
- products or services are tailored to customer specifications
- some products or services are sold in large numbers but others are sold in small numbers.

In these situations, ABC will often result in significantly different product or service overhead costs, compared with traditional absorption costing.

The difference between traditional costing and ABC costing will also be dependent on the makeup of the overhead cost. Overhead costs can be divided into 4 different types of activities

(i)   Unit-level activities – where the consumption of resources is very strongly correlated with the number of units produced.

(ii) Batch-level activities – where the consumption of resources is very strongly correlated with the number of batches produced.

(iii) Product-level activities – where consumption of resources may be related to the existence of particular products.

(iv) Facility-level activities – where the cost cannot be related in any way to the production of any particular product line.

Comparison to traditional costing

Any unit cost, no matter how it is derived, can be misinterpreted. There is temptation to adopt a simplistic approach, which would say, for example, that if it cost $1,000 to produce ten units, it will cost $10,000 to produce 100 units. As we know, this in incorrect in the short term, owing to the existence of short-term fixed costs. The ABC approach does not eliminate this problem anymore than the traditional approach. The alternative to presenting full absorption costing information in a traditional costing system has been to provide the user with a marginal costing statement which distinguishes clearly between the variable cost of production and the fixed cost of production. This carries an implication for the decision-maker that if the variable cost of production is $50 for 10 units, the additional cost of producing a further 40 units will be 40 × $5 = $200.

Activity-based costing, on the other hand, can provide the user with a more sophisticated breakdown of cost. This breakdown relates cost to the level of activities undertaken. The structure of reporting will vary from company to company, but Cooper (1992) has suggested that four levels of activity, which he terms a hierarchy of cost, will commonly be found in practice.

These are shown below:

(i)   *Unit-level activities.* These are activities where the consumption of resources is very strongly correlated with the number of units produced. Costs traditionally defined as direct costs would fall into this category, for example direct material and direct labour.

(ii)   *Batch-level activities.* Some activities – for example, machine set-up, materials handling and batch inspection – consume resources in proportion to the number of batches produced, rather than in proportion to the number of units produced. By identifying the consumption of resources at a batch rather than a unit level, it is easier than in a traditional costing system for a user to visualise the changing cost that will come about in the long term by changing a product mix or production schedule.

(iii) *Product-level activities.* Consumption of resources by, for example, administration, product specification or purchasing may be related to the existence of particular products. If the activity is performed to sustain the existence of a particular product line, it is a product-level activity.

(iv)   *Facility-level activities.* Even within an ABC system, it is accepted that there are some costs that relate simply to being in business and that therefore cannot be related in any way to the production of any particular product line. Grounds maintenance, plant security and property taxes would be examples of this type of cost.

Consideration of (i)–(iv) shows that the difference between traditional costing and ABC costing will be dependent on the proportion of overhead cost that falls into each of the four categories. If this overhead is made up primarily of (i) and (iv), it is obvious that the traditional approach and the ABC approach will lead to very similar product costs. However, if the bulk of overhead cost falls into category (ii) and/or category (iii), there will be a very significant difference between the two.

The debate as to whether ABC is actually a new technique, or whether it simply encourages a more accurate tracing of costs to products in a manner that is perfectly consistent with the traditional approach, is interesting but sterile – and misses the point of ABC, as is demonstrated in the rest of this chapter. Nevertheless, it is worth pointing out that ABC product costs are full absorption costs and, as such, suffer from the same type of deficiencies in a decision-making context as do traditional full absorption costs – they are historical, based on current methods of organisation and operation and, at the level of the product, contain allocations of joint/common costs, etc.

However, it can be strongly argued that ABC has an important 'attention-directing' role to play in both cost management and decision-making. ABC is defined in the CIMA Official Terminology as:

> *an approach to the costing and monitoring of activities which involves tracing resource consumption and costing final outputs. Resources are assigned to activities, and activities to cost objects based on consumption estimates. The latter utilise cost drivers to attach activity costs to outputs.*

In decision-making, it is arguable that activity-based costs are much more helpful than traditional costs in determining the costs relevant for decision-making and, more particularly, in drawing attention to the likely impact on long-run variable costs of short-term decisions.

Advantages and disadvantages of ABC

Advantages	Disadvantages
• improved accuracy	• not always relevant
• better cost understanding	• still need arbitrary cost allocations
• fairer allocation of costs	• need to choose appropriate drivers and activities
• better cost control	• complex
• can be used in complex situations	• expensive to operate
• can be applied beyond production	
• can be used in service industries	

Advantages and disadvantages of ABC

ABC has a number of advantages:

- It provides a more accurate cost per unit. As a result, pricing, sales strategy, performance management and decision making should be improved (see next section for detail).

- It provides much better insight into what drives overhead costs.

- ABC recognises that overhead costs are not all related to production and sales volume.

- In many businesses, overhead costs are a significant proportion of total costs, and management needs to understand the drivers of overhead costs in order to manage the business properly. Overhead costs can be controlled by managing cost drivers.

- It can be applied to derive realistic costs in a complex business environment.

- ABC can be applied to all overhead costs, not just production overheads.

- ABC can be used just as easily in service costing as in product costing.

Disadvantages of ABC:

- ABC will be of limited benefit if the overhead costs are primarily volume related or if the overhead is a small proportion of the overall cost.

- It is impossible to allocate all overhead costs to specific activities.

- The choice of both activities and cost drivers might be inappropriate.

- ABC can be more complex to explain to the stakeholders of the costing exercise.

- The benefits obtained from ABC might not justify the costs.

The implications of switching to ABC

The use of ABC has potentially significant commercial implications:

- Pricing can be based on more realistic cost data.

  - Pricing decisions will be improved because the price will be based on more accurate cost data

- Sales strategy can be more soundly based.

  - More realistic product costs as a result of the use of ABC may enable sales staff to:

    - target customers that appeared unprofitable using absorption costing but may be profitable under ABC

    - stop targeting customers or market segments that are now shown to offer low or negative sales margins.

- Decision making can be improved.

  - Research, production and sales effort can be directed towards those products and services which ABC has identified as offering the highest sales margins.

- Performance management can be improved.

  - Performance management should be enhanced due to the focus on selling the most profitable products and through the control of cost drivers.

  - ABC can be used as the basis of budgeting and longer term forward planning of overhead costs. The more realistic budgeted overhead cost should improve the system of performance management.

5   Chapter summary

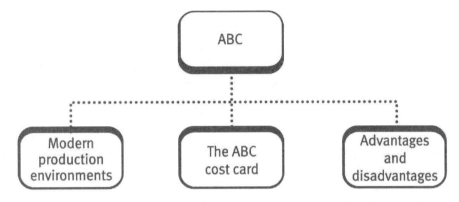

Modern production environments

- Less use of direct labour
- Overheads becoming more important
- More detail needed on overheads
- Need fairer ways to share overheads

The ABC cost card

- Allocates costs to pools rather than departments
- Costs in pools are charged to products using cost drivers
- Cost drivers are more representative of the cause of the cost

Advantages and disadvantages

- More detail is provided on overheads
- Overheads are shared better between products
- Impacts on pricing
- But it is complex
- Some arbitrary allocations remain

6 Practice questions

Test your understanding 1

An organisation has a single production process with expected material receipt and inspection costs of $35,000 for the next period. The following budgeted information has been obtained for the period:

	Product A	Product B	Product C
Production quantity (units)	2,000	1,500	800
Batches of material	20	10	5

The organisation uses an activity based costing system.

The amount of material and inspection costs attributed to each unit of Product B in the period will be:

A $6.67

B $6.98

C $10.89

D $19.97

Test your understanding 2

PB manufactures and sells three products, E, F and G. Budgeted costs for machine running time for the next year are $4,560,000.

The following information is given on budgeted plans for each product:

	Product E	Product F	Product G
Production quantity (units)	5,000	4,000	6,000
Machine hours per unit	2	4	2
Labour hours per unit	1	2	4
Machine set ups	10	6	8

To the nearest $, the machine running cost per unit for Product F using activity based costing will be $ 480

Test your understanding 3

A bank regularly samples business customer accounts and reviews these for risks to the bank. These review costs totalled $1,050,280 in the last period. The following budgeted information has been obtained for the period:

	Sole traders	Partnerships	Companies
Number of customers	250,000	10,000	90,000
Number of reviews	100,000	3,000	18,000

The bank uses an activity based costing system.

To the nearest $, the total amount of review costs attributed to sole trader customers is $ 868,000

Test your understanding 4

A company manufacturers three products with total production overheads of $2,600,000. The company uses an ABC system and has identified associated cost drivers:

Activity cost pool	Cost driver	Cost associated with activity cost pool
Receiving/inspecting quality assurance	Purchase requisitions	$1,400,000
Production scheduling/machine set-ups	Number of batches	$1,200,000

Details on the three products are as follows

	P	R	S
Number of customers	10,000	20,000	30,000
Number of purchase requisitions	1,200	1,800	2,000
Number of set ups	240	260	300

The receiving/inspecting quality assurance cost per unit attributed to product P is:

A $25.20

B $33.60

C $36.00

D $280.00

Test your understanding 5

A company manufacturers three products with total production overheads of $2,600,000. The company uses an ABC system and has identified associated cost drivers:

Activity cost pool	Cost driver	Cost associated with activity cost pool
Receiving/inspecting quality assurance	Purchase requisitions	$1,400,000
Production scheduling/machine set-ups	Number of set-ups	$1,200,000

Details on the three products are as follows

	P	R	S
Production (units)	10,000	20,000	30,000
Number of purchase requisitions	1,200	1,800	2,000
Number of set ups	240	260	300

The charge out rate for production scheduling/machine set-ups is $ 1,500

Test your understanding 6

An organisation has a single production process with expected material handling costs of $13,650 for the next period.

The following budgeted information has been obtained for the period:

	Product X	Product Y	Product Z
Production quantity (units)	2,000	1,500	800
Batches of material	10	5	16
Data per product unit	240	260	300
Direct material (sq. metres)	4	6	3
Direct material ($)	5	3	6

The organisation uses an activity based costing system and the cost driver for material handling is the quantity of material (sq. metres) handled.

The amount of material handling costs attributed to each unit of Product X in the period will be:

A $2.81

B $2.83

C $14.05

D $14.15

Test your understanding 7

A small accountancy firm provides three services as follows:

	Statutory audit	Tax services	Other services
Budgeted services	5,000	10,000	40,000
Budgeted labour hours per service	18	2	4
Average number of reviews per service	3	0.5	2

Other services include services such as pension planning, business consultancy and business valuations.

The budgeted activity cost for reviews was $55,000.

To the nearest cent, if an ABC system is used by the accountancy firm, how much review cost is attached to each statutory audit service?

A $0.55

B $1.65

C $3.00

D $3.67

Test your understanding 8

Machine set up costs are likely to be classed as which type of activity in the hierarchy of costs?

A Unit level activity

B Batch level activity

C Product level activity

D Facility level activity

Test your understanding 9

Scenario

Fixed overhead absorption rates are often calculated using a single measure of activity. It is suggested that fixed overhead costs should be attributed to cost units using multiple measures of activity (Activity Based Costing).

Task

Explain Activity Based Costing and how it may provide useful information to managers.

(Your answer should refer to both the setting of cost driver rates and subsequent overhead cost control).

(Time allowed: 10 minutes)

Test your understanding 10

Explain the benefits of using multiple activity bases for variable overhead absorption.

(Time allowed: 10 minutes)

Test your understanding 11

Explain the factors that should be considered when selecting cost drivers for an activity based costing system.

(Time allowed: 10 minutes)

Test your understanding 12

Scenario

An organisation manufactures three products in a single process. It has used absorption costing in the past and absorbed overheads on the basis of direct labour hours. It has prepared the following standard cost card for each product on that basis:

	Product X	Product Y	Product Z
Direct material	5.00	3.00	6.00
Direct labour	3.60	6.00	9.00
Production overhead	7.53	12.50	18.75
	$16.10	$21.50	$33.75

The accountant has proposed a switch to activity based costing and has prepared revised standard cost cards on that basis as follows:

	Product X	Product Y	Product Z
Direct material	5.00	3.00	6.00
Direct labour	3.60	6.00	9.00
Production overhead			
Material receipt/inspection	2.52	1.69	10.08
Process power	6.46	3.23	2.15
Material handling	2.61	4.22	2.11
Cost per unit	$20.39	$18.13	$29.32

Process power has been charged to products on the basis of the number of drill operations carried out on each product. A cost driver for drill operations of $1.0773 has been determined.

Task:

Using the power drill costs as an illustration, explain the relevance of cost drivers in activity based costing.

(Time allowed: 10 minutes)

 Test your understanding 13

Scenario

Cabal makes and sells two products, Plus and Doubleplus. The direct costs of production are $12 for one unit of Plus and $24 per unit of Doubleplus.

Information relating to annual production and sales is as follows:

	Plus	**Doubleplus**
Annual production and sales	24,000 units	24,000 units
Direct labour hours per unit	1.0	1.5
Number of orders	10	140
Number of batches	12	240
Number of setups per batch	1	3
Special parts per unit	1	4

Information relating to production overhead costs is as follows:

	Cost driver	**Annual cost**
		$
Setup costs	Number of setups	73,200
Special parts handling	Number of special parts	60,000
Other materials handling	Number of batches	63,000
Order handling	Number of orders	19,800
Other overheads	–	216,000
		_____
		432,000
		_____

Other overhead costs do not have an identifiable cost driver, and in an ABC system, these overheads would be recovered on a direct labour hours basis

The following cost cards were created for the products using a traditional absorption costing system:

	Plus	Doubleplus
	$	$
Direct costs	12.00	24.00
Production overhead	7.20	10.80
Full production cost	19.20	34.80

The accountant has also prepared the following standard cost card to support a suggestion that the company switch to an ABC costing system:

	Plus	Doubleplus
	$	$
Direct costs	12.00	24.00
Production cost per unit	4.33	13.67
Full cost	16.33	37.67

Tasks:

(a) Explain the reasons for the differences in the production cost per unit between the two methods.

(Time allowed: 10 minutes)

(b) Explain the implications for management of using an ABC system instead of an absorption costing system.

(Time allowed: 10 minutes)

Note:

	Plus	Doubleplus
	$	$
Assume the selling prices are	$25.00	$40.00
Using absorption costing sales margins are	23.2%	13.0%
ABC sales margins are	34.7%	5.8%

Test your understanding answers

 Example 1

Solution

(a)

Workings	M1	M2	Total
Number of batches	4	80	84
Number of setups	4	240	244
Special parts	16,000	64,000	80,000
Direct labour hours	16,000	20,000	36,000

Activity	Cost		M1	M2
	$		$	$
Setups	97,600	Cost per setup $400	1,600	96,000
Materials handling	42,000	Cost per batch $500	2,000	40,000
Special parts handling	50,000	Cost per part $0.625	10,000	40,000
Invoicing	31,000	Cost per order $100	6,000	25,000
Other overheads	108,000	Cost per hour $3	48,000	60,000
	328,600		67,600	261,000

	M1		M2	
	$	$	$	$
Sales		$432,000		584,000
Direct materials	88,000		168,000	
Direct labour	128,000		160,000	
Overheads	67,600		261,000	
Total costs		283,600		589,000
Profit/(loss)		148,400		(5,000)
Profit/loss per unit		18.55		(0.625)

(b) The figures suggest that model M2 is less profitable than M1. The sales manager should try to persuade the customer to buy model M1. Note that the apparent loss on M2 does not necessarily mean that production should be ceased. To assess this management should consider the incremental relevant cash flows involved – e.g. is the product making positive contribution, how many overheads are avoidable? They could also consider ways to reduce the cost drivers for the product to reduce its share of the overheads and convert the product loss into a profit.

Test your understanding 1

Firstly a cost driver must be determined. For material receipts and inspections this is likely to be based on the number of batches produced:

$$\text{Material receipt and inspection} = \frac{\$35,000}{20 + 10 + 5} = \$1,000 \text{ per batch}$$

These should then be charged to each product. For product B, the cost per unit will be:

Product Y $1,000/batch × 10 batches/1,500 units

          = $6.67/unit

Option **A** is the correct answer

Test your understanding 2

Machine running time cost is likely to be driven by the machine hours. Total number of machine hours

	Product E	Product G	Product F
Machine hours (Production units × hours per unit)	10,000	16,000	12,000

Charge out rate = $4,560,000/38,000 machine hours = $120 per machine hour

Cost per unit for Product F = $120 per machine hour × 4 hours per unit = **$480**

Test your understanding 3

Firstly a cost driver must be determined for the review costs:

$$\text{Review costs driver rate} = \frac{\$1,050,280}{100,000 + 3,000 + 18,000} = \$8.68 \text{ per review}$$

The total amount charged to sole trader accounts will be:

$8.68 per review × 100,000 reviews

= $868,000

Test your understanding 4

Cost driver rate:

Receiving/inspecting quality assurance (based on purchase requisitions) $= \dfrac{\$1,400,000}{5,000} = \$280$

Charge to product P = $280 × 1,200/10,000 = $33.60

Option **B** is the correct answer.

Test your understanding 5

Cost driver rate:

Production scheduling/machine set-ups (based on no. set-ups) $= \dfrac{\$1,200,000}{800} = \$1,500 \text{ per set-up}$

Test your understanding 6

Firstly a cost driver must be determined:

$$\text{Material handling} = \frac{\$13,650}{(2,000 \times 4) + (1,500 \times 6) + (800 \times 3)}$$

$$= \$0.70361 \text{ per sq. metre handled}$$

These should then be charged to each product. For product X, the cost per unit will be:

Product X $0.70361/m^2 of material × 4m^2 = $2.81

Option **A** is the correct answer.

Test your understanding 7

The most appropriate cost driver for reviews would be the number of reviews per service.

Total number of reviews = (5,000 × 3) + (10,000 × 0.5) + (40,000 × 2) = 100,000

Cost per review = $55,000/100,000 = $0.55

The review cost for statutory audit services = $0.55 × 3 = $1.65

The correct answer is option **B**.

Test your understanding 8

Machines are likely to be set-up for production of a batch of units. The associated costs would therefore be classed as a batch level activity.

Option **B** is the correct answer.

Test your understanding 9

Activity Based Costing (ABC) is a system of full costing which recognises that the more traditional method of absorption costing using cost centre absorption rates may not provide accurate product costs.

ABC identifies the activities of a production process and the extent to which individual products make use of those activities. Costs are then estimated for each of these activities which are referred to as cost pools. The number of times which the activity is expected to be carried out is also estimated and a cost driver rate calculated:

$$\frac{\text{Estimated cost of pool}}{\text{Estimated number of times activity is to be performed}}$$

An individual product will probably make use of a number of different activities, and a proportion of the cost of each activity will be attributed to the product using these predetermined cost driver rates.

The actual costs of each cost pool together with the number of times the activity is performed will be collected and a comparison made with the corresponding estimated values. This is similar to the comparison of actual and budgeted costs and volumes using the traditional absorption costing approach except that there are likely to be a greater number of cost driver rates using ABC than the one per cost centre absorption rate found in traditional absorption costing.

Test your understanding 10

Such an approach is beneficial because it identifies overhead costs with their cause, rather than assuming that they are all driven by a single cause. The costs are then allocated to the cost units in a more relevant way, providing the user with a more sophisticated breakdown of cost.

Having a more realistic estimate of the true cost of the product then means that:

– Pricing can be improved

– Decision making can be improved

– Performance management can be improved.

This should enable management to control such costs more easily, the variances reported will be more meaningful and this will help management to control costs.

Test your understanding 11

The cost driver for a particular activity is the factor that causes a change in the cost of the activity. For the cost driver to be useful there must be an identifiable relationship between the cost and the cost driver, i.e. changes in the number of cost drivers must cause corresponding changes in the total cost incurred on the activity.

Another major consideration is the ease of accurately recording the number of cost drivers incurred. If the process of recording the cost drivers is very complex and time-consuming then the cost of the recording system might outweigh the benefits derived from the information obtained.

Test your understanding 12

A cost driver is that factor which is most closely related to the way in which the costs of an activity are incurred. It could be said to cause the costs. Under ABC an organisation does not need to restrict itself to just one overall overhead absorption rate. An organisation can choose whatever basis it considers suitable to charge overheads to the product.

Examining process power in this organisation, under traditional absorption costing Product Z was the dearest for process power merely because it used the most labour hours per unit – a fact completely and utterly unconnected with the way in which process power costs are incurred. Under ABC the accountant has likely investigated the business and actually taken the time to find out what factor is most closely related to the cost and use that factor to charge overheads. The outcome is that Product X should be the dearest because it uses the most power drill operations.

ABC supporters would argue that this cost/power drill operation is useful information. The costs of power drill operations for product X is not insignificant and in fact is nearly as much as the direct material cost and direct labour cost combined. It would be inconceivable that the direct material costs and direct labour costs would not be very carefully controlled and yet under traditional absorption costing the process power costs would be included within the general overheads and would not be subject to such severe scrutiny.

Under ABC, once we realise that power drill operations cost $1.0773 each then when designing new products, the organisation would have better cost information and thus would be able to make better informed decisions.

Test your understanding 13

(a) **The reasons for the difference in the production cost per unit between the two methods**

- The allocation of overheads under absorption costing was unfair. This method assumed that all of the overheads were driven by labour hours and, as a result, the Double Plus received 1.5 times the production overhead of the Plus.

- However, this method of absorption is not appropriate. The overheads are in fact driven by a number of different factors. There are five activity costs, each one has its own cost driver. By taking this into account we end up with a much more accurate production overhead cost per unit.

- Using ABC, the cost per unit of a Double Plus is significantly higher. This is because the Double Plus is a much more complex product than the Plus. For example, there are 140 orders for the Double Plus but only 10 for the Plus and there are 4 special parts for the Double Plus compared to only one for the Plus. As a result of this complexity, the Double Plus has received more than three times the overhead of the Plus.

- This accurate allocation is important because the production overhead is a large proportion of the overall cost.

(b) **The implications of using ABC**

- Pricing – pricing decisions will be improved because the price will be based on more accurate cost data.

- Decision making – this should also be improved. For example, research, production and sales effort can be directed towards the most profitable products.

- Performance management – should be improved. ABC can be used as the basis of budgeting and forward planning. The more realistic overhead should result in more accurate budgets and should improve the process of performance management. In addition, an improved understanding of what drives the overhead costs should result in steps being taken to reduce the overhead costs and hence an improvement in performance.

- Sales strategy – this should be more soundly based. For example, target customers with products that appeared unprofitable under absorption costing but are actually profitable, and vice versa.

Other costing techniques

Chapter learning objectives

Lead outcome	Component outcome
A2. Costing concepts	(b) Costing concepts for different organisations and cost objects.
A3. Costing methods	(e) Digital costing
C3. Techniques to support short-term decision-making	(c) Product mix decisions with constraints

1 Chapter overview diagram

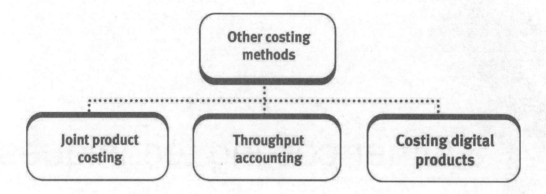

Previous chapters have looked at the most common costing methods used by organisations. However, there are other costing methods which may be used by organisations, either because it suits the way that the organisation operates or because the organisation wants to more fully understand its costs. Better costing methods may lead to better decision making.

The purpose of costing is to calculate the cost of each cost unit of an organisation's products. In order to do this the costs of each unit should be gathered together and recorded in the costing system. This is the overall aim, but the methods and system used will differ from organisation to organisation as the type of products and production methods differ between organisations.

There are two main types of costing system:

- **Specific order costing**, where the costs of distinct products or services are collected. Individual cost units are different according to individual customer's requirements. The main example of specific order costing is job costing where costs are attributed to a specific job (such as, for example, the cost of providing a service to one particular client).

  Batch costing is also a form of specific order costing, although costs will be attributed to specific batches rather than specific orders or customers.

  These costing systems are usually associated with absorption or activity based costing methodology, and the costs calculated for each batch or each job produced are normally a fully absorbed production cost.

- **Continuous costing**, where a series of similar products or services are produced. Costs are collected and averaged over the number of products or services produced to arrive at a cost per unit. An example of continuous costing is **joint product costing**.

Cost units

The cost units of different organisations will be of different types and this will tend to necessitate different costing systems. The main types of cost unit are as follows:

• Individual products designed and produced for individual customers. Each individual product is a cost unit. Job costing is used.

• Groups of different products possibly in different styles, sizes or colours produced to be held in inventory until sold. Each of the batches of whatever style, size or colour is a cost unit. Batch costing is used.

• Many units of identical products produced from a single production process. These units will be held in inventory until sold. Each batch from the process is a cost unit. Process costing is used. Process costing often requires the use of joint product costing

2 Joint product costing

Some products may be produced at the same time in the same process before being separated for sale or further individual processing. These products are known as joint products and the separation point is known as the split-off point.

For example, different types of carbonated drinks might use a common starting process where syrup, sweeteners and malt are added before they are split up and individual flavourings added.

Joint costs are the total of the raw material, labour, and overhead costs incurred up to the initial split-off point.

Joint costs and common costs

A joint cost is the cost of a process that results in more than one main product. A common cost is a cost relating to more than one product or service.

The term 'joint cost' refers to the cost of some common process before a split-off point after which various joint products and by-products can be identified. 'Common costs' is a wider term that need not relate to a process. For example, the absorption of fixed production overheads in total absorption costing described in an earlier chapter is an example of assigning common costs to cost units.

The joint costs can not normally be directly attributable to individual joint products or by-products. Therefore, arbitrary allocations may have to be used instead.

Joint products and by-products

The nature of process costing is that the process incurs joint costs and often produces more than one product. These additional products may be described as either joint products or by-products. Essentially joint products are all the main products, whereas by-products are incidental to the main products.

- Joint products are two or more products produced by the same process and separated in processing, each having a sufficiently high saleable value to merit recognition as a main product.

- A by-product is output of some value produced incidentally in manufacturing something else (main product).

These definitions still leave scope for subjective judgement, but they provide a basis for such judgement. The distinction is important because the accounting treatment of joint and by-products differs. Costs incurred in processing prior to the separation of the products are known as **joint costs.**

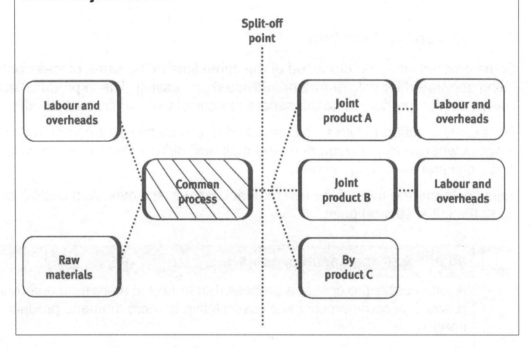

Methods of joint cost apportionment

There are many ways in which joint costs can be apportioned to products such as:

- physical measurement
- market value at point of separation
- net realisable value/net relative sales value

In turn, the methods will result in different inventory valuations and, therefore, different recorded profits.

Further details and explanation

Accounting for joint products

Joint products are, by definition, subject to individual accounting procedures.

Joint costs will require apportionment between products for inventory valuation purposes. The main bases for appointment are as follows:

- *Physical measurement of joint products:* Joint costs can be apportioned to the units of output of each joint product. When the unit of measurement is different, e.g. litres and kilos, some method should be found of expressing them in a common unit. Some joint costs are not incurred equally for all joint products: such costs can be separated and apportioned by introducing weighting factors. Alternatively, a technical estimate of relative usage by each product may be made by the organisation.

- *Market value:* Joint costs can be apportioned on the basis of the market value of each joint product at the point of separation. The effect is to make each product appear to be equally profitable.

- *Net realisable value:* Where certain products are processed after the point of separation, further processing costs may be deducted from the market values before joint costs are apportioned.

It is essential to realise that apportionment is, of necessity, an arbitrary calculation and product costs that include such an apportionment can be misleading if used as a basis for decision-making.

Accounting for by-products

Either of the following methods may be adopted: the proceeds from the sale of the by-product may be treated as pure profit, or the proceeds from the sale, less any handling and selling expenses, may be used to reduce the cost of the main products.

If a by-product needs further processing to improve its marketability, the cost will be deducted in arriving at net revenue. Note that recorded profits will be affected by the method adopted if inventories of the main product are maintained.

Example 1

An organisation produces two joint products Product A and Product B. The total joint costs are $750 and the following information is provided on each product:

	Kgs produced	Kgs sold	Selling price per kg	Joint Cost
Product A	100	80	$5	
				$750
Product B	200	150	$2	

Further information needed:

Further processing costs	Selling price after further processing
$280 + $2.00 per kg	$8.40
$160 + $1.40 per kg	$4.50

Apportion the joint costs between the products using the following apportionment methods:

- physical measurement

- market value at point of separation

- net realisable value/net relative sales value

3 Throughput accounting

Throughput accounting is very similar to marginal costing, but it can be used to make longer-term decisions about capacity/production equipment.

Throughput accounting is based on three concepts: throughput, inventory (or investment) and operating expenses. The basic premise is that managers should aim to increase throughput while simultaneously reducing inventory and operational expenses.

Throughput

In throughput accounting, the only cost that is deemed to relate to volume of output is the direct material cost. All other costs (including all labour costs) are deemed to be fixed. These fixed costs may be called Total Factory Costs (TFC). Throughput is a measure of profitability and is defined by the following equation:

Throughput contribution = Revenue – Totally variable costs

The aim of throughput accounting is to maximise this measure of throughput contribution.

Since totally variable costs are normally just raw materials and bought-in components, it is often convenient to define throughput contribution as:

Throughput contribution = Revenue – direct material costs

Conversion costs

A distinction can be made between material and other manufacturing costs. These other manufacturing costs are sometimes collectively referred to as conversion costs. Therefore, costs such as direct labour, factory rent, equipment depreciation, inspection costs etc. will come together under the heading of conversion costs. This is a term that you may encounter in questions on this topic.

Investment

This is defined as all the money the business invests to buy the things that it intends to sell and all the money tied up in assets so that the business can make the throughput. Investment therefore includes unused raw materials, work-in-progress and unsold finished goods. It can also include non-current assets if these are used for buying or creating materials (such as equipment and buildings used to produce materials or research and development costs that can be attributed to its creation).

Operating expenses

Operating expenses are defined as all the money a business spends to produce the throughput (i.e. to turn the inventory into throughput). It is not correct to think of operating expenses as fixed costs. They are costs that are not totally variable.

Profit reporting

Since a business makes its money from throughput, management accounting systems should focus on the value of throughput created. Profit should therefore be reported as follows (illustrative figures are included):

		$
Revenue		750,000
Raw material cost	(totally variable cost)	200,000
Throughput contribution		550,000
Operating expenses		400,000
Net profit		150,000

Super variable costing

Throughput accounting has been described as a form of 'super-variable costing' because the concept of throughput has similarities to the concept of contribution. It could therefore be seen as an alternative to marginal costing as a costing method. However, this is not an accurate description. This is because in throughput accounting, the concept of product cost is rejected. The throughput earned by individual products is calculated, but no attempt is made to charge operating expenses to products. This makes throughput accounting radically different from both traditional cost accounting systems such as absorption costing and marginal costing and also from activity based costing.

Inventory valuation

Inventory should be valued at the purchase cost of its raw materials and bought-in parts.

It should not include any other costs, not even labour costs. No value is added by the production process, not even by labour, until the item is sold.

Example 2

A company makes 1,000 units of an item during a period and sells 800 units for $8,000. Costs of production were as follows:

	$
Materials	3,000
Direct labour	2,000
Fixed production overhead	1,000
Other overhead	1,000

Actual production volume and production overhead expenditure were both the same as budgeted.

Required:

Calculate the profit for the period using:

(a) absorption costing

(b) marginal costing

(c) throughput accounting.

4 Multi-product decision making in throughput accounting

The usual requirement in questions is to maximise contribution (given that fixed costs are unaffected by the production decision in the short run) per unit of the limiting factor. In throughput accounting the approach should be to maximise the throughput contribution earned.

Maximising throughput

Using throughput accounting, the aim should be to maximise throughput, on the assumption that operating expenses are a fixed amount in each period.

- If the business has more capacity than there is customer demand, it should produce to meet the demand in full.

- If the business has a constraint that prevents it from meeting customer demand in full, it should make the most profitable use that it can of the constraining resource. This means giving priority to those products earning the highest throughput contribution for each unit of the constraining resource that it requires.

This goal is achieved by determining what factors prevent the throughput being higher. This constraint is called a **bottleneck.** A bottleneck may be a machine whose capacity limits the output of the whole production process. The aim is to identify the bottlenecks and remove them, or, if this is not possible, ensure that they are fully utilised at all times. Non-bottleneck resources should be scheduled and operated based on the constraints within the system, and should not be used to produce more than the bottlenecks can absorb.

The following provides a step-by-step technique for resolving the problem

Step 1: identify the bottleneck constraint.

Step 2: calculate the throughput contribution per unit for each product.

Step 3: calculate the throughput contribution per unit of the bottleneck resource for each product.

Step 4: rank the products in order of the throughout contribution per unit of the bottleneck resource.

Step 5: allocate resources using this ranking and answer the question.

Example 3

The following data relates to two products manufactured by DJ

	Product X	Product Y
Selling price per unit	$15	$20
Direct material cost per unit	$10	$11
Maximum demand (units)	25,000	30,000
Time required on the bottleneck (hours per unit)	2	6

The firm has 80,000 bottleneck hours available each period.

Total factory costs amount to $128,000 in the period.

Required:

Calculate the optimum product mix and the maximum profit.

Throughput accounting measures

Various performance measures have been devised to help measure throughput:

$$\text{Return per factory hour} = \frac{\text{Throughput contribution}}{\text{Product's time on the bottleneck resource}}$$

$$\text{Cost per factory hour} = \frac{\text{Total factory cost}}{\text{Total time on the bottleneck resource}}$$

$$\text{Throughput accounting ratio} = \frac{\text{Return per factory hour}}{\text{Cost per factory hour}}$$

Explanation of the ratios

The return per factory hour shows the value added by the organisation and managers are encouraged to maximise this (for example, by increasing throughput or reducing the time taken in the process).

The cost per factory hour shows the cost of operating the factory in terms of overheads, labour costs etc.

The throughput accounting ratio measures the return from a product against the cost of running the factory. Some people would argue that only products with a throughput accounting ratio greater than 1 are worthwhile. This is because the ratio is telling us that the return that is made at this point is less than the cost of producing that return. For example, if the return was $2 per hour but it was costing $4 per hour to operate the factory, then the throughput accounting ration would be 0.5. This could easily be benchmarked against the target of 1 to tell us that production is not worthwhile.

But notice that the return per factory hour and the throughput accounting ratios are for each individual product, whereas the cost per factory hour is for the company as a whole. So it could be argued that a throughput accounting ratio of less than 1 does not reveal the full story.

Example 4

Calculate the throughput accounting ratio for each product in the previous example.

Criticism of throughput accounting

A criticism of throughput accounting is that it concentrates on the short term, when a business has a fixed supply of resources and operating expenses are largely fixed.

It is more difficult to apply throughput accounting concepts to the longer term, when all costs are variable, and vary with the volume of production and sales or another cost driver.

This criticism suggests that although throughput accounting could be a suitable method of measuring profit and performance in the short term, an alternative management accounting method, such as activity based costing, might be more appropriate for measuring and controlling performance from a longer-term perspective.

5 Costing digital products

Up to this point in the study text, we have been focussing on cost estimation for tangible products, or services, where we are able to readily identify the costs associated with production, such as direct materials, labour, delivery. However, in today's digital era we are seeing a huge increase in the availability of information in electronically accessible formats, such as eBooks, graphics, online courses and a multitude of apps. The costs associated with the creation of these products differs greatly from the tangible costs we have seen so far, and it therefore stands to reason that the way we cost these digital products will also need to be different. This is what we will investigate in the following sections.

A digital product typically refers to a product that is stored, delivered and consumed in an electronic format.

The products can be delivered in many ways such as through a website, a mobile phone application or email. One digital product may be offered in various forms. For example, a company may release a game that can be played on its website or via IOS or Android apps. A digital product can also refer to digital media that will be distributed such as a television programme or music album.

Digital products as bundles of features

Digital products can sometimes be seen as a gathering together of individual product features.

Features can be added and changed by individual consumers giving each user a bespoke experience through choosing the features that they want and don't want. It may therefore be that individual features need to be costed in order to determine selling prices for each feature. It is common, for example, for computer or console games to launch with a basic set of features which gamers can then add to through additional downloadable content.

> It may even be that features become products in their own right when unbundled from the product. For example, Facebook's messenger feature is now available as a separate app and has its own development team that is separate from Facebook's core activities.

Digital products are often undertaken as individual jobs so that, to some extent, job costing techniques can be very relevant in costing digital products. But products are often much more difficult to cost than traditional products for a number of reasons, such as:

- Marginal costs can be virtually zero for many digital products and most costs are likely to be fixed in nature. This means that digital products are expensive to produce but cheap to reproduce, since the unit cost of reproduction is negligible.

- There is often no standard time or cost that can be attributed to digital products making the use of standard costing inappropriate.

- Drivers for overheads can be very difficult to determine.

- The timing of costs can be difficult to estimate and can extend over a number of accounting periods. Many of the product costs will be upfront and pre-launch such as design and development. Many other costs will be post-launch such as royalties and marketing costs. But some costs may be incurred over both periods such as testing and platform costs.

- The lifespan of digital products can vary greatly. Some products, say a weather forecast, may last and have value for only a day, whilst others, such as an e-book, can have a life that spans decades. It will be necessary to establish the total costs over the lifetime of the app and then compare this to the expected benefits in terms of increased revenue. Determining the lifetime of an app can be very difficult particularly when there are rapid changes in technology as there is at the present time.

- Many product features or functions might be shared amongst a number of products. The finance function then needs to determine how to absorb these costs into each individual product.

Illustration 1 – costing digital products

A private educational training company is looking to develop a new app to provide its students with tailored personal study advice and tuition programmes which they can access at home. The directors are unsure of the types off costs which need to be considered.

The cost of developing the app itself, whilst significant, is not the only cost which needs to be considered. There are four main categories of costs associated with maintaining and operating apps post-development which also need to be considered:

Functional services:

Functional services are those needed to execute the functionalities and features of the app. While the apps developer will have provided a certain functionality, the app will not work unless there is a subscription to a service that will provide a delivery mechanism. This will allow functionality such as push notifications; social media and chat; SMS and email messaging.

Administrative services:

There will need to be an intuitive, powerful, accessible and user-friendly administration dashboard to enable effective administration of the app. Administrative costs are the most difficult to anticipate as they will largely depend and differ based on each individual app. The administration dashboard allows management of the content of the app; management of the functional services detailed above; updating of the app; management of user profiles; collection and analysis of user behaviour; control access by users and enabling of data or user segmentation.

Infrastructure services:

These services include infrastructural components such as where the app is hosted, where data is stored and how the data is delivered. This will include the cost of servers (where the app is hosted); data storage; content delivery network (CDN) and images data.

IT support services:

Ongoing technical support is a critical component of any app deployment. Technical support will be needed to deal with iOS and Android updates; updates to application programming interfaces (APIs) and bug fixing. IT specific maintenance costs for infrastructure will also be required since servers, data storage, CDN and image data will all require some level of monitoring and maintenance.

Example 5

Which of the following would be a reason as to why throughput accounting would not be suitable for costing a digital product?

A   The lifespan of digital products can vary greatly

B   The timing of costs can be difficult to estimate

C   Marginal costs are virtually zero

D   Drivers for overheads can be difficult to determine

More details on digital product costs

Digital products will have a wide variety of costs that may be very different to the costs incurred in traditional products. There are likely to be little or no material costs and more overheads, for example.

The cost structure for digital media may be very different. Much of the cost will be fixed in nature and incurred upfront. For example, in making a music album there will be studio costs, fees for session musicians, editing and mastering costs and artwork and photography costs. But there will then be costs associated with marketing that may be incurred over the next 6 to 12 months. There will, finally, be royalty costs paid to the recording artist and writer(s) that may be paid for numerous years. It is likely that it is only this final cost that will be truly variable in nature as it is likely to be payable based on each distribution of the content (for example, each time the album is played on a platform such as Spotify).

Much of these costs reflect only the direct costs of the music album. There may be many more indirect costs that are attributed to the album that come from the record label etc.

Digital product costs can be difficult to budget as there is often no standard cost for cost items or other standard costing elements such as a standard time for activities. For example, studio costs are normally incurred per day but it can be difficult to estimate the number of days that will be required. It is also very common for the time taken to exceed the budget and therefore there may be an argument for including some initial slack in the budget and adding extra days in order to account for such eventualities. Also, when budgeting costs such as royalty fees some estimate needs to be made regarding actual sales or distribution levels.

Some typical costs and cost patterns are explored below.

Staff costs

Many staff costs will be specific to the product or project. For example, particularly in mobile phone app design, staff tend to be employed for the development of that particular app / product. Staff are typically paid a fixed fee or a fee per day. Once the app has been developed these staff are no longer required or used. It means that, although there may be some permanent staff costs for preparing updates and providing product maintenance, the majority of staff costs are often upfront and pre-launch with very little ongoing costs post-launch.

Infrastructure, platform and payment types

There will be costs associated with the platform on which digital products will be launched. Many organisations choose to launch on one platform as a trial of the product before launching into other platforms.

This means that these costs can be a combination of immediate and predictable costs for the initial target platform with then potential further costs if the product is launched on other platforms in the future.

Infrastructure services include infrastructural components such as where the app is hosted, where data is stored and how the data is delivered. This will include the cost of servers (where the app is hosted); data storage; content delivery network (CDN) and images data.

Similar decisions will be taken on acceptable payment types where an organisation might only initially accept one type of payment type but over time start to accept more methods. Each payment type added to the product would incur additional costs for the product.

Functionality

Individual product functions may be costed separately. For example, features may be required to allow functionality such as push notifications; social media and chat; SMS and email messaging.

It may be that functions can be re-used in other products and costs absorbed accordingly. For example, in a mobile phone app there may be a payment function for accessing additional content. This payment function may be usable across a number of applications.

Likewise, if a product uses functions or designs from previously created products then these will need to be costed to the new product in some way.

Design and development

Likewise there may be shareable design elements for products. Many computer games, for example, use the same game 'engine'. For example, the Frostbite engine is used in games as varied as FIFA, Battlefield and Need for Speed. The cost of employing the engine would have to be absorbed into each individual product, most likely as an overhead cost.

But each product is also likely to have its own design and development costs. These would be direct costs and are most likely to be pre-launch costs.

Marketing

The majority of marketing costs will be incurred post launch although some may be incurred prior to launch if the organisation wants to build expectations, provide previews, do open market testing pre-launch etc. Many digital products will be allocated a fixed marketing budget which will need to be carefully planned.

IT Support services and testing

Ongoing technical support is a critical component of any app deployment. IT specific maintenance costs for infrastructure will also be required since servers, data storage, CDN and image data will all require some level of monitoring and maintenance.

Testing will be a key factor and cost before the digital product is launched. But it is a cost that may be an ongoing one as developers may be required to provide updates to application programming interfaces (APIs) and fix bugs after the product launch. This will incur additional post-launch costs.

Royalty and license costs

There may also be royalty and license costs for the product. Royalties are often based on sales and will therefore be difficult to budget for and incurred post-launch, possibly over a number of accounting periods. License fees tend to be a fixed amount paid on production of the product pre-launch.

Inventory costs

A major advantage of digital products is that there will be no inventory of the product. This not only eliminates the associated inventory holding costs but avoids the need for inventory valuation by the accounting function.

Administrative services

We will need an intuitive, powerful, accessible and user-friendly administration dashboard to enable the organisation to effectively administer the apps. Administrative costs are the most difficult to anticipate as they will largely depend and differ based on each individual app. The administration dashboard will allow the organisation to manage the content of the apps; manage the functional services detailed above; update the apps; manage user profiles; collect and analyse user behaviour; control access by users and enable data or user segmentation.

Digital products and decision making

Digital products have low marginal costs and, once created, the majority of fixed costs are sunk (i.e. money has already been spent on areas such as developing the product and cannot be recovered so should be ignored for any future decisions). In decision making, for example when trying to decide on a selling price for the product, normally only marginal costs are considered and sunk (or historic) costs are ignored.

Decisions are also complicated by the fact that digital products can be consumed simultaneously by more than one user (for example, more than one user might be reading the same e-book at the same time). It means that the same, identical product can be sold over and over again at virtually no extra cost to the business.

Cost benefit analysis for launching new products, for example, will be complicated for digital products due to many of the problems explored in this section such as:

- The timing and frequency of costs will be difficult to estimate. Some costs may be upfront (such as development costs), others will be ongoing (such as royalties) whilst others (such as the cost of providing updates or for moving to new platforms) will be one-off future costs. Forecasts will have to be made for the time taken for each activity, the number of staff required for each element, prospective sales volumes, etc.

- Some costs for shared functions (such as payments or digital images) may have to be shared and absorbed across a number of products and it can be difficult to determine the drivers associated with these costs.

- Determining benefits will be complicated by the unknown lifespan of the product and the fact that the same product can be sold over and over again.

Many of the decision making techniques that follow in this syllabus (such as, say, linear programming) are therefore very complicated for digital products. But using these techniques on digital products is beyond the scope of this syllabus and the decision making techniques which follow will focus only on physical products (and services).

 ## 6   Digital costing

We have seen so far in this study text that determining the cost of a product or service is an important but sometimes complex task for organisations. We have only had to deal with one or two types of materials, labour and overheads.

Some organisations may make a product requiring hundreds or thousands of components. Boeing, for example, estimate that their B737 aircraft has 367,000 parts. A typical car will have over 30,000 components. To cost such a product using techniques covered so far in this syllabus would be a very long and cumbersome task.

Thankfully, in the age of technology, digital costing systems have been developed in order to perform this task. A digital costing system is dynamic and involves linking internal digital systems (for example, digital production machinery, purchasing and sales systems) with those of suppliers, customers and the external market. In a digital costing system, data is gathered from all of these resources and from the internet in real time, to give up-to-date costing information which reflects current information on components and product parts.

The systems can provide information on marginal, total and average product costs that are much more detailed than those produced from non-digital systems, the information is obtained more quickly and product costs become more accurate.

Digital costing systems use technology to allow them to understand and 'read' product designs and plans in order to find the best components to achieve product goals. They can gather and feed information into manufacturing times to make the entire operation more efficient, flexible and effective.

These can bring large operational and strategic benefits to organisations who employ such systems.

Features and benefits of digital costing systems

Real-time/up-to-date information:

Digital costing systems gather information from the internet in real time. This is done by linking systems with those of suppliers and marketplaces. This allows the system to automatically compare prices and suppliers, giving the organisation access to the cheapest (or best lead times, if that is what is desired) components available. This can give significant cost savings to the organisation.

The system will be constantly up-to-date and reflecting current information. This allows the organisation to change and adapt to changes in its supply chain environment.

Access to a wider variety of resources:

The organisation will have access to more suppliers. This can bring other benefits (outside of cost savings) such a quicker lead times and access to more variety of resources. It can also help alleviate scarcity problems for organisations who face a shortage of resources in the short term.

Reduced operational costs:

Although digital costing systems can be expensive to implement when they are up and running they have low operational costs. Because the process is fully automated there is no time burden for cost accountants. The time saved by cost accountants in the long term can vastly outweigh the cost of implementing the system.

Better understanding of costs:

Digital costing systems have built in analytics and intelligence capabilities. They can analyse changes over time, supplier flexibility etc. This can allow organisations to better understand the changing nature of costs, and provide a more detailed split of semi-variable costs so that organisation's better understand the costs which are truly variable.

These systems allow for the calculation of cost per customer, cost per location etc. This allows better customer profitability evaluation which can lead into customer decision making such as offering discounts to particular customers or setting prices for bespoke products or services.

Digital costing allows for granular decisions. Prices for components, for example, may only differ by a fraction of a cent. Traditional costing would have ignored this detail, but if an organisation is dealing in very large volumes moving from one component supplier to another in order to save a fraction of a cent per component may make significant overall cost savings.

More advanced systems have the capability to make suggestions to buying behaviour. They may suggest newly available types of components (subject to limits expressed within product design set up) which can change and improve product design. In this way the organisation can achieve improved, cheaper and more efficient operations that are constantly evolving.

Digital costing systems have the ability to accurately cope with hundreds of purchasing decisions at one time. They are also easy to use and quickly understood by decision makers.

More accurate costing:

The organisation will receive better, more up-to-date information on the cost of its product(s). This will include better knowledge of drivers and absorption of costs to products. Digital costing systems will automate this process and their better understanding of cost drivers should result in a more accurate and useful product cost.

Digital costing allows for a more detailed break-down of overheads with more personalised cost drivers. This can help in cost control and pricing decisions.

Improved communication/faster decision making:

Digital costing systems are fully integrated systems and make large use of microservices. For example, the technology might have a microservice that computes lead times, another that tells the factory manager to make provisions for the delivery, another that tells the finance department when and who to pay etc. (The microservices can be built in-house, bought in as off-the-shelf packages or, for larger organisation, purchased as bespoke, personalised services from developers). This all happens digitally so that there is much less bureaucracy and the entire system is quicker, easier and cheaper to operate.

More accurate pricing:

The product cost may constantly change as market prices and conditions change. Many organisations are moving towards adaptive or dynamic pricing of their products which is facilitated by digital costing. This allows selling prices to be changed quickly and easily based on new information on the cost of the product or market conditions.

Other organisations may use a system known as target costing. This system is used when the selling price is less controllable so that profit is very much dependent on meeting a target cost rather than adjusting selling prices. A digital costing system can determine whether (and how) a target cost can be achieved in order to reach a target level of profit.

Improved cost control:

Standards are being regularly updated, whereas with more traditional systems the standards would be updated less frequently, resulting in potentially out of date standards where prices are changing.

Where these standards are used to calculate variances and measure the performance of managers (such as the procurement or production manager), it is important for values to reflect current market conditions.

As a result of the standards being real time there should be no planning variances and any operational variances will arise because the manager is not acting in accordance with the current environment. For example, instead of holding a procurement manager responsible for a large price variance based on an out of date standard, the performance of this manager can be assessed against the current standard and through detailed information about how, for example, the cost of the raw material is being controlled over time.

Example 6

Which of the following would not be a typical feature of digital costing?

A   There is a focus on a smaller number of suppliers

B   Improved knowledge of cost drivers

C   Fully integrated systems

D   Improved performance management

7 Chapter summary

```
                    ┌──────────────────┐
                    │  Other costing   │
                    │    methods       │
                    └──────────────────┘
```

Joint product costing

- Allocate costs using
  - Net realisable value
  - Physical output
  - Market value
- By-product revenue can be deducted from joint costs

Throughput accounting

- Throughput contribution = Revenue – direct material costs
- Rank products in order of the contribution per unit of the bottleneck resource
- TAR = Return per factory hour divided by cost per factory hour

Costing digital products

- Fewer marginal costs
- Most costs are fixed
- Costs span a number of time frames
- Less standardisation
- Impacts on decision making

8   Practice questions

Test your understanding 1

The total production cost of joint products can be apportioned between products using which of the following methods? (Tick all that apply)

(1)   Weight

(2)   Sales revenue

(3)   Selling prices

(4)   Net realisable value

Test your understanding 2

Products A and B are manufactured in a joint process. The following data is available for a period:

Joint process costs		$30,000
Output	Product A	2,000 kg
	Product B	4,000 kg
Selling price:	Product A	$12 per kg
	Product B	$18 per kg

What is Product B's share of the joint process costs if the sales value method of cost apportionment is used?

A $7,500

B $18,000

C $20,000

D $22,500

Test your understanding 3

Charleville operates a continuous process producing three products and one by-product. Output from the process for a month was as follows:

Product	Selling price per unit	Units of output from process
1	$18	10,000
2	$25	20,000
3	$20	20,000
4 (by product)	$2	3,500

Total output costs were $277,000.

The unit valuation for Product 3 (using the sales revenue basis for allocating joint costs) was $ 5 (Fill in the missing number)

Test your understanding 4

Scenario

A business makes four products, W, X, Y and Z. Information relating to these products is as follows:

	W	X	Y	Z
Sales price/unit	$20	$25	$18	$40
Materials required/unit	$10	$15	$11	$22
Labour hours/unit	4	5	2	6
Monthly sales demand (units)	500	800	1,000	400

There is a limit to the availability of labour, and only 8,000 hours are available each month.

Task:

Identify which products the business should produce using a throughput accounting approach.

Test your understanding 5

A company manufactures a product that requires machine time of 1.5 hours per unit. Machine time is a bottleneck resource, due to the limited number of machines available. There are 10 machines available and each machine can be used for up to 40 hours each week. The product is sold for $85 per unit and the material cost per unit is $42.50. Total operating expenses are $8,000 each week.

Required:

Calculate the throughput accounting ratio.

Test your understanding 6

Scenario

Justin Thyme manufactures four products, A, B, C and D. Details of sales prices, costs and resource requirements for each of the products are as follows.

	Product A	Product B	Product C	Product D
	$	$	$	$
Sales price	1.40	0.80	1.20	2.80
Materials cost	0.60	0.30	0.60	1.00
Direct labour cost	0.40	0.20	0.40	1.00
	Minutes	Minutes	Minutes	Minutes
Machine time per unit	5	2	3	6
Labour time per unit	2	1	2	5
	Units	Units	Units	Units
Weekly sales demand	2,000	2,000	2,500	1,500

Machine time is a bottleneck resource and the maximum capacity is 400 machine hours each week. Operating costs, including direct labour costs, are $5,440 each week. Direct labour costs are $12 per hour, and direct labour workers are paid for a 38-hour week, with no overtime.

Tasks:

(a) Identify the quantities of each product that should be manufactured and sold each week to maximise profit using a throughput accounting approach and calculate the weekly profit.

(b) Calculate the throughput accounting ratio at this profit-maximising level of output and sales.

(Time allowed: 15 minutes)

Test your understanding 7

The following data relate to the single product made by Squirrel Ltd:

Selling price per unit	$16
Direct material cost per unit	$10
Maximum demand (units) per period	40,000
Time required (hours) in Process X, per unit	1
Time required (hours) in Process Y, per unit	1.5

The capacities are 35,000 hours in Process X and 42,000 hours in Process Y.

The total factory costs are $105,000 in the period.

Tasks:

(a) Identify the process bottleneck.

(b) Calculate the throughput accounting ratio.

(**Note:** This would be two separate questions in an examination)

Test your understanding 8

A company manufactures three products: W, X and Y. The products use a series of different machines, but there is a common machine that is a bottleneck. The standard selling price and standard cost per unit for each product for the next period are as follows:

	W $	X $	Y $
Selling price	180	150	150
Cost:			
Direct material	41	20	30
Direct labour	30	20	50
Variable production overheads	24	16	20
Fixed production overheads	36	24	30
Profit	49	70	20
Time (minutes) on bottleneck machine	7	10	7

Using a throughput accounting approach, the rank order (best first) of the products would be:

A   W, X, Y

B   W, Y, X

C   X, W, Y

D   Y, X, W

Test your understanding 9

Which of the following is most likely to be true of a digital product?

A   Marginal costing will be the most appropriate costing system

B   Activity based costing could be used to absorb indirect overheads

C   Standard costing will play a vital role in costing the product

D   Throughput accounting will be commonly used

Test your understanding 10

Which of the following is not likely to be a benefit of a digital costing system?

A   Costing information is more up-to-date

B   The costing system can deal with a higher volume of components

C   The number of cost drivers will be reduced

D   The costing system will be cheaper to operate than non-digital systems

Test your understanding 11

Hard Tiles recorded a profit of $120,000 in the accounting period just ended, using marginal costing. The contribution/sales ratio was 75%.

Material costs were 10% of sales value and there were no other variable production overhead costs. Fixed costs in the period were $300,000.

Required:

What was the value of throughput in the period?

Test your understanding 12

A company manufactures three products: Alpha, Beta and Gamma. Each product has to go through three processes: 'Assembly', 'Quality' Control' and 'Packaging'. The following information is available:

	Alpha	Beta	Gamma
Sales price per unit	$2.00	$2.25	$1.75
Direct materials cost per unit	$0.50	$0.81	$0.35
Direct labour cost per unit	$0.30	$0.60	$0.50
Machine time per unit:			
Assembly (in minutes)	2	3	2.5
Quality Control (in minutes)	3	4	2
Packaging (in minutes)	4	5	3
Weekly sales demand	1,000 units	1,500 units	850 units

Operating expenses, including labour, are $4,000. The maximum hours available for the machines are 150 hours (Assembly), 170 hours (Quality Control) and 250 hours (Packaging).

How many units of 'Beta' should be produced each week to maximise profit?

A   850 units

B   1,000 units

C   1,375 units

D   1,500 units

Test your understanding 13

A company is considering implementing a digital costing system. Which of the following statements regarding digital costing systems is correct?

A   Operating variances would be eliminated

B   Standards would be more up to date

C   Operating costs would be higher than non-digital systems

D   The costing system cannot be linked with external parties

Test your understanding 14

Which of the following statements regarding cost benefit analysis of a digital product are true?

i   The timing and frequency of costs will be difficult to estimate

ii   It can be difficult to determine the drivers associated with some costs

iii   Determining the benefits can be complicated due to the unknown lifespan of the products

A   i only

B   i and ii only

C   ii and iii only

D   i, ii and iii

Example and test your understanding answers

Example 1

Tutorial note: This is a comprehensive question. The notes provided below are much more detailed that you would need for your assessment. However, it is useful to work through examples like this to improve your understanding of the topic as a whole.

Apportionment by physical measurement

$$\frac{\text{Joint cost}}{\text{Kgs produced}} = \frac{\$750}{300} = \$2.50 \text{ per kg for A+B}$$

Trading results

	Product A		Product B		Total
		$		$	$
Sales	80 × $5.00	400	150 × $2.00	300	700
Cost of sales	80 × $2.50	200	150 × $2.50	375	575
		___		___	___
Profit/(Loss)		200		(75)	125
		___		___	___
Value of closing inventory	20 × $2.50	50	50 × $2.50	125	
		___		___	
Total share of joint costs (Cost of sales + inventory)		250		500	

The main point to emphasise about joint products is the production mix. In this case the production ratio is 100:200 which means that, in order to obtain 1 kg of A, it is necessary also to produce 2 kg of B. Although in the longer term it may be possible through research and development work to change the mix, in many processes this is not possible and for exam purposes you should assume that the ratio of output is fixed.

In attempting to assess the profitability of the common process it is necessary to assess the overall position as follows:

		$
Sales value of product A	100 × $5	500
Sales value of product B	200 × $2	400
		___
		900
Joint cost		750
		___
Profit		150
		___

This total profit figure should be used to evaluate the viability of the common process.

Referring back to the trading results, it is important to appreciate that the 'loss' on B has been created by the joint cost apportionment, i.e.:

	$
Selling price	2.00
Share of joint cost	2.50
Loss	0.50

A decision not to produce and sell product B is not possible because, if product B were not produced, then neither could product A be produced. A further point to note is that inventory of B could not be valued in the financial statements at $2.50 bearing in mind that inventory should be valued at the lower of cost and net realisable value.

Apportionment by market value at point of separation

	Sales value of production	Proportion	Joint cost apportionment	Per kg
	$	$	$	$
A 100 × $5	500	5/9	417	4.17
B 200 × $2	400	4/9	333	1.67
			750	

Trading results:

	A	B	Total
Sales	400	300	700
Cost of sales	333.6	250.5	584.1
Profit	66.4	49.5	115.9
Profit/sales	16.6%	16.5%	
Closing inventory	(20 × 4.17)	(50 × 1.67)	
	83	83	

Notes:

(1) Apportionment is on the basis of proportionate sales value of production.

(2) Profit margin for each product is the same (with a small rounding difference).

(3) This approach provides a more realistic estimate of cost to use for valuing inventory of B, i.e. $1.67

Apportionment by net realisable value

This approach should be used in situations where the sales value at the split-off point is not known – either because the product is not saleable, or if the examiner does not tell you – or if specifically asked for by the examiner.

Further information needed:

Further processing costs	Selling price after further processing
$280 + $2.00 per kg	$8.40
$160 + $1.40 per kg	$4.50

Apportionment of joint costs:

	Product A $	Product B $
Final sales value of production	840	900
(100 × $8.40; 200 × $4.50)	480	440
Further processing cost		
280 + 100 × $2; 160 + 200 × $1.40)		
	360	460
Joint cost apportionment (360 : 460)	329	421
Joint cost per kg	$3.29	$2.10

Trading result (for common process only):

	$	$	$
Sales			700
Joint cost		750	
Less: Closing inventory			
A 20 × $3.29	66		
B 50 × $2.10	105		
		(171)	
Cost of sales			579
Profit			121

Notes:

(1)   As we know sales value of product B at the point of separation is $2, we can see that this method results in an unrealistic inventory value of $2.10. Bear in mind that this approach should only be used where the sales value at the split-off point is not known, or if instructed to use it by the examiner.

Example 2

The valuation of closing inventory is:

- $1,200 ($6,000 × 200/1,000) in absorption costing

- $1,000 ($5,000 × 200/1,000) in marginal costing

- $600 ($3,000 × 200/1,000) in throughput accounting.

Profit statements

(a)   **Absorption costing**

Value of closing inventory = $1,200

	$	$
Sales		8,000
Cost of production	6,000	
Less: Closing inventory	1,200	
Cost of sales		4,800
Gross profit		3,200
Non-production overhead		1,000
Profit		2,200

(b) **Marginal costing**

Value of closing inventory = $1,000

	$	$
Sales		8,000
Cost of production	5,000	
Less: Closing inventory	1,000	
Cost of sales		4,000
Contribution		4,000
Fixed overhead		1,000
Non-production overhead		1,000
Profit		2,000

(c) **Throughput accounting**

Value of closing inventory = $600

	$	$
Sales		8,000
Material costs	3,000	
Less: Closing inventory	600	
Cost of sales		2,400
Throughput		5,600
Operating expenses		4,000
Profit		1,600

Example 3

	Product	
	$	$
	X	**Y**
Selling price	15	20
Direct material	10	11
	—	—
Throughput	5	9
No. of bottleneck hours per unit	2	6
Return per factory hour	2.50	1.50
	1st	2nd

	Units	Bottleneck hrs per unit	Bottleneck hrs	Throughput $
Product X	25,000	2	50,000	125,000
Product Y	5,000[Bal]	6	30,000[Bal]	45,000
			—	—
			80,000	170,000
			—	—
Total factory cost				128,000
				—
Gross profit				42,000
				—

Example 4

	Product X	**Product Y**

$$\text{Return per factory hour} = \frac{\text{Throughput per unit}}{\text{Bottleneck hrs per unit}} = \frac{15-10}{2 \text{ hrs}} \quad \frac{20-11}{6 \text{ hrs}}$$

$$= \$2.50 \quad = \$1.50$$

$$\text{Cost per factory hour} = \frac{\text{Total factory cost}}{\text{Total bottleneck}} = \frac{\$128{,}000}{80{,}000 \text{ hrs}}$$

$$= \$1.60$$

$$\text{Throughput accounting ratio} = \frac{\text{Return per factory hour}}{\text{Cost per factory hour}} = \frac{\$2.50}{\$1.60} \quad \frac{\$1.50}{\$1.60}$$

$$= 1.56 \quad = 0.94$$

Product X has the higher throughput accounting ratio and thus should be given priority over Product Y.

Example 5

Correct solution is C.

In throughput accounting, the only cost that is deemed to relate to volume of output is the direct material cost. With digital products there is likely to be very little or zero direct material costs and therefore throughput accounting is unlikely to be useful.

Example 6

Correct solution is A.

Digital costing provides access to real-time information from a greater number of suppliers.

Test your understanding 1

1, 2 and 4 are all recognised ways of splitting joint costs. Selling prices (i.e. per unit) are not an acceptable basis as this does not take into account the relative volumes of each joint product.

Test your understanding 2

The correct answer is answer **D**.

	Output (kg)	Sales value ($)	Apportionment	Joint costs ($)
Product A	2,000	24,000	(24/96)	7,500
Product B	4,000	72,000	(72/96)	22,500
		96,000		30,000

Test your understanding 3

The unit valuation for Product 3 (using the sales revenue basis for allocating joint costs) was **$5**

Total sales revenue +	= ($18 × 10,000) + ($25 × 20,000) ($20 × 20,000) = $1,080,000
Joint costs to be allocated	= $277,000 – ($2 × 3,500) = $270,000
Allocation rate	= (270,000/1,080,000) = 0.25 of sales revenue
Joint costs allocated to Product 3	= 0.25 × ($20 × 20,000) = $100,000
Per unit	= $100,000/20,000 units = **$5** per unit

Test your understanding 4

The business should seek to maximise the total throughput.

	W $	X $	Y $	Z $
Sales price/unit	20	25	18	40
Materials required/unit	10	15	11	22
Throughput/unit	10	10	7	18
Labour hours/unit	4	5	2	6
Throughput/labour hour	$2.50	$2.00	$3.50	$3.00
Priority	3rd	4th	1st	2nd

The production volumes that will maximise throughput and net profit are:

Product	Units	Labour hours	Throughput $
Y	1,000	2,000	7,000
Z	400	2,400	7,200
W	500	2,000	5,000
		6,400	
X (balance)	320	1,600	3,200
		8,000	22,400

Test your understanding 5

Throughput per bottleneck machine hour = ($85 − $42.50)/1.5 hours = $28.33

Operating expenses per bottleneck machine hour = $8,000/(10 × 40) = $20

Throughput accounting ratio = $28.33/$20 = 1.42

Test your understanding 6

(a) **Step 1:** Determine the bottleneck constraint

The bottleneck resource is machine time. 400 machine hours available each week = 24,000 machine minutes.

Step 2: Calculate the throughput per unit for each product

	A	B	C	D
	$	$	$	$
Sales price	1.40	0.80	1.20	2.80
Materials cost	0.60	0.30	0.60	1.00
Throughput/unit	0.80	0.50	0.60	1.80

Step 3: Calculate the throughput per machine minute

Machine time per unit	5 minutes	2 minutes	3 minutes	6 minutes
Throughput per minute	$0.16	$0.25	$0.20	$0.30

Step 4: Rank

Rank	4th	2nd	3rd	1st

Step 5: Allocate resources using this ranking and answer the question.

The profit-maximising weekly output and sales volumes are as follows.

Product	Units	Machine minutes	Throughput per unit	Total throughout
			$	$
D	1,500	9,000	1.80	2,700
B	2,000	4,000	0.50	1,000
C	2,500	7,500	0.60	1,500
		20,500		
A (balance)	700	3,500	0.80	560
		24,000		5,760
Operating expenses				5,440
Profit				320

(b) Throughput per machine hour: $5,760/400 hours = $14.40

Cost (operating expenses) per machine hour: $5,440/400 hours = $13.60.

TPAR: $14.40/$13.60 = 1.059

Test your understanding 7

(a) **Process bottleneck**

$$\text{Capacity in Process} \times \frac{35.000}{1} = 35{,}000 \text{ units per period}$$

$$\text{Capacity in Process} \times \frac{42.000}{1.5} = 28{,}000 \text{ units per period}$$

Process Y has the lower capacity and therefore this is the bottleneck.

(b) **Throughput accounting ratio**

Throughput per unit = $16 – $10 = $6

$$\text{Return per factory hour} = \frac{\$6}{1.5} = \$4$$

$$\text{Cost per factory hour} = \frac{\$105{,}000}{42{,}000 \text{ hours}} = \$2.50$$

$$\text{Throughput accounting ratio} = \frac{\$4}{\$2.50} = \$1.60$$

As the throughput accounting ratio is greater than 1 it provides a satisfactory result.

Test your understanding 8

B

	W	X	Y
	$	$	$
Throughput*	139	130	120
Time at bottle neck	7	10	7
Throughput per minute	20	13	17
Rank	1	3	2

* throughput = sales less material costs

Test your understanding 9

The correct answer is answer **B**.

There is likely to be very little material or marginal costs for digital products and therefore marginal costing and throughput accounting are unlikely to be useful for digital products.

There is also likely to be very little standardisation of costs between digital products which reduces the role of standard costing.

But activity based costing could be used to absorb indirect overheads as long as cost drivers and levels of activity could be reasonably estimated.

Test your understanding 10

The correct answer is answer **C**.

The number of cost drivers is likely to increase. Overheads will be split by more detailed analysis and each will have its own cost driver. This is likely to increase the number of cost drivers in the system.

The other statements are true.

Test your understanding 11

	$
Profit	120,000
Fixed costs	300,000
Contribution	420,000
Contribution/sales ratio	75%
	$
Sales	560,000
Material costs (10% of sales)	56,000
Throughput	504,000

Test your understanding 12

C

First, we need to establish the bottleneck:

The 'Assembly' hours needed for maximum production are 143.75 ((2 × 1,000) + (3 × 1,500) + 2.5 × 850)/60. This is less than the 150 hours available and so assembly is not the bottleneck resource.

The 'Quality Control' hours needed for maximum production are 178.33 ((3 × 1,000) + (4 x 1,500) + (2 × 850))/60. This is greater than the 170 hours available and so 'quality control hours' is the limiting resource/bottleneck. The 'Packaging' hours needed for maximum production are 234.17 ((4 × 1,000) + (5 × 1,500) + (3 × 850))/60. This is less than the 250 hours available and so is not a bottleneck resource.

Next, we calculate the throughput per unit:

	Alpha	Beta	Gamma
Sales price per unit	$2.00	$2.25	$1.75
Direct materials cost per unit	$0.50	$0.81	$0.35
Throughput per unit	$1.50	$1.44	$1.40

Then, we calculate the throughput per unit of bottleneck resource:

	Alpha	Beta	Gamma
Throughput per unit	$1.50	$1.44	$1.40
Time on bottleneck resource (quality control)	3 minutes	4 minutes	2 minutes
Throughput per minute	$0.50	$0.36	$0.70

Test your understanding 13

B

With a digital costing system, standards are regularly updated.

As a result of the standards being in real time, there should be no planning variances. Operational variances will still arise, through differences between up to date standards and actual results.

Although digital costing systems can be expensive to implement, when they are up and running they have low operational costs.

In a digital costing system, internal digital systems are linked with suppliers, customers and external markets.

Test your understanding 14

D

Determining the lifetime of digital products can be very difficult, particularly when there are rapid changes in technology as there is at the present time. This also makes it complicated to predict the benefits.

Some of the costs incurred on the development of features or updates are common to all the apps (such as payment features) and an appropriate method will need to be determined to share the costs between the apps.

5

Chapter

Variance analysis

Chapter learning objectives

Lead outcome	Component outcome
A3. Apply costing methods to determine the costs for different purposes	(b) Standard costing (c) Variance analysis (without mix and yield variance)

1 Chapter overview diagram

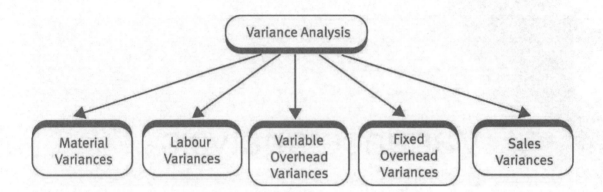

2 Standard costing and variance analysis

 Standard costing is a technique which establishes predetermined estimates of the costs of products and services and then compares these predetermined costs with actual costs as they are incurred. The predetermined costs are known as standard costs and the difference between the standard cost and actual cost is known as a variance.

 Further explanation of standard costing

Whenever identical operations are performed or identical products are manufactured many times over, it should be possible to decide in advance not merely what they are expected to cost, but also what they ought to cost.

Similarly, when a standard service is provided many times over, it should be possible to establish in advance how the service should be provided, how long it should take and how much it should cost.

- A **standard** is 'a benchmark measurement of resource usage or revenue or profit generation, set in defined conditions' (CIMA Official Terminology).

- A **standard cost** for a product or service is a predetermined (planned) unit cost, based on a standard specification of the resources needed to supply it and the costs of those resources.

  A standard cost is based on technical specifications for the materials, labour time and other resources required and the prices and rates for the materials and labour.

  Standard costs can be prepared using either absorption costing or marginal costing.

- A **standard price** for a product or service is the expected price for selling the standard product or service. When there is a standard sales price and a standard cost per unit, there is also a **standard profit per unit** (absorption costing) or **standard contribution per unit** (marginal costing).

Types of standard

There are four main types of standard:

Attainable standards

- They are based upon efficient (but not perfect) operating conditions.

- The standard will include allowances for normal material losses, realistic allowances for fatigue, machine breakdowns, etc.

- These are the most frequently encountered type of standard.

- These standards may motivate employees to work harder since they provide a realistic but challenging target.

Basic standards

- These are long-term standards which remain unchanged over a period of years.

- Their sole use is to show trends over time for such items as material prices, labour rates and efficiency and the effect of changing methods.

- They cannot be used to highlight current efficiency.

- These standards may demotivate employees if, over time, they become too easy to achieve and, as a result, employees may feel bored and unchallenged.

Current standards

- These are standards based on current working conditions.

- They are useful when current conditions are abnormal and another standard would provide meaningless information.

- The disadvantage is that they do not attempt to motivate employees to improve upon current working conditions and, as a result, employees may feel unchallenged.

Ideal standards

- These are based upon perfect operating conditions.

- This means that there is no wastage or scrap, no breakdowns, no stoppages or idle time; in short, no inefficiencies.

- In their search for perfect quality, Japanese companies use ideal standards for pinpointing areas where close examination may result in large cost savings.

- Ideal standards may have an adverse motivational impact since employees may feel that the standard is impossible to achieve.

The process by which the total difference between actual cost and standard is broken down into its different elements is known as **Variance Analysis.**

Variance analysis

Variances can be calculated for both costs and sales. Cost variances analyse the difference between actual costs and standard costs. Sales variances analyse the difference between actual and budgeted sales prices and sales volumes.

Where standard costing is used, variance analysis can be an important aspect of performance measurement and control. It is defined in the CIMA Official Terminology as 'the evaluation of performance by means of variances, whose timely reporting should maximise the opportunity for managerial action'.

Variance reports comparing actual results with the standards or budget are produced regularly, perhaps monthly.

A variance is the difference between actual results and the budget or standard.

Taken together, cost and sales variances can be used to explain the difference between the budgeted profit for a period and the actual profit.

When actual results are better than expected results, a **favourable (F)** variance occurs.

When actual results are worse than expected results, an **adverse variance (A)** occurs.

The difference between budgetary control and variance analysis

Budgetary control is covered in a later chapter and is concerned with controlling total costs across an area of responsibility, whereas standard costing and variance analysis are concerned with unit costs.

In order to use standard costing, a standard unit must be made or a standard action be performed. Budgetary control is more flexible and can be used to control costs even when a wide variety of activities are undertaken. It can even be applied to discretionary expenditure such as research, which is much harder to use for standard costing.

One disadvantage of using budgetary control is that whilst it limits expenditure it does not provide a basis for measuring the efficiency of that expenditure.

A standard costing system is integrated with the actual accounting system whereas budgetary control operates as a reporting system external to the accounting system.

Variance groups

Variances can be divided into three main groups:

- sales variances
- variable cost variances
    - material variances
    - labour variances
    - variable overhead variances
- fixed overhead variances

3   Sales variances

Sales variances explain the effect of differences between:

- actual and standard sales prices, and
- budgeted and actual sales volumes

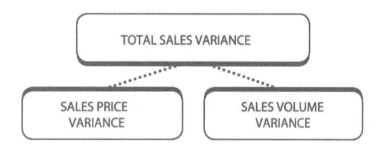

Sales price variance

A sales price variance shows the effect on profit of a 'change in revenue caused by the actual selling price differing from that budgeted' (CIMA Official Terminology). It is calculated as the difference between:

(a)   Standard selling price multiplied by the actual number of units sold, and

(b)   Actual selling price multiplied by the actual number of units sold.

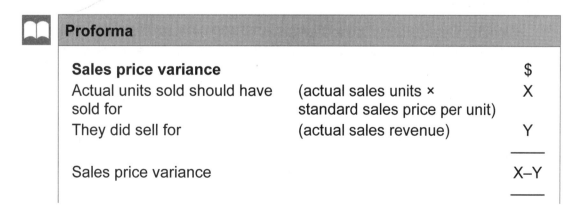

Proforma		
Sales price variance		$
Actual units sold should have sold for	(actual sales units × standard sales price per unit)	X
They did sell for	(actual sales revenue)	Y
Sales price variance		X–Y

This variance is favourable if actual sales revenue is higher than sales at the standard selling price, and adverse if actual sales revenue is lower than standard.

Sales volume variance

The sales volume variance is a 'measure of the effect on contribution/profit of not achieving the budgeted volume of sales' (CIMA Official Terminology). It is the difference between actual and budgeted sales volumes valued at either standard profit, in an absorption costing system, or standard contribution in a marginal costing system.

Proforma

Sales volume variance	Units of sale
	Units
Actual sales volume	X
Budgeted sales volume	Y
Sales volume variance	X–Y

This variance is favourable if actual sales revenue is higher than sales at the standard selling price, and adverse if actual sales revenue is lower than standard.

The variance in units can then be valued in one of three ways:

- at the **standard profit per unit** – if using absorption costing
- at the **standard contribution per unit** – if using marginal costing
- at the **standard revenue per unit** – this is rarely used and you should only do so if it is specifically asked for in an exam question.

Example 1

Walter Dean Ltd has budgeted sales of 400 units at $25 each. The variable costs are expected to be $18 per unit, and there are no fixed costs.

The actual sales were 500 units at $20 each and costs were as expected.

Calculate the selling price variance and the sales volume contribution variance.

> **Example 2**
>
> The following data is available for the most recent month of sales:
>
> | | Budget | Actual |
> |---|---|---|
> | Sales units | 320 | 380 |
> | Selling price per unit | $45 | $42 |
> | Total cost per unit | $23 | $22 |
> | Variable cost per unit | $17 | $15 |
>
> Calculate the sales variances, calculating the sales volume variance using absorption costing, marginal costing and standard revenue per unit.

As well as calculating variances you may also have to determine possible causes for variances.

Here are potential causes of the sales variances:

Sales price

(1) Higher-than-expected discounts offered to customers to persuade them to buy larger, bulk quantities.

(2) Lower-than-expected discounts, perhaps due to strength of sales demand.

(3) The effect of low-price offers during a marketing campaign.

(4) Market conditions forcing an industry-wide price change.

Sales volume

(1) Successful or unsuccessful direct selling efforts.

(2) Successful or unsuccessful marketing efforts (for example, the effects of an advertising campaign).

(3) Unexpected changes in customer needs and buying habits.

(4) Failure to satisfy demand due to production difficulties.

(5) Higher demand due to a cut in selling prices, or lower demand due to an increase in sales prices.

4   Direct material cost variances

This section has three variances. The direct material total variance, which shows the total difference in the amount spent on materials, and this can also be split into two further components – the materials price and materials usage variances:

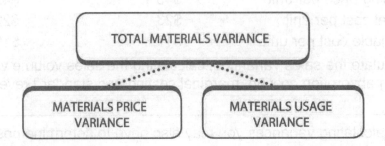

Direct material total variance

The difference between:

(a)   the standard direct material cost of the actual production and

(b)   the actual direct material cost.

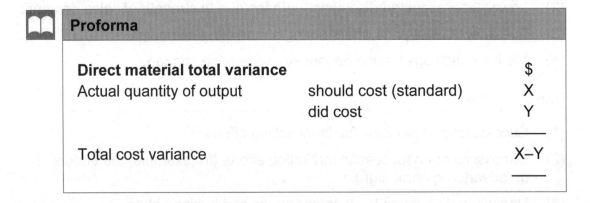

Proforma		
Direct material total variance		$
Actual quantity of output	should cost (standard)	X
	did cost	Y
Total cost variance		X–Y

Illustration 1

An extract from the standard cost card of Product X is provided below:

Direct materials: 40 kg @ $5.30 per kg

Actual results:

Output 1,000 units

Material purchased and used 39,000 kg

Material cost $210,600

Calculate the direct material total variance.

Solution:

		$
Actual quantity of output (1,000 units)	should cost (40 kg per unit @ $5.30 per kg)	212,000
	did cost	210,600
Total cost variance		1,400 F

The direct materials for the production of 1,000 units of Product X *should* have cost $212,000, based on standard quantities and costs. However, they only cost $210,000, which means that less was spent on materials than planned, which results in a favourable variance.

Example 3

James Marshall Ltd makes a single product with the following budgeted material costs per unit:

   2 kg of material A at $10/kg

Actual details:

   Output 1,000 units

   Material purchased and used 2,200 kg

   Material cost $20,900

Calculate the direct material total variance.

A total material variance actually conveys very little useful information. It needs to be analysed further. It can be analysed into two sub-variances:

(1)   a direct material price variance, i.e. paying more or less than expected for materials and

(2)   a direct material usage variance, i.e. using more or less material than expected for the actual output.

> **CIMA definitions**
>
> The total direct material variance is defined as:
>
> > *measurement of the difference between the standard material cost of the output produced and the material cost incurred.*
>
> The material price variance is defined as:
>
> > *the difference between the actual price paid for purchased materials and their standard cost.*
>
> The material usage variance is defined as a variance which:
>
> > *measures efficiency in the use of material, by comparing standard material usage for actual production with actual material used, the difference is valued at standard cost.*
>
> *(all taken from CIMA Official Terminology).*

Direct material price variance

It is calculated as the difference between:

(a)   standard purchase price per kg (or per litre for liquids) and

(b)   actual purchase price

multiplied by the actual quantity of material purchased or used.

Note that the material price variance can be calculated either at the time of purchase or at the time of usage.

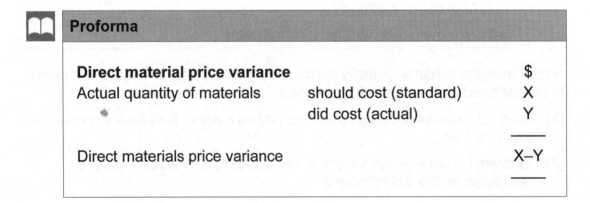

> **Proforma**
>
> | **Direct material price variance** | | $ |
> |---|---|---|
> | Actual quantity of materials | should cost (standard) | X |
> | | did cost (actual) | Y |
> | | | |
> | Direct materials price variance | | X–Y |

e.g **Illustration 2**

Continuing with the information from Illustration 1, calculate the direct materials price variance.

Solution:

		$
Actual quantity of materials	should cost (39,000 kg @ $5.30 per kg)	206,700
	did cost	210,600
Direct materials price variance		3,900 A

The direct materials purchased should have only cost $5.30 per kg. However, as the total purchase price of the materials was $210,600, then this means that the amount paid per kg must have been $210,600/39,000 kg = $5.40. This is greater than the standard, which leads to an adverse variance.

Direct material usage variance

The difference between:

(a) the standard quantity of material specified for the actual production and

(b) the actual quantity used

multiplied by the standard purchase price.

Proforma

Direct materials usage variance		$
Actual output produced	should use (standard quantity)	X
	did use (actual quantity)	Y
Direct materials usage variance	(in material quantity)	X–Y
× standard price	(per unit of material)	$P
Direct materials usage variance		(X–Y)

Illustration 3

Continuing with the information from Illustration 1, calculate the direct materials usage variance.

Solution:

		Kg
Actual output produced (1,000 units)	should use (40 kg per unit)	40,000
	did use (39,000 kg)	39,000
Direct materials usage variance	(in material quantity)	1,000 F
× standard price per kg		$5.30
Direct materials usage variance		$5,300 F

Production of 1,000 units should have used 40,000 kg of direct materials (based on standard). However, only 39,000 kg were purchased and used. This is therefore a favourable usage variance, as less was used than expected.

Example 4

For example 3, calculate the price and usage variances for materials.

An alternative method

Using the data in Example 3, calculate the same variances for materials using the following format:

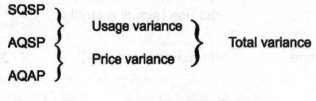

Where	SQ	means Standard Quantity
	SP	means Standard Price
	AQ	means Actual Quantity
and	AP	means Actual Price

Standard Quantity means the standard quantity of the actual output.

Note: This assumes purchases = issues and/or the price variance is calculated at the time of issue.

					$	
SQSP						
	2 kg/unit x 1,000 units	x	$10/kg	=	20,000	Usage
AQSP						$2,000 A
	2,200 kg	x	$10/kg	=	22,000	
AQAP						$1,100 F
		x		=	20,900	Price

The potential causes of the material variances are as follows:

Material price

(1) Using a different supplier, who is either cheaper or more expensive.

(2) Buying in larger-sized orders, and getting larger bulk purchase discounts. Buying in smaller-sized orders and losing planned bulk purchase discounts.

(3) An unexpected increase in the prices charged by a supplier.

(4) Unexpected buying costs, such as high delivery charges.

(5) Efficient or inefficient buying procedures.

(6) A change in material quality, resulting in either higher or lower purchase prices.

Material usage

(1) A higher-than-expected or lower-than-expected rate of scrap or wastage.

(2) Using a different quality of material (higher or lower quality) could affect the wastage rate.

(3) Defective materials.

(4) Better quality control.

(5) More efficient work procedures, resulting in better material usage rates.

(6) Changing the labour mix which impacts on wastage if different types of labour make more/less errors.

(7) Changing the materials mix to obtain a more expensive or less expensive mix than the standard.

The impact of inventory valuation

In the examples we have just looked at, the quantity of material purchased was the same as the quantity of material used.

However, this may not always be the case.

We also need to consider situations where all of the material purchased is not used and inventory therefore remains at the end of the period.

If inventory is valued at standard cost, then the calculation should be performed using the quantity of materials purchased. This will ensure that all of the variance is eliminated as soon as purchases are made and the inventory will be held at standard cost.

If inventory is valued at actual cost, then the calculation should be performed using the quantity of materials used. This means that the variance is calculated and eliminated on each item of inventory as it is used up. The remainder of the inventory will then be held at actual price, with its price variance still 'attached', until it is used and the price variance is calculated.

The materials usage variance is based on the quantity of materials used as before.

For example:

X Ltd purchases 4,000 kg of material at a cost of $8,400. It uses 3,300 kg to produce 600 units of Product A. Product A's standard cost card for material A is as follows:

Material: 5 kg @ $2 per kg

Required:

Calculate the direct material price variance, the usage variance and the value of closing inventory.

Solution

Price variance: (this is calculated on all of the materials purchased, whether they were used in production or not)

		$
Actual quantity of materials (4,000 kg)	should cost ($2 per kg)	8,000
	did cost	8,400
Direct materials price variance		400 A

162

Usage variance: (this is based on the amount of material used)

		Kg
Actual output produced (600 units)	should use (5 kg per unit)	3,000
	did use (3,300 kg)	3,300
Direct materials usage variance	(in material quantity)	300 A
× standard price per kg		$2
Direct materials usage variance		$600 A

The value of the **closing inventory** is the difference between the quantity purchased and used, valued at standard price. This is therefore 4,000 kg − 3,300 kg = 700 kg @ $2 = $1,400.

Example 5

Patio Ltd manufactures and sells wooden gazebos.

The budget and actual results for materials in May are as follows:

Budget:

> 7,500 units using 22,500 kg of materials costing $90,000.

Actual:

> 6,500 units, 20,800 kg purchased @ $91,520.

There was no opening inventory of raw materials at the start of May but there was 500 kg of closing inventory at the end of May.

Required:

Calculate the material price variance, the material usage variance and the valuation of the closing inventory at standard cost.

5 Direct labour cost variances

This section has four variances. The direct labour total cost variance, which shows the impact of any overall change in the amount spent on labour, and this can also be split into two further components – the labour rate and labour efficiency variances. In some scenarios we might also see a labour idle time variance.

Direct labour total variance

The difference between:

(a) the standard direct labour cost of the actual production and

(b) the actual cost of direct labour.

Proforma

Direct labour total variance		$
Actual quantity of output	should cost (standard)	X
	did cost	Y
Total cost variance		X–Y

Illustration 4

The following information relates to the production of Product J18.

Extract from the standard cost card of Product J18:

Direct labour:

Bonding (24 hours @ $5 per hour) $120

Actual results for wages:

Production	1,000 units produced
Bonding	23,900 hours costing $131,450 in total

Required:

Calculate the direct labour total variance.

Solution:

		$
Actual quantity of output (1,000 units)	should cost (1,000 units @ 24 hours @ $5 per hour)	120,000
	did cost	131,450
Total cost variance		11,450A

The direct labour for actual production should have only cost $120,000 based on standards. However, as it actually cost $131,450 then this means that more was paid in total for labour, which is an adverse variance.

A total labour variance can also be analysed further. It can be analysed into two sub-variances:

(1) a direct labour rate variance, i.e. paying more or less than expected per hour for labour and

(2) a direct labour efficiency variance, i.e. using more or less labour hours per unit than expected.

CIMA definitions

The total direct labour variance is defined as one which:

indicates the difference between the standard direct labour cost of the output which has been produced and the actual direct labour cost incurred.

The direct labour rate variance is defined as one which:

indicates the actual cost of any change from the standard labour rate of remuneration.

The direct labour efficiency variance is defined as:

standard labour cost of any change from the standard level of labour efficiency.

(all taken from CIMA Official Terminology).

Direct labour rate variance

The difference between:

(a) standard rate per hour and the

(b) actual rate per hour

multiplied by the actual hours that were paid for.

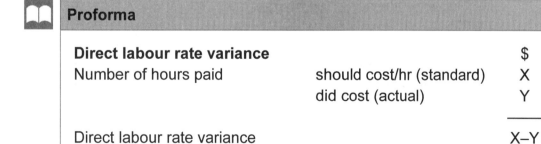

Proforma

Direct labour rate variance		$
Number of hours paid	should cost/hr (standard)	X
	did cost (actual)	Y
Direct labour rate variance		X–Y

Continuing with the information in Illustration 4 above, calculate the labour rate variance for Product J18.

Solution:

		$
Number of hours paid (23,900)	should cost/hr ($5)	119,500
	did cost (actual)	131,450
		———
Direct labour rate variance		11,950A
		———

As the total payment for the 23,900 hours was $131,450, this equates to a rate per hour of $131,450/23,900 = $5.50. This is more than the standard rate of $5 per hour and so this variance is adverse; more was paid per hour than expected.

Direct labour efficiency variance

The difference between:

(a) the standard hours specified for the actual production and

(b) the actual hours worked

multiplied by the standard hourly rate.

Proforma

		$
Direct labour efficiency variance		
Actual output produced	should take (standard hours)	X
	did take(actual hours)	Y
		———
Direct labour efficiency variance	(in hours)	X–Y
		———
× standard rate per hour		$P
Direct labour efficiency variance		$P × (X–Y)

Illustration 6

Continuing with the information in Illustration 4 above, calculate the direct labour efficiency variance for Product J18.

Solution:

Actual output produced (1,000 units)	should take (24 hours)	24,000
	did take(actual hours)	23,900
Direct labour efficiency variance	(in hours)	100 F
× standard rate per hour		$5
Direct labour efficiency variance		$500 F

Actual production was completed in fewer hours than expected. This is therefore a favourable variance as the employees were more efficient than expected per the standard.

Example 6

Ivan Korshunov provides a pension consultancy service and has the following budgeted/standard information:

Budgeted services	1,000
Labour hours per unit	3
Labour rate per hour	$80
Actual results	
Number of services provided	1,100
Hours paid for and worked	3,400 hours
Labour cost	$283,000

Calculate rate and efficiency variances for labour.

Idle time and idle time variances

During a period, there might be idle time, when the work force is not doing any work at all.

When idle time occurs, and if it is recorded, the efficiency variance should be separated into two parts:

- an idle time variance

- an efficiency variance during active working hours.

If there is no standard idle time set, then **the idle time variance is always adverse**, because it represents money 'wasted'.

Idle time definition

The purpose of an efficiency variance should be to measure the efficiency of the work force in the time they are actively engaged in making products or delivering a service. CIMA Official

The direct labour idle time variance is defined as:

> *this variance occurs when the hours paid exceed the hours worked and there is an extra cost caused by this idle time. Its computation increases the accuracy of the labour efficiency variance. (CIMA Official Terminology).*

Illustration 7

A product has a standard direct labour cost of $15, consisting of 1.5 hours of work for each unit at a cost of $10 per hour. During April, 100 units were produced. The direct labour workers were paid $2,000 for 160 hours of attendance, but the idle time records show that 30 hours in the month were recorded as idle time.

(a) We can record an idle time variance of 30 hours (A). This is costed at the standard rate per hour, $10, to give an idle time variance of $300(A).

(b) The efficiency variance should then be calculated using the active hours worked, not the total hours paid for.

Direct labour efficiency variance

		Hours $
Actual output produced should take (standard hours)	(100 hrs × 1.5 hrs per unit)	150
	did take (160 – 30 hrs)	130
Direct labour efficiency variance	(in hours)	20F
× standard rate per hour		$10/hr
Direct labour efficiency variance		$200 F

Example 7

Melanie Mitchell Ltd makes a single product with the following information:

Budget/Standard

Output	1,000 units
Hours	6,000
Labour cost	$42,000

Actual

Output	900 units
Hours paid	5,500
Hours worked	5,200
Labour cost	$39,100

Calculate appropriate variances for labour

Expected idle time

Some organisations may experience idle time on a regular basis. For example, if demand is seasonal or irregular, but the organisation wishes to maintain and pay a constant number of workers, they will experience a certain level of 'expected' or 'normal' idle time during less busy periods.

In this situation the standard labour rate may include an allowance for the cost of the expected idle time. Only the impact of any unexpected or abnormal idle time would be included in the idle time variance. If actual idle time is greater than standard then the variance is adverse; if it is less than standard then it would be favourable.

Example

LBC offer a public bus service for local journeys at a popular holiday resort. It experiences seasonal demand for its product. During the next period the company expects that there will be an average level of idle time equivalent to 20% of hours paid. The company's standard labour rate is $9 per hour before the adjustment for idle time payments.

The standard time for each journey is 3 active (productive) hours.

Actual results for the period were as follows:

Number of journeys	3,263
Actual hours paid for	14,000
Actual active (productive) hours	10,304

Required:

Calculate the following variances for the period:

(i)   the idle time variance

(ii)   the labour efficiency variance.

Solution

The basic standard rate per hour must be increased to allow for the impact of the idle time:

$$\text{Standard rate per hour worked} = \frac{\$9.00}{0.8} = \$11.25$$

The variances can now be evaluated at this increased hourly rate.

Idle time variance

	Hours	
Expected idle time = 20% × 14,000 hours paid	2,800	
Actual idle time = 14,000 – 10,304 hours	3,696	
	———	
Variance (hours)	896	A
Standard rate per hour worked	$11.25	
	———	
Idle time variance	$10,080	A
	———	

Labour efficiency variance

	Hours	
3,263 journeys should have taken (×3)	9,789	
But did take (productive hours)	10,304	
	———	
Variance (hours)	515	A
Standard rate per hour worked	$11.25	
	———	
Labour efficiency variance	$5,794	A
	———	

Possible operational causes of the labour variances are as follows:

Labour rate

(1)   An unexpected increase in basic rates of pay.

(2)   Payments of bonuses, where these are recorded as direct labour costs.

(3)   Using labour that is more or less experienced (and so more or less expensive) than the 'standard'.

(4)   A change in the composition of the work force, and so a change in average rates of pay.

Labour efficiency

(1) Taking more or less time than expected to complete work, due to inefficient or efficient working.

(2) Using labour that is more or less experienced (and so more or less efficient) than the 'standard'.

(3) A change in the composition or mix of the work force, and so a change in the level of efficiency.

(4) Improved working methods.

(5) Industrial action by the work force: 'working to rule'.

(6) Poor supervision.

(7) Improvements in efficiency due to an unexpected 'learning effect' amongst the work force.

(8) Unexpected lost time due to production bottlenecks and resource shortages.

6   Variable overhead variances

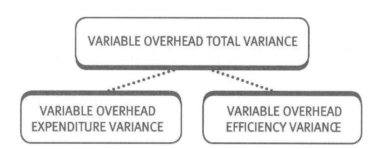

Variable overhead variances are similar to direct labour variances.

*   In standard product costing, a variable production overhead total variance can be calculated, and this can be analysed into an expenditure variance and an efficiency variance.

*   With service costing, a variable overhead total variance can be calculated, but this might not be analysed any further.

Since variable production overheads are normally assumed to vary with labour hours worked, **labour hours are used in calculations**. This means, for example, that the variable production overhead efficiency variance uses exactly the same hours as the direct labour efficiency variance.

Details on the variances

Variable production overhead total variance

The difference between:

(a) the standard variable overhead cost of the actual production and

(b) the actual cost of variable production overheads.

Variable production overhead total variance	$
Actual quantity of output should cost (standard)	X
did cost	Y
Total variance	X–Y

A total variable production overhead variance can also be analysed further. It can be analysed into two sub-variances:

(1) a variable production overhead expenditure variance, i.e. paying more or less than expected per hour for variable overheads and

(2) a variable production overhead efficiency variance, i.e. using more or less variable overheads per unit than expected.

The official CIMA definitions are as follows:

The variable production overhead total variance is defined as one which:

> *measures the difference between the variable overhead that should be used for actual output and variable production overhead actually used.*

> *(CIMA Official Terminology).*

The variable production overhead expenditure variance is defined as one which:

> *indicates the actual cost of any change from the standard rate per hour. Hours refer to either labour or machine hours depending on the recovery base chosen for variable production overhead.*

> *(CIMA Official Terminology).*

The variable production overhead efficiency variance is defined as the:

> *standard variable overhead cost of any change from the standard level of efficiency.*

> *(CIMA Official Terminology).*

Variable production overhead expenditure variance

		$
Number of hours worked	should cost/hr (standard)	X
	did cost (actual)	Y
Variable production overhead expenditure variance		X–Y

Variable production overhead efficiency variance

		$
Actual output produced	should take (standard hours)	X
	did take (actual hours)	Y
Efficiency variance	(in hours)	X–Y
× standard variable overhead rate per hour		$P
Variable production overhead efficiency variance		$P × (X–Y)

Example 8

The budgeted output for KB for May was 1,000 units of product A. Each unit requires 2 direct labour hours. Variable overheads are budgeted at $3 per labour hour.

Actual results:

Output	900 units
Labour hours worked	1,980 hours
Variable overhead	$5,544

Calculate appropriate variances for variable overheads.

Alternative method

Using the same example, calculate appropriate variances for variable overhead using the following format:

SHSR

    Efficiency variance

AHSR   } Total variance

    Expenditure variance

AHAR }

Where	SH	means Standard Hours
	SR	means Standard Rate
	AH	means Actual Hours
and	AR	means Actual Rate

Standard Hours means the standard hours of the actual output.

		$	
SHSR			
2 hrs/unit x 900 units x $3/hr =	5,400 }	Efficiency $540 A	
AHSR			
1,980 hrs x $3/hr =	5,940 {		
AHAR		$396 F	
=	5,544 }	Expenditure	

Idle time variances and variable production overhead

The analysis of variable production overhead variances is affected by the existence of idle time. It is usually assumed that variable production overhead is incurred during active hours only.

The variable production overhead efficiency variance is calculated in the same way that the direct labour efficiency variance is calculated when there is idle time.

The variable production overhead expenditure variance, when there is idle time, is the difference between:

- the standard variable overhead cost of the active hours worked, and

- the actual variable overhead cost.

Example 9

Extracts from the standard cost card of a product are as follows:

		$/unit
Direct labour	2 hours × $15 per hour	30
Variable production overhead	2 hours × $4 per hour	8

During May, 200 units were produced. The direct labour workers were paid $6,600 for 440 hours of work, but the idle time records show that 20 hours in the month were recorded as idle time. Actual variable production overhead expenditure incurred was $1,530.

Calculate the labour and variable overhead variances.

7 Fixed production overhead cost variances

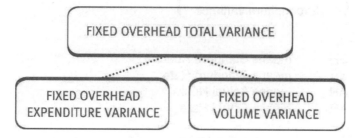

Fixed production overhead total variance

The amount of overhead absorbed for each unit of output is the standard fixed overhead cost per unit. The total cost variance is therefore calculated as follows:

The difference between:

(a)   the standard fixed production overhead cost absorbed by the actual production (i.e. the amount of fixed overhead actually absorbed into production using the standard absorption rate), and

(b)   the actual fixed production overheads incurred.

Proforma

Fixed production overhead total variance

		$
Overheads absorbed	(Actual output × standard fixed production overhead absorption rate)	X
Actual fixed overhead incurred		Y
Fixed production overhead total variance		X – Y

Under/over-absorption

In a standard absorption costing system, fixed overheads are related to cost units by using absorption rates. The total cost variance for fixed production overhead variances is the amount of over-absorbed or under-absorbed overhead. Over-absorbed overhead is a favourable variance, and under-absorbed overhead is an adverse variance.

Under/over-absorption is the difference between the overheads incurred and the overheads absorbed

The under/over-absorption occurs because the OAR is based upon two predictions – the budgeted fixed overhead and the budgeted level of activity. If either or both predictions are wrong there will be under/over-absorption and there will be a fixed overhead total variance.

- If the actual expenditure is different from the budgeted expenditure there is an expenditure variance and

- If the actual production is different from the budgeted production there is a volume variance. A fixed production overhead volume variance represents the amount of fixed overhead that has been under- or over-absorbed due to the fact that actual production volume differed from the budgeted production volume.

Fixed production overhead expenditure variance

The difference between:

(a)   budgeted fixed production overhead and

(b)   actual fixed production overhead.

> **Proforma**
>
> **Fixed production overhead expenditure variance**
>
> | | $ |
> |---|---|
> | Budgeted fixed overhead | X |
> | Actual fixed production overhead incurred | Y |
> | Fixed production overhead expenditure variance | X–Y |
>
> An expenditure variance can be calculated for fixed production overhead. A similar variance can be calculated (if required) for other fixed overhead costs:
>
> - a fixed administration overhead expenditure variance
>
> - a fixed sales and distribution overhead expenditure variance.

Fixed production overhead volume variance

The volume variance is calculated as the difference between:

(a)   Budgeted output in units and

(b)   Actual output in units multiplied by the standard fixed overhead cost (FOAR) per unit.

⚠ The fixed overhead volume variance does not occur in a marginal costing system.

> **Proforma**
>
> **Fixed production overhead volume variance**
>
> | | | Units |
> |---|---|---|
> | Actual output produced | | X |
> | Budgeted output | | Y |
> | Volume variance | (in units) | X–Y |
> | × standard fixed overhead rate per unit | | $F |
> | Fixed production overhead volume variance | | $F × (X–Y) |

You may be aware that the fixed production overhead volume variance can be sub-divided into a fixed production overhead capacity and fixed production overhead efficiency (explained later).

Illustration 8

The following information relates to the production of Product M17 in June:

Budget:

Fixed overheads	$22,960
Units	6,560

Actual:

Fixed overheads	$24,200
Units	6,460

The company uses a standard absorption costing system.

Required:

Calculate the following

(i)   fixed production overhead total variance

(ii) fixed production overhead expenditure variance

(iii) fixed overhead volume variance

Solution:

(i)   fixed production overhead total variance:

		$
Overheads absorbed	(6,460 units × $3.50 per unit (W1)	22,610
Actual fixed overhead incurred		24,200
Fixed production overhead total variance		1,590A

(W1) FOAR = budgeted overheads / budgeted activity

= $22,960 / 6,560 = $3.50 per unit

(ii) fixed production overhead expenditure variance:

	$
Budgeted fixed overhead	22,960
Actual fixed production overhead incurred	24,200
Fixed production overhead expenditure variance	1,240 A

(iii) fixed production overhead volume variance:

		Units
Actual output produced		6,460
Budgeted output		6,560
Volume variance	(in units)	100 A
× FOAR		$3.50
Fixed production overhead volume variance		$350 A

Example 10

The following data relates to the fixed production overhead costs of producing widgets in March:

Budgeted fixed production overhead expenditure	$4,375
Budgeted production volume (widgets)	1,750 units
Standard fixed production overhead cost:	
(0.25 hours @ $10 per hour)	$2.50
Number of widgets produced in March	1,800 units
Actual fixed production overhead expenditure	$4,800

Required:

Calculate the fixed production overhead expenditure and volume variances in March

It has been shown in an earlier chapter that, where products take different times to produce, it is not always suitable to have fixed overheads allocated on a per unit basis. A labour hour basis may be more suitable, for example.

It may therefore be necessary to work out the fixed overhead volume variance based on the fixed overhead absorption rate per hour, rather than the rate per unit. This is needed when an organisation has more than one product and an absorption rate per unit is not appropriate.

The variance is calculated by comparing the cost of the standard hours for actual production with the total budgeted fixed overhead.

Illustration 9

A cosmetic dental practice offers two types of treatment, teeth whitening and teeth straightening. The treatments last for varying amounts of time and fixed overheads are allocated to treatments based on labour hours spent on the treatment. In the month of September total fixed overheads were budgeted to be $40,000 and the services were budgeted to have the following total labour hours:

Service	Whitening	Straightening
Budgeted hours	460	540

During September there were 190 teeth straightening treatments which took on average 2.8 hours per treatment compared to a standard time of 3 hours per treatment.

Calculate the fixed overhead volume variance for the teeth straightening service for September.

Solution

The fixed overhead absorption rate per hour is:

= $40,000 / (460 hours + 540 hours) = $40 per hour

The budgeted overhead cost for the teeth straightening treatment is:

= 540 hours × $40 per hour = $21,600

The standard cost of the standard hours worked is:

= 190 treatments × 3 hours per treatment × $40 per hour = $22,800

The variance = $22,800 – $21,600 = $1,200 Favourable

Fixed overhead capacity and efficiency variances

In absorption costing systems, if the fixed overhead is absorbed based on **hours**, then the fixed overhead volume variance can be subdivided into capacity and efficiency variances.

- The capacity variance measures whether the workforce worked more or fewer hours than **budgeted** for the period:

	$
Actual hours × FOAR per hour	X
Less Budgeted expenditure	(X)
Fixed overhead capacity variance	X

The efficiency variance measures whether the workforce took more or less time than **standard** in producing their output for the period:

	$
Standard hours for actual production × FOAR per hour	X
Less Actual hours × FOAR per hour	(X)
Fixed overhead efficiency variance	X

Together, these two sub-variances explain why the level of activity was different from that budgeted, i.e. they combine to give the fixed overhead volume variance.

Illustration 10

Following on from Illustration 8, suppose now that we are told that the production overheads are absorbed based on labour hours and not on a per unit basis.

The following information relates to the production of Product M17 in June:

Budget:

Fixed overheads	$22,960
Units	6,560
Direct labour per unit	2 hours

Actual:

Fixed overheads	$24,200
Units	6,460
Direct labour	12,600 hours

Required:

Calculate the following

(i)   fixed overhead capacity variance

(ii) fixed overhead efficiency variance

(iii) fixed overhead volume variance

Solution:

(i)   fixed overhead capacity variance:

	$
Actual hours × FOAR per hour (12,600 × $1.75 (W1))	22,050
Less Budgeted expenditure	(22,960)
Fixed overhead capacity variance	910 A

(W1)   FOAR = budgeted overheads / budgeted activity

         = $22,960 / (6,560 units @ 2 hours per unit)

         = $22,960 / 13,120 hours = $1.75 per labour hour

(ii)   fixed overhead efficiency variance:

	$
Standard hours for actual production × FOAR per hour (6,460 × 2 hours × $1.75)	22,610
Less Actual hours × FOAR per hour (12,600 × $1.75)	(22,050)
Fixed overhead efficiency variance	560 F

(iii) fixed overhead volume variance:

This is the sum of the capacity and efficiency variances calculated in parts (i) and (ii) which is $910A + $560F = $350A. This agrees to the previous calculation we made for the volume variance in Illustration 8.

Example 11

The following information is available for a company for Period 4.

Fixed production overheads	$22,960
Units	6,560

The standard time to produce each unit is 2 hours

Actual

Fixed production overheads	$24,200
Units	6,460
Labour hours	12,600 hrs

Required:

Calculate the following:

(a)   fixed overhead absorption rate per hour

(b)   fixed overhead capacity variance

(c)   fixed overhead efficiency variance

(d)   fixed overhead volume variance.

> ### Marginal costing fixed production overhead variances
>
> In marginal costing, fixed production overheads are not absorbed into the cost of production. For this reason, there is no fixed production overhead volume variance.
>
> The only fixed production overhead variance reported in standard marginal costing is a fixed production overhead expenditure variance. This is the difference between actual and budgeted fixed production overhead expenditure, as described above for absorption costing.

Potential causes of fixed and variable overhead variances are as follows:

(1) Fixed overhead expenditure adverse variances are caused by spending in excess of the budget. A more detailed analysis of the expenditure variance would be needed to establish why actual expenditure has been higher or lower than budget.

(2) The fixed overhead volume variance (and therefore the capacity and efficiency variance) is caused by changes in production volume (which in turn might be caused by changes in sales volume or through increased or decreased labour productivity).

(3) Variable production overhead expenditure variances are often caused by changes in machine running costs (for example, if electricity rates have changed).

(4) Variable production overhead efficiency variances: the causes are similar to those for a direct labour efficiency variance.

8 Possible interdependence between variances

In many cases, the explanation for one variance might also explain one or more other variances in which case the variances are inter-related.

For control purposes, it might therefore be necessary to look at several variances together and not in isolation.

Some examples of interdependence between variances are listed below.

• Using cheaper materials will result in a favourable material price variance, but using the cheaper material in production might increase the wastage rate (adverse material usage) and cause a fall in labour productivity (adverse labour and variable overhead efficiency).

• Using more experienced labour to do the work will result in an adverse labour rate variance, but productivity might be higher as a result (favourable labour and variable overhead efficiency).

• Workers trying to improve productivity (favourable efficiency variance) in order to win a bonus (adverse rate variance) might use materials wastefully in order to save time (adverse materials usage).

• Cutting sales prices (adverse sales price variance) might result in higher sales demand from customers (favourable sales volume variance).

9 Operating statements

An operating statement is a top-level variance report, reconciling the budgeted and actual profit for the period.

An operating statement starts off with the expected figure, e.g. budgeted or standard profit or contribution or cost, etc. and ends up with the corresponding actual figure. In between we list all the appropriate variances in as much detail as possible.

The format will be similar to the following, the numbers have no significance. They are purely for illustration purposes.

Operating Statement for Period 12

		$	$	$	
Budgeted gross profit				100,000	
Sales volume profit variance				15,000	F
Budgeted profit from actual sales volume				115,000	
Sales price variance				28,750	F
				143,750	

		Adverse	Favourable		
Cost variances					
Direct material A	Price	3,100			
	Usage		10,000		
Direct material B	Price		3,050		
	Usage		7,500		
Direct labour	Efficiency		7,000		
	Rate		12,000		
	Idle time		3,000		
Variable overhead	Efficiency	4,000			
	Expenditure		3,500		
Fixed Prod overhead	Expenditure		11,500		
	Volume	30,400			
		37,500	57,550	20,050	F
Actual gross profit				163,800	

Variance reporting

Variances should be reported to management at the end of each control period, for example at the end of each month. There might be a hierarchy of control reports:

- a top level report reconciling budgeted and actual profit should be prepared for senior management

- variance reports might be prepared for individual managers with responsibility for a particular aspect of operations.

For example, regional sales managers might be sent variance reports showing sales price and sales volume variances for their region. Production managers might be sent variance reports relating to materials usage, labour efficiency and other items of expenditure under their control. Similarly, detailed reports on overhead expenditure variances might be sent to the managers responsible for departmental spending.

Variance reports should be provided as soon as possible after the end of each control period, since there is a risk that variance information might be considered 'out of date' if it is received several weeks after the control period has ended.

Example 12

SM is a manufacturing company which produces a variety of products. The following information relates to one of its products – Product W:

Standard cost data

		$	$
Selling price			100
Direct Material X	5 kg	15	
Direct Material Y	4 kg	20	
Direct labour	@ $8/hr	24	
Variable overheads	$ ₵/hr	18 ⅓	
Fixed overheads		6	
			83
Profit per unit			17

The budgeted production is 24,000 units per annum evenly spread throughout the year, with each calendar month assumed to be equal. March is a bad month in terms of sales revenue and it is expected that sales will only be 1,700 units during the month. Fixed overheads were expected to be $144,000 per year and are absorbed on a labour hour basis.

Actual results for the month of March were that sales were 2,200 units at a price of $90. There was no change in inventory of finished goods or raw materials.

The purchases during the month were 11,300 kg of material X at $2.80 per kg and 8,300 kg of material Y at $5.30 per kg.

4,800 labour hours were worked at a rate of $8.10 per hour and 1,600 hours at $8.30.

The actual variable overheads for the period were $33,000 and the fixed overheads were $12,500.

The company uses an absorption costing system and values its raw materials at standard cost.

Required:

Calculate appropriate variances for the month of March in as much detail as possible and present an operating statement reconciling budgeted profit with actual profit.

Variances in service industries

In the exam, you are just as likely to encounter service industries as manufacturers. These could be law firms, healthcare providers, accountants, banks etc. The calculations, however, will still follow the same principles as in manufacturing.

Illustration

The standard cost schedule for hospital care for a minor surgical procedure is shown below.

Staff: patient ratio is 0.75:1

		$
Nursing costs	2 days × 0.75 × $320 per day	480
Space and food costs	2 days × $175 per day	350
Drugs and specific materials		115
Hospital overheads	2 days × $110 per day	220
		————
Total standard cost		1,165
		————

The actual data for the hospital care for one patient having the minor surgical procedure showed that the patient stayed in hospital for three days. The cost of the drugs and specific materials for this patient was $320. There were 0.9 nurses per patient on duty during the time that the patient was in hospital. The daily rates for nursing pay, space and food, and hospital overheads were as expected.

Prepare a statement that reconciles the standard cost with the actual costs of hospital care for this patient. The statement should contain FIVE variances that will give useful information to the manager who is reviewing the cost of hospital care for minor surgical procedures.

Solution

		$	$
Standard cost for 2-day procedure			1,165
Length of stay variances			
Nursing costs	1 day × 0.75 × $320 per day	240A	
Space and food costs	1 day × $175 per day	175A	
Hospital overheads	1 day × $110 per day	110A	
			525 A
Standard cost for 3-day stay			1,690
Drug and specific cost variances			205 A
Nursing staff variance	3 days × (0.90 – 0.75) × $320 per day		144 A
Actual cost			2,039

10 Variance analysis using ABC costing

As part of variance analysis managers will need to establish standard costs. Activity based costing is one method for determining costs and hence will have implications of some of the variances calculated.

Compared to traditional absorption costing, the use of ABC is most likely to impact overhead variances.

Typically, standard costs can be compared to actual and an overhead expenditure and efficiency variance calculated.

Illustration 11

An ABC approach to the analysis of overhead costs is possible. This follows the ABC logic that all overheads are variable if one understands what they vary with. Let us illustrate the approach with a simple example.

Example

XX produces the Unit and all overheads are associated with the delivery of Units to its customers. Budget details for the period include $8,000 overheads, 4,000 Units output and 40 customer deliveries. Actual results for the period are $7,800 overheads, 4,200 Units output and 38 customer deliveries.

The overhead cost variance for the period is

	$	
Actual cost	7,800	
Standard cost (4,200 units × $2 per unit)	8,400	
Cost variance	600	F

Applying the traditional fixed overhead cost variance analysis gives the following result:

		$	
Volume variance	($8,400 standard – $8,000 budget)	400	F
Expenditure variance	($8,000 budget – $7,800 actual)	200	F
Cost variance		600	F

Adopting an ABC approach gives the following result:

		$	
Efficiency variance	(42 standard – 38 actual deliveries) × $200	800	F
Expenditure variance	[(38 deliveries × $200) – $7,800]	200	A
Cost variance		600	F

The ABC approach is based on an assumption that the overheads are essentially variable (but variable with the delivery numbers and not the Units output). The ABC cost variances are based on a standard delivery size of 100 Units and a standard cost per delivery of $200. Both of these figures are derived from the budget. The activity variance reports the cost impact of undertaking more or less activities than standard, and the expenditure variance reports the cost impact of paying more or less than standard for the actual activities undertaken.

11 Chapter summary

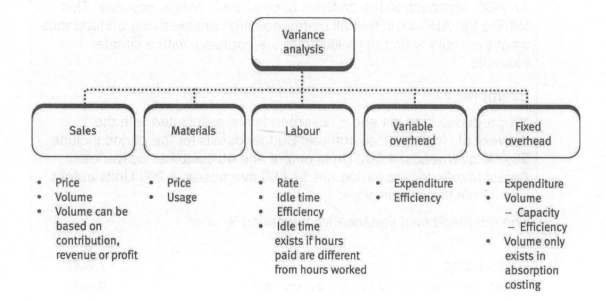

Variance analysis

Sales
- Price
- Volume
- Volume can be based on contribution, revenue or profit

Materials
- Price
- Usage

Labour
- Rate
- Idle time
- Efficiency
- Idle time exists if hours paid are different from hours worked

Variable overhead
- Expenditure
- Efficiency

Fixed overhead
- Expenditure
- Volume
  - Capacity
  - Efficiency
- Volume only exists in absorption costing

11 Practice questions

Test your understanding 1

The following data relates to the budget for a company producing widgets in March:

Budgeted production and sales (widgets)	1,750 **units**
Standard cost per unit:	$
Direct materials	6.00
Direct labour	3.00
Variable production overhead	0.75
Fixed production overhead	2.50
	12.25
Standard sales price	18.25
Standard profit per unit	6.00
Number of widgets produced and sold in March	1,800 units
Actual sales revenue	$32,300

Required:

Calculate the sales price and sales volume profit variance. What would be the sales volume contribution variance if standard marginal costing were used?

Test your understanding 2

Major Caldwell makes and sells a single product. Each unit of the product requires 3 kg of material at $4 per kg.

The actual details for last period were that 1,200 units of finished goods were produced, 3,600 kg of material were purchased for $14,800 and 3,520 kg were used.

Major Caldwell maintains its raw materials account at standard.

Calculate appropriate variances for materials.

Test your understanding 3

The standard direct material and labour costs for a product are:

		$
Direct material A	2 kg × $ 4 per kg	8
Direct material B	0.5 litres × $6 per litre	3
Direct labour	0.75 hours × $12 per hour	9
		20

During November, the company made 3,200 units and sold 2,900. Actual production costs were:

		$
Direct material A	6,100 kgs	25,000
Direct material B	1,750 litres	11,600
Direct labour	2,200 hours paid	28,000
	(only 2,000 hours worked)	

Required:

Calculate the following variances:

- direct materials price

- direct materials usage

- direct labour rate

- direct labour idle time

- direct labour efficiency.

Test your understanding 4

Jack Doherty makes a single product with the following standard cost details per unit.

		$
Direct materials	5 kg @ $4/kg	20
Direct labour	4 hrs @ $6/hr	24

Actual results were that 1,000 units were produced and sold. The actual hours paid for were 4,100 and the hours worked were 3,900. The actual labour cost was $27,060. The number of kg purchased in the month was 5,200 kg for $21,320 and the number of kg used was 4,900 kg. The company calculates the material price variance at the time of purchase.

Calculate appropriate variances for materials and labour.

Test your understanding 5

Axelrod makes and sells a single product with the following information:

Standard/Budget

Output	1,000 units
Material	3,000 kg @ $5 per kg
Labour	5,000 hours @ $6 per hour

Actual

Output	1,100 units		
Material	Purchased	3,600 kg	for $18,720
	Used	3,400 kg	
Labour hrs	Paid for	5,200 hrs	for $32,760
	Worked	4,900 hrs	

Axelrod maintains its raw material account at standard cost. Calculate the variances for materials and labour.

Test your understanding 6

IR hospital provides surgical treatments which require 3 standard hours per treatment. Fixed overheads are budgeted at $12,000 and are absorbed on a labour hour basis. The hospital budgeted to provide 1,000 treatments during March.

Actual results:

Treatments	1,100
Labour hours	3,080 hours
Overheads incurred	$13,000

Calculate appropriate variances for fixed overhead.

Test your understanding 7

The electronic crime division of a local police station had the following information for Period 4:

Budget	
Fixed overheads	$35,200
Reported crimes	4,400

The standard time to deal with each crime is 2.5 hours

Actual	
Fixed overheads	$33,910
Reported crimes	4,560
Labour hours	12,100 hrs

Required:

If the division uses an absorption costing system, calculate the following:

(a) FOAR per labour hour

(b) Fixed overhead expenditure variance

(c) Fixed overhead capacity variance

(d) Fixed overhead efficiency variance

(e) Fixed overhead volume variance.

Test your understanding 8

Last month, 40,000 production hours were budgeted in CTD, and the budgeted fixed production overhead cost was $250,000. Actual results show that 38,000 hours were worked and paid, and the standard hours for actual production were 35,000. CTD operates a standard absorption costing system.

What was the fixed production overhead capacity variance for last month?

A $12,500 Adverse

B $12,500 Favourable

C $31,250 Adverse

D $31,250 Favourable

Test your understanding 9

Scenario

Malcolm Reynolds makes and sells a single product, Product Q, with the following standard specification for materials:

	Quantity	Price per kg
	kg	$
Direct material X	12	40
Direct material Y	8	32

It takes 20 direct labour hours to produce one unit with a standard direct labour cost of $10 per hour.

The annual sales/production budget is 2,400 units evenly spread throughout the year. The standard selling price was $1,250 per unit.

The budgeted production overhead, all fixed, is $288,000 and expenditure is expected to occur evenly over the year, which the company divides into 12 calendar months. Absorption is based on direct labour hours.

For the month of October the following actual information is provided.

	$	$
Sales (220 units)		264,000
Cost of sales		
Direct materials used	159,000	
Direct wages	45,400	
Fixed production overhead	23,000	
		227,400
Gross profit		36,600
Administration costs	13,000	
Selling and distribution costs	8,000	
		21,000
Net profit		$15,600

Costs of opening inventories, for each material, were at the same price per kilogram as the purchases made during the month but there had been changes in the materials inventory levels as follows:

	1 October	30 October
	kg	kg
Material X	680	1,180
Material Y	450	350

Material X purchases were 3,000 kg at $42 each.

Material Y purchases were 1,700 kg at $30 each.

The number of direct labour hours worked was 4,600 and the total wages incurred $45,400.

Work-in-progress inventories and finished goods inventories may be assumed to be the same at the beginning and end of October.

Tasks:

(a) to prepare a standard product cost for one unit of product Q showing the standard selling price and standard gross profit per unit

(b) to calculate appropriate variances for the materials, labour, fixed production overhead and sales, noting that it is company policy to calculate material price variances at time of issue to production and that Malcom Reynolds does not calculate mix and yield variances

(c) to prepare a statement for management reconciling the budgeted gross profit with the actual gross profit.

Test your understanding 10

Flexed budgets for the cost of medical supplies in a hospital, based on a percentage of maximum bed occupancy, are shown below:

Bed occupancy	82%	94%
Medical supplies cost	$410,000	$429,200

During the period, the actual bed occupancy was 87% and the total cost of the medical supplies was $430,000.

Identify the medical supplies expenditure variance:

A $5,000 adverse

B $12,000 adverse

C $5,000 favourable

D $12,000 favourable

Test your understanding 11

A company has a sales budget of $145,000 per month for the financial year January to December. However, by the end of May, the cumulative sales variances for the year to date are:

Sales price variance	$30,000 (A)
Sales volume contribution variance	$16,000 (A)

The standard contribution/sales ratio is 40%. The marketing department has now estimated that sales for the next three months will be $120,000 per month, but for the rest of the year, monthly sales should rise to $148,000.

Required:

Prepare a statement as at the end of May that compares budgeted and forecast sales revenue and contribution for the year as a whole. Ignore variable cost variances.

Test your understanding 12

A company has prepared an activity-based budget for its stores department. One activity concerns inventory counts which has an activity based cost driver of $800 per inventory count (based on a budgeted activity of 50 counts per year).

During the year there were 52 counts and the actual cost for inventory counts was $40,560.

To the nearest $, the value of the variance for inventory counts in the year was $ 1,040 F

Test your understanding 13

One activity for the tax department of a large accountancy firm is to perform follow-up visits to clients to investigate and resolve issues that have arisen as part of its tax work for that client. Information for this activity for the year was as follows:

	Budget	Actual
Clients	2,000	2,100
Follow up visits	4,000	3,600
Activity cost	$180,000	$168,000

Required:

Calculate the overhead expenditure variance and the overhead efficiency variance for the follow up activity.

Test your understanding 14

A dental practice uses standard costing and variance analysis. Match the variance to the most likely cause:

Variance:

(a) adverse materials price

(b) adverse labour efficiency

(c) favourable fixed overhead volume

(d) adverse sales price

Potential causes:

(i)   more dental treatments were carried out than was budgeted   c ✓

(ii) new competition entered the market   d ✓

(iii) new dentists were recruited   b ✓

(iv) new suppliers were used   a ✓

Test your understanding 15

ML produces a single product for which the following data are given:

Standards per unit of product:

Direct material   4 kg at $3 per kg

Direct labour   2 hours at $6.40 per hour

Actual details for given financial period:

Output produced in units		38,000
Direct materials:		$
purchased	180,000 kg for	504,000
issued to production	154,000 kg	
Direct labour	78,000 hours worked for	546,000

There was no work in progress at the beginning or end of the period.

From this information the following variances have been calculated:

Variance	Favourable	Adverse
	$	$
Direct labour efficiency		12,800
Direct labour rate		46,800
Direct materials usage		6,000
Direct materials price	30,800	
(based on issues to production)		

State whether in each of the following cases, the comment given and suggested as the possible reason for the variance, is consistent or inconsistent with the variance calculated: *(place a tick in the appropriate column)*

Variance	Consistent?	Inconsistent?
Direct labour efficiency variance: the efficiency of labour was commendable		
Direct labour rate variance: the union negotiated wage increase was $0.60 per hour lower than expected		
Direct materials usage variance: material losses in production were less than had been allowed for in the standard		
Direct materials price variance: the procurement manager has ignored the economic order quantity and, by obtaining bulk quantities, has purchased material at less than the standard price		

Example and test your understanding answers

Example 1

Selling price variance

	$	
Standard selling price	25	
Actual selling price	20	
	5	A
× Actual no of units sold	× 500	
	2,500	A

Sales volume contribution variance

	Units	
Actual sales volume	500	
Budgeted sales volume	400	
	100	F
× Standard contribution per unit	× $7	
	$700	F

In this scenario there are no fixed costs, so the answer is the same whether we are using marginal or absorption costing.

Example 2

		$	
Sales price variance			
Units sold should have sold for	(380 units × $45 per unit)	17,100	
They did sell for	(actual sales revenue)	15,960	
Sales price variance		1,140	A

Absorption costing

	Units	
Sales volume profit variance		
Actual sales volume	380	
Budgeted sales volume	320	
Sales volume variance	60	F
× standard profit per unit ($45 – $23)	× $22	
Sales volume profit variance	$1,320	F

Marginal costing

	Units	
Sales volume contribution variance		
Actual sales volume	380	
Budgeted sales volume	320	
Sales volume variance	60	F
× standard contribution per unit ($45 – $17)	× $28	
Sales volume contribution variance	$1,680	F

Standard revenue per unit

	Units	
Sales volume contribution variance		
Actual sales volume	380	
Budgeted sales volume	320	
Sales volume variance	60	F
× standard selling per unit	× $45	
Sales volume revenue variance	$2,700	F

Example 3

Direct material total variance

	$	
Standard cost of actual output		
2 kg × 1,000 units × $10/kg	20,000	
Actual cost	20,900	
	900	A

Example 4

Direct materials price variance:		$
Actual quantity of materials	should cost (standard)	
2,200 kgs	$10/kg	22,000
	did cost (actual)	20,900
Direct materials price variance		1,100 F

Direct materials usage variance:		$
Actual output produced	should use (standard quantity)	
1,000 units	2 kgs/unit	2,000
	did use (actual quantity)	2,200
Direct materials usage variance	(in material quantity)	200 A
× standard price	(per unit of material)	$10
Direct materials usage variance		2,000 A

Example 5

Direct materials price variance:		$
Actual quantity of materials	should cost (standard)	
20,800 kgs	($90,000 / 22,500 kg) = $4 per kg)	83,200
	did cost (actual)	91,520
Direct materials price variance		8,320 A

Direct materials usage variance:		kg
Actual output produced	should use (standard quantity)	
6,500 units	(22,500 kg / 7,500 kg per unit = 3 kg per unit)	19,500
	did use (actual quantity)	20,300
	20,800 kg – 500 kg	
Direct materials usage variance	(in material quantity)	800 A
× standard price	(per unit of material)	$4
Direct materials usage variance		3,200 A

Closing inventory = quantity purchased – closing inventory = 500 kg
Valued at standard price per kg = 500 kg @ $4 = $2,000.

Example 6

Direct labour rate variance:		$
Number of hours worked	should cost/hr (standard)	
3,400 hours	$80/hr	272,000
	did cost (actual)	283,000
Direct materials price variance		11,000 A

Direct labour efficiency variance:		Hours
	should take (standard hours)	
Actual services provided 1,100	3 hrs per service	3,300
	did take (actual hours)	3,400
Direct materials usage variance	(in hours)	100 A
× standard rate per hour		$80/hr
Direct labour efficiency variance		$8,000 A

Example 7

					$
SHSR					
	6 hrs/unit x 900 units	x	$7/hr	=	37,800
AHSR					
	5,200 hrs	x	$7/hr	=	36,400

} Efficiency $1,400 F

The efficiency variance looks at whether people **WORK** fast or slow and looks at hours **WORKED**.

					$
AHSR					
	5,500 hrs	x	$7/hr	=	38,500
AHAR					
				=	39,100

} $600 A Rate

The rate variance looks at the rate of **PAY** so it looks at the hours **PAID**.

Idle time variance

(5,500 – 5,200) × $7 per hour $2,100 A

Or the idle time variance is simply the difference between the $38,500 and the $36,400 above = $2,100 A.

Example 8

Variable production overhead expenditure variance:		$
Number of hours worked	should cost/hr (standard)	
1,980 hours	$3/hour	5,940
	did cost (actual)	5,544
Variable production overhead expenditure variance		396 F

Variable production overhead efficiency variance:		**Hours**
Actual output produced	should take (standard hours)	
900 units	2 hours/unit	1,800
	did take (actual hours)	1,980
Efficiency variance	(in hours)	180 A
× standard variable overhead rate per hour		$3
Variable production overhead efficiency variance		$540 A

Example 9

(a) The idle time variance is 20 hours × $15 = $300 (A).

(b) The efficiency variances are then calculated based on the active hours worked, not on the total hours paid for.

Efficiency variances:		**Hours**
Actual output produced	should take (standard hours)	
200 units	2 hours/unit	400
	did take (440 – 20)	420
Efficiency variance	(in hours)	20 A

Hours × standard direct labour rate per hour	$15
Direct labour efficiency variance	$300 A
Hours × standard variable overhead rate per hour	$4
Variable production overhead efficiency variance	$80 A

(c) The variable production overhead expenditure variance is based on active hours only, since variable production overhead cost is not incurred during idle time.

Variable production overhead expenditure variance:		$
Number of hours worked	should cost/hr (standard)	
420 hours	$4/hour	1,680
	did cost (actual)	1,530
Variable production overhead expenditure variance		150 F

Example 10

Fixed production overhead expenditure variance:	$
Budgeted fixed overhead	4,375
Actual fixed overhead incurred	4,800
Fixed production overhead expenditure variance	425 (A)

Fixed production overhead volume variance:	**Units**
Actual output produced	1,800
Budgeted output	1,750
Volume variance (in units)	50
× standard fixed overhead rate per unit	$2.50
Fixed production overhead volume variance	$125 (F)

 Example 11

(a)   FOAR = $22,960/(6,560 units × 2 hours) = $1.75 per hour

(b)   Actual hours × FOAR
   12,600 × $1.75
   Less Budgeted expenditure

	$
12,600 × $1.75	22,050
Less Budgeted expenditure	(22,960)
Capacity variance	$910 A

(c)   Standard hours × FOAR
   6,460 × 2 × $1.75
   Less Actual hours × FOAR
   12,600 × $1.75

	$
6,460 × 2 × $1.75	22,610
Less Actual hours × FOAR	
12,600 × $1.75	(22,050)
Efficiency variance	$560 F

(d) The fixed overhead volume variance is the sum of the capacity and efficiency variances, i.e.

$910 (A) + $560 (F) = 350 (A).

This can be proved as follows:

	$
Standard hours × FOAR per hour	
(6,460 × 2 hours × $1.75)	22,610
Less: Budgeted expenditure	(22,960)
Total variance	$350 A

Example 12

Standard product cost

		$	$
Standard selling price			100
Material X	5 kg @ $3/kg	15	
Material Y	4 kg @ $5/kg	20	
Direct labour	3 hrs @ $8/hr	24	
Variable overheads	3 hrs @ $6/hr	18	
Fixed overheads (W1)	3 hrs @ $2/hr	6	
			83
Standard profit per unit			17

Material X variances

				$	
SQSP					
5 kg/unit x 2,200 units	x	$3/kg	=	33,000	Usage
AQSP					$900 A
11,300 kg	x	$3/kg	=	33,900	
AQAP					$2,260 F
11,300 kg	x	$2.8/kg	=	31,640	Price

Material Y variances

				$	
SQSP					
4 kg/unit x 2,200 units	x	$5/kg	=	44,000	Usage
AQSP					$2,500 F
8,300 kg	x	$5/kg	=	41,500	
AQAP					$2,490 A
8,300 kg	x	$5.30/kg	=	43,990	Price

Fixed overhead expenditure variance

	$	
Budgeted cost	12,000	
Actual cost	12,500	
	500	A

Fixed overhead volume variance

	Units	
Budgeted output	2,000	
Actual output	2,200	
	200	F
× Standard fixed overhead cost per unit	× $6	
	$1,200	F

Sales volume profit variance

	Units	
Actual sales	2,200	
Budgeted sales	1,700	
	500	F
× Standard profit per unit	× $17	
	$8,500	F

Sales price variance

	Units	
Actual selling price	90	
Standard selling price	100	
	10	A
× Actual no of units sold	× 2,200	
	$22,000	A

Operating statement

		$	$	$
Budgeted gross profit (W2)				28,900
Sales volume profit variance				8,500 F
				———
Budgeted profit on actual sales				37,400
Selling price variance				22,000 A
				———
				15,400

		Favourable	Adverse	
Cost variances				
Material X	Usage		900	
	Price	2,260		
Material Y	Usage	2,500		
	Price		2,490	
Direct labour	Efficiency	1,600 ✓		
	Rate		960	
Variable overhead	Efficiency	1,200		
	Expenditure	5,400		
Fixed prod overhead	Expenditure		500	
	Volume	1,200		
		———	———	
		14,160	4,850	9,310 F
		———	———	
				24,710
				———

Workings

(W1) Budgeted fixed overheads are $144,000 per year and the budgeted output is 24,000 units for the year. Thus the budgeted/standard fixed cost per unit is $6.

The overheads are absorbed on direct labour hours and each unit takes 3 hours. Therefore the budgeted/standard fixed overhead is $2 per hour ($6 ÷ 3 hours).

(W2) Budgeted profit = $17 per unit × Budgeted **sales** of 1,700 units = $28,900

(W3)

		$	$
Sales	2,200 units × $90		198,000
Material X	11,300 kg × $2.80/kg	31,640	
Material Y	8,300 kg × $5.30/kg	43,990	
Direct labour	(4,800 hrs × $8.10) + (1,600 hrs × $8.30)	52,160	
Variable overhead		33,000	
Fixed overhead		12,500	
			173,290
Actual profit			24,710

Test your understanding 1

Sales price variance		$
Units sold should have sold for (1.800 units × $18.25 per unit)		32,850
They did sell for	(actual sales revenue)	32,300
Sales price variance		550 (A)

Sales volume variance	**Units**
Actual sales volume	1,800
Budgeted sales volume	1,750
Sales volume variance	50
× standard profit per unit	× $6
Sales volume profit variance	$300 (F)

Marginal costing

The contribution per unit is $8.50 ($18.25 – 6.00 – 3.00 – 0.75)

	Units
Sales volume variance	
Actual sales volume	1,800
Budgeted sales volume	1,750
Sales volume variance	50
× standard contribution per unit	× $8.50
Sales volume contribution variance	$425 (F)

Test your understanding 2

				$	
SQSP					
3 kg/unit x 1,200 units	x	$4/kg	=	14,400	} Usage
AQSP					$320 F
3,520 kg	x	$4/kg	=	14,080	

For a **USAGE** variance the quantity must be the quantity **USED**

				$	
AQSP					
3,600 kg	x	$4/kg	=	14,400	} $400 A
AQAP					Price
			=	14,800	

As the price variance is calculated at the time of **PURCHASE** then the quantity must be the quantity **PURCHASED** and we had to use the more complicated format.

Test your understanding 3

Direct material A price variance:		$
Actual quantity of materials	should cost (standard)	
6,100 kgs	$4/kg	24,400
	did cost (actual)	25,000
Direct material A price variance		600 A ✓

Direct material A usage variance

Actual output produced	should use (standard quantity)	
3,200 units	2 kgs/unit	6,400
	did cost (actual quantity)	6,100

Direct materials price variance	(in kgs)	300 F
× standard price	(per kg)	$4

Direct material A usage variance		$1,200 F

Direct material B price variance: $

Actual quantity of materials	should cost (standard)	
1,750 litres	$6/litre	10,500
	did cost (actual)	11,600

Direct material B price variance		1,100 A✓

Direct material B usage variance:

Actual output produced	should use (standard quantity)	
3,200 units	0.5 litres/unit	1,600
	did cost (actual quantity)	1,750

Direct materials price variance	(in litres)	150A
× standard price	(per litre)	$6

Direct material B usage variance		$900 A ✓

Direct labour rate variance: $

Number of hours paid	should cost (standard)	
2,200 hours	$12/hr	26,400
	did cost (actual)	28,000

Direct labour rate variance		1,600 A

Idle time variance:

There are 200 hours of idle time. At a standard cost of $12 per hour, this

gives an idle time variance of

> = 200 hours × $12/hour
>
> = $2,400 A

Direct labour efficiency variance:		$
Actual output produced	should use (standard hours)	
3,200 units	0.75 hrs per unit	2,400
	did take (actual hours)	2,000
Direct labour efficiency variance (in hours)		400 F
× standard rate per hour		$12/hr
Direct labour efficiency variance		$4,800 F

Test your understanding 4

Material variances

SQSP

					$	
5 kg/unit x 1,000 units	x	$4/kg	=	20,000	Usage
					$400 F

AQSP

4,900 kg	x	$4/kg	=	19,600

For a **USAGE** variance the quantity must be the quantity **USED**

AQSP

				$	
5,200 kg	x	$4/kg	=	20,800	$520 A

AQAP

	=	21,320	Price

As the price variance is calculated at the time of **PURCHASE** then the quantity must be the quantity **PURCHASED** and we had to use the more complicated format.

Labour variances

SHSR

				$	
4 hrs/unit x 1,000 units	x	$6/hr	=	24,000	Efficiency

AHSR

3,900 hrs	x	$6/hr	=	23,400	$600 F

The efficiency variance looks at whether people **WORK** fast or slow and looks at hours **WORKED.**

AHSR

				$	
4,100 units	x	$6/hr	=	24,600	$2,460 A

AHAR

	=	27,060	Rate

The rate variance looks at the rate of **PAY** so it looks at the hours **PAID**.

Idle time variance

(4,100 – 3,900) × $6 per hour $1,200 A

Or the idle time variance is simply the difference between the $23,400 and the $24,600 above = $1,200 A

Test your understanding 5

Material variances

						$	
SQSP							
	3 kg/unit x 1,100 units	x	$5/kg	=	16,500	}	Usage $500 A
AQSP							
	3,400 kg	x	$5/kg	=	17,000		

For a **USAGE** variance the quantity must be the quantity **USED**.

					$	
AQSP						
	3,600 kg	x	$5/kg	=	18,000	} $720 A Price
AQAP						
				=	18,720	

As the price variance is calculated at the time of **PURCHASE** then the quantity must be the quantity **PURCHASED** and we had to use the more complicated format.

Labour variances

					$	
SHSR						
	5 hrs/unit x 1,100 units	x	$6/hr	=	33,000	} Efficiency $3,600 F
AHSR						
	4,900 hrs	x	$6/hr	=	29,400	

The efficiency variance looks at whether people **WORK** fast or slow and looks at hours **WORKED**.

					$	
AHSR						
	5,200 hrs	x	$6/hr	=	31,200	} $1,560 A Rate
AHAR						
				=	32,760	

The rate variance looks at the rate of **PAY** so it looks at the hours **PAID**.

Idle time variance

(5,200 – 4,900) × $6 per hour $1,800 A

Or the idle time variance is simply the difference between the $29,400 and the $31,200 above = $1,800 A

Test your understanding 6

Fixed overhead total variance

	$
Standard cost of actual output	
$12/unit × 1,100 treatments	13,200
Actual cost	13,000
	————
	200 F
	————

Fixed overhead expenditure variance

	$
Budgeted cost	12,000
Actual cost	13,000
	————
	1,000 A
	————

Fixed overhead volume variance

	Units
Budgeted treatments	1,000
Actual treatments	1,100
	————
	100 F
× Standard fixed overhead cost per treatment	× $12
	————
	$1,200 F
	————

Under-/over-absorption

	$
Overheads incurred	13,000
Overheads absorbed	
$4/direct labour hour × (3 hours × 1,100 treatments)	13,200
	————
Over-absorption	200
	————

The overhead absorption rate is based on direct labour hours and =

$$\frac{\text{Budgeted overheads}}{\text{Budgeted level of activity}}$$

$$\text{OAR} = \frac{\$12,000}{1,000 \text{ treatments} \times 3 \text{ hrs}} = \$4/\text{direct labour hour}$$

It would now be very natural to calculate the overheads absorbed by multiplying the OAR by the actual number of hours, i.e. 3,080, but in a standard costing system, the overheads are absorbed on the standard hours, not the actual hours.

The standard hours are the standard hours of actual output, 3 hours × 1,100 units = 3,300 hours.

Fixed overhead capacity variance

	$
Actual hours × FOAR	
3,080 hours × $4	12,320
Less: Budgeted expenditure	(12,000)
	———
Capacity variance	$320 (F)
	———

Fixed overhead efficiency variance

	$
Standard hours × FOAR	
3,300 hours × $4	13,200
Less: Actual hours × FOAR	
3,080 × $4	(12,320)
	———
Efficiency variance	$880 (F)
	———

Test your understanding 7

(a) FOAR = $35,200 ÷ (4,400 crimes × 2.5 hours per reported crime)
= $3.20 per labour hour

(b) **Fixed overhead expenditure variance**

	$
Budgeted fixed overhead	35,200
Actual fixed overhead	33,910
Variance	1,290 F

Fixed overhead expenditure variance – three line method

AH AR = $33,910

Variance = $1,290 F

BH SR = $35,200

(c) **Fixed overhead capacity variance**

	$
Actual hours (12,100 × standard FOAR $3.20/hr)	38,720
Less budgeted expenditure	35,200
Variance	3,520 F

Fixed overhead capacity variance – three line method

BH SR = $35,200

Variance = $3,520 F

AH SR = 12,100 × $3.20 = $38,720

(d) **Fixed overhead efficiency variance**

	$
Standard hours for actual production × FOAR per hour (4,560 × 2.5 hours × $3.20)	36,480
Less actual hours × FOAR (12,100 × $3.20)	38,720
Variance	2,240 A

Fixed overhead efficiency variance – alternative method

AH SR = 12,100 × $3.20 = $38,720

Variance = $2,240 A

SH SR = (4,560 × 2.5) × $3.20 = $36,480

(e) **Fixed overhead volume variance**

	Units
Budgeted reported crimes	4,400
Actual reported crimes	4,560
Variance	160 F

Variance in $ = 160 F reported crimes × standard hours of 2.5 × standard FOAR per hour $3.20 = $1,280 F

Fixed overhead volume variance – alternative method

BH SR = $35,200

Variance = $1,280 F

SH SR = (4,560 × 2.5) × $3.20 = $36,480

Note: The fixed overhead volume variance of $1,280F is the total of the capacity and efficiency variances ($3,520 F + $2,240 A).

Test your understanding 8

A

Actual hours × FOAR per hour	$
38,000 × $250,000/40,000 hours	237,500
Budgeted expenditure	250,000
Capacity variance	$12,500 A

Test your understanding 9

(a) **Standard product cost**

		$	$
Standard selling price			1,250
Material X	12 kg @ $40/kg	480	
Material Y	8 kg @ $32/kg	256	
Direct labour	20 hrs @ $10/hr	200	
Production overhead (W1)		120	
			1,056
			194

(b) **Material X variances**

					$	
SQSP						
12 kg/unit x 220 units	x	$40/kg	=		105,600	Usage
AQSP						$5,600 F
2,500 kg (W2)	x	$40/kg	=		100,000	
AQAP						$5,000 A
2,500 kg	x	$42/kg	=		105,000	Price

Material Y variances

					$	
SQSP						
8 kg/unit x 220 units	x	$32/kg	=		56,320	Usage
AQSP						$1,280 A
1,800 kg (W2)	x	$32/kg	=		57,600	
AQAP						$3,600 F
1,800kg	x	$30/kg	=		54,000	Price

Direct labour variances

					$	
SHSR						
20 hrs/unit x 220 units	x	$10/hr	=		44,000	Efficiency
AHSR						$2,000 A
4,600 hrs	x	$10/hr	=		46,000	
AHAR						$600 F
			=		45,400	Rate

Fixed Overhead Expenditure variance

	$
Budgeted Cost (W3)	24,000
Actual Cost	23,000
	1,000 F

Fixed overhead variance

	Units
Budgeted output (2,400 units p.a. ÷ 12 months)	200
Actual output	220
	20 F
× Standard fixed overhead cost per unit	×120
	$2,400 F

This can be sub-divided into the efficiency and capacity variances:

Fixed overhead efficiency variance

	Hours
Standard hours for actual production	4,400
Less Actual hours	(4,600)
Fixed overhead efficiency variance – hours	200 A
FOAR	$6
	1,200 A

Fixed overhead capacity variance

	$
Actual hours × FOAR per hour (4,600 hours × $6 per hour)	27,600
Less Budgeted expenditure ($288,000/12 months)	(24,000)
Fixed overhead capacity variance	3,600 F

Sales price variance

	$
Standard selling price	1,250
Actual selling price ($264,000/220 units)	1,200
	50 A
× Actual no of units sold	× 220
	$11,000 A

Selling volume profit variance

	Units
Budgeted sales	200
Actual sales	220
	20 F
× Standard profit per unit	×194
	$3,880 F

(c) **Operating statement**

		$	$	$
Budgeted gross profit (W4)				38,800
Sales volume profit variance				3,880 F
				———
Standard profit on actual sales				42,680
Sales price variance				11,000 A
				———
				31,680

		Favourable	Adverse	
Cost variances				
Material X	Usage	5,600		
	Price		5,000	
Material Y	Usage		1,280	
	Price	3,600		
Direct labour	Efficiency		2,000	
	Rate	600		
Fixed prod overhead	Expenditure	1,000		
	Efficiency		1,200	
	Capacity	3,600		
		———	———	
		14,400	9,480	4,920 F
		———	———	———
Actual gross profit				36,600
				———

Workings:

(W1) Fixed overhead per unit = $288,000/2,400 units = $120 per unit. With labour taking 20 hours per unit this equates to a FOAR of $6 per hour

(W2)

	Material X	Material Y
	Kg	Kg
Op inventory	680	450
+ Purchases	3,000	1,700
	———	———
	3,680	2,150
– Cl inventory	1,180	350
	———	———
Materials issued/used	2,500	1,800
	———	———

(W3) Budgeted fixed overhead per month = $288,000/12 = $24,000

(W4) Budgeted profit = 200 units × $194 = $38,800

Test your understanding 10

B

Contribution margin	=	$\dfrac{429,200 - 410,000}{94\% - 82\%}$
	=	$1,600 for every 1% change
Budget for 87% occupancy	=	$429,200 − (7 × 1600)
	=	$418,000
Medical expenditure variance	=	418,000 − 430,000
	=	$12,000 Adverse

Test your understanding 11

	$
Sales volume (contribution) variance	16,000 (A)
Standard contribution/sales ratio:	40%
Sales volume variance in sales revenue	40,000 (A)
Sales price variance	30,000 (A)
Budgeted sales for the first 5 months (× 145,000)	725,000
Actual sales revenue for the first five months	655,000
Expected sales for the next 3 months (× 120,000)	360,000
Expected sales for the final 4 months (× 148,000)	592,000
Forecast sales for the year	**1,607,000**

	$
Forecast sales for the year (actual revenue)	1,607,000
Cumulative sales price variances	30,000 (A)
Forecast sales at standard sales prices	1,637,000
Standard contribution/sales ratio	40%
Forecast contribution at standard sales price	$654,800
Cumulative sales price variances	$30,000(A)
Forecast contribution at actual sales prices	$624,800

Statement of budgeted and forecast annual results, as at end May

	Budget $	Forecast $	Variance $
Sales revenue (145,000 × 12)	1,740,000	1,607,000	133,000 (A)
Contribution (1,740,000 × 40%)	696,000	624,800	71,200 (A)

Test your understanding 12

Activity	Expected cost $	Actual cost $	Variance $
Inventory counts (based on 52 counts)	41,600	40,560	**1,040** (F)

Test your understanding 13

Variable overhead expenditure variance

		$
3,600 actual visits should cost	($180,00/4,000 visits =) $45 per visit	162,000
3,600 actual visits did cost		168,000
Variance		$6,000 A

Variable overhead efficiency variance

		Visits
2,100 actual clients should require	(4,000 visits/2,000 clients =) 2 visits per client	4,200
2,100 actual clients did require		3,600
Variance		600 F

Variance = 600 F visits × standard cost of $45 per visit = $27,000 F

Test your understanding 14

Variance	Most likely cause
adverse materials price	new suppliers were used
adverse labour efficiency	new dentists were recruited
favourable fixed overhead carried volume	more dental treatments were out than was budgeted
adverse sales price	new competition entered the market

Test your understanding 15

(i)   Direct labour efficiency variance: Inconsistent. The workforce were inefficient.

(ii) Direct labour rate variance: Inconsistent. In fact the wage increase was $0.60 per hour higher than expected.

(iii) Direct materials usage variance: Inconsistent. If the losses had been less than expected then the usage variance would have been favourable.

(iv) Direct materials price variance: Consistent. A bulk purchase discount should lead to cheaper materials and hence a favourable material price variance.

Further variance analysis

Chapter learning objectives

Lead outcome	Component outcome
A3. Apply costing methods to determine the costs for different purposes	(c) Variance analysis (without mix and yield variance)

1 Chapter overview diagram

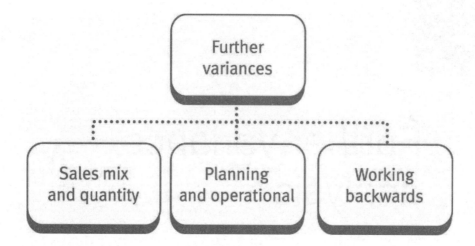

This chapter examines how some of the variances calculated in the previous chapter can be further analysed in order to give more detailed information to management. It is critical that you have gained a thorough understanding of the variances in the previous chapter before embarking on your studies of this chapter.

2 Sales mix and quantity variances

The sales volume variances that we have calculated so far have been based on organisations that sell only one product, but many organisations will sell more than one product.

If these products are related and substitutable then the organisation might want to determine the impact that this has on profits. This is the aim of sales mix and quantity variances. They take the sales volume variance and provide more detail by splitting it into these two component parts.

This might prove very useful to, say, a movie franchise which may set targets for a mix of cinema ticket sales, disc sales, streaming sales and merchandising sales. The franchise might, for example, expect 30% of sales to come from merchandising. The sales mix variance then becomes very useful to the franchise by examining the impact on profits if this 30% target is not met or if it is exceeded.

Note: No valid information would be obtained if these variances are calculated for unrelated products sold to different markets since the factors which influence demand and preferences in these markets would be different. For example, no meaningful information would result if these variances were calculated by a company who, say, make beds as well as an android tablet.

There are a number of steps involved in calculating the sales mix and quantity variances.

Step 1 – the standard mix

The first step is to compare the changes in the proportion of sales made up by each product. This means determining what the actual sales for each product would have been if the sales proportions had remained unchanged. This is known as the **standard mix**. This is the key part of the mix calculation.

> The actual total sales is split between the products based on the originally planned proportions.

Illustration 1

Marco Ltd operates a marginal costing system and sells three products, A15, B14 and E1 which are substitutes for each other. The following information relates to the three products:

	A15	B14	E1
Budgeted production and sales (units)	13,800	11,700	4,500
Budgeted contribution per unit	$3	$5	$7
Actual production and sales (units)	11,100	15,500	4,900

Required:

Calculate the actual production units at standard mix.

Solution:

To calculate the standard mix we need to take the actual sales and apply the standard proportion of sales for each product in the budget. In this example the total budgeted sales are 13,800 + 11,700 + 7,500 = 30,000 units.

Budgeted sales of product A15 make up 10,800 of the 30,000 units, which is a proportion of 13,800/30,000 or 46%.

Budgeted sales of product B14 make up 11,700 of the 30,000 units, which is a proportion of 11,700/30,000 or 39%.

Budgeted sales of product E1 make up 4,500 of the 30,000 units, which is a proportion of 4,500/30,000 or 15%.

Note: these proportions should add up to 100% (or 1 if you are working in decimals rather than percentages).

We then apply these proportions to the total sales in the period, to arrive at the actual sales at budget mix figures:

Product	Actual sales quantity		Actual sales at budget mix
A15	11,100	31,500 × 46%	14,490
B14	15,500	31,500 × 39%	12,285
E1	4,900	31,500 × 15%	4,725
	31,500		31,500

The sales mix variance (in units) is the difference between the actual sales quantity and the actual sales that would have been made if the total actual sales had been made in the standard mix.

Product	Actual sales quantity	Actual sales at budget mix	Difference
A15	11,100	14,490	3,390 A
B14	15,500	12,285	3,215 F
E1	4,900	4,725	175 F
	31,500	31,500	0

The total on the difference column should always be zero as we are only looking here at the differences caused due to the mix of the actual sales changing and not the volume of sales.

Example 1

A car wash and valeting business offers two services to customers which had the following budgeted information for the next budget period:

Service	Exterior	Full
Volume	800	200
Contribution per service	$4	$12

The actual results for the period were:

Service	Exterior	Full
Volume	720	480
Contribution per service	$5	$10

Required:

Calculate the sales mix variance (in units) for each type of service.

Step 2 – valuation

The first step showed us that there has been a change in mix – customers have bought less of the exterior and more of the full service (as a percentage of sales) than the company was expecting.

The next step is to determine the impact that this has had on profits. The mix and quantity variances are calculated using the **standard margin**. Where marginal costing is used this will be the standard contribution and where absorption costing is used this will be the standard profit.

There are two ways to do this (and it is important to learn how to use both methods so that you are able to follow the instructions in questions as to which to use):

- the individual units method

- the weighted average contribution method

The individual units method

In the individual units method each product's variance is multiplied by the standard margin.

Illustration 2

Following on from Illustration 1, Marco Ltd, we can value the variances using the individual units method.

We need to multiply the variance (in units) with the **standard** contribution per unit, to arrive at the variance per unit in $. We then total the variance column to arrive at the total sales mix variance.

Product	Actual sales quantity	Actual sales at budget mix	Difference	Contribution per unit $	Variance $
A15	11,100	14,490	3,390 A	3	10,170 A
B14	15,500	12,285	3,215 F	5	16,075 F
E1	4,900	4,725	175 F	7	1,225 F
	31,500	31,500	0		7,130 F

We can see here that the total mix variance is favourable. This is because the mix of sales has changed, with fewer of the least profitable product (A15) being sold and more of the more profitable product (E1) being sold than in the standard mix.

Example 2

Required:

Value the variances calculated in Example 1 using the individual units method.

The size of this impact on profits is useful to the management of the company. Management can further investigate as to why the change may have happened (i.e. why did customers switch from one product to another?). When favourable, the management can look to replicate this change, or when adverse the management can look to counteract the reasons for customers switching to the product/service with the lower contribution.

The weighted average contribution method

The first step in this approach is to calculate a weighted average contribution for the products. This is based on the budgeted sales and contribution. For the products in our example the weighted average contribution would be calculated as follows:

Product	Budgeted sales	Contribution	Total contribution
Exterior	800	$4	$3,200
Full	200	$12	$2,400
	1,000		$5,600

The weighted average contribution is ($5,600 / 1,000 units) $5.60.

To value the sales mix variance the weighted average contribution is deducted from the contribution per unit for each product.

Illustration 3

Following on from Illustration 1, Marco Ltd, we can calculate the standard weighted average margin per unit as follows:

Product	Budgeted sales	Contribution	Total contribution
A15	13,800	$3	$41,400
B14	11,700	$5	$58,500
E1	4,500	$7	$31,500
	30,000		$131,400

The weighted average contribution is therefore ($131,400 / 30,000 units) $4.38.

This is then deducted from the standard contribution per unit to value the differences:

Product	AQ	AQSM	Diff	SM – weighted average cont. per unit $	Var $
A15	11,100	14,490	3,390A	$3 – $4.38 = $0.138A	4,678F
B14	15,500	12,285	3,215F	$5 – $4.38 = $0.62F	1,993F
E1	4,900	4,725	175F	$7 – $4.38 = $2.62F	459F
	31,500	31,500			7,130F

We can see that the total mix variance is still the same ($7,130F) but the breakdown between the products has changed.

Product A15 has sold fewer units than expected in the standard mix. However, as this has the lowest contribution per unit, then it could be argued that this reduction is actually in the company's favour. They would prefer to sell a higher proportion of the more profitable products and a lower proportion of the least profitable product. This is why we see a change from the adverse variance for A15 in the individual method, to a favourable variance here.

This demonstrates how the weighted average method provides a more superior analysis of the variance than the individual units method. It clearly shows the impact of selling more or less of each product when it is measured against the average margin.

Example 3

Required:

Value the variances calculated in Example 1 using the weighted average contribution method.

Superiority of the weighted average method

The weighted average method for the mix variance is seen as being superior to the individual units method. It is easier to see the impact of each individual product or service when it is measured against the average margin.

The weighted average method provides better variances for control purposes. In the example above, the exterior service now shows as having a favourable variance (the variance was adverse when we used the individual units method). This is more representative of what has happened in this scenario: by selling less of the least profitable product (and therefore more of the most profitable product) the impact on the profits will be greater. Switching sales away from the exterior services into full services has a positive (favourable) impact on profits for both products.

Step 3 – sales quantity variance

The sales quantity variance ignores the change in mix and focuses on the impact on profit from selling more or less units than was budgeted.

The difference between actual sales and budgeted sales is valued at the weighted average margin per unit.

Sales quantity variance = (actual sales quantity – budgeted sales quantity) × weighted average margin

Illustration 4

Following on from the previous Illustrations, Marco Ltd, we can calculate the sales quantity variance by taking the difference between the total budgeted sales (30,000 units) and the actual sales figure (31,500 units).

This is a favourable variance of 1,500 units.

We then value this at the weighted average contribution per unit of $4.38:

Sales quantity variance = 1,500 @ $4.38 = $6,570 F.

An alternative way to arrive at the difference would be to calculate it by individual product (showing below). However it is important to note that the resulting individual variances that are showing here do not have any meaning in themselves; it is only the total that we are interested in with the sales quantity variance. You would therefore only use this method if you didn't have the weighted average contribution per unit figure.

Product	Actual sales at budget mix	Budget sales	Difference	Contribution	Variance
A15	14,490	13,800	690 F	$3	$2,070 F
B14	12,285	11,700	585 F	$5	$2,925 F
E1	4,725	4,500	225 F	$7	$1,575 F
	31,500	30,000	1,500 F		$6,570 F

Example 4

Required:

Calculate the sales quantity variance for Example 1.

This gives useful information to managers as it explains the impact on profits for the change in volume (assuming that the mix between products had remained unchanged).

Benefits and problems of mix and quantity variances

Benefits

- The sales mix variance can allow an organisation to identify trends in sales of individual elements of its total product sales. For example, they may find that although overall sales are improving (as suggested by the sales quantity or sales volume variance being favourable), that one individual product has shown a period-on-period decline in volume.

- The sales quantity variance can be used to indicate changes in the size of the market and/or the change in the market share for an organisation.

- The sales mix variance may indicate future directions for sales strategies – organisations would aim to repeat any favourable variances by identifying and exploiting their causes.

- The sales mix variance can be used to gauge the success or failure of new marketing campaigns. For example, if an organisation were to launch a special edition of its product, it might be able to determine the impact that this has had on its profits as well as any adverse impact it might have had on sales of its regular product.

- Responsibility accounting is improved when the sales volume variance is split between the sales mix and quantity variance as different managers might be responsible for different elements of sales. The sales quantity variance, for example, will indicate whether the sales team have performed well overall, whereas the mix variance will then provide information on the success of those responsible for applying the mix of sales.

Problems

- Like any variance, it will be important for the user to consider the controllability of the variance before making performance review decisions based on the output. For example, an adverse sales quantity variance might have been caused by an uncontrollable change in government restrictions on sales of the product, rather than having been caused by the actions of the sales team/manager. Also, it may be that a strategy to change the mix also has an impact on the quantity variance. For example, it may be that the car wash company has improved quantity overall because it has moved upmarket by deliberately targeting more full services and changing its mix.

- Likewise, variances should be considered as a whole rather than on an individual basis due to their interdependence. Managers would have to be aware, for example, that sales volume variances might be affected by decisions taken in production (such as a change in materials or labour used).

- The sales mix variance is only relevant if the products have some sort of relationship between them. Examples of this are:

  - the products are of the same type but of a different variety (for example, where there are 'normal' and 'special' editions of a product

  - the products are complementary (for example, where a company sells both ebooks and ereaders)

  - the products can be substituted for each other (for example, a company might sell European and Asian holidays).

- It can sometimes be difficult to apply these techniques in organisations which have very broad product ranges. It can be difficult to determine which products are complementary, which are substitutes etc. and often computer based techniques are needed to perform the detailed calculations.

Overall, these can be complex calculations that might only apply for certain organisations. But for managers who can interpret these well, sales mix and quantity variance analysis can provide vital information on sales trends, marketing effects, marketing position and variance responsibility.

3 Planning and operational variances

One reason that a variance may arise may be that the original plan has subsequently been found to be inappropriate. This might arise, for example, if suppliers have increased the cost of raw materials and this has not been accounted for in the original standard cost card. In that case the total variance must be split into two constituent parts:

- the **planning variance** – this is the part of the variance caused by an inappropriate original (ex-ante) standard, and

- the **operational variance** – this is the part of the variance attributable to decisions taken within the business that has caused a change between the revised (ex-post) standard and the actual results.

Traditional variance

– Compares actual results with the original (flexed) budget.

Planning variance

– Compares the revised (flexed) budget and the original (flexed) budget.

– Often deemed to be uncontrollable. Management should not be held accountable.

Operational variance

– Compares actual results with the revised (flexed) budget.

– Deemed controllable. Management held responsible for operational variances.

Further explanation

Forecasts by their nature are unreliable, and yet most standards are set on a forecast basis, i.e. **ex ante** or before the event. A planning variance arises from an inability to make exact predictions of future costs and revenues at the budgeting stage.

If it were possible to set standards with the benefit of hindsight, i.e. **ex post** or after the event, managers would be able to see more clearly what amount of variances was genuinely attributable to operating performance **(operational variances)** and what amount to difficulties or errors in setting the original standard **(planning variances).** Such information should improve operational control and may also provide guidance for the improvement of planning procedures.

The planning variance is usually regarded as uncontrollable and has arisen because the original standard was not reflective of the attainable standard. The operational variance is controllable.

Operational variances

Operational variances are variances that are assumed to have occurred due to operational factors. These are materials price and usage variances, labour rate and efficiency variances, variable overhead expenditure and efficiency variances, fixed overhead expenditure variances, and sales variances.

Operational variances are calculated with the 'realistic' ex post standard. They are calculated in exactly the same way as described in earlier chapters, the only difference being that the ex post standard is used, not the original standard.

Planning variances

A planning variance measures the difference between the budgeted and actual profit that has been caused by errors in the original standard cost. It is the difference between the ex-ante and the ex post standards.

- A planning variance is **favourable** when the ex post standard cost is lower than the original ex ante standard cost.

- A planning variance is **adverse** when the ex post standard cost is higher than the original ex ante standard cost.

Controllability and responsibility

Management will wish to draw a distinction between these two variances in order to gain a realistic measure of operational efficiency. As planning variances are self-evidently not under the control of operational management, it cannot be held responsible for them, and there is thus no benefit to be gained in spending time investigating such variances at an operational level. Planning variances may arise from faulty standard-setting, but the responsibility for this lies with senior, rather than operational management.

Illustration 5 – planning and operational variances for labour

The standard hours per unit for of production for product B3 is 4 hours of semi-skilled labour time. Actual production for the period was 850 units and actual hours worked were 3,050. The standard rate per hour was $12.

Because of a shortage of semi-skilled labour in the period, it has been necessary to use skilled workers instead and it is estimated that this has reduced the time taken to produce each unit by 25%.

Actual labour costs were $42,400.

Required:

Calculate the conventional variances for direct labour rate and efficiency and also the planning and operational variances.

Solution:

Conventional variances:

Direct labour rate variance			$
3,050 hours	should cost/hr ($12)		36,600
	did cost (actual)		42,400
Direct labour rate variance			5,800A

Direct labour efficiency variance			$
Actual output produced (850 units)	should take (4 hours)		3,400
	did take(actual hours)		3,050
Direct labour efficiency variance	(in hours)		350F
× standard rate per hour			$12
Direct labour efficiency variance			$4,200F

If we combine the rate and efficiency variances we have a total direct labour rate variance of $1,600A.

Planning and operational variances:

Using planning and operational variances, we can split this total variance into variances which were controllable (operational) and those which were uncontrollable (planning).

First of all we need to revise the original standard for the reduction in labour time per unit. This will fall from 4 hours to 4 hours × 75% = 3 hours.

The planning variance is found by taking the original flexed budget and the revised flexed budget and calculating the variance as follows:

	$
Original budget:	
850 units × 4 hours per unit × $12 per hour	40,800
Revised budget:	
850 units × 3 hours per unit × $12 per hour	30,600
Planning variance	10,200 F

We next need to calculate the operational variances for labour efficiency, as follows:

	$
Direct labour efficiency variance:	
850 units should take (3 hours per unit × $12 per hour)	30,600
850 units did take (3,050 hours × $12 per hour)	36,600
Operational efficiency variance	6,000 A

The operational labour rate variance remains unchanged as we are not told that a different rate per labour hour was paid for the different grade of employees.

If we total the planning and operational variances we have just calculated, this gives us $10,200F + $6,000A + $5,800A = $1,600A which is the same as we calculated using the traditional approach.

What this breakdown enables us to do, is to ensure that managers only have their performance measured against the variances that were within their control (operational variances). This is something that will be covered in later chapters.

If we look at the results here, using the traditional approach, it would appear that the workers have been much more efficient than planned, with a favourable efficiency variance of $4,200.

However, upon investigating this further, and revising the standards for the fact that skilled labour is now being used (which ought to be more efficient), then we can see that we in fact have an adverse operational variance for labour efficiency. This means that the workers are not being as efficient as expected. The initial favourable outcome was due to incorrect standards being used and formed the planning variance.

Illustration 6 – planning and operational variances for sales

The sales volume variance can also be subdivided into a planning and operational variance using the pro-forma below:

Actual sales quantity x standard margin

Revised budgeted sales x standard margin
(to achieve target share of actual market)

Original budgeted sales x standard margin

Market share variance (operational)

Market size variance (planning)

Suppose a company sets its budget based on an average price of $14 per unit and sales volume of 250,000 units. Competition was more intense than expected and the company only achieved sales of 220,000 and had to sell at a discounted price of $12.50 per unit.

The company was unable to reduce costs so profit per unit fell from $4 per unit to $2.50 per unit.

It was estimated that the total market volume grew by 10% from 1,000,000 units to 1,100,000 units.

Using traditional variances, we can calculate the sales price and volume variances as follows:

Sales price variance		$000
Actual units sold should have sold for	(220,000 × $14)	3,080
They did sell for	(220,000 × $12.50)	2,750
Sales price variance		330A

Sales volume variance

	Units
Actual sales volume	220,000
Budgeted sales volume	250,000
Sales volume variance (in units)	30,000A
@ standard contribution per unit $4	$120 A

Now we will investigate the planning and operational variances.

Market size (planning) variance:

The budgeted market share was 250,000 units of a total market of 1,000,000 units = 25%.

Therefore, as the total market grew to 1,100,000 units then the company should expect sales of 25% × 1,100,000 = 275,000 units.

The market size variance is therefore calculated as:

= (Revised budget sales – original budget sales) × standard margin

= (275,000 – 250,000) × $4 = $100,000 F.

Market share (operational) variance:

= (Actual sales - revised budget sales) × standard margin

= (220,000 – 275,000) × $4 = $220,000 A

We can see that the total of the planning and operational variances agree to the original sales volume variance that we calculated.

Illustration 7 – planning and operational variances for materials

The standard cost per unit of raw material was estimated to be $5.20 per unit. However, due to subsequent improvements in technology, the general market price at the time of purchase was $5.00 per unit. The actual price paid was $5.18 per unit.

10,000 units of the raw materials were purchased and used during the period.

Using traditional variances, we can calculate the materials variance as follows:

Direct material price variance		$
Actual quantity of materials (10,000 units)	should cost ($5.20)	52,000
	did cost ($5.18)	51,800
Direct materials price variance		200 F

Now we will investigate the planning and operational material price variances.

Planning variance:

Actual quantity (10,000 units)	Original standard ($5.20)	52,000
Actual quantity	Revised standard ($5.00)	50,000
Planning materials price variance		2,000F

Operational variance:

Actual quantity (10,000 units)	Actual price ($5.18)	51,800
Actual quantity	Revised standard ($5.00)	50,000
		———
Operational materials price variance		1,800A
		———

We can see that the total of the planning and operational variances agree to the original material price variance of $200F that we calculated.

Example 5

A government department is responsible for awarding entry visas for overseas residents wishing to enter the country. Details of actual and budget labour costs for the department for period 9 are:

	Budget	Actual
Applications	500	550
Labour hours	1,000	1,200
Labour cost	5,000	5,100

However, a relaxation in the government's legal entry checks for overseas residents subsequent to the preparation of the budget resulted in a 25% increase in standard labour efficiency, such that it is now possible to assess 5 applications instead of 4 applications using 8 hours of labour – giving a revised standard labour requirement of 1.6 hours (thus $8 labour cost) per application.

Required:

Calculate all relevant labour variances for the period.

Example 6

A company budgets to sell 1,000 units of its new product with the following standard information:

	$	$
Standard sales price per unit		200
Standard costs per unit		
Raw materials (10 kg at $10)	100	
Labour (6 hours at $8)	48	(148)
Standard contribution per unit		52

Actual results for the first year were as follows:

	$000	$000
Sales (1,000 units)		316
Production costs (1,000 units)		
Raw materials (10,800 kg)	194.4	
Labour (5,800 hours)	69.6	(264)
Actual contribution (1,000 units)		52

The managing director made the following observations on the actual results:

In total, the performance agreed with budget; nevertheless, in every aspect other than volume, there were large differences.

Sales were made at what was felt to be the highest feasible price, but we now feel that we could have sold for $330 with no adverse effect on volume. Labour costs rose dramatically with increased demand for the specialist skills required to produce the product, and the general market rate was $12.50 per hour – although we always paid below the general market rate whenever possible.

The raw material cost that was expected at the time the budget was prepared was $10 per kilogram. However, the market price relating to efficient purchases of the material during the year was $17 per kilogram.

It is not proposed to request a variance analysis for the first year's results. In any event, the final contribution was equal to that originally budgeted, so operations must have been fully efficient.

Required:

Despite the managing director's reluctance to calculate it, produce an operating statement for the period ignoring the impact of any planning variances.

Calculate the impact of the planning variances for the business.

4   Causes of planning variances

There must be a good reason for deciding that the original standard cost is unrealistic. Deciding in retrospect that expected costs should be different from the standard should not be an arbitrary decision, aimed perhaps at shifting the blame for poor results from poor operational management to poor cost estimation.

A good reason for a change in the standard might be:

- a change in one of the main materials used to make a product or provide a service

- an unexpected increase in the price of materials due to a rapid increase in world market prices (for example, the price of oil or other commodities)

- a change in working methods and procedures that alters the expected direct labour time for a product or service

- an unexpected change in the rate of pay to the work force.

More than one planning error

A situation might occur where the difference between the standards is in two (or more) items.

In these circumstances, the rules for calculating planning and operational variances are as follows:

- Operational variances are calculated against the most up-to-date revision

- The total planning variance will be the difference between the original standard or budget and the most up-to-date revision. This can then be further divided between each individual planning error.

For example, the original standard cost for a product was $4 per kg and the actual cost was $6 per kg. Two planning variances were discovered. Firstly, the accountant had assumed that a bulk discount on purchases would arise but this was never likely, and it meant that the standard should have been set at $4.60 per kg. Secondly, a worldwide shortage of materials led to an industry wide increase of $1 per kg to the cost of materials. This means that the most up-to-date standard cost would have been $5.60 per kg. The operational variance would therefore be $0.40 ($6 − $5.60) per kg adverse and the total planning variance would be $1.60 ($5.60 − $4) per kg. The planning variance could then be split between the two effects: there is a $0.60 per kg adverse variance caused by the failure to gain the bulk discount, and a $1 per kg adverse variance caused by the market conditions.

5 Benefits and problems of planning variances

Benefits	Problems
• More useful	• Subjective
• Up-to-date	• Time consuming
• Better for motivation	• Can be manipulated
• Assesses planning	• Can cause conflict

 Further explanation

Benefits of planning and operational variances

(1) In volatile and changing environments, standard costing and variance analysis are more useful using this approach.

(2) Operational variances provide up to date information about current levels of efficiency.

(3) Operational variances are likely to make the standard costing system more acceptable and to have a positive effect on motivation.

(4) It emphasises the importance of the planning function in the preparation of standards and helps to identify planning deficiencies.

Problems of planning and operational variances

(1) There is an element of subjectivity in determining the ex-post standards as to what is 'realistic'.

(2) There is a large amount of labour time involved in continually establishing up to date standards and calculating additional variances.

(3) There is a great temptation to put as much as possible of the total variances down to outside, uncontrollable factors, i.e. planning variances.

(4) There can then be a conflict between operating and planning staff. Each laying the blame at each other's door.

On the face of it, the calculation of operational and planning variances is an improvement over the traditional analysis. However, you should not overlook the considerable problem of data collection for the revised analysis: where does this information come from, and how can we say with certainty what should have been known at a particular point in time?

6 Working backwards

An excellent way of testing whether you really understand the reasons for and the calculation of operating variances is to 'work backwards' from standard cost data and variances to arrive at the actual results.

In these scenarios the examiner will provide you with the variance and give you one other piece of information (either the original standard or the actual results). You then must use this information to determine the missing information.

For example, we know that:

Total materials variance = Standard material cost for actual production – Actual material cost

If the question gave you the variance and the actual material cost you would rearrange this formula to calculate the standard material cost:

Standard material cost = Total materials variance + Actual material cost

A useful approach is to use the formula or proforma from the previous chapter, fill in the information that you have been given in the scenario, then re-arrange the equations to determine the missing information.

 Detailed example on working backwards

Q operates a system of standard costing and in respect of one of its products, which is manufactured within a single cost centre, the following information is given.

For one unit of product the standard material input is 16 litres at a standard price of $2.50 per litre. The standard labour rate is $5 per hour and 6 hours are allowed to produce one unit. Fixed production overhead is absorbed at the rate of 120% of direct labour cost. During the last 4 weeks accounting period the following occurred.

- The material price variance was extracted on purchase and the actual price paid was $2.45 per litre.

- Total direct labour cost was $121,500.

- Fixed production overhead cost incurred was $150,000.

Variances included:

	Favourable $	Adverse $
Direct material price	8,000	
Direct material usage		6,000
Direct labour rate		4,500
Direct labour efficiency	3,600	
Fixed production overhead expenditure		6,000

Required:

Calculate the following for the 4-week period:

(a)   budgeted output in units ✓

(b)   number of litres purchased ✓

(c)   number of litres used above standard allowed ✓

(d)   actual units produced

(e)   actual hours worked ✓

(f)   average actual direct labour rate per hour.

Solution

The best thing to do as a first step is to pull together all of the standard cost information to calculate a standard cost per unit.

	$
Direct material (16 litres × 2.5 per litre)	40
Direct labour (6 hours × $5 per hour)	30
Fixed production overhead ($30 × 120%)	36
Total	106

Calculating the required figures is now just a series of exercises in logic. These exercises can seem difficult to the novice – but the logic becomes simple and obvious with familiarity.

(a)   If actual fixed production overhead was $150,000 and the fixed production overhead expenditure variance was $6,000 adverse, then it follows that the budget fixed overhead was $144,000. From this it follows that the budget must have been 4,000 units (that is, $144,000 budgeted overhead/$36 standard overhead cost per unit).

(b)   If the standard material purchase price was $2.50 per litre and the actual purchase price was $2.45, then it follows that the material price variance is $0.05 per litre favourable. We are told that the material price variance was $8,000 favourable, so it follows that 160,000 litres must have been purchased (that is, $8,000 price variance/$0.05 price variance per litre). ✓

(c)   If the direct material usage variance was $6,000 adverse and the standard price of materials is $2.50 per litre, then it follows that the number of litres used above the standard allowance is 2,400 ($6000/$2.50 per litre).

(d) If the actual direct labour cost was $121,500 and labour cost variances totalling $900 adverse ($4,500 adverse rate plus $3,600 favourable efficiency) were experienced, then the standard labour cost for the output achieved was $120,600. It follows that the units produced were 4,020 (that is, $120,600 standard labour cost/$30 standard labour cost per unit).

(e) The total hours actually worked is 24,120 standard hours worked (that is, 4,020 units produced at 6 standard hours per unit) minus the 720-hour favourable labour efficiency variance (that is, $3,600 efficiency variance/$5 standard rate per hour). This gives a total of 23,400 actual hours worked.

(f) If the actual labour cost was $121,500 and the actual hours worked was 23,400, then it follows that the actual wage rate per hour was $5.1923.

Example 7

A government department is responsible for awarding entry visas for overseas residents wishing to enter the country. Details of actual and budget labour costs for the department for period 9 are:

A manufacturer has the following information on labour costs for July:

	Budget	Actual
Production (units)	180,000	200,000
Labour costs ($)	$720,000	$760,000

The standard cost for labour is based on a labour rate of $30 per hour. The labour rate variance was $10,000 adverse.

What was the actual labour rate per hour in July?

A $29.61 per hour

B $30.00 per hour

C $30.40 per hour

D $30.81 per hour

7   Chapter summary

Further variances

Sales mix and quantity
-   Splits the sales volume variance
-   Requires the calculation of the standard mix
-   Comparing to actual mix = mix variance
-   Comparing to budgeted sales = quantity variance

Planning and operational
-   Revised standard for errors in the plan
-   Planning variance = difference between original standard and revised standard
-   Operational variance = difference between revised standard and actual results

Working backwards
-   Given the variance and the standard results to calculate the actual results
-   Set up the calculation and enter the figures from the question
-   Missing figures will be the answer

8   Practice questions

Test your understanding 1

A beauty salon offers two types of treatment, Standard and Deluxe, details for the current period as follows:

	Standard mix (treatments)	Standard profit ($ per treatment)	Average profit ($ per treatment)
Standard	2	5	
Deluxe	3	6	
Total	5	((2 × 5) + (3 × 6))/5	5.60

Budget sales – 200 units Standard and 300 units Deluxe

Actual sales – 180 units Standard and 310 units Deluxe

Required:

(a)   calculate the sales quantity profit variance

(b)   calculate the sales mix profit variance using the individual method

(c)   calculate the sales mix profit variance using the weighted average method.

Test your understanding 2

Holmes uses one raw material for one of their products. The standard cost per unit at the beginning of the year was $28, made up as follows:

Standard material cost per unit = 7 kg per unit at $4 per kg = $28.

In the middle of the year the supplier had changed the specification of the material slightly due to problems experienced in the country of origin, so that the standard had to be revised as follows:

Standard material cost per unit = 8 kg per unit at $3.80 per kg = $30.40.

The actual output for November was 1,400 units. 11,000 kg of material was purchased and used at a cost of $41,500.

Calculate

(a)   material price and usage variances using the traditional method

(b)   the planning and operational material variances.

Test your understanding 3

The following data relates to Skilled Labour Grade ST1

Standard labour hours per unit	5 hours
Standard labour rate	$10 per hour
Actual production	250 units
Actual labour hours	1,450 hours
Actual labour cost	$13,050

During the month there was an unforeseen shortage of the Skilled Labour Grade ST1. Semi-skilled workers (Grade ST2) were hired. As a consequence of this, the standard time was revised to 6 hours per unit.

Required:

Calculate labour rate and efficiency variances using a planning and operational approach.

Test your understanding 4

A company uses standard marginal costing. Last month the standard contribution on actual sales was $44,000 and the following variances arose:

Total variable costs variance	$6,500 Adverse
Sales price variance	$2,000 Favourable
Sales volume contribution variance	$4,500 Adverse

What was the actual contribution for last month?

A $33,000
B $35,000
C $37,500
D $39,500

Test your understanding 5

WC is a company that installs kitchens and bathrooms for customers who are renovating their houses. Some installations are highly customised designs for specific jobs.

The company operates with three divisions: Kitchens, Bathrooms and Central Services. The costs of the Central Services division are charged to the other divisions based on the budgeted number of jobs to be undertaken by the other two divisions.

The budgeting and reporting system of WC is not very sophisticated and does not provide much detail for the Directors of the company. The budgeted details for last year were:

	Kitchens	Bathrooms
Number of jobs	4,000	2,000
	$	$
Average price per job	10,000	7,000
Average direct costs per job	5,500	3,000
Central services recharge per job	2,500	2,500
Average profit per job	2,000	1,500

The actual results were as follows:

	Kitchens	Bathrooms
Number of jobs	2,600	2,500
	$	$
Average price per job	13,000	6,100
Average direct costs per job	8,000	2,700
Central services recharge per job	2,500	2,500
Average profit per job	2,500	900

The actual costs for the Central Services division were $17.5 million.

Required:

(a) Calculate the budgeted and actual profits for both the Kitchen and Bathroom division and for the whole company for the year.

(b) Calculate the sales price variances and the sales mix profit and sales quantity profit variances.

(c) Prepare a statement that reconciles the budgeted and actual profits and shows appropriate variances in as much detail as possible.

(d) Using the statement that you prepared in part (c) above, discuss the performance of the company for the year.

Test your understanding 6

The expected contribution per unit of the product manufactured by ATS is $26, ascertained as below:

		$	$
Selling price			110
Material	8 kg × $3/kg	24	
Labour	6 hours × $10/hour	60	
		___	
			84
			___
Contribution/unit			26
			___

The expected contribution was $31,200. The actual contribution was $38,800 as shown below:

		$	$
Actual sales revenue	1,000 units @ $135		135,000
Actual material cost	7,800 kg × $4/kg	31,200	
Actual labour cost	6,250 hours × $10.40/hour	65,000	
		_____	
			96,200
			_____
Actual contribution/unit			38,800
			_____

The Sales Director made the policy decision to sell at $5 above the prevailing market price of $125, suggesting that if they did suffer a decrease in volume, ATS would still be better off. It was also accepted that an efficient purchasing officer could have purchased at around $4.50 per kg.

There was no inventory movement of either materials or finished goods in the period.

Required:

Prepare a variance statement which would be most helpful to the management of ATS, which clearly takes planning and operational variances into consideration.

Test your understanding 7

A company budgeted to make and sell 2,000 units of its only product, for which the standard marginal cost is:

		$
Direct materials	4 kilos at $2 per kilo	8
Direct labour	3 hours at $6 per hour	18
		26

The standard sales price is $50 per unit and the standard contribution $24 per unit. Budgeted fixed costs were $30,000, giving a budgeted profit of $18,000.

Due to severe material shortages, the company had to switch to a less efficient and more expensive material, and it was decided in retrospect that the realistic (ex post) standard direct material cost should have been 5 kilos at $3 per kilo = $15 per unit.

Actual results were as follows:

Actual production and sales: 2,400 units

		$	$
Sales revenue			115,000
Direct materials	12,300 kilos at $3 per kilo	36,900	
Direct labour	7,500 hours at $6.10 per hour	45,750	
Total variable costs			82,650
Actual contribution			32,350
Actual fixed costs			32,000
			350

Required:

Prepare an operating statement with planning and operational variances that reconciles the budgeted and actual profit figures.

Test your understanding 8

Gooch makes a single product and operates a standard costing system. The following variances, standard costs and actual results relate to period 6:

Variances

	Favourable	Adverse
Direct material price variance		1,012
Direct material usage variance		1,380
Direct labour rate variance		920
Direct labour efficiency variance	3,680	
Variable overhead expenditure variance		1,288
Variable overhead efficiency variance	920	

Standard cost data

		$/unit
Direct materials	2 kg @ $3/kg	6
Direct labour	3 hrs @ $8/hr	24
Variable overheads	3 hrs @ $2/hr	6
Fixed overheads	3 hrs @ $4/hr	12
		____
		$48

Fixed overheads were budgeted at $24,000 and the budgeted profit per unit was 20% of the selling price. Budgeted sales were 1,900 units.

Actual results

Material purchased and used	$16,192
Labour cost	$52,440
Variable overhead cost	$14,168
Fixed overhead cost	$23,500

Selling price per unit was $3 lower than budget and there was no change in inventory levels.

You are required to calculate the:

(a) actual output

(b) actual material price per kg

(c) labour hours worked

(d) fixed overhead volume variance

(e) fixed overhead expenditure variance

(f) sales volume profit variance

(g) selling price variance

(h) budgeted profit

(i) actual profit

Test your understanding 9

Scenario

RBF Transport, a haulage contractor, operates a standard costing system and has prepared the following report for April 20X0:

Operating statement

		$	$	$
Budgeted profit				8,000
Sales volume profit variance				880 (A)
				7,120
Selling price variance				3,560 (F)
				10,680

Cost variances		A	F	
Direct labour	– rate		1,086	
	– efficiency	240		
Fuel	– price	420		
	– usage	1,280		
Variable overhead	– expenditure		280	
	– efficiency	180		
Fixed overhead	– expenditure		400	
	– volume	1,760		
		3,880	1,766	2,114 (A)
Actual profit				8,566

The company uses delivery miles as its cost unit, and the following details have been taken from the budget working papers for April 20X0:

(1) Expected activity   200,000 delivery miles

(2) Charge to customers $0.30 per delivery mile

(3) Expected variable cost per delivery mile:

     Direct labour (0.02 hours) $0.08

     Fuel (0.1 litres) $0.04

     Variable overhead (0.02 hours) $0.06

The following additional information has been determined from the actual accounting records for April 20X0.

- Fixed overhead cost $15,600
- Fuel price $0.42 per litre
- Direct labour hours   3,620

Tasks:

(a) Calculate for April 20X0:

  (i) the actual number of delivery miles

  (ii) the actual direct labour rate per hour

  (iii) the actual number of litres of fuel consumed

  (iv) the actual variable overhead expenditure.

(b) State TWO possible causes of the fuel usage variance.

(Time allowed for part (b): 5 minutes)

(c) Prepare a report, addressed to the transport operations manager, explaining the different types of standard which may be set, and the importance of keeping standards meaningful and relevant.

(Time allowed for part (c): 15 minutes)

Test your understanding 10

Scenario

It might be argued that only operational variances have significance for performance measurement. Planning variances cannot be controlled and so have little or no value for performance reporting.

Task:

State briefly, with your reason(s), whether you agree with this point of view.

(Time allowed: 10 minutes)

Test your understanding 11

Which of the following statements regarding market size variances are true?

(1) A fall or increase in market size is uncontrollable by management and therefore results in a planning variance.

(2) The sales volume planning variance reveals the extent of which the original standard (estimation of market size) was at fault.

(3) Managers should be appraised on both the operational and planning variances for sales.

A   Statements (1) and (2)

B   Statements (2) and (3)

C   Statements (1) and (3)

D   Statements (1), (2) and (3)

Test your understanding answers

Example 1

Firstly, we record the actual sales for each product:

Product	Actual sales quantity
Exterior	720
Full	480
	1,200

Then we determine the standard mix. This takes the actual sales and applies the proportion of sales for each product in the budget. In this example the exterior service was budgeted to be 800 out of 1,000 total services i.e. 80% of budgeted sales. If this 'mix' hadn't changed it should have made up 80% of actual sales i.e. 80% × 1,200 services = 960 services. A similar calculation can be done for the full service.

Product	Actual Sales quantity	Actual sales at budget mix
Exterior	720	960
Full	480	240
	1,200	1,200

The difference between these (actual sales less the standard mix) is the mix variance in units.

Product	Actual Sales quantity	Actual sales at budget mix	Difference
Exterior	720	960	240 A
Full	480	240	240 F
	1,200	1,200	

The total in the 'Difference' column should always be nil.

Example 2

We are given a contribution for each service (the company must be using marginal costing):

Product	Actual sales quantity	Actual sales at budget mix	Difference	Contribution	Mix variance
Exterior	720	960	240 A	$4	960 A
Full	480	240	240 F	$12	2,880 F
	1,200	1,200			1,920 F

The proportion of sales (mix) has moved away from exterior services and towards full services. Because full services have a greater contribution per service this has a positive impact overall on company profits.

Example 3

We are given a contribution for each service (the company must be using marginal costing):

Product	Actual sales quantity	Actual sales at budget mix	Difference	Contribution	Mix variance ($000)
Exterior	720	960	240 A	$4 – $5.60	384 F
Full	480	240	240 F	$12 – $5.60	1,536 F
	1,200	1,200			1,920 F

The total mix variance is still the same but the breakdown between the products has changed.

Example 4

Actual sales = 1,200 units

Budgeted sales = 1,000 units

Variance = 200 units Favourable

Valued at the weighted average contribution = 200 units × $5.60 = 1,120 Favourable

Example 5

The total labour cost variance for period 9 is $400 favourable (i.e. $5,500 standard cost less $5,100 actual cost). This may be analysed as follows:

Planning variance:

Original (ex-ante) standard less the revised (ex-post) labour cost

(550 applications × $10) – (550 applications × $8) = $1,100 favourable

Operational variances:

Labour efficiency:

(standard (ex-post) hours less actual hours) × standard hourly rate
((550 applications × 1.6 hours) – 1,200 hours) × $5 = $1,600 adverse

Labour rate:

(standard rate – actual rate) × actual hours
($5 – $4.25) × 1,200 = $900 favourable

Note that the three component variances add up to $400 favourable.

In this case, the separation of the labour cost variance into operational and planning components indicates a larger problem in the area of labour efficiency than might otherwise have been indicated. The operational variances are based on the revised standard and this gives a more meaningful performance benchmark than the original standard.

Example 6

Operating statement

				$	
Budgeted contribution				52,000	
Sales price variance				116,000	F
				———	
				168,000	

Cost variances		Fav	Adv		
Direct material price	($10 × 10,800) − $194,400		86,400		
Direct material usage	(10,000 − 10,800) × $10		8,000		
Direct labour rate	($8 × 5,800) − $69,600)		23,200		
Direct labour efficiency	(6,000 − 5,800) × $8	1,600			
		———	———		
		1,600	117,600	116,000	A
		———	———	———	
				52,000	
				———	

As the managing director states, and the above analysis shows, the overall variance for the company was zero: the adverse cost variances exactly offset the favourable sales price variance. However, this analysis does not clearly indicate the efficiency with which the company operated during the period, as it is impossible to tell whether some of the variances arose from the use of inappropriate standards, or whether they were due to efficient or inefficient implementation of those standards. In order to determine this, a revised ex post plan should be constructed, setting out the standards that, with hindsight, should have been in operation during the period. These revised ex post standards are shown under (B) below.

	(A) Original plan	$	**(B)** Revised ex ante plan	$	**(C)** Actual result	$
Sales	200,000		330,000		316,000	
	(1,000 × $200)		(1,000 × $330)		(1,000 × $316)	
Materials	100,000		170,000		194,400	
	(10,000 × $10)		(10,000 × $17)		(10,800 × $18)	
Labour	48,000		75,000		69,600	
	(6,000 ×$8)		(6,000 × $12.50)		(5,800 × $12)	

	$	$
Planning variances (A – B)		
Sales price	130,000 F	
Materials price	70,000 A	
Labour rate	27,000 A	
	———	
		33,000 F
Operational variances		
Sales price (B – C)	14,000 A	
Materials price (10,800 × $1)	10,800 A	
Materials usage (800 × $17)	13,600 A	
Labour rate (5,800 × $0.50)	2,900 F	
Labour efficiency (200 hrs × $12.50)	2,500 F	
	———	
		33,000 A

A comparison of (B) and (C) produces operational variances, which show the difference between the results that were actually achieved and those that might legitimately have been achievable during the period in question. This gives a very different view of the period's operations. For example, on the cost side, the labour rate variance has changed from adverse to favourable, and the material price variance, while remaining adverse, is significantly reduced in comparison to that calculated under the traditional analysis; on the sales side, the sales price variance, which was particularly large and favourable in the traditional analysis, is transformed into an adverse variance in the revised approach, reflecting the fact that the company failed to sell at prices that were actually available in the market.

A comparison of the original plan (A) with the revised plan (B) allows the planning variances to be identified. As noted at the beginning of this section, these variances are uncontrollable by operating, staff, and may or may not have been controllable by the original standard-setters at the start of the budget period. Where a revision of standards is required due to environmental changes that were not foreseeable at the time the budget was prepared, the planning variances are truly uncontrollable. However, standards that failed to anticipate known market trends when they were set will reflect faulty standard-setting: it could be argued that these variances were controllable (avoidable) at the planning stage.

Example 7

C $30.40

The standard cost of actual hours worked = actual cost – labour rate variance = $760,000 – $10,000 = $750,000

The actual hours worked = $750,000 / $30 per hour = 25,000 hours

The actual rate per hour = $760,000 / 25,000 hours = $30.40 per hour

Test your understanding 1

(a) **Sales quantity profit variance**

It is apparent that the overall sales volume profit variance for the period is $40 adverse (that is (20 units adverse of Standard times $5) plus (10 units favourable of Deluxe times $6).

We can split this into a sales quantity profit variance and a sales mix profit variance. The sales quantity profit variance is calculated as follows:

(Actual units – budgeted units) × weighted average profit per unit

(500 units budget – 490 units actual) × $5.60 average profit = $56 A

(b) **Sales mix profit variance (using the individual units method)**

	Standard mix	Actual mix	Variance (treatments)	Profit per treatment ($)	Variance ($)
Standard	196	180	16 (A)	5	80 (A)
Deluxe	294	310	16 (F)	6	96 (F)
	———	———			———
Total	490	490			16 (F)
	———	———			———

The standard mix is the total unit sales (490) multiplied by 2/5 to give X and 3/5 to give Y.

(c) **Sales mix profit variance (using the weighted average method)**

	Standard mix	Actual mix	Variance (treatments)	Profit per treatment ($)	Weighted average profit ($)	Difference	Variance ($)
Standard	196	180	16 (A)	5	5.60	0.60 (A)	9.60 (F)
Deluxe	294	310	16 (F)	6	5.60	0.40 (F)	6.40 (F)
Total	490	490					16.00 (F)

The Standard variance is favourable overall because, although the company sold less of that treatment than the standard mix, this is the less profitable treatment.

This perhaps explains the superiority of the weighted average method overall. Overall we have sold more of the more profitable treatment and less of the least profitable treatment so that it can be argued that both variances are in the company's favour and should be favourable.

Test your understanding 2

(a) **Traditional variances**

Actual quantity × Actual price =	$41,500	
Price variance		$2,500 F
Actual quantity × Standard price = (11,000 × $4)	$44,000	
Usage variance		$4,800 A
Standard quantity × Standard price = (1,400 × 7 × $4)	$39,200	

(b) **Planning variances**

	$
Original standard quantity × Original standard price (1,400 × 7 × $4)	39,200
Revised standard quantity × Revised standard price (1,400 × 8 × $3.80)	42,560
Planning variance	$3,360 A

Operational variances

AQ × AP =	$41,500	
Price variance		$300 F
AQ × RSP = (11,000 × $3.80)	$41,800	
Usage variance		$760 F
RSQ × RSP = (1,400 × 8 × $3.80)	$42,560	

Test your understanding 3

Conventional approach

					$	
SHSR						
5 hrs/unit x 250 units	x	$10/hr	=	12,500		Efficiency
AHSR						$2,000 A ✓
1,450 hrs	x	$10/hr	=	14,500		
AHAR						$1,450 F ✓
			=	13,050		Rate

Planning and operational approach

Planning variance

Efficiency   (5 hrs/unit − 6 hrs/unit) x 250 units x $10/hr $2,500 A

Operational variances

					$	
SHSR						
6 hrs/unit x 250 units	x	$10/hr	=	15,000		Efficiency
AHSR						$500 F
1,450 hrs	x	$10/hr	=	14,500		
AHAR						$1,450 F
			=	13,050		Rate

Test your understanding 4

D $39,500

	$
Standard contribution on actual sales	44,000
Add: Favourable sales price variance	2,000
Less: Adverse total variable costs variance	(6,500)
Actual contribution	$39,500

Test your understanding 5

(a) Budgeted and actual profits

Budget	Kitchens $m	Bathrooms $m	Total $m
Sales	40	14	54
Direct costs	(22)	(6)	(28)
Central services	(10)	(5)	(15)
Budgeted profit	8	3	11

Actual	Kitchens $m	Bathrooms $m	Total $m
Sales	33.8	15.25	49.05
Direct costs	(20.8)	(6.75)	(27.55)
Central services	(6.5)	(6.25)	(17.50)
Actual profit	6.5	2.25	4.00

(b) Sales variances

Sales price variance	Kitchens $000	Bathrooms $000	Total $000
Standard sales price	10	7.0	
Actual sales price	13	6.1	
Variance	3 F	0.9 A	
Actual sales quantity	× 2,600	× 2,500	
Sales price variance	7,800 F	2,250 A	5,550 F

Sales mix profit variances

	Standard mix	Actual mix	Variance (units)	Profit per unit ($)	Variance ($m)
Kitchens	3,400	2,600	800 (A)	$2,000	1.60 (A)
Bathrooms	1,700	2,500	800 (F)	$1,500	1.20 (F)
Total	5,100	5,100			0.40 (A)

Sales quantity profit variances

Sales quantity variance = (actual sales quantity – budgeted sales quantity) × weighted average margin

Sales quantity variance = (5,100 – 6,000) × ((3,400/5,100 × $2,000) + (1,700/5,100 × $1,500))

Sales quantity variance = $1,650,000 A

Alternative method:

	Standard mix	Budgeted Sales	Variance (units)	Profit per unit ($)	Variance ($m)
Kitchens	3,400	4,000	600 (A)	$2,000	1.20 (A)
Bathrooms	1,700	2,000	300 (A)	$1,500	0.45 (A)
Total	5,100	6,000			1.65 (A)

Check

Sales volume variances

Kitchens	(4,000 – 2,600) × $2,000 = $2.8m A
Bathrooms	(2,000 – 2,500) × $1,500 = $0.75m F

Total $2.05m

Sales volume variance = mix variance + quantity variance

= $0.4m A + $1.65m A = $2.05 m

(c) **Reconciliation of profits**

		$m
Budgeted profit (from part a)		11

	Favourable ($m)	Adverse ($m)
Sales price variances (from part b)		
– kitchens	7.80	
– bathrooms		2.25
Sales mix variance (from part b)		
– kitchens		1.60
– bathrooms	1.20	
Sales quantity variance (from part b)		
– kitchens		1.20
– bathrooms		0.45
Direct costs (W1)		
– kitchens		6.50
– bathrooms	0.75	
Central services (W2)		
– volume (kitchens)		3.50
– volume (bathrooms)	1.25	
– expenditure		2.50
	11.00	18.00

	7 A
Actual profit (from part a)	4

Workings

(W1) **Direct cost variances:**

Kitchens 2,600 × (5,500 – 8,000) = $6.5m A

Bathrooms 2,500 × (3,000 – 2,700) = $0.75m F

(W2) **Central services volume variances:**

Kitchens (4,000 – 2,600) × $2,500 = $3.5m A

Bathrooms (2,500 – 2,000) × $2,500 = $1.25m F

Central services expenditure variance = $15m – $17.5m = $2.5m A

(d) **Performance of the company for the year**

(Actual profit at $4m is $7m below budgeted profit, a shortfall of 64%). The main causes are as follows:

– an overall fall in the total volume of sales resulting in a sales quantity variance of $1.65m A. The lower than expected volume has also resulted in central services costs being under absorbed as shown by the volume variances (net impact $2.25A).

– the sales mix has also switched from more profitable kitchens to less profitable bathrooms and this is reflected in the sales mix variance of $0.4m A.

– the impact of the lower volume of kitchen sales has been partially offset by the favourable price variance for kitchens. It is possible that a higher proportion of jobs are of the highly customised category rather than the 'off the shelf' packages. This has led to higher average prices being charged but also higher direct costs being incurred. The opposite seems to have occurred with bathrooms.

– Central services costs have exceeded budget by $2.5m. This may be due to higher costs incurred designing customised jobs.

It would be worth investigating whether the extra price charged for customised designs is covering all of the additional costs incurred. Higher prices may be necessary or better control of costs.

Tutorial note: For part (a): The information given in the question suggests that an OAR of $2,500 per job is used to absorb central services costs. This means that there is under absorbed central services cost of 17.5 – 6.5 – 6.25 = $4.75m. There is no indication that this is charged to the other divisions, but total costs must be shown to arrive at total profit.

Test your understanding 6

Operating statement for ATS

		$	$
Original budgeted contribution	1,200 × $26		31,200
Sales volume contribution variance	(1,000 – 1,200) × $26		5,200 A
			———
Budgeted contribution on actual sales			26,000

Planning variances

		$	$
Sales price	($110 – $130) × 1,000	20,000 F ✓	
Material price	($3 – $4.50) × 8 × 1,000	12,000 A	
			8,000 F
			———
Revised contribution on actual sales			34,000

Operational variances

		$	$
Sales price	($130 – $135) × 1,000	5,000 F	
Material price	($4.50 – $4) × 7,800	3,900 F	
Material usage	(8,000 – 7,800) × $4.50	900 F	
Labour rate	($10 – $10.40) × 6,250	2,500 A	
Labour efficiency	(6,000 – 6,250) × $10	2,500 A	
		———	
		4,800 F	
		———	
Actual contribution		38,800	
		———	

Test your understanding 7

In this example, since the change in both the material usage and material price are inter-related, the total planning variance only is reported in the operating statement below.

	$	
Budgeted profit	18,000	
Budgeted fixed costs	30,000	
Budgeted contribution	48,000	
Planning variance	16,800	(A)
Revised budgeted contribution	31,200	
Sales volume contribution variance	9,600	(F)
	40,800	
Operational variances		
Sales price	5,000	(A)
Materials usage	900	(A)
Direct labour rate	750	(A)
Direct labour efficiency	1,800	(A)
Actual contribution	32,350	
Budgeted fixed costs	30,000	
Fixed cost expenditure variance	2,000	(A)
Actual profit	350	

Operational variances

Materials price	$	
12,300 kilos should cost (× $3)	36,900	
They did cost	36,900	
Direct materials price variance	0	

Materials usage	*Kilos*	
2,400 units of product should use (× 5 kilos)	12,000	
They did use	12,300	
Direct materials usage variance (in kilos)	300	(A)
Standard price per kilo (ex post)	$3	
Direct materials usage variance	$900	(A)

Labour rate	$	
7,500 hours should cost (× $6)	45,000	
They did cost	45,750	
	———	
Direct labour rate variance	750	(A)
	———	

Labour efficiency	Hours	
2,400 units of product should take (× 3 hours)	7,200	
They did take	7,500	
Direct labour efficiency variance (in hours)	300	(A)
Standard rate per hour	$6	
	———	
Direct labour efficiency variance	$1,800	(A)
	———	

Sales price	$	
2,400 units should sell for (× $50)	120,000	
They did sell for	115,000	
	———	
Sales price variance	5,000	(A)
	———	

Fixed overhead expenditure	$	
Budgeted fixed costs	30,000	
Actual fixed costs	32,000	
	———	
Fixed cost expenditure variance	2,000	(A)
	———	

Sales volume	Units	
Budgeted sales	2,000	
Actual sales	2,400	
	———	
Sales volume variance (in units)	400	(F)
	———	
Standard contribution per unit	$24	
Sales volume contribution variance	$9,600	(F)
	———	

Planning variances

Material costs	$/unit
Ex ante standard per unit (4 kilos × $2)	8.0
Ex post standard per unit (5 kilos × $3)	15.0
	———
Planning variance per unit	7.0 (A)
Actual units produced	× 2,400
	———
Total planning variance	$16,800 (A)
	———

Test your understanding 8

(a)   This is a 'backwards' question. Rather than calculating the variances ourselves, we have been given some of them. We have to find some other information which is missing. We will use the variances to work backwards to find that missing information.

The starting point is usually to find a variance which mentions the missing information, i.e. for part (a) we are asked for the actual output. We need to find a variance which mentions the actual output somewhere along the line.

One set of variances which would work are the material variances. The first line of the format is SQSP, where SQ is the standard quantity of the **actual output.**

We plug in the information that we know, and we can then work backwards to find the missing information.

Material variances

				$		
SQSP						
2 kg/unit x ? units	x	$3/kg	=	?	}	Usage $1,380 A
AQSP						
? kg	x	$3/kg	=	?	}	
AQAP						$1,012 A
? kg	x	$?/kg	=	16,192	}	Price

We know that AQAP is 16,192 and we know that the price variance is 1,012 A, so we can work backwards to find AQSP.

AQSP = 16,192 - 1,012 = 15,180

Material variances

				$		
SQSP						
2 kg/unit x ? units	x	$3/kg	=	?	}	Usage $1,380 A
AQSP						
? kg	x	$3/kg	=	15,180 Bal 1	}	
AQAP						$1,012 A
? kg	x	$?/kg	=	16,192	}	Price

Now, we know AQSP is 15,180 and the usage variance is 1,380 A, so we can work backwards to find SQSP.

SQSP = 15,180 - 1380 A = 13,800

Material variances

						$		
SQSP								
2 kg/unit x ? units	x	$3/kg	=	13,800$^{Bal\ 2}$			}	Usage $1,380 A
AQSP								
? kg	x	$3/kg	=	15,180$^{Bal\ 1}$				
AQAP								$1,012 A
? kg	x	$?/kg	=	16,192				Price

Finally, for the first line, we know SQSP, i.e. we know 2 kg x something x $3/kg = 13,800. We can work backwards to find the actual output.

Actual output = 13,800 ÷ 2kg ÷ $3/kg = 2,300 units

Material variances

					$		
SQSP							
2 kg/unit x 2,300 $^{Bal\ 3}$ units	x	$3/kg	=	13,800$^{Bal\ 2}$		}	Usage $1,380 A
AQSP							
? kg	x	$3/kg	=	15,180$^{Bal\ 1}$			
AQAP							$1,012 A
? kg	x	$?/kg	=	16,192			Price

(b) We have already worked out a lot of the figures that we need for the material variances. We can carry on from where we left off in part (a).

Material variances

					$		
SQSP							
2 kg/unit x 2,300 $^{Bal\ 3}$ units	x	$3/kg	=	13,800 $^{Bal\ 2}$		}	Usage $1,380 A
AQSP							
? kg	x	$3/kg	=	15,180$^{Bal\ 1}$			
AQAP							$1,012 A
? kg	x	$?/kg	=	16,192			Price

For the second line, we know AQSP = 15,180, i.e. we know that AQ x 3 = 15,180.

Actual quantity = 15,180 ÷ 3 = 5,060 kg

AQ appears on both the second line and the third line, so we can write 5,060 kg on both lines.

Material variances

					$		
SQSP							
2 kg/unit x 2,300 $^{Bal\ 3}$ units	x	$3/kg	=	13,800 $^{Bal\ 2}$		}	Usage $1,380 A
AQSP							
5,060 $^{Bal\ 4}$ kg	x	$3/kg	=	15,180 $^{Bal\ 1}$			
AQAP	⇓						$1,012 A
5,060 $^{Bal\ 4}$ kg	x	$?/kg	=	16,192			Price

Finally for the third line, AQAP = 5,060 Kg x something = 16,192

Actual price = 16,192 ÷ 5,060 = $3.20 per kg.

Material variances

					$		
SQSP							
2 kg/unit x 2,300 $^{Bal\ 3}$ units	x	$3/kg	=	13,800 $^{Bal\ 2}$		}	Usage $1,380 A
AQSP							
5,060 $^{Bal\ 4}$ kg	x	$3/kg	=	15,180 $^{Bal\ 1}$			
AQAP	⇓						$1,012 A
5,060 $^{Bal\ 4}$ kg	x	$3.20/kg$^{Bal\ 5}$	=	16,192			Price

(c) **Labour variances**

				$	
SHSR					
3 hrs/unit x 2,300 units	x	$8/hr	=	55,200	Efficiency $3,680 F
AHSR					
? hrs	x	$8/hr	=	?	$920 A Rate
AHAR					
? hrs	x	$?/hr	=	52,440	

To find out the labour hours we can use the labour variances format. We can find AHSR by subtracting the efficiency variance of 3,680 F from SHSR to get 51,520 or by adding the adverse rate variance of 920 to AHAR.

Once we know that AHSR is $51,520, we know that something x $8/hr = $51,520.

Actual hours = 51,520 ÷ 8 = 6,440 hours

Labour variances

				$	
SHSR					
3 hrs/unit x 2,300 units	x	$8/hr	=	55,200	Efficiency $3,680 F
AHSR					
6,440 $^{Bal 2}$ hrs	x	$8/hr	=	51,520 $^{Bal 1}$	$920 A rate
AHAR					
? hrs	x	$?/hr	=	52,440	

(d) **Fixed overhead volume variance**

	Units
Budgeted output	2,000
Actual output	2,300
	300 F
× Standard fixed overhead cost per unit	×12
	$3,600 F

(e) **Fixed overhead expenditure variance**

	$
Budgeted output	24,000
Actual output	23,500
	500 F

(f) **Sales volume profit variance**

	Units
Actual sales	2,300
Budgeted sales	1,900
	400 F
× Standard profit per unit	×12
=	$4,800 F

The profit margin is 20% of selling price. A profit margin of 20% is the same as a mark-up of 25%. Thus we know standard cost to be $48 per unit, standard profit must be 25% of that, must be $12 per unit.

(g) **Selling price variance**

	$
Actual selling price	57
Standard selling price	60
	3 A
× Actual no of units sold	× 2,300
=	6,900 A

We know that standard cost is $48 per unit and we the standard profit (from part (f)) is $12. Therefore standard selling price = $48 + $12 = $60.

(h) Budgeted profit = 1,900 units × $12 per unit = $22,800.

(i)

		$	$
Sales	2,300 units × $57		131,000
Direct material		16,192	
Direct labour		52,440	
Variable overhead		14,168	
Fixed overhead		23,500	
			106,300
Actual profit			24,800

Test your understanding 9

Key answer tips

This is a very good test of the depth of your knowledge of variances. The basic technique is to set out your normal computations of the variances, putting in the figures you know and working back to those you don't. Often the results from one will be needed in another, so do all the related variances together.

(a) (i)   Budgeted fixed overhead cost/mile

$$= \frac{(\$15,600 + \$400)}{200,000} = \$0.08/\text{mile}$$

Volume variance	= $1,760 (A)
Volume difference	= $1,760 ÷ $0.08
	= 22,000 miles (A)
	= 200,000 – 22,000
	178,000

(ii)

$$\text{Standard rate/hr} = \frac{\$0.08}{0.02}$$

Rate variance	= $4/hour
	= $1,086 (F)
	= $1,086 / 3,620 = $0.30/hr (F)
Actual rate	$4.00 – $0.30 = $3.70/hr

(iii)

$$\text{Standard price/litre} = \frac{\$0.04}{0.1}$$

	= $0.40/litre
Actual price/litre	= $0.42/litre
Price variance/litre	= $0.02 (A)
Total price variance	= $420 (A)
Actual number of litres =	$\frac{\$420}{\$0.02}$ = 21,000

(iv) Variable overhead variances

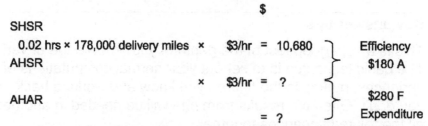

We know all the above infor mation, but are trying to find the missing information represented by question marks. In particular we are trying to find the bottom question mark, the actual hours at the actual rate, i.e. the actual variable overhead expenditure. We can do this in one step or two. Taking it in two steps, we can find the middle question mark:

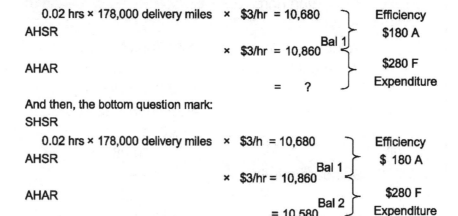

And then, the bottom question mark:

SHSR

    0.02 hrs × 178,000 delivery miles × $3/h = 10,680   Efficiency

AHSR $ 180 A

                               Bal 1

                × $3/hr = 10,860

AHAR $280 F

                        Bal 2

                  = 10,580   Expenditure

The actual variable overhead expenditure is $10,580´

(b)   Two possible causes of an adverse fuel usage variance are:

(i)   Spillage of fuel occurred on filling vehicle fuel tanks.

(ii)   Vehicles are in need of servicing and as a result fuel usage is excessive.

(c) **To:** Transport Operations Manager

From: Management Accountant

Date: XX – XX – XX

Subject: Standard costs

Introduction

This report explains the type of standard cost which may be set and importance of keeping standards meaningful and relevant.

Types of standard

A standard cost is a prediction of the cost per unit expected in a future period. It is dependent on estimates of resource requirements per output unit and the price to be paid per resource unit.

There are four types of standard which may be set and these are often referred to as:

- current standard

- basic standard

- attainable standard; and

- ideal standard.

The current standard uses existing efficiency and achievement levels as the standard for the future period. This does not encourage improvement and may also allow existing inefficiencies to continue unnoticed.

The basic standard is a long-term standard which remains unchanged over a period of years. Their sole use is to show trends over time and so are not used to highlight current efficiency and not as useful as other standards. These standards may demotivate employees if, over time, they become too easy to achieve and employees start to feel bored and unchallenged.

The attainable standard sets a target which requires improvements in performance if it is to be achieved, but these are small and are considered to be achievable (or attainable). This form of standard is believed to be the best motivator to a manager.

The ideal standard assumes a perfect working environment (which never exists for a prolonged period). This is impossible to achieve.

Keeping standards useful

Standards are useful as a basis for performance evaluation. If such comparisons are to be valid the standard must reflect the current method of working AND resource prices which are realistic. If standards are not kept up to date they are no longer meaningful and thus their usefulness is reduced.

Conclusion

I recommend that attainable standards should be used, and that they should be reviewed regularly. Please contact me if you wish to discuss this further.

Test your understanding 10

A performance reporting and management control system depends on both reliable planning as well as control over operating activities.

Some planning variances might be caused by factors that could not have been foreseen in advance. However, some planning variances might be caused by weaknesses in the planning process. If so, they can be significant and indicate the need for better planning procedures in the future.

Test your understanding 11

Correct solution is A.

Statement (3) is not correct. Managers should only be appraised on what they can control, i.e. on the operational variances for sales.

Preparing budgets

Chapter learning objectives

Lead outcome	Component outcome	
B1. Distinguish between the different rationales for budgeting	(a)	Explain the role of budgets
	(b)	Distinguish between the different rationales for budgeting
B2. Prepare budgets	(b)	Prepare master budgets
	(c)	Conduct what-if analysis in budgeting
	(d)	Describe the technologies available for improving budgeting
D1: Apply basic risk management tools in the short term	(b)	Apply basic sensitivity analysis to budgeting and short term decision making.

1 Chapter overview diagram

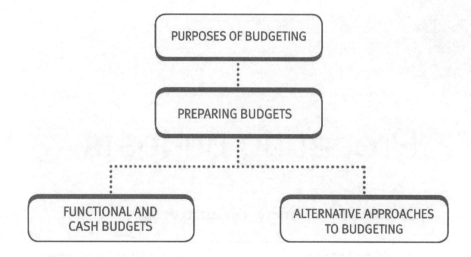

2 Budget

A quantitative or financial plan relating to the future. It can be for the company as a whole or for departments or functions or products or for resources such as cash, materials, labour, etc. It is usually for one year or less.

3 Purposes of budgeting

Budgets have several different purposes:

(1) planning

(2) control and evaluation

(3) co-ordination

(4) communication

(5) motivation

(6) authorisation

Purposes of budgets explained

Budgets have several different purposes:

(1) **Planning**

Budgets compel planning. The budgeting process forces management to look ahead, set targets, anticipate problems and give the organisation purpose and direction. Without the annual budgeting process the pressures of day-to-day operational problems may tempt managers not to plan for future operations. The budgeting process encourages managers to anticipate problems before they arise, and hasty decisions that are made on the spur of the moment, based on expediency rather than reasoned judgements, will be minimised. Corporate planners would regard budgeting as an important technique whereby long-term strategies are converted into shorter-term action plans.

(2) **Control and evaluation**

The budget provides the plan against which actual results can be compared. Those results which are out-of-line with the budget can be further investigated and corrected. The performance of a manager is often evaluated by measuring their success in achieving their budgets. The budget might quite possibly be the only quantitative reference point available.

(3) **Co-ordination**

The budget serves as a vehicle through which the actions of the different parts of an organisation can be brought together and reconciled into a common plan. Without any guidance managers may each make their own decisions believing that they are working in the best interests of the organisation. A sound budgeting system helps to co-ordinate the different activities of the business and to ensure that they are in harmony with each other.

(4) **Communication**

Budgets communicate targets to managers. Through the budget, top management communicates its expectations to lower-level management so that all members of the organisation may understand these expectations and can co-ordinate their activities to attain them.

(5) **Motivation**

The budget can be a useful device for influencing managerial behaviour and motivating managers to perform in line with the organisational objectives.

(6) **Authorisation**

A budget may act as formal authorisation to a manager for expenditure, the hiring of staff and the pursuit of the plans contained in the budget.

Advantages and disadvantages of budgeting

Advantages	Disadvantages
• budgets ensure that the organisation's actions are matched to the organisation's goals and that these goals are communicated throughout the organisation	• preparing budgets can be time consuming for staff and management and may distract from the business' core operations
• creating a budget forces management to consider the future and how the business' environment (both internally and externally) might change	• predicting future changes is very subjective and relies on the ability of the preparer of the budget to make these predictions as accurately as possible
• it means that organisations are better placed to cope with change and can act as an early warning system for problems	• budgets can create conflicts and barriers between budget holders rather than knowledge sharing and coordination
• budgets force management to consider the cost and profitability of products, departments, functions etc.	• the use of budgets can encourage short-termism where, for example, discretionary expenditure such as staff training is reduced in order to meet budget targets
• this in turn can force management to consider the value added by these products, departments or functions	• budgets focus on financial outcomes rather than broader measures of success such as customer satisfaction, quality etc.
• budgets improve decisions on resource and cash allocation, financing and investment	• budgets can encourage managers to spend what is in the budget, even if it is not necessary, to guard against reductions to next year's budget.
• having budgets facilitates performance evaluation in areas such as the use of variance analysis	• using budgets can deter innovation and enterprise as staff become focused on meeting the targets rather than exceeding them or responding to changing market needs

Difficulties in budgeting for global companies

Many organisations will operate across many countries and continents. This can make the budgeting process more difficult as these organisations will be facing a high level of diversity in these markets in areas such as:

Area of diversity	Complexity in budgeting
Currency	Although dealing in multiple currencies can easily be accommodated by most budgeting systems, the problem lies in that currencies are not stable and are instead likely to fluctuate regularly. It means that targets set in one currency will be constantly moving when converted to another currency. It will also mean that a business unit that has reported performance in its local currency may see that it's performance is viewed very differently when the results are translated back to the 'home' or central currency.
Legal framework	Plans will have to be adjusted for different laws and regulations relevant to the location of the business unit. It may mean, for example, that sources of supply have to be changed if some components must be sourced locally (which may, in turn, impact on product quality) or that staff training and welfare must be changed to reflect local rules and customs. This makes it much more difficult to have central rules and policies that apply across the global organisation and may even result in greater conflict between business units if each one is treated differently.
Customer tastes and competitor actions	Differences in taste in culture can force organisations to adapt products and services. This can require different types of materials and labour, for example, meaning that more localised targets and standards are required, adding further complexity to the budgeting system. Likewise, local competitors will compete in different ways such as having different pricing and promotional strategies. It means that the budgeting system may have be further decentralised in order to allow local business unit managers the ability to react to this. But this can lead to a lack of consistency across the organisation if, say, one local manager decides to pursue a strategy of under-cutting rivals on price whilst a manager in a different location, facing different competitors, decides to offer enhanced services and quality.

Political climate	Business units operating in different countries will be dealing with different governments. They therefore might experience different levels of political 'interference'. Governments can have policies and laws on what type of labour can be used, how much labour should be paid, what goods can be brought into or out of the country, etc. This therefore can require further decentralisation of the budgeting process and adds further layers of complexity for budget prepares and evaluators.

Example 1

Which of the following is NOT a purpose of setting budgets?

A   To help co-ordinate the different activities of the business

Ⓑ   To prevent adverse variances from arising

C   To motivate managers

D   To encourage managers to look ahead and anticipate problems

4   Functional budgets and the master budget

A **master budget** for the entire organisation brings together the departmental or activity budgets for all the departments or responsibility centres within the organisation.

The structure of a budget depends on the nature of the organisation and its operations. In a manufacturing organisation, the budgeting process will probably consist of preparing several **functional budgets**, beginning with a sales budget. All budgets will be prepared for the same budget period.

The budget period

Before preparing a budget, the organisation should decide the budget period.

The **budget period** is the time for which the budget is prepared. This is typically 1 year which reflects the fact that the financial reports for most organisations cover 1 year periods. But a budget can be for any length of time that suits management purposes.

The budget period must not be too short otherwise too much time is spent in regularly preparing the budget and evaluating performance against the budget. But it also should not be too long as things are likely to change more over longer periods which means the budget becomes out of date and also evaluation happens less often as is less useful as targets are less relevant.

Principal budget factor

When a key resource is in short supply and affects the planning decisions, it is known as the **principal budget factor** or **limiting budget factor.**

It is usually assumed in budgeting that sales demand will be the key factor setting a limit to what the organisation can expect to achieve in the budget period.

When the principal budget factor has been determined this should be the starting point for all other budgets.

Other limiting factors
In most organisations the principal budget factor is sales demand: a company is usually restricted from making and selling more of its products because there would be no sales demand for the increased output at a price which would be acceptable and/or profitable to the company.
Occasionally, however, there might be a shortage of a resource, such as cash, raw material supplies, skilled labour or equipment. If a resource is in restricted supply, and the shortage cannot be overcome, the budget for the period should be determined by how to make the best use of this limited resource, rather than by sales demand.
Principles such as linear programming, limiting factor analysis and throughput accounting could then be used to determine production plans. These will be investigated in later chapters.

Budget preparation

These stages in budgeting are illustrated in the following diagram:

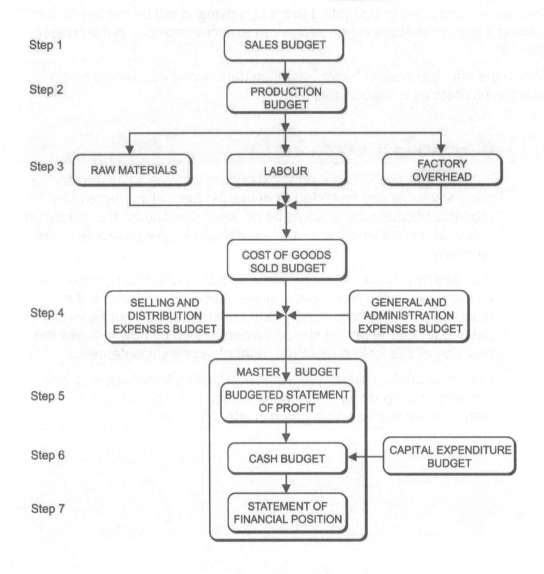

Explanation of each budget

You can see from this that the principal budget factor is the starting point in the process. It is generally sales, as shown in the diagram.

Step 1: The sales budget considers how many units can be sold.

Step 2: The production budget considers how many units must be produced to meet the budgeted sales level.

Note: The difference between the sales and the production budgets is the inventory of finished goods:

	Units
Sales budget	X
Add closing inventory finished goods	X
Less opening inventory finished goods	(X)
Production budget	X

An additional point to note here is with regards to wastage/loss of finished goods. This may be due to items rejected as inferior by quality control, items damaged in the warehouse or theft, for example. Where there is such loss, the production budget would need to be adjusted to account for this, as follows:

	Units
Sales budget	X
Add closing inventory finished goods	X
Less opening inventory finished goods	(X)
Good/fault free production required	X
Faulty production/wastage	X
Total production	X

Step 3: The material, labour and overhead budgets can be established, based on the production budget.

Note: The material budget is generally calculated in two parts, firstly the quantity of material required in production, then the quantity of material required to be purchased. The difference between these will be the inventory of raw materials:

	Quantity
Material required in production	X
(e.g. production budget (units) × kgs per unit)	
Add closing inventory raw materials	X
Less opening inventory raw materials	(X)
Materials purchases budget	X

As with the production budget in step 2 above, there may also be material losses during the production process itself. This 'wastage' may be due to such things as evaporation, faulty materials supplied or materials damaged during the process. This loss will need to be adjusted for in the materials usage budget, as follows:

	Quantity
Material required in production	X
(e.g. production budget (units) × kgs per unit)	
Wastage	X
Total material requirement	X
Add closing inventory raw materials	X
Less opening inventory raw materials	(X)
Materials purchases budget	X

Step 4: Non-production budgets. Budgets for non-production costs, such as selling and distribution costs, must also be considered.

Steps 5, 6 and 7: The master budget, comprising the statement of profit or loss, cash budget and statement of financial position can be pulled together from the individual budgets.

More specifics on each budget:

- **Sales budget.** Budget for future sales, expressed in revenue terms and possibly also in units of sale. The budget for the organisation as a whole might combine the sales budgets of several sales regions.

- **Production budget.** A production budget follows on from the sales budget, since production quantities are determined by sales volume. The production volume will differ from sales volume by the amount of any planned increase or decrease in inventories of finished goods (and work-in-progress).

In order to express the production budget in financial terms (production cost), subsidiary budgets must be prepared for materials, labour and production overheads. Several departmental managers could be involved in preparing these subsidiary budgets.

- **Direct materials usage budget.** This is a budget for the quantities and cost of the materials required for the planned production quantities.

- **Materials purchases budget.** This is a budget for the cost of the materials to be purchased in the period. The purchase cost of direct materials will differ from the material usage budget if there is a planned increase or decrease in direct materials inventory. The purchases budget should also include the purchase costs of indirect materials.

- **Direct labour budget**. This is a budget of the direct labour costs of production. If direct labour is a variable cost, it is calculated by multiplying the production quantities (in units) by the budgeted direct labour cost per unit produced. If there is expected to be any idle time, then this will need to be incorporated into the budgeted labour hours for the period. If direct labour is a fixed cost, it can be calculated by estimating the payroll cost.

- **Production overheads.** Budgets can be produced for production overhead costs. Where a system of absorption costing is used, overheads are allocated and apportioned, and budgeted absorption rates are determined.

- **Administration and sales and distribution overheads.** Other overhead costs should be budgeted.

- **Budgeted statement of profit or loss, cash budget and balance sheet.** Having prepared budgets for sales and costs, the master budget can be summarised as a statement of profit or loss for the period, a cash budget and a balance sheet (or statement of financial position) as at the end of the budget period.

If the budgeted profit, cash position or balance sheet are unsatisfactory, the functional budgets should be revised until a satisfactory planned outcome is achieved

Illustration 1

Toys Ltd budgets to sell 10,000 play cubes at $10 per cube in the following month.

Inventory of finished cubes was 3,000 cubes at the start of the month and was budgeted to be 4,000 cubes at the end of the month.

Each cube requires 0.5kg of raw material that costs $1 per kg. Opening inventory of raw material was 1,000 kg at the start of the month and is budgeted to reduce by 25% at the end of the month.

Each cube requires 0.25 hours of direct labour, which is paid at a rate of $12 per hour.

Required:

Prepare the budgets for sales, production, materials usage, materials purchases and labour.

Step 1: Sales budget

The sales budget has already been provided, which is 10,000 units.

Step 2: Production budget

	Units
Sales budget	10,000
Add closing inventory finished goods	4,000
Less opening inventory finished goods	(3,000)
Production budget	11,000

Step 3: Materials and labour budgets

Materials usage budget = production in units × quantity per unit

$$= 11,000 \text{ units} \times 0.5 \text{ kg per unit}$$

$$= 5,500 \text{ kg}$$

Materials purchase budget needs to take into account the opening and closing raw materials, as follows:

	Kg
Material required in production	5,500
Add closing inventory raw materials	750 (W1)
Less opening inventory raw materials	(1,000)
Materials purchases budget	5,250

(W1) Closing inventory is 25% less than opening inventory. This will therefore be 1,000 kg × (1 – 25%) = 750 kg.

Each kg costs $1 and so the materials purchase budget in $ will be $5,250.

Labour budget:

To calculate the cost of labour we have to return to the production budget, as the cost of labour is determined by the level of production.

Number of labour hours required for production of 11,000 units = 11,000 units × 0.25 hours per unit = 2,750 hours.

Cost of direct labour = 2,750 hours × $12 = $33,000.

Example 2

What is the formula to calculate the production budget?

A   Sales budget + opening inventory – closing inventory

B   Sales budget – opening inventory + closing inventory

C   Sales budget – opening inventory – closing inventory

D   Sales budget + opening inventory + closing inventory

Example 3

A business manufactures a single product and is preparing its production budget for the year ahead. It is estimated that 100,000 units of the product can be sold in the year and the opening inventory is currently 14,000 units. The inventory level is to be reduced by 40% by the end of the year.

Calculate the production budget.

Example 4

A business is preparing its budget for the forthcoming period. The following information is known:

Budgeted sales	2,300 units
Current inventory of finished goods	400 units
Required inventory of finished goods	500 units

Each unit of the product uses 6 kg of material X and details of this are as follows:

Current inventory of X	2,000 kg
Required closing inventory of X	2,600 kg

Calculate the materials purchases budget, in kgs.

Example 5

A company has a budget for two products Alpha and Beta as follows:

	Alpha	Beta
Sales (units)	450	600
Production (units)	500	710
Labour:		
Skilled at $20 per hour	3 hrs/unit	4 hrs/unit
Semi-skilled at $12 per hour	4.5 hrs/unit	6 hrs/unit

Calculate the budgeted cost for skilled labour for the period.

Example 6

Newton manufactures three products; the expected sales for each product are shown below.

	Product 1	Product 2	Product 3
Sales in units	3,000	4,500	3,000

Opening inventory is expected to be:

Product 1	500 units
Product 2	700 units
Product 3	500 units

Management have stated their desire to reduce inventory levels and closing inventories are budgeted as:

Product 1	200 units
Product 2	300 units
Product 3	300 units

Three types of material are used in varying amounts in the manufacture of the three products. Material requirements per unit are shown below:

	Product 1	Product 2	Product 3
Material M1	2 kg	3 kg	4 kg
Material M2	3 kg	3 kg	4 kg
Material M3	6 kg	2 kg	4 kg

The opening inventory of material is expected to be:

Material M1	4,300 kg
Material M2	3,700 kg
Material M3	4,400 kg

Management are keen to reduce inventory levels for materials as well and closing inventories are to be much lower. Expected levels are shown below:

Material M1	2,200 kg
Material M2	1,300 kg
Material M3	2,000 kg

Material prices are expected to be 10% higher than this year and current prices are $1.10/kg for material M1, $3.00/kg for material M2 and $2.50/kg for material M3.

Two types of labour are used in producing the three products. Standard hours per unit are shown below:

	Product 1	Product 2	Product 3
Skilled labour	3	1	3
Semi-skilled labour	3	3	4

Skilled labour are to be paid at the rate of $6/hour and semi-skilled labour at the rate of $4/hour.

Required:

Prepare budgets for:

(a) production (in quantity)

(b) materials usage (in quantity)

(c) materials purchases (in quantity and value)

(d) labour (in hours and value).

Cash budgets and cash flow forecasts

 A **cash forecast** is an estimate of cash receipts and payments for a future period under existing conditions.

A **cash budget** is a commitment to a plan for cash receipts and payments for a future period after taking any action necessary to bring the forecast into line with the overall business plan.

Cash budgets are used to:

- assess and integrate operating budgets
- plan for cash shortages and surpluses
- compare with actual spending.

There are two different techniques that can be used to create a cash budget:

- a receipts and payments forecast
- a balance sheet forecast.

Receipts and payments forecast

This is a forecast of cash receipts and payments based on predictions of sales and cost of sales and the timings of the cash flows relating to these items.

Preparing forecasts from planned receipts and payments

Every type of cash inflow and receipt, along with their timings, must be forecast. Note that cash receipts and payments differ from sales and cost of sales in the statement of profit or loss because:

- not all cash receipts or payments affect the statement of profit or loss, e.g. the issue of new shares or the purchase of a non-current asset

- some statement of profit or loss items are derived from accounting conventions and are not cash flows, e.g. depreciation or the profit/loss on the sale of a non-current asset

- the timing of cash receipts and payments does not coincide with the statement of profit or loss accounting period, e.g. a sale is recognised in the statement of profit or loss when the invoice is raised, yet the cash payment from the receivable may not be received until the following period or later

- irrecoverable debts will never be received in cash and an allowance for irrecoverable debts may not be received at all. When you are forecasting the cash receipts from customers you must remember to adjust for these items.

Tutorial note: The following approach is a comprehensive step-by-step guide to how a management accountant might go about preparing a full cash budget. Understanding this process should help you in your understanding and interpretation of cash budgets, but note that you will not be required to prepare a full cash budget in an examination.

Step 1 – Layout

There is no definitive layout that should be used for a cash budget. However, it will typically include the following:

(i)   A clear distinction between the cash receipts and cash payments for each control period. Your budget should not consist of a jumble of cash flows. It should be logically arranged with a subtotal for receipts and a subtotal for payments.

(ii)   A figure for the net cash flow for each period. It could be argued that this is not an essential feature of a cash budget. However, managers find in practice that a figure for the net cash flow helps to draw attention to the cash flow implications of their actions during the period.

(iii) The closing cash balance for each control period. The closing balance for each period will be the opening balance for the following period.

The following is a typical layout:

Month:	1	2	3	4
	$	$	$	$
Receipts (few lines)				
Sub total				
Payments (Many lines)				
Sub total				
Net cash flow				
Opening balance				
Closing balance				

Step 2 – Fill in the simple figures

Some payments need only a small amount of work to identify the correct figure and timing and can be entered straight into the proforma. These would usually include:

- wages and salaries

- fixed overhead expenses

- dividend payments

- purchase of non-current assets.

Step 3 – Work out the more complex figures

The information on sales and purchases can be more time consuming to deal with, e.g.:

- timings for both sales and purchases must be found from credit periods

- variable overheads may require information about production levels

- purchases may require calculations based on production schedules and inventory balances.

Example 7

	January $	February $	March $	April $
Sales	6,000	8,000	4,000	5,000

All sales are on credit and receivables tend to pay in the following pattern:

	%
In month of sale	10
In month after sale	40
Two months after sale	45

The organisation expects the rate of irrecoverable debts to be 5%.

Calculate the forecast cash receipts from receivables in April.

Example 8

The following details have been extracted from the payables' records of X Ltd:

	%
Invoices paid in month of purchase	30
Invoices paid in the first month after purchase	60
Invoices paid in the second month after purchase	10

Purchases for January to March are budgeted to be as follows:

January	$300,000
February	$310,000
March	$295,000

For suppliers paid in the month of purchase, a settlement discount of 3% is received.

Calculate the forecast cash payments to suppliers in March.

Interpretation of a cash budget

Examples of factors to consider when interpreting a cash budget include:

- Is the balance at the end of the period acceptable/matching expectations?
- Does the cash balance become a deficit at any time in the period?
- Is there sufficient finance (e.g. an overdraft) to cover any cash deficits? Should new sources of finance be sought in advance?
- What are the key causes of cash deficits?

- Can/should discretionary expenditure (such as asset purchases) be made in another period in order to stabilise the pattern of cash flows?

- Is there a plan for dealing with cash surpluses (such as reinvesting them elsewhere)?

- When is the best time to make discretionary expenditure?

Example 9

HT has prepared a cash budget for the first three months of the year as follows:

	January $	February $	March $
Receipts			
From sales	56,000	58,000	54,000
Payments			
Capital expenditure	–	–	30,000
For direct materials	21,000	17,500	16,500
For direct labour (30% × prod'n cost)	15,000	16,500	9,750
For fixed production overheads	2,000	2,000	2,000
For variable production overheads	13,000	10,600	8,800
For admin/selling overhead	15,000	–	–
Total outflow	66,000	46,600	67,050
Net cash flow for month	(10,000)	11,400	(13,050)
Opening balance	(5,000)	(15,000)	(3,600)
Closing balance	(15,000)	(3,600)	(16,650)

Required:

Explain the usefulness of this budget to the business and the issues that it raises.

---

5 Sensitivity analysis and stress testing budgets

Budgets are based on assumptions about the future. Each and every one of these assumptions could be wrong. It will therefore be important to test what might happen to a budget if the assumptions change.

There are various approaches to this issue and one of the most widely used is 'sensitivity analysis'.

A sensitivity analysis exercise involves revising the budget on the basis of a series of varied assumptions. **One assumption can be changed at a time** to determine the impact on the budget overall. For example, if sales quantities were to be changed the impact on profits, cash flow etc. could be observed.

When changing more than one variable at a time it may be better to use spreadsheets to simplify and speed up the process.

Example of sensitivity analysis

An organisation has a budget for the first quarter of the year as follows:

	$
Sales: 100 units @ $40 per unit	4,000
Variable costs: 100 units @ $20 per unit	(2,000)
Fixed costs	(1,500)
Profit	500

There is some uncertainty over the variable cost per unit and that cost could be anywhere between $10 and $30, with $20 as the 'expected' outcome. We are required to carry out a sensitivity analysis on this.

One approach to this would be to present the budget shown above as an 'expected' case but with two other cases as 'worst' and 'best' possible outcomes.

Worst-case budget ($30 unit variable cost)

	$
Sales: 100 units @ $40 per unit	4,000
Variable costs: 100 units @ $30 per unit	(3,000)
Fixed costs	(1,500)
Profit	(500)

Best-case budget ($10 unit variable cost)

	$
Sales: 100 units @ $40 per unit	4,000
Variable costs: 100 units @ $10 per unit	(1,000)
Fixed costs	(1,500)
Profit	1,500

Example 10

Company SL Ltd makes and sells one product, the Q, for which the budgeted cost and revenue structure is as follows:

	%
Sales revenue	100
Variable costs	45
Fixed costs	25
	───
Profit	30
	───

Latest estimates have shown that the sales price will now only be 80% of the budgeted figure.

Required:

Calculate the revised profit margin.

Example 11

A company produced a budgeted marginal costing statement based on selling 5,000 units of Product H, details showing below:

	$
Direct materials (3 kg × $20 per kg)	60
Direct labour (5 hours × $9 per hour)	45
Variable production overhead (5 hours × $3 per labour hour)	15

Final production overheads were budgeted at $60,000 and the selling price was based on a 30% mark-up on prime cost.

Managers would like to perform sensitivity analysis, to examine the effect of changes in the original budget. Note that the budgeted sales price will not be changed with changes to prime cost.

Required:

(i)   Calculate the effect on profit if direct materials are 25% more expensive than planned.

(ii) Calculate the effect on profit if employees are 20% more efficient than budgeted.

 Stress testing budgets

Stress testing a budget involves a more substantial examination of how a budget would cope under pressure from changes. It is more complex than simply changing one assumption (which is what occurs in sensitivity analysis).

A stress test examines how a budget would perform or function under severe or unexpected pressure.

For example, it may test a budget to examine the consequences of the loss of a major customer. Budgets rarely go to plan (as can be seen from our chapter on variance analysis). But if an organisation has stress tested its budgets it will be better prepared for when things go wrong and have a better idea of whether it can cope and how to react

 Illustration 2

Some organisations run stress tests drills in order to get a full understanding of their financial and strategic position. Consider the following example:

A business wants to test its ability to cope with the loss of a major customer. It has therefore placed all income from that customer in a certain month in a separate bank account that can't be accessed for normal business use. The business then continues to operate as normal but does not access these funds and when funds are required the business needs to find ways to adapt without the funds that would be available from this customer.

This will indicate whether the business could survive without this customer for a month and what stresses it might put on the business. Perhaps it had to extend its overdraft or delay the purchase of new equipment. Or the company might find that it is not happy with the interest received on the money that it placed on deposit from the customer. There may have been some positives – maybe there was a better focus on getting cash in earlier from other customers.

The stress test drill can identify new areas of efficiencies (such as in credit control over other customers) or inefficiencies (getting effective returns on cash invested). These lessons learnt can be built into budgets and plans and make the business perform better in the future by building on its successes and removing its failures during the stress test period.

Stress testing ensures that budgets and the organisation can withstand the pressures, both expected and unexpected, that are likely to be put on the business over the budget period.

The need for stress testing

Stress testing can play a strategic role. The results of a stress test can indicate why a strategy may not be successfully realised or implemented, it can identify areas of inefficiency and it can make a business more 'agile' and adaptable to changes in its business environment.

Stress testing allows risks to be quantified. Many businesses might be able to state that sales will fall if the economy were to move into a recession but a company who has stress tested its budgets for such an event would be able to say not only by how much sales would fall, but also to explain the impact on profits and cash as well as the company's plans to minimise the impact and adjust its strategies.

Stress tests may be imposed on the business by lenders. If, say, a company is borrowing money in order to finance a new project and the loan will last 10 years, a lender may want to know how the company will cope with a rise in interest rates or if the project returns are only half of what the company are expecting.

There may also be infrequent expenditure that is not accounted for in the budget. For example, if an employee leaves and has to be replaced there will be costs involved in recruitment, training and lost productivity. These are often not planned for in the budget but should be stress tested. In simple terms, the organisation can then set cash aside for these instances of infrequent and sometimes unexpected elements of expenditure rather than have all 'available' cash tied up in investments meaning that there is a short-term shortage of cash available to meet the extra burden placed on the organisation.

Stress testing is not just testing for the survival of the organisation. It may be that an organisation expects sales to increase by 40% this year and has therefore put in place an employee recruitment programme throughout the year. If sales fail to increase by 40% the company may not go out of business, but it will need to consider what to do with any staff recruited or how to delay or cancel any outstanding recruitment. Warning signs need to be identified and plans put in place for when these warning signs are triggered.

If, for example, sales fail to increase at all in the first quarter then it is unlikely that annual sales will rise by 40%. So the company could place on hold all second quarter recruitment and look for ways to redeploy any staff already recruited (which might in itself create growth elsewhere in the business).

Considering these events prior to the budget launch will allow the company to more quickly and effectively react to the stresses placed on the budget. This proactivity is much better than being reactive to changes in the organisation's environment. In choosing to outline the ways in which stresses might affect the company's position, more informed decisions can be made about where it is the company's focus should lie.

Sources of business stress

There are many sources of stress that may be placed on an organisation (both internally and externally) such as:

- technology which makes the product obsolete or uncompetitive

- changes in customer or consumer tastes

- the economy changes from a boom to a recession (or vice versa)

- rivals creating a better product or finding ways to stand out better to customers

- a cybersecurity attack

- a workforce strike

- failure of or faults in production systems.

This list is not comprehensive and every organisation will face many more risks than these. But the list should illustrate that the stresses can come from both internal and external events.

Organisations should be constantly assessing these stresses and then testing their budgets to evaluate their ability to cope with any or all of these at any point in time. Stress testing will also identify correlations between events – how, for example, changes in the strength of the economy might also impact on the relative strength of a country's currencies. The impact of both events happening concurrently might then be stress tested.

Stress testing goes beyond simple 'what-if' analysis which often focuses on changing one or two variables in the budget. Stress testing evaluates the impact of entire scenarios on an organisation. For example, a company that exports to foreign markets might assess how a change in currency movements might impact on its business. The currency fluctuations may impact on the company sales price but it may also impact on the entire domestic economy so that unemployment rates change, consumer spending levels change or inflation rates change. These would impact on a number of variables in the budget system such as sales volume, wage rates, import costs etc.

Stress testing for industries

Stress tests may even be employed to an industry as a whole rather than to or by individual companies within that industry. Every year, for example, the International Monetary Fund conducts its own stress testing of various countries banking sectors, with the aim of giving an independent overview of bank solvency. This can have many uses. For example, governments in the country might have an indication of whether financial aid is required for particular banks, whether public funds need to be better safeguarded or whether more regulation is required for banks to provide better safeguards or to implement their own stress tests.

Stress testing and software

Stress tests are usually computer-generated simulation models that test hypothetical scenarios. Major organisations will have developed their own software and systems which tailors the tests to their situations. But smaller organisations should also be stress testing their budgets even if it is using bespoke and simple software such as Excel.

The scenarios that are planned for and tested for should be plausible. Stress testing can be a complicated, time-consuming and expensive exercise. It is therefore important that risks and events are evaluated for plausibility before the stress testing process is initiated. The resources available for the testing must also be considered so that smaller organisations might only test 5 or 6 events whereas larger organisations might test up to 20 events.

In objective test questions you may have to adjust budgets for events or stresses that impact on more than one variable in the budget.

Example 12

A manufacturer is concerned about the potential loss of a major client. The manufacturer has already prepared the following budget for the year:

	$000
Revenue	480
Cost of sales	200
Other operating costs	80
	___
Net profit	200

The manufacturer wants to stress test the budget for the loss of the major customer who makes up 25% of its total sales. This customer provides a gross margin of 15% on sales.

What would be the revised budgeted profit if the customer's sales were lost?

A $182,000

B $80,000

C $110,000

D $150,000

Stress testing is actually an element of budgetary control (which is covered in more detail in a later chapter). It has, however, been covered in this chapter as it typically requires the preparation of a new budget.

6 Budget data

There are many sources of information that can be used as the basis for budgeting. If, for example, sales is the principal budget factor the following are examples of where information on expected future sales levels might come from:

- General economic data – information on changes to the economy such as expected growth in the economy or changes in consumer spending is regularly published

- Public announcements – competitors and customers may publicly announce their plans for the future which may impact on sales and pricing expectations

- Historic sales trends – these can be examined to identify patterns and changes in existing buyer habits and tastes

- Market research – all of the above can be verified through independent market research

- Business unit consultation – for organisations where budgets are set centrally, regular communication with managers of individual business unit managers may provide better insight into local conditions and expectations

A new, growing area of information for budgeting setting is in the use of big data analytics. This can supplement and enhance the data from sources such as those listed above.

 Using big data in budgeting

Big data is used to refer to the large volume of data, both structured and unstructured, that is available to organisations on a day-to-day basis. This information is often in digital form and created outside the organisation and available to everyone.

 Big data can be analysed in order to provide insights that lead to better decisions based on more informed knowledge.

Big data analytics has become the catch-all term for gathering, analysing, and using massive amounts of digital information to improve business operations. Big data analytics enable organisations to make decisions based on data instead of business instinct.

Sources of big data

Big data can come from a range of sources such as:

- Media (including social media). This involves tracking media such as press reports, podcasts and industry briefings as well as social media such as YouTube, Twitter or Facebook visits and comments etc. It is often free and easy to obtain and can quickly provide valuable insights on consumer preferences and changing trends.

- The web. Data on the web is widely available and can often have more structure (such as on sites such as Wikipedia or Investopedia). Data can be accessed quickly and there is a vast, diverse repository of information available.

- Machine generated. Machines can be programmed to gather data. For example, a household device such as Amazon Alexa might gather data on what was searched for, what media was accessed and from where, what are devices are connected etc.

- Databases. There is likely to be a wide variety of unstructured and unanalysed data within an organisations own databases on customers, suppliers, inventory etc.

Organising this data into structured and useful information can be time consuming and expensive. Many larger organisations will use specialist staff and software to perform this task.

But big data is not just useful for large businesses with high budgets set aside for its collection and analysis. There is lots of information available to organisations of any size. There are already tools built into the programs businesses use each day.

Businesses of all sizes can take advantage of the analytics available in their Twitter, Facebook and other social media accounts. For example, organisations can examine which types of posts get the most likes or retweets. Website analytics can tell which pages are most popular, how long users spent on individual pages, how many visitors returned to the website etc. Accounting software may be able to tell which days are more popular for certain types of products, which day of the week a particular customer is likely to place an order etc.

As well as (sometime expensive) specific data analytic software, many new business software applications are having built-in analytic tools, with dashboards that can pull it all together. But it should be noted that even the best technology cannot deliver benefits without the knowledge to use it properly. This is why many organisations are creating specific roles for data analytic experts.

Benefits of big data analytics for budgeting

The principal budget factor is often the sales forecast. But this can often be very subjective and due to a high degree of uncertainty. There can also be uncertainty when estimating costs and other assumptions within the budgets. It may even be that some data is not included in the budget as it is seen as being unquantifiable.

The use of big data can reduce many of these problems.

Benefits of big data

Big data can help to answer what were previously thought to be unanswerable questions such as 'what will rivals do next?', 'how will consumer tastes change?', 'why are customers switching to substitute products?' etc.

Some of the benefits of using big data include:

- Organisations can react more quickly than rivals in the marketplace giving them a competitive edge. This can be achieved by better tracking of consumer trends as well as the actions of competitors themselves.

- This, in turn, can allow organisations to be better prepared and more proactive towards expected changes in the industry.

- Tracking consumer feedback and tastes can mean that non-value adding activities or failures in systems can more easily be identified and removed.

- Customer interactions and relationship management can be improved resulting in better repeat business and customer loyalty.

- Business operations can be examined and analysed in order to find areas for streamlining and simplification resulting in cost reductions and efficiencies.

- Employees can be provided with better information and make better local and operational decisions.

- Customer needs are more readily identified meaning that new product ideas can be more easily formulated and market tested.

- Business performance can be better tracked and analysed against a wider set of criteria.

Big data and stress testing

Big data analytics can play a key role in stress testing. It can help in the following ways:

- Identify stress events

- Help quantify the effects of stress events

- Help test the validity of assumptions in measures to deal with stress

- Identify correlations for stress events

- Create and identify warning signs / triggers for stress events

Big data can reduce the uncertainty in budget estimates, validate budget assumptions, fill in the gaps for missing data, create expectations for business and environment changes and identify correlations in those changes. It will provide valuable insights and make an organisation more proactive to changes which should lead to better budgets and better decisions which will aid strategic implementation and development and generate greater success for the organisation.

Real world examples

Logistics

UPS uses telematics to improve performance. Delivery vehicles are equipped with sensors which monitor data on speed, direction, braking performance, drive train performance and other mechanical aspects of the vehicle. This information is then used to optimise maintenance schedules and improve efficiency of delivery routes saving time, money and reducing wastage.

Data from the vehicles is combined with customer data, GPS information and data concerning the normal behaviour of delivery drivers. Using this data to optimise vehicle performance and routes has resulted in several significant improvements:

- Over 15 million minutes of idling time were eliminated in one year. This saved 103,000 gallons of fuel.

- During the same year 1.7 million miles of driving was eliminated, saving 183,000 gallons of fuel.

Retail

It is widely reported that Walmart tracks data on over 60% of adults in the US. Data gathered includes online and instore purchasing patterns, Twitter interactions and trends, weather reports and major events. This data, according to the company, ensures a highly personalised customer experience. Walmart detractors criticise the company's data collection as a breach of human rights and believe the company uses the data to make judgements and conclusions on personal information such as sexual orientation, political view and even intelligence levels.

Entertainment

Netflix has 150 million users worldwide who watch 140 million hours of programmes per day. The company uses information gathered from analysis of viewing habits to inform decisions on which shows to invest in. Analysing past viewing figures and understanding viewer populations and the shows they are likely to watch allows the analysts to predict likely viewing figures before a show has even aired. This can help to determine if the show is a viable investment.

Problems in using big data

Big data analytics must overcome a number of problems, often explained by the characteristics of big data (often referred to as the 3V's):

- Volume – there is often too much data to analyse
- Variety – the data comes in various forms
- Velocity – it is created and changed at great speed.

More details

- Volume – there is a massive amount of big data available and not all of it will be of use to the organisation. Someone in the organisation will have to decide what data to collect, how to store it, most importantly, how to structure it into something useful. Big data is typically unstructured and messy and it can only be of use to an organisation if these characteristics can be removed.

- Variety – there is no consistent way in which big data is presented. It can be tweets, text, pictures, videos, graphs etc. The data needs to be organised and interpreted before it can be analysed.

- Velocity – digital information is uploaded and updated on a second-by-second basis. It will need to be processed quickly and constantly monitored. This is why software often play a critical role in big data analytics in that it can collect, organise and change information at greater speeds than organisations could do using traditional analytical techniques.

There may be other problems in performing big data analytics such as:

- Because the data is often freely available it can be used and analysed by rivals so that any competitive advantage gained may be very short lived.

- It requires a significant investment in IT in order to store, organise and manage the data.

- The 3V's is often extended to a 4th V, veracity. This suggests that users of big data must determine whether the data is accurate, representative and can be trusted. Earlier it was suggested that sites such as Wikipedia or Investopedia might be used as sources of information, for example, but these sites are openly edited and their accuracy cannot be taken for granted.

- Likewise, the data can be distorted by data outliers. This is data that does not appear to fit in with other data that has been gathered.

Example 13

One of the problems associated with the use of Big Data is that the data may not be accurate.

Which of the characteristics of Big Data does this relate to?

A   Volume

B   Veracity

C   Variety

D   Velocity

Data outliers

Data outliers are pieces of data that do not appear to fit into the pattern of normal results.

For example, consider the following data for website visitors over the last year (in thousands):

	Jan	Feb	Mar	Apr	May	Jun	July	Aug	Sep	Oct	Nov	Dec
Visitors	140	150	145	150	140	65	145	150	140	150	150	140

It can be seen that most months are within five thousand visitors of 145,000. But June does not appear to follow this pattern. It is well below the normal results. June's result is an outlier.

Note: outliers are often more easily spotted through the use of data graphs. For example, if the data above was represented as a scatter graph then the June results would very quickly stand out.

If data outliers are included in data the results are skewed towards the outlier. In our example, if June's result is ignored completely and we calculate the average number of monthly visitors to the website we get an average of 145.5 which would give a very fair representation of the data.

But when June's result is included in the average the average falls to 138.8 giving a very different impression of the overall data. Analysis and interpretation of the data would likewise be very different.

This is not to say that outliers should be ignored completely. The outliers themselves could contain valuable data. In our example, June's result could indicate some seasonality, the impact of negative press reports in the month of June, a website failure in June etc. For that reason data outliers are often investigated separately from data that more readily fits into overall patterns.

Data outliers are more common in big data – due to its obvious size and variability. One way of coping with data outliers in big data is to use a trimming approach. For example, if we wanted to examine the average time taken per page on visits to a particular page on our website we might 'trim' the data by ignoring the longest and shortest 5% of visitors. This would exclude people who have clicked on the page but left it open long after they have finished reading it as well as excluding people who clicked on the page by accident. The remaining 90% of data would be used in the website analytics to give a more useful piece of information.

Care must therefore be taken when using big data to make decisions.

7   Periodic vs rolling budgets

Periodic budget

A periodic budget shows the costs and revenue for one period of time, e.g. a year and is updated on a periodic basis, e.g. every 12 months.

Rolling budgets (continuous budgets)

A rolling budget is a 'budget continuously updated by adding a further accounting period (month or quarter) when the earliest accounting period has expired' (CIMA Official Terminology). Rolling budgets are also called 'continuous budgets'. Rolling budgets are for a fixed period, but this need not be a full financial year.

Reasons for rolling budgets

The reason for preparing rolling budgets is to deal with the problem of uncertainty in the budget, when greater accuracy and reliability are required. A common example is **cash budgeting**. Cash management is often a critical element of financial management in organisations, and it is essential to have reasonably reliable forecasts of cash flows, especially over the course of the next few days, weeks or months. An organisation might therefore produce rolling budgets (= revised forecasts) for cash flow. The cash budget period might be three or six months, and rolling cash budgets might be prepared monthly.

Illustration 3

If rolling annual budgets are prepared quarterly, four rolling budgets will be prepared each year, each for a 12-month period. A new quarter is added at the end of the new budget period, to replace the current quarter just ending:

- One budget might cover the period 1 January – 31 December Year 1.

- The next rolling budget will cover 1 April Year 1 to 31 March Year 2.

- The next rolling budget will cover 1 July Year 1 to 30 June Year 2.

- The next quarterly rolling budget will cover 1 October Year 1 to 30 September Year 2, and so on.

Reasons for rolling budgets

A key reason for preparing rolling budgets, as we've just seen, is to deal with the problem of uncertainty in the budget.

Another reason would be where budgeting conditions are subject to rapid financial change. When a budget is prepared, the forecasts on which it is based might be uncertain due to the probability of significant financial changes during the budget period. For example:

- The forecast rate of cost inflation/price inflation might be high

- The business might be affected by changes in an exchange rate, such as the sterling/US dollar rate and the exchange rate might be extremely volatile and subject to large movements within relatively short periods of time

- When there is a large amount of uncertainty in the budget, it might be appropriate to prepare rolling budgets at regular intervals, in order to have plans that are reasonably realistic and achievable.

Example 14

A company uses rolling budgeting and has a sales budget as follows for the next 12 month period:

	Qtr 1	Qtr 2	Qtr 3	Qtr 4	Total
	$	$	$	$	$
Sales	125,750	132,038	138,640	145,572	542,000

Actual sales for Quarter 1 were $123,450. The adverse variance is fully explained by competition being more intense than expected and growth being lower than anticipated. The budget committee has proposed that the revised assumption for sales growth should be 3% per quarter for Quarters 2,3 and 4.

Required:

Update the budget figures for Quarters 2-4 as appropriate.

Advantages and disadvantages of rolling budgets

Advantages

- They reduce uncertainty in budgeting.

- They can be used for cash management.

- They force managers to look ahead continuously.

- When conditions are subject to change, comparing actual results with a rolling budget is more realistic than comparing actual results with a fixed annual budget.

Disadvantages

- Preparing new budgets regularly is time-consuming.

- It can be difficult to communicate frequent budget changes.

Real world example

For years, senior managers at REL Consultancy Group handled budgeting and revenue forecasting much the way most other companies do. As year-end approached, they would evaluate performance, set sales targets for the upcoming year and then work to see that everyone met or exceeded the goals.

Unfortunately, the process didn't always produce the intended results.

'Invariably,' recalls Stephan Payne, president of the London-based global management consulting firm, 'one of the account directors would land a couple of good clients early in the year and make his annual budget well before the year closed. More often than not, he'd then take his foot off the gas and coast.' To make the budgeting process more timely and relevant, the firm embraced a more complex, albeit intuitive, approach to financial forecasting – the **rolling budget.** Rather than creating an annual financial forecast that remains static for the year, he and his colleagues now produce an 18-month budget and then update projections every month – in effect, recalculating the whole budget. As the firm's actual sales figures come in each month, directors plug them into their forecasting model in place of what they had projected, then roll the budget forward one more month.

No more free rides

The result: an always-current financial forecast that reflects not only the company's most recent monthly results but also any material changes to its business outlook or the economy. In addition, it provides fewer opportunities for account directors to ride the coattails of past performance.

'Now, even the guy who booked a million dollars' worth of business in one month can't sit still because 30 days later, we're going to have an entirely new forecast,' Payne says, adding, 'It's a dynamic process that makes a lot more sense.'

Although traditional 1-year budgets are still the norm at most companies large and small, many accountants argue that rolling budgets can be a far more useful tool. Unlike static budgets, they encourage managers to react more quickly to changing economic developments or business conditions. They discourage what is too often a fruitless focus on the past ('Why didn't we meet our numbers?') in favour of a realistic focus on the future. And they produce forecasts that, over the near term, are never more than a few months old, even when companies are rolling them forward on a quarterly basis – the more common approach – rather than REL's monthly basis.

'A static budget simply doesn't reflect the pace of business today,' says Jill Langerman, CPA, president and CFO of the accounting firm Fair, Anderson & Langerman in Las Vegas. 'If at mid-year you add a new product to your line-up, you want to calculate the costs and profit margins associated with that and reflected those calculations in your budget OSC to reflect the impact that it will have on your remaining product lines. That way, you can set an accurate performance target and make informed decisions about whether you're now free to invest more in the remaining product lines or perhaps add a new line. If you're not incorporating these new analyses into your budget, it becomes a rather useless document.'

Implementing rolling budgets doesn't necessarily require any fundamental change in the way a company has been doing its budgets – except, of course, it no longer does the job just once a year. However, companies that decide to step up to rolling budgets may want to take advantage of the decision to make a change and consider what else they can do to improve the process. After all, if a company can get everyone on board to make such a fundamental change, a further nudge to make the process more effective and efficient in other ways may be possible, too.

Taken from:

'Budgets on a roll: recalculating a business's outlook several times a year'

Randy Myers, Journal of Accountancy, December 2001. © 2001. Reprinted with permission of AICPA

8   Alternative approaches to budgeting

There are many different starting positions in the creation of budgets. In this section we look at three different ways in which the budgeting process might begin.

Incremental budgeting

 The traditional approach to budgeting is to take the previous year's budget and to add on a percentage to allow for inflation and other cost increases. In addition there may be other adjustments for specific items such as an extra worker or extra machine.

Further explanation

- Fairly small changes are made to the current year's budget. For example, adjustments might be made to allow for a planned increase or decline in sales volume, and for inflationary increases in sales prices and costs.

- A check is then made to ensure that the budget produced in this way meets the performance targets of the organisation. For example, the company might have a target of keeping the operating costs to sales ratio at less than, say, 60%.

In a static business environment, incremental budgets are little more than 'last year's budget plus a percentage amount for inflation'.

Advantages and disadvantages of incremental budgeting

Advantages	Disadvantages
• simple	• backward looking
• cheap	• builds on previous inefficiencies
• suitable in stable environments	• doesn't remove waste/inefficiencies
• most practical	• unsuited to changing environments
	• targets are too easy
	• activities are not justified
	• encourages over-spending

Further explanation

The advantage of incremental budgeting is that it is an easy, quick and cheap method of preparing budgets for what may be many cost centres in a large organisation. However, the traditional approach has severe disadvantages.

Advantages

(1) It is a simple, low-cost budgeting system.

(2) If the business is fairly stable, the budgets produced by this method might be sufficient for management needs.

(3) There are some items of cost where an incremental budgeting approach is probably the most practical. For example, the easiest way of budgeting telephone expenses for the next year might be to base the planned cost on the previous year's budget (or possibly actual costs in the current year).

Disadvantages

(1) The main disadvantage is that it assumes that all current activities should be continued at the current level of operations and with the same allocation of resources.

(2) It is backward-looking in nature, since next year's budget is based on what has happened in the past. In a dynamic and rapidly-changing business environment, this approach to planning is inappropriate.

(3) It is often seen as a desk-bound planning process, driven by the accounts department.

(4) The performance targets in the budget are often unchallenging, based on past performance. Incremental budgeting does not encourage managers to look for ways of improving the business.

(5) When there are excessive costs in the budget for the current year, these will be continued in the future. Incremental budgeting is not a planning system for cutting out waste and overspending.

(6)   Consideration will not be given to the justification for each activity. They will be undertaken merely because they were undertaken the previous year.

(7)   Different ways of achieving the objective will not be examined.

(8)   Past inefficiencies will be continued.

(9)   Managers know that if they fail to spend their budget, it is likely to be reduced next period. They therefore try to spend the whole budget, regardless of whether or not the expenditure is justified

ZBB is one method which may be used to overcome these problems.

Zero-based budgeting

 ZBB may be defined as:

'A method of budgeting whereby all activities are re-evaluated each time a budget is formulated. Each functional budget starts with the assumptions that the function does not exist, and is at zero cost. Increments of costs are compared with increments of benefits, culminating in the planned maximum benefit for a given budgeted cost.'

Zero-based budgeting (ZBB) is a radical alternative to incremental budgeting. In ZBB, all activities and costs are budgeted from scratch (a zero base). For every activity, managers look at its costs and its purpose, and consider whether there are alternative ways of doing it. Inessential activities and costs are identified and eliminated, by removing them from next year's budget.

 ZBB in practice

Implementing ZBB

All activities are subjected to the most basic scrutiny, and answers sought to such fundamental question as:

(a)   Should the activity be undertaken at all?

(b)   If the company undertakes the activity, how much should be done and how well should it be done (e.g. should an economy or a deluxe service level be provided)?

(c)   How should the activity be performed – in-house or subcontracted?

(d)   How much would the various alternative levels of service and provision cost?

In order to answer these questions, all existing and potential organisational activities must be described and evaluated in a series of 'decision packages', giving the following four-step process to a ZBB exercise:

(1) Determine the activities that are to be used as the object of decision packages – the provision of home support for the elderly or provision of catering facilities for the workforce, for example – and identify the manager responsible for each activity.

(2) Request the managers identified in (1) above to prepare a number of alternative decision packages for those individual activities for which they are responsible. (At least three packages are normally requested: one that sets out what could be delivered with funding maintained at the current level; one for a reduced level of funding, e.g. 80% of the current level; and one for an enhanced level of funding, e.g. 120% of the current level.)

(3) Rank the decision packages in order of their contribution towards the organisation's objectives.

(4) Fund the decision packages according to the ranking established under (3) above until the available funds are exhausted.

Adoption of ZBB

ZBB has been adopted more widely in the public sector than the private, although examples of organisations regularly adopting a full ZBB approach are rare. Full-scale ZBB is so resource-intensive that critics claim that its advantages are outweighed by its implementation costs. However, it is not necessary to apply ZBB to the whole of an organisation; benefits can be gained from its application to specific areas. For example, in the public sector, a decision could be made regarding the overall size of the childcare budget, and ZBB could be applied to allocate resources within that particular field; similarly, in a business organisation, ZBB could be applied to individual divisions on a rotational basis. This selective application ensures that a thorough reappraisal of activities is undertaken regularly, but not so regularly that the process itself is a major drain on organisational resources.

Notwithstanding the criticisms, the main plank of the ZBB approach – the rejection of past budgets as a planning baseline – is being increasingly accepted.

Illustration 4

A company is conducting a ZBB exercise, and a decision package is being prepared for its materials handling operations.

- The manager responsible has identified a base package for the minimum resources needed to perform the materials handling function. This is to have a team of five workers and a supervisor, operating without any labour-saving machinery. The estimated annual cost of wages and salaries, with overtime, would be $375,000.

- In addition to the base package, the manager has identified an incremental package. The company could lease two fork lift trucks at a cost of $20,000 each year. This would provide a better system because materials could be stacked higher and moved more quickly. Health and safety risks for the workers would be reduced, and there would be savings of $5,000 each year in overtime payments.

- Another incremental package has been prepared, in which the company introduces new computer software to plan materials handling schedules. The cost of buying and implementing the system would be $60,000, but the benefits are expected to be improvements in efficiency that reduce production downtime and result in savings of $10,000 each year in overtime payments.

The base package would be considered essential, and so given a high priority. The two incremental packages should be evaluated and ranked. Here, the fork lift trucks option might be ranked more highly than the computer software.

In the budget that is eventually decided by senior management, the fork lift truck package might be approved, but the computer software package rejected on the grounds that there are other demands for resources with a higher priority.

Advantages and disadvantages of ZBB

Advantages

- creates an environment that accepts change
- better focus on goals
- forward looking
- improves resource utilisation

- better performance measures

- focuses managers to examine activities

Disadvantages

- time-consuming

- expensive
- encourages short-termism
- management may lose focus on the true cost drivers
- managers require new budgeting skills
- can result in arbitrary decisions

Further explanation

Advantages

- It helps to create an organisational environment where change is accepted.

- It helps management to focus on company objectives and goals. It moves budgeting away from number-crunching, towards analysis and decision-making.

- It focuses on the future rather than on the past.

- It helps to identify inefficient operations and wasteful spending, which can be eliminated.

- Establishing priorities for activities provides a framework for the optimum utilisation of resources. This assists decision-makers when some expenditures are discretionary.

- It establishes a measure of performance for each decision package. This measure can be used to monitor actual performance and compare actual with budget.

- It involves managers in the budgeting process. Unlike incremental budgeting, it is not a desk-bound exercise driven by the accounting department. Preparation of the decision packages will normally require the involvement of many employees, and thus provides an opportunity for their view to be considered. This involvement may produce useful ideas, and promote job satisfaction among the wider staff.

Disadvantages

- It is a time-consuming exercise. It is unlikely that an organisation will have the time to carry out a ZBB exercise every year.

- There is a temptation to concentrate on short-term cost savings at the expense of longer-term benefits.

- It might not be useful for budgeting for production activities or service provision, where costs and efficiency levels should be well-controlled, so that budgets can be prepared from forecasts of activity volume and unit costs.

- In applying ZBB, 'activities' may continue to be identified with traditional functional departments, rather than cross-functional activities, and thus distract the attention of management from the real cost-reduction issues. For example, it could be argued that the costs incurred in a warranty department are largely a function of the reliability of products, which itself is a function of actions and decisions taken elsewhere. If the warranty department is treated as an activity under ZBB, the focus of the decision packages is likely to be on providing the same level of customer service at reduced cost, or enhancing the level of customer service for the same cost. The main driver behind the department's cost – product reliability – may remain unaddressed in ZBB, as it is with the blanket cut approach.

- It might require skills from management that the management team does not possess.

- The ranking process can be difficult, since widely-differing activities cannot be compared on quantitative measures alone. For example, it might be difficult to rank proposals for spending on better service quality, improvements in safety in the work place or more spending on new product development.

Activity-based budgeting

Introduction

In a manufacturing business, budgeting for direct costs is relatively straightforward. The costs of direct materials and direct labour are assumed to vary with production, and once production levels have been estimated, budgeting the direct costs of production is a matter of simple arithmetic.

Budgeting for overhead costs is not so simple. Traditionally, there has been a tendency to take an incremental approach in budgeting for overhead costs, and prepare next year's budget by simply adding a percentage to the current year budget, to allow for inflation. Zero-based budgeting is one method of bringing greater discipline to the process of budgeting for overhead activities and costs. Another method is activity-based budgeting.

As its name should suggest, activity-based budgeting (ABB) takes a similar approach to activity-based costing. ABB is defined as: 'a method of budgeting based on an activity framework and utilising cost driver data in the budget-setting and variance feedback processes' (CIMA Official Terminology).

Whereas ZBB is based on budgets (decision packages) prepared by responsibility centre managers, ABB is based on budgeting for activities.

In its simplest form, ABB is simply about using costs determined via ABC to prepare budgets for each activity. The basic approach of ABB is to budget the costs for each cost pool or activity as follows:

(1) The cost driver for each activity is identified. A forecast is made of the number of units of the cost driver that will occur in the budget period.

(2) Given the estimate of the activity level for the cost driver, the activity cost is estimated. Where appropriate, a cost per unit of activity, known as the **cost driver rate**, is calculated.

(There will also be some general overhead costs that are not activity-related, such as factory rental costs and the salary cost of the factory manager. General overhead costs are budgeted separately.)

Illustration 5

Consider the following example:

Septran operates two rail services. The Northern line operated for 20,000 hours last year. It had 200 full time staff. The Southern line operated for 39,000 hours last year. It had 300 full time staff. Eight train staff are needed for each journey on both lines. The total overhead for indirect wages was $39m.

Next year the government want to promote greater use of train services in the north of the country. Septran expect this to result in approximately 10,000 more journey hours for the Northern line. Because of transfers between services and other knock on effects, this is also likely to result in an extra 5,000 journey hours for the Southern line.

The company want to use an ABB approach to budget for the indirect wages cost next year.

Step 1

Firstly, the company need to determine how costs should be allocated to each service (each service effectively becomes a 'cost pool'). This might be the number of journeys or the number of full time employees. For indirect wages Septran believe that the number of full time staff would be the most appropriate way to allocate costs to each cost pool.

Step 2

The total overheads are then allocated to each cost pool on this basis.

	Northern line	Southern line	Total
	$m	$m	$m
Indirect wage cost – split 200:300	15.6	23.4	39.0

Step 3

The company then need to determine the cost driver. Septran believe that the cost is driven by the number of journey hours in operation.

	Northern line	Southern line
Indirect wage cost – split 20:30	$15.6m	$23.4m
Number of journey hours	20,000	39,000
Cost driver rate	$780 per journey hour	$600 per journey hour

Step 4

These established cost drivers will then be used to prepare the budget for next year:

	Northern line	Southern line
Cost driver rate	$780 per journey hour	$600 per journey hour
Budgeted level of activity	30,000 hours	44,000 hours
Budgeted indirect wage cost	$23.4m	$26.4m

The total budgeted indirect wage cost for next year will be $49.8m.

Advantages and disadvantages of ABB

Advantages	Disadvantages
• useful when overheads are significant	• expensive to implement
• better cost control	• only suited to ABC users
• management	
• useful for TQM environments	

Further explanation

The advantages of ABB are similar to those provided by activity-based costing.

- It draws attention to the costs of 'overhead activities'. This can be important where overhead costs are a large proportion of total operating costs.

- It provides information for the control of activity costs, by assuming that they are variable, at least in the longer term.

- It provides a useful basis for monitoring and controlling overhead costs, by drawing management attention to the actual costs of activities and comparing actual costs with what the activities were expected to cost.

- It also provides useful control information by emphasising that activity costs might be controllable if the activity volume can be controlled.

- ABB can provide useful information for a total quality management (TQM) programme, by relating the cost of an activity to the level of service provided (for example, stores requisitions processed) – Do the user departments feel they are getting a cost-effective service?

The system however does have some disadvantages:

- It is an expensive system to implement. New information systems are required and managers need to be trained in its use.

- It will also rely on the use of activity based costing (ABC) as the standard costing system.

Example 15

Tiddleypeeps is a private childcare provider and operates from two different sites. Site 1 currently employs 15 staff and has 120 children registered for childcare provision. Site 2 employs 24 staff and has 160 children registered. The total overhead for salaries at Tiddleypeeps this year was $624,000.

Tiddleypeeps is looking to expand both of its premises next year such that it can provide childcare for an additional 15 more children at Site 1 and 24 additional children at Site 2.

Management use staff numbers to allocate costs between the sites and believe that the number of registered children is the most appropriate cost driver for salaried costs.

Required:

Using an activity based budgeting approach, calculate the budgeted cost for salaries for both sites at Tiddleypeeps for next year.

 ## 9 Beyond budgeting

Beyond budgeting is an approach to budgeting that tries to resolve the weaknesses and limitations of traditional approaches to budgeting explored earlier in this chapter. In particular, many organisations complain that budgets do not fully prepare an organisation for potential changes in its environment and are too often based on assumptions that things won't change and that last year's assumptions will continue to be valid.

Beyond budgeting is: 'An idea that companies need to move beyond budgeting because of the inherent flaws in budgeting especially when used to set contracts. It is argued that a range of techniques, such as rolling forecasts and market related targets, can take the place of traditional budgeting.' CIMA Official Terminology

Beyond budgeting approaches are commonly used in organisations that face regular environmental changes or where continuous improvement is critical to the organisation's success. There are some common features of 'beyond budgeting' systems such as:

- The use of rolling budgets, produced on a quarterly or monthly basis, as an alternative to annual budgeting. These are flexible, do not rely on obsolete figures and should result in more timely allocation of resources. It also means that budgets are quickly adjusted for changes in the organisation's environment.

- A wider range of performance measures are assessed such as customer satisfaction, production times, innovation, staff utilisation etc.

- Targets are often set based on 'benchmarks' observed externally. For example, if Amazon can offer guaranteed next day delivery on products then this may become the benchmark for an organisation's own distribution department.

- There is a greater focus on determining and explaining what might happen in the future (for example, how might product design be changed to reduce material usage) rather than on what has happened in the past (for example, examining why a material usage variance has occurred).

- Innovation is encouraged and rewarded.

- Budgets are set at a local level rather than being prepared centrally based on organisational goals and then having these provided to local managers who might actually understand the local environment better.

Advantages and disadvantages of beyond budgeting

Advantages	Disadvantages
- planning is continuous and the organisation is more likely to be proactive rather than reactive to changes in its environment	- planning, coordination and performance evaluation become more complicated. This has the added impact that reward systems also become more complex
- targets become more challenging and more market focused. They stretch staff and encourage staff to find better ways to do things. They also make the organisation more customer focused.	- if benchmarks and targets are seen as being unachievable then effort to achieve them is reduced rather than improved

- the organisation becomes more innovative and continuously improves

- managers are more involved in the decision making process which provides better information for decisions as well as providing better motivation for managers

- managers can take decisions much more quickly

- it creates information systems which provide fast and open information throughout the organisation.

- organisational goals are less clear and are not communicated throughout the organisation. This means that many key stakeholders such as providers of finance and shareholders lose out as the organisation focuses more on customers and innovation

- organisations who move to a beyond budgeting structure can often face a lot of resistance from staff and managers where traditional budgets may be very deeply ingrained in the organisation's culture. Is staff fail to fully embrace the new systems and targets then the system is set to fail.

- it may be very difficult or impractical for organisations to adopt the culture of decentralisation on which successful BB depends

- the need for more up-to-date and accurate information requires costly investment

10   Chapter summary

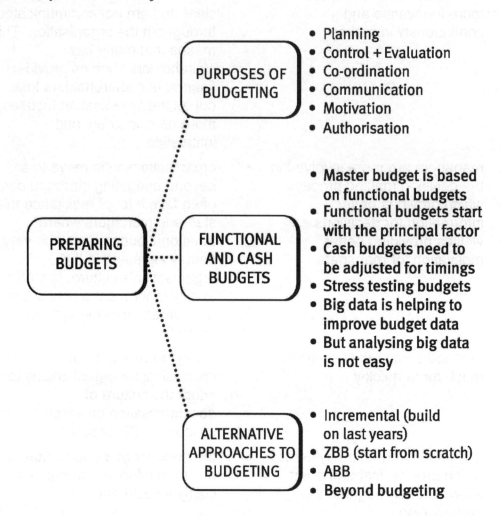

PURPOSES OF BUDGETING
- Planning
- Control + Evaluation
- Co-ordination
- Communication
- Motivation
- Authorisation

PREPARING BUDGETS

FUNCTIONAL AND CASH BUDGETS
- Master budget is based on functional budgets
- Functional budgets start with the principal factor
- Cash budgets need to be adjusted for timings
- Stress testing budgets
- Big data is helping to improve budget data
- But analysing big data is not easy

ALTERNATIVE APPROACHES TO BUDGETING
- Incremental (build on last years)
- ZBB (start from scratch)
- ABB
- Beyond budgeting

11 Practice questions

Test your understanding 1

Hopper manufactures two products, X and Y. Budgeted information for the next financial year is as follows

	Product X Units	Product Y Units
Budgeted sales	4,000	6,000
Budgeted closing inventory	500	300
Opening inventory	200	400

	Product X Kg per unit	Product Y Kg per unit
Direct materials requirements		
Material DM1	1.2	2.0
Material DM2	0.8	–

	Material DM1 Kg	Material DM2 Kg
Budgeted closing inventory	1,000	200
Opening inventory	3,000	600
Standard price per kg	$0.80	$0.50

Required:

In the boxes below, enter the purchase quantities and cost for both materials from a materials purchases budget for the year.

	Material DM1	Material DM2
Budgeted purchase quantities (kgs)	16,960	3,440
Budgeted cost of purchases ($)	11,968	1,520

Test your understanding 2

Note: This is a comprehensive question. It is much bigger than you will see in your assessment but it is useful to work through examples like this to improve your understanding of the topic as a whole.

Scenario

SRW makes two similar products, the Alpha and Beta, and operates a five-day week for both production and sales. Both products use the same material and labour, but Beta requires more labour and materials than the Alpha. The company divides its year into five-week periods for budgetary purposes. One of your responsibilities is to prepare budgets for the Alpha and the Beta.

You are given the following information to help you prepare the production and resource budgets for period 8.

Forecast sales volumes (units)	Days in period	Alpha	Beta
Period 8	25	8,460	9,025
Period 9	25	10,575	12,635

Finished inventories

- There will be 1,692 Alphas and 3,610 Betas in finished inventory at the beginning of Period 8.

- The closing inventory of both Alphas and Betas depends on the forecast sales in period 9.

- Period 8's closing inventory of Alphas must equal 5 days sales of Alphas in period 9.

- Period 8's closing inventory of Betas must equal 10 days sales of Betas in period 9.

- The first-in-first-out inventory valuation method is used to value closing inventory.

Production and failure rates

- 10% of Alpha finished production and 5% of Beta finished production is faulty and has to be destroyed. This faulty production has no value.

- The faulty production arises from the production technology and is only discovered on completion. The cost of faulty production is part of the cost producing fault-free Alphas and Betas.

Materials

- Each Alpha produced requires 20 kg of materials and each Beta produced requires 40 kg of materials.

- The opening inventory of materials at the beginning of period 8 is 64,800 kg.

- The closing inventory of materials at the end of period 8 must be 52,600 kg.

- The material costs 50c per kilogram.

Labour

- Each Alpha produced requires two labour hours and each Beta produced requires three labour hours.

- SRW employs 300 production staff who work 35 hours per five-day week.

- The hourly rate per employee is $10 and if any overtime is required the overtime premium is $3 per employee per hour of overtime.

- Any overtime premium is charged to factory overheads and not to the cost of production.

Factory overheads

- Budgeted overheads are charged to production on the basis of labour hours.

- For Alpha, the budgeted factory overheads are $62 per labour hour. For Beta, they are $58 per labour hour.

Tasks:

(a) Prepare the following information for Period 8:

    (i)   Production budgets for Alpha and Beta

    (ii)   Material purchases budget in kilograms and $

    (iii) Budgeted labour hours to be worked, including any overtime hours

    (iv) Labour cost budget

    (v)   Total (full) cost of production budget for Alpha and Beta

    (vi) Full cost of GOOD production per unit for Alpha and Beta

(Time allowed for part a: 30 minutes)

The Sales Director has just informed you that the Alpha sales in period 8 will be 2,000 units more than originally forecast. You are told the following:

- SRW production employees can work up to a maximum of 5,000 overtime hours in any five-week period.

- The material used in Alpha and Beta production can only be made by one company and SRW is the only user of the material. Currently there is a shortage of the material and the maximum additional material that can be obtained is 34,000 kg.

- The demand for Beta in period 8 will remain at 9,025 units.

(b)

    (i)   Prepare calculations to show whether it is the material or labour hours that limits the extra production of Alpha in period 8.

    (ii)   Prepare a revised production budget in units for Alphas in period 8.

    (iii) Calculate the shortfall in the planned extra sales of Alpha caused by the limit in extra production.

    (iv) Suggest three ways how this shortfall may be overcome.

(Time allowed for part b: 30 minutes)

Test your understanding 3

Twenty per cent of a company's sales are made to cash customers. The records show that the credit customers settle their bills as follows:

Paid in the month following the sale 60%

Paid two months after the sale 38%

Bad debts 2%

Credit customers paying in the month following the sale receive a 3% discount.

Budgeted sales for the forthcoming period are as follows:

January	February	March
$20,400	$29,500	$26,800

Required:

Calculate the amount to be shown as receipts from sales in the cash budget for March.

Test your understanding 4

A manufacturing business makes and sells widgets. Each widget requires two units of raw materials, which cost $3 each. Production and sales quantities of widgets each month are as follows:

Month	Sales and production units
December (actual)	50,000
January (budget)	55,000
February (budget)	60,000
March (budget)	65,000

In the past, the business has maintained its inventories of raw materials at 100,000 units. However, it plans to increase raw material inventories to 110,000 units at the end of January and 120,000 units at the end of February. The business takes one month's credit from its suppliers.

Required:

In the following boxes, enter the forecast payments to suppliers each month, for raw material purchases.

	January $	February $	March $
Payment to suppliers	300,000	360,000	390,000

Test your understanding 5

A company operates on a single continent which is divided into a number of individual states, each with their own government. Each state shares the same single currency. The company wants to set budgets for each business unit in each state from a central head office.

Which TWO of the following statements are most likely to be true:

A   Budgeting will be made easier by the presence of a single currency

B   Budgeting will be made easier as one single language will be used across the continent

C   Budgeting will be more complex if the currency constantly fluctuates

D   Budgeting will be made more complex if strategic rivals are different in each individual state

Test your understanding 6

Scenario

A company makes and sells two products, X and Y, for which the budgeted sales price and variable costs per unit are:

	Product X	Product Y
Variable cost	$2	$4
Sales price	$5	$8

Budgeted fixed costs are $140,000. Budgeted sales are 30,000 units of Product X and 15,000 units of Product Y.

Tasks

(a)   Calculate the budgeted profit.

(b)   Calculate how profit would be affected in each of the following separate circumstances:

  (i)   if the variable cost of Product Y were 25% higher than expected

  (ii)   if sales volumes of Product X were 10% less than budgeted

  (iii)   if sales volumes of Product X were 5% less than budgeted and unit variable costs of X were 10% higher than budgeted

  (iv)   if total sales revenue is the same as in the original budget, but the sales mix (by revenue) is 50% of Product X and 50% of Product Y.

(Time allowed: 20 minutes)

Test your understanding 7

Which of the following statements regarding the use of big data is most likely to be true?

A   Big data can be cheap to acquire

B   The veracity of big data is easy to confirm

C   Using big data makes stress testing budgets less useful

D   Big data stays the same for a long period

Test your understanding 8

An importer has produced the following budget for next month:

	$000
Sales	64,000
Material costs	(28,000)
Labour costs	(12,000)
Overhead costs	(18,000)
Gross profit	6,000

The importer wants to stress test the budget for a potential change in currency rates on the products that it imports. A currency change would increase material costs by 10%, only half of which could be passed on to the importers powerful customers.

The revised gross profit for the month would be $ _4,600_ ✓

Test your understanding 9

Note: This is a comprehensive question. It is much bigger than you will see in your assessment but it is useful to work through examples like this to improve your understanding of the topic as a whole.

Scenario

For a number of years, the research division of Z has produced its annual budget (for new and continuing projects) using incremental budgeting techniques. The company is now under new management and the annual budget for 20X4 is to be prepared using zero based budgeting techniques.

Tasks:

(a) Explain the differences between incremental and zero based budgeting techniques.

(b) Explain how Z could operate a zero based budgeting system for its research projects.

The operating divisions of Z have in the past always used a traditional approach to analysing costs into their fixed and variable components. A single measure of activity was used which, for simplicity, was the number of units produced. The new management does not accept that such a simplistic approach is appropriate for budgeting in the modern environment and has requested that the managers adopt an activity-based approach to their budgets for 20X4.

Tasks:

(c) (i) Briefly explain activity-based budgeting (ABB).

(ii) Explain how activity-based budgeting would be implemented by the operating divisions of Z.

(Time allowed: 40 minutes)

Test your understanding 10

AW Inc produces two products, A and C. In the last year (20X4) it produced 640 units of A and 350 units of C incurring costs of $672,000. Analysis of the costs has shown that 75% of the total costs are variable. 60% of these variable costs vary in line with the number of A produced and the remainder with the number of C.

The budget for the year 20X5 is now being prepared using an incremental budgeting approach. The following additional information is available for 20X5:

• All costs will be 4% higher than the average paid in 20X4.

• Efficiency levels will remain unchanged.

• Expected output of A is 750 units and of C is 340 units.

Required:

Calculate the budgeted total variable cost of products A and C for the full year 20X5?

(Time allowed: 10 minutes)

Test your understanding 11

Identify which of the following budgets is likely to be the most time consuming to construct and manage?

A   A periodic budget based on incremental budgeting principles

B   A periodic budget based on ZBB principles

C   A rolling budget based on incremental budgeting principles

D   A rolling budget based on ZBB principles

Test your understanding 12

Identify which of the following statements is correct regarding the benefits to be gained from using ABB?

A   If there is much inefficiency within the operations of a business then ABB will identify and remove these areas of inefficiency

B   In a highly direct labour intensive manufacturing process, an ABB approach will assist management in budgeting for the majority of the production costs

C   In an organisation currently operating efficiently, where the next period will be relatively unchanged from the current one, then ABB will make the budgeting process simpler and quicker

D   If an organisation produces many different types of output using different combinations of activities then ABB can provide more meaningful information for budgetary control

Test your understanding 13

Branch makes and sells two products, P and Q. The following budget has been prepared:

	Product P	Product Q
Sales price per unit	$3	$6
Variable cost per unit	$2	$3

Budgeted fixed costs are $140,000. Budgeted sales are 20,000 units of Product P and 50,000 units of Product Q.

Tasks:

(a) Calculate the budgeted profit.

(b) Calculate by how much the profit would be reduced if the variable cost of Product P were 15% higher than budgeted and the variable cost of Product Q were 10% higher than budgeted.

(c) Calculate by how much the profit would be reduced or increased if total sales revenue is the same as in the original budget, but the sales mix (by revenue) is one-third Product P and two-thirds Product Q.

(Time allowed: 15 minutes)

Test your understanding 14

A company makes 2 products, X and Y, which are sold in the ratio 2:5. The selling prices are $100 and $150 respectively. The company wants to generate revenue of $712,500 in the next period.

How many units of X and Y should be included in the sales budget?

Test your understanding 15

A company has an overdrawn bank balance at the start of the month of $12,500, trade receivables of $25,800 and trade payables of $37,000. The company can sell goods costing $74,000 for $98,200 next month. One half of all sales are collected in the month of sale and the remainder in the following month. All purchases are made on credit and paid during the following month. Inventory levels will remain constant during the month. General cash expenses will be $60,000 during the month.

What is the cash balance at the end of the month?

A $9,600 overdrawn

(B) $34,600 overdrawn

C $48,300 overdrawn

D $14,500

Test your understanding answers

Example 1

Correct answer is B.

Whilst the budget provides the plan against which actual results can be compared, this does not mean that adverse variances will not arise. Any results which are out-of-line with the budget will be investigated and corrected.

Example 2

Correct answer is B.

Production budget:

Sales budget – opening inventory + closing inventory

Example 3

Production budget:

	Units
Sales budget	100,000
Add closing inventory finished goods (14,000 × 0.6)	8,400
Less opening inventory of finished goods	(14,000)
	94,400

Example 4

Production budget:

	Units
Sales budget	2,300
Add closing inventory finished goods	500
Less opening inventory of finished good	(400)
	2,400

Materials usage budget:

2,400 units × 6 kg per unit = 14,400 kg

Materials purchases budget:

	kg
Materials usage	14,400
Add closing inventory raw material	2,600
Less opening inventory raw material	(2,000)
Materials purchases	15,000 kg

Example 5

Note: remember that the labour budget is calculated in relation to the production budget and not the sales budget.

	Alpha	**Beta**
Production (units)	500	710
Skilled labour per unit (hours)	3	4
Total required skilled hours	1,500	2,840
Paid @ $20 per hour	$30,000	$56,800
Total cost of skilled labour	$86,800	

Example 6

(a) **Production budget**

	Product 1 units	**Product 2** units	**Product 3** units
Sales	3,000	4,500	3,000
+ Closing inventory	200	300	300
	3,200	4,800	3,300
– Opening inventory	(500)	(700)	(500)
Production quantity	2,700	4,100	2,800

(b) **Material usage budget**

	Material M1 kg	Material M2 kg	Material M3 kg
Production requirement			
2,700 Product 1	5,400	8,100	16,200
4,100 Product 2	12,300	12,300	8,200
2,800 Product 3	11,200	11,200	11,200
Usage quantity	28,900	31,600	35,600

(c) **Material purchases budget**

	Material M1 kg	Material M2 kg	Material M3 kg
Usage quantity	28,900	31,600	35,600
+ Closing inventory	2,200	1,300	2,000
– Opening inventory	4,300	3,700	4,400
Purchase quantity	26,800	29,200	33,200
	× $1.21 (W1)	× $3.30 (W1)	× $2.75 (W1)
Total purchases	$32,428	$96,360	$91,300

(d) **Labour budget**

	Skilled hrs	Semi-skilled hrs
Production requirement		
2,700 Product 1	8,100	8,100
4,100 Product 2	4,100	12,300
2,800 Product 3	8,400	11,200
Usage quantity	20,600	31,600
	× $6/hr	× $4/hr
Total labour cost	$123,600	$126,400

(W1) Current year material prices have been increased by 10% for use in the budget.

Material M1 price per kg = $1.10 × 1.1 = $1.21 per kg

Material M2 price per kg = $3.00 × 1.1 = $1.30 per kg

Material M3 price per kg = $2.50 × 1.1 = $2.75 per kg

Example 7

Cash from:		$
April sales:	10% × $5,000	500
March sales:	40% × $4,000	1,600
February sales:	45% × $8,000	3,600
		———
		5,700

Example 8

The amount budgeted to be paid to supplier is $301,845

	$
30% of March invoices (30% × $295,000, less 3% discount (i.e. × 0.97))	85,845
60% of February invoices (60% × $310,000)	186,000
10% of January invoices (10% × $300,000)	30,000
	301,845

Example 9

Interpretation of the cash budget

The company will be overdrawn throughout the three-month period, therefore it is essential that it should have access to borrowings to cover the shortfall. The bank might already have agreed an overdraft facility, but this should be at least $16,650 and ideally higher, to allow for the possibility that the actual cash flows will be even worse than budgeted.

The business may decide to delay the purchase of the capital equipment for one month in order to allow the cash position to move to a positive one before the investment is made. Alternatively, an extension of the overdraft facilities may be arranged for the appropriate period.

If it is decided that overdraft facilities are to be arranged, it is important that due account is taken of the timing of the receipts and payments within each month.

For example, all of the payments in January may be made at the beginning of the month but receipts may not be expected until nearer the end of the month. The cash deficit could then be considerably greater than it appears from looking only at the month-end balance.

If the worst possible situation arose, the overdrawn balance during January could become as large as $5,000 (Opening balance) minus $66,000 (January payments) = $71,000 before the receipts begin to arise. If management had used the month-end balances as a guide to the overdraft requirement during the period then they would not have arranged a large enough overdraft facility with the bank. It is important, therefore, that they look in detail at the information revealed by the cash budget, and not simply at the closing cash balances.

Example 10

The best way to approach questions such as this is to assume a sales price and work the figures through, as follows.

If revenue falls to 80%, then variable costs will also reduce accordingly.

Fixed costs will remain unchanged.

Suppose the original sales price was $100:

	$
Sales revenue (100%)	100
Variable costs (45% of $100)	45
Fixed costs (25% of $100)	25
Profit	30

Now when the sales price falls to 80%, this will become:

	$
Sales revenue (80% of $100)	80
Variable costs (45% of $80)	36
Fixed costs (remains unchanged)	25
Profit	19

The revised profit margin is therefore 19 / 80 × 100 = 23.75%.

Example 11

Original budget:

	$
Revenue $136.50 (W1) × 5,000 units	682,500
Less direct costs $105 × 5,000 units	(525,000)
Less variable overheads $15 × 5,000 units	(75,000)
Less fixed costs	(60,000)
Profit	22,500

(W1) Selling price is based on a 30% mark-up on prime cost. This is therefore $105 × (1 + 30%) = $136.50.

(W2) Prime cost = direct materials + direct labour

$$= \$60 + \$45 = \$105$$

(i) Direct materials 25% more than budget.

Revised direct material cost per unit: 3kg × ($20 × 1.25) = $75

Revised prime cost per unit: $75 + $45 = $120

	$
Revenue (unchanged)	682,500
Less direct costs $120 × 5,000 units	(600,000)
Less variable overheads $15 × 5,000 units	(75,000)
Less fixed costs	(60,000)
Loss	(52,500)

Profits will fall by $75,000 if material prices increase by 25%.

Note, a quicker way to arrive at the solution would be to calculate the increased cost per unit and multiply by the number of units:

Extra material cost = 25% × ($20 × 3kg) × 5,000 units = $75,000.

(ii) If employees are 20% more efficient, this means it will take 20% less time to produce each unit. The direct labour required per unit will fall from 5 hours to 5 × 0.80 = 4 hours per unit. This will impact on the direct labour cost and also the variable overhead per unit.

Revised labour cost per unit: 4 hours × $9 per hour = $36

Revised prime cost per unit: $60 + $36 = $96

Revised variable overhead per unit: 4 hours × $3 per hour = $12

	$
Revenue (unchanged)	682,500
Less direct costs $96 × 5,000 units	(480,000)
Less variable overheads $12 × 5,000 units	(60,000)
Less fixed costs	(60,000)
Profit	82,500

Profits will increase by $60,000 if workers are 20% more efficient.

Again, there is a quicker way to arrive at the change in profits, by calculating the total labour saving per unit and multiplying by the number of units:

1 hour × ($9 + $3) × 5,000 units = $60,000.

Example 12

A

Revised budget

	Original $000	Adjustment	Revised $000
Revenue	480	Less: 25% × 480k = 120k	360
Cost of sales	200	Less: 85% × 120k = 102k	98
Other operating costs	80		80
Net profit	200		182

Alternatively:

Lost sales = 25% × 480k = 120k

Reduction in profit: = 15% × 120k = 18k

Revised profit = 200k − 18k = 182k

Example 13

Correct solution B.

Veracity refers to the trustworthiness and accuracy of the data.

Example 14

The revised budget should incorporate 3% growth starting from the actual sales figure of Qtr 1.

	Qtr 2	Qtr 3	Qtr 4
	$	$	$
Sales	127,154	130,969	134,898

Workings:

Quarter 2: $123,450 × 103% = $127,154 ✓

Quarter 3: $127,154 × 103% = $130,969 ✓

Quarter 4: $130,969 × 103% = $134,898 ✓

Example 15

	Site 1	Site 2
Salary cost (W1)	$240,000	$384,000
Number of children	120	160
Cost driver rate	$2,000 per child	$2,400 per child
Budgeted children next year	135	184
Budgeted salary cost next year (W2)	$270,000	$441,600

(W1)

Total staff: 15 site 1 + 24 site 2 = 39

Salary cost site 1 = 15/39 × $624,000

Salary cost site 2 = 24/39 × $624,000

(W2)

Budgeted salary cost site 1 = $2,000 per child × 135 children = $270,000

Budgeted salary cost site 2 = $2,400 per child × 184 children = $441,600

Test your understanding 1

Materials purchases budget

	Material DM1 Kg	Material DM2 Kg
To make 4,300 units (W1) of X	5,160	3,440
To make 5,900 units (W1) of Y	11,800	0
Required for production	16,960	3,440
Add: closing inventory	1,000	200
Deduct: opening inventory	(3,000)	(600)
Budgeted purchase quantities	14,960	3,040
Standard price per kg	$0.80	$0.50
Budgeted cost of purchases	$11,968	$1,520

(W1) Production budget:

	Units	Units
Sales budget	4,000	6,000
Closing inventory	500	300
	4,500	6,300
Opening inventory	(200)	(400)
Production budget	4,300	5,900

Test your understanding 2

(a) (i)   **Production budget (Period 8)**

	Alpha Units	**Beta** Units
Sales budget	8,460	9,025
Add: Closing inventory (W1)	2,115	5,054
Less: Opening inventory	(1,692)	(3,610)
Good production	8,883	10,469
Wastage	987	551
Total production	9,870	11,020

Working 1 – Closing inventory

Alpha	Beta
$\dfrac{5}{25} \times 10,575 = 2,115$ units	$\dfrac{10}{25} \times 12,635 = 5,054$ units

(ii) **Materials purchases**

	Kilograms	$
Alpha 9,870 × 20 kgs	197,400	98,700
Beta 11,020 × 40 kgs	440,800	220,400
	638,200	319,100
Add: Closing	52,600	
Less: Opening	(64,800)	
Purchases	626,000	313,000

(iii) **Labour hours**

	Hours
Alpha 9,870 × 2	19,740
Beta 11,020 × 3	33,060
	52,800
Normal hours 300 × 35 × 5 weeks	52,500
Overtime hours	300

(iv) **Labour cost budget**

Direct labour cost	52,800 × $10 =	$528,000
Overtime premium (OH)	300 × $3 =	$900

(v) **Full production cost**

	Alpha	Beta
	$	$
Direct material	98,700	220,400
Direct labour	197,400	330,600
Overhead: 19,740 hours × $62	1,223,880	
Overhead: 33,060 hours × $58		1,917,480
	1,519,980	2,468,480
÷ Good units	÷ 8,883	÷ 10,469
Full cost per unit	$171.11	$235.79

(b) (i)

Increase in demand	2,000 units
	÷ 0.90
Therefore, increase in production	2,223 units

Hours required	2,223 units × 2 hours =	4,446 hours
Overtime hours available	(5,000 hours – 300 hours)	4,700 hours

Therefore, labour hours are not a scarce resource.

Kilograms of material required	2,223 units × 20 kgs =	44,460 kgs
Available		34,000 kgs

Therefore, material is a scarce resource.

(ii)

$$\text{Allowable increase in production:} \quad \frac{34,000 \text{ kg}}{20 \text{ kg per unit}} = 1,700 \text{ units}$$

New production budget: 9,870 + 1,700 = 11,570 units

(iii)

New production budget:		= 11,570 units
The extra production		= 11,570 – 9,870
(new production – existing production)		
		= 1,700 units
Good units produced:	(1,700 × 90%)	= 1,530 units
Shortfall (when compared to the increase in demand of 2,000 units)		= 470 units

(iv)

- Reduce planned closing inventory levels

- Improve wastage rate

- Reduce production of Beta

Test your understanding 3

	$
March sales = 20% for cash ($26,800 × 0.2)	5,360.00
February credit sales = 80% × 60% received less 3% discount ($29,500 × 0.8 × 0.6 × 0.97)	13,735.20
January credit sales = 80% × 38% received ($20,400 × 0.8 × 0.38)	6,201.60
	25,296.80

Test your understanding 4

When inventories of raw materials are increased, the quantities purchased will exceed the quantities consumed in the period.

Figures for December are shown because December purchases will be paid for in January, which is in the budget period.

Quantity of raw material purchased in units:

	Units of widgets produced	Material (@ 2 units per widget)			
		December	January	February	March
	Units	Units	Units	Units	Units
December	50,000	100,000			
January	55,000		110,000		
February	60,000			120,000	
March	65,000				130,000
Increase in inventories			10,000	10,000	–
Total purchase quantities		100,000	120,000	130,000	130,000
At $3 per unit		300,000	360,000	390,000	390,000

Having established the purchases each month, we can go on to budget the amount of cash payments to suppliers each month. Here, the business will take one month's credit

	January $	February $	March $
Payment to suppliers	300,000	360,000	390,000

At the end of March, there will be payables of $390,000 for raw materials purchased, which will be paid in April.

Test your understanding 5

A and D

A single currency will simplify the budgeting process in each individual state and avoid problems caused by fluctuating exchange rates. As the company only operates in this one continent currency fluctuations will not cause major budgeting problems in the short-term (removing option C as a possible correct answer).

Budget setters should not assume that one single language is used across an entire continent and the presence of more than one language or dialect will complicate the budgeting process (ruling out option B).

Having different strategic rivals in each state will change product pricing, design etc. and further complicate the budgeting process.

Test your understanding 6

The original budget and 'what if' budgets can be constructed quickly using a marginal costing approach

	Product X $	Product Y $	Total $
Budgeted sales	150,000	120,000	270,000
Variable costs	60,000	60,000	120,000
Contribution	90,000	60,000	150,000
Fixed costs			140,000
Budgeted profit			10,000

(b) (i)

		Product X $	Product Y $	Total $
Budgeted sales		150,000	120,000	270,000
Variable costs		60,000	75,000 (+25%)	135,000
Contribution		90,000	45,000	135,000
Fixed costs				140,000
Budgeted profit				(5,000)

(ii)

		Product X $	Product Y $	Total $
Budgeted sales	(−10% X)	135,000	120,000	255,000
Variable costs	(−10% X)	54,000	60,000	114,000
Contribution		81,000	60,000	141,000
Fixed costs				140,000
Budgeted profit				1,000

(iii)

		Product X	Product Y	Total
Sales units		28,500	15,000	
		$	$	$
Budgeted sales	(at $5)	142,500	120,000	262,500
Variable costs	(at $2.20)	62,700	60,000	122,700
Contribution		78,800	60,000	139,800
Fixed costs				140,000
Budgeted loss				(200)

(iv)

		Product X		Product Y	Total
Sales units	(135,000/5)	27,000	(135,000/8)	16,875	
		$		$	$
Budgeted sales	(50%)	135,000	(50%)	135,000	270,000
Variable costs	(at $2)	54,000	(at $4)	67,500	121,500
Contribution		81,000		67,500	148,500
Fixed costs					140,000
Budgeted profit					8,500

In practice, budget models are usually much more detailed and complex, but 'what if' analysis can be carried out simply and quickly.

In the example above, the 'what if' scenarios show that profit might be less than expected if actual results are less favourable than the assumptions and forecasts in the budget. If any of these results are unacceptable, management would need to consider alternative budget strategies for improving budgeted performance or reducing the risk.

Test your understanding 7

A

Some big data, such as information held on social media sites, is quickly, readily and cheaply available. For example, the number of likes that a particular new product video has received on a service such as YouTube can be seen by almost anyone.

But it is difficult to determine the veracity of data such as this (ruling out option B) and big data will be constantly changing (ruling out option D). But if the data can be transformed into useful information then it can improve the usefulness of stress testing budgets by improving accuracy and considering wider impacts (ruling out option C).

Test your understanding 8

The revised profit for the month would be $4,600

	Original $	Adjustment	Revised $
Sales	64,000	+(30,800 – 28,000) / 2	65,400
Material costs	(28,000)	× 110%	(30,800)
Labour costs	(12,000)		(12,000)
Overhead costs	(18,000)		(18,000)
Gross profit	6,000		4,600

Test your understanding 9

(a) An incremental budget starts off with last year's budget or last year's actual results and adds on a certain percentage to take account of expected inflation and/or any expected changes in the level of activity. It is a very simple, quick and cheap budget to produce, but it does not promote a questioning attitude. Activities are undertaken without thought. They are simply incorporated into the next budget because they were in the last budget and nobody has given any thought as to whether the activity is still really worthwhile.

With ZBB, each manager sets out what he or she wishes to accomplish over the forthcoming period. For each activity they want to undertake, they look at different ways of achieving the objective and they look at providing the service at different levels. They estimate the costs and benefits and the activity only takes place if the benefits exceed the costs. Also once all the activities have been evaluated, they can be ranked against each other and the company's resources directed to the best activities.

(b) The managers/researchers responsible for each project should decide which projects they wish to undertake in the forthcoming period. These projects will be a mixture of continued projects and new projects. For the projects which have already been started and which the managers want to continue in the next period, we should ignore any cash flows already incurred (they are sunk costs), and we should only look at future costs and benefits. Similarly, for the new projects we should only look at the future costs and benefits. Different ways of achieving the same research goals should also be investigated and the projects should only go ahead if the benefit exceeds the cost.

Once all the potential projects have been evaluated if there are insufficient funds to undertake all the worthwhile projects, then the funds should be allocated to the best projects on the basis of a cost-benefit analysis.

ZBB is usually of a highly subjective nature. (The costs are often reasonably certain, but usually a lot of uncertainty is attached to the estimated benefits.) This will be even truer of a research division where the researchers may have their own pet projects which they are unable to view in an objective light.

(c) (i) Activity based budgeting is where the budget is based upon a number of different levels of activity, i.e. on a number of different cost drivers, rather than being based on just one level of activity such as machine hours or output in units.

   The activity based budget will be based upon the number of units of the cost driver multiplied by the cost per unit of cost driver. The cost driver is that factor which actually causes the cost and therefore should lead to a more accurate budget as the budgeted cost will be based on the thing that should influence that cost. The alternative is to use absorption costing and assume that all overheads vary with output or machine hours or labour hours or that they are fixed.

(ii) Z may employ an outside specialist such as a management consultant who will investigate the business and determine what activities the business undertakes during the course of its operations.

   The consultant will discuss matters with the staff and the process will normally be time consuming. For each activity, efforts will be made to determine the factor which is most closely related to the costs of that activity, i.e. the cost driver. The investigation may bring to light non-value-added activities which can then be eliminated. It should improve the understanding of all those involved as to the true relationship between cost and level of activity.

   Managers would then estimate the expected incidence of their cost drivers and multiply by the budgeted cost driver rate to get the budget for the forthcoming period. ABB would be more complicated than a traditional budget and the overheads would be broken down into many activities such as set-up costs, materials, handling costs, etc rather than expenses such as rent, heating, depreciation, etc.

   With ABB the majority of the overhead costs would be perceived as variable rather than fixed. Of course it is not necessary to employ an outside consultant. The company may feel that they have their own managers with sufficient skills and time to undertake the exercise.

Test your understanding 10

Total variable cost	Variable cost per unit
20X4:	
Product A $672,000 × 75% × 60% = $302,000	$302,000 ÷ 640 units = $472.50
Product C $672,000 × 75% × 40% = $201,600	$201,600 ÷ 350 units = $576
20X5:	
Product A $472.50 × 1.04 × 750 units = $368,550	n/a
Product C $576 × 1.04 × 340 units = $203,674	n/a

Test your understanding 11

D

Rolling budgets are more time consuming to manage than periodic budgets as they must be update more regularly. ZBB is a more expensive system to manage than incremental budgeting as every item must be fully justified and investigated before being included in the budget.

Test your understanding 12

D

Situation A would be best suited by implementing Zero Base Budgeting.

Situation B does not require ABB since it has relatively low overheads.

Situation C would be suitable for incremental budgeting. ABB will certainly not be quicker.

Test your understanding 13

Part (a)

The budgeted profit is $30,000

	Product P $	Product Q $	Total $
Budgeted sales	60,000	300,000	360,000
Variable costs	40,000	150,000	190,000
Contribution	20,000	150,000	170,000
Fixed costs			140,000
Budgeted profit			30,000

Part (b)

The profit would fall by $21,000.

	Product P $	Product Q $	Total $
Budgeted sales	60,000	300,000	360,000
Variable costs	46,000 (+15%)	165,000 (+10%)	211,000
Contribution	14,000	135,000	149,000
Fixed costs			140,000
Revised profit			9,000
Original budgeted profit			30,000
Reduction in profit			21,000

Part (c)

The profit would fall by $10,000

	Product P	Product Q	Total
Sales units	40,000	40,000	
	$	$	$
Budgeted sales	120,000	240,000	360,000
	(at $3)	(at $6)	
Variable costs	80,000	120,000	200,000
	(at $2)	(at $3)	
Contribution	40,000	120,000	160,000
Fixed costs			140,000
Revised profit			20,000
Original budgeted profit			30,000
Reduction in profit			10,000

Test your understanding 14

If 2X and 5Y are sold, this generates revenue of (2 × $100) + (5 × $150) = $950. Call this a batch.

$712,500 / $950 per batch = 750 batches.

This is therefore equal to sales as follows:

750 × 2X = 1,500X

750 × 5Y = 3,750Y

Test your understanding 15

Correct solution B

	$
Opening overdraft	(12,500)
Opening receivables received in month	25,800
Opening payables paid in month	(37,000)
50% sales made in month ($98,200 × 50%)	49,100
General cash expenses paid in month	(60,000)
	(34,600)

Forecasting techniques

Chapter learning objectives

Lead outcome	Component outcome
B2. Prepare budgets	(a) Explain forecasting and its relationship with budgeting

1 Chapter overview diagram

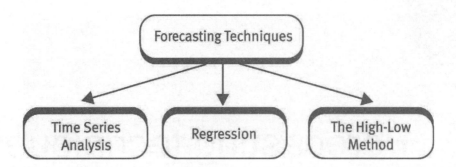

Forecasts in budgeting

Budgets are based on forecasts. Forecasts might be prepared for:

- the volume of output and sales

- sales revenue (sales volume and sales prices)

- costs.

The purpose of forecasting in the budgeting process is to establish realistic assumptions for planning. Forecasts might also be prepared on a regular basis for the purpose of feedforward control reporting.

A forecast might be based on simple assumptions, such as a prediction of a 5% growth in sales volume or sales revenue. Similarly, budgeted expenditure might be forecast using a simple incremental budgeting approach, and adding a percentage amount for inflation on top of the previous year's budget.

On the other hand, forecasts might be prepared using a number of forecasting models, methods or techniques. The reason for using these models and techniques is that they might provide more reliable forecasts.

This chapter describes:

- the high-low method

- the uses of linear regression analysis

- techniques of time series analysis

These methods are based on data gathered from the budgeting process (covered in an earlier chapter). As discussed in the earlier chapter this data can come from areas such as historic sales and cost data, economic data and market research. But there is a growing use of big data to support these other sources of data in spotting trends, identifying relationships between sets of data or in forecasting which costs, for example, may change in terms of behaviour in the future.

Forecasting can also be carried out using a diagram (known as a scatter diagram). The data is plotted on a graph. The y-axis represents the dependent variable, i.e. that variable that depends on the other. The x-axis shows the independent variable, i.e. that variable which is not affected by the other variable. From the scatter diagram, the line of best fit can be estimated. The aim is to use our judgement to draw a line through the middle of data with the same slope as the data. Because it is based on judgement it is potentially less accurate than some of the more mathematical approaches used in this chapter.

More complex models might be used in practice, but these are outside the scope of the syllabus.

2 The high-low method

High-low method revision

In your previous studies you will have seen the use of the high-low method for breaking semi-variable costs into their two components. A semi-variable cost being a cost which is partly fixed and partly variable.

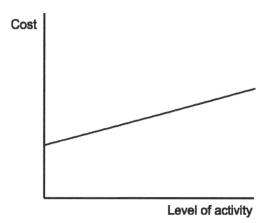

In the exam in computational questions, semi-variable costs must be broken down into their 2 components using the *high-low method.*

Step 1 Determine the variable costs

It is important that we start with the **highest and lowest output (activity)** and their associated costs.

$$\text{Variable cost per unit} = \frac{\text{Increase in cost}}{\text{Increase in activity}}$$

Choose either the highest or lowest output and multiply it by the variable cost per unit just calculated. This will tell us the total variable costs at that output.

Step 2 Find the fixed cost

A semi-variable cost consists of two components:

Total semi-variable cost = Fixed cost + (Variable cost per unit × number of units)

We have found the variable component. What is left must be the fixed component. If we take the total cost and deduct the variable costs (just calculated) then we are left with the fixed costs.

Step 3 Calculate the expected cost

Once the variable cost per unit and the total fixed costs are known, these can be used to predict future cost levels. The total expected future costs will be:

= total fixed costs (from step 2) + [forecast production (in units) × variable cost per unit (from step 1)]

Illustration 1

A factory has incurred the following power costs in the last three months with different levels of production in each month:

	Activity	Power costs
February	16,000	$16,500
March	18,000	$17,500
April	24,000	$20,500

If production levels of 30,000 units are anticipated next month, what is the expected power cost?

Step 1

Find the highest and lowest levels of production (activity) and their related costs.

		Activity	Cost
Highest	April	24,000	$20,500
Lowest	February	16,000	$16,500
		———	———
Difference		8,000	$4,000

Variable cost = $4,000 / 8,000 = $0.50 per unit.

Step 2

Using either the highest or the lowest production level (from step 1), find the fixed cost.

At activity level for 24,000 units:

Total semi-variable cost = Fixed cost + (Variable cost per unit × number of units)

$20,500 = Fixed cost + ($0.50 × 24,000 units)

$20,500 = Fixed cost + $12,000

Fixed cost = $20,500 – $12,000 = $8,500

Step 3

The semi-variable power cost consists of the fixed cost ($8,500) and a variable cost per unit ($0.50). Therefore for an activity level of 30,000 units the total cost is predicted to be:

Variable cost 30,000 × $0.50	$15,000
Fixed cost	$8,500
Total cost	$23,500

Example 1

Great Auk Limited has had the following output and cost results for the last 4 years:

	Output units	Cost $
Year 1	5,000	26,000
Year 2	7,000	34,000
Year 3	9,000	42,000
Year 4	10,000	46,000

In year 5 the output is expected to be 13,000 units. Calculate the expected costs.

Inflation may be ignored.

The high-low method with stepped fixed costs

Sometimes fixed costs are only fixed within certain levels of activity and increase in steps as activity increases (i.e. they are stepped fixed costs).

The high/low method can still be used to estimate fixed and variable costs. Simply choose two activity levels where the fixed cost remains unchanged.

Adjustments need to be made for the fixed costs based on the activity level under consideration.

Illustration

An organisation has the following total costs at three activity levels:

Activity level (units)	4,000	6,000	7,500
Total cost	$40,800	$50,000	$54,800

Variable cost per unit is constant within this activity range and there is a step up of 10% in the total fixed costs when the activity level exceeds 5,500 units.

What is the total cost at an activity level of 5,000 units?

Calculate the variable cost per unit by comparing two output levels where fixed costs will be the same:

Variable cost per unit = [(54,800 – 50,000)/(7,500 – 6,000)] = $3.20

Total fixed cost above 5,500 units = [54,800 – (7,500 × 3.20)] = $30,800

Total fixed cost below 5,500 units = 30,800/110 × 100 = $28,000

Total cost for 5,000 units = [(5,000 × 3.20) + 28,000] = $44,000

Example 2

Total costs in a factory have been recorded for the final five months of 20X8, as follows:

	Output units	Cost $
August	1,200	30,150
September	900	29,050
October	1,100	29,990
November	1,500	31,750
December	1,800	58,910

When output is 1,700 units or more, another factory unit must be rented and fixed costs therefore increase by 100%.

Variable cost per unit is also forecast to rise by 10% in 20X9.

> **Required:**
>
> Calculate the estimated total costs of producing 2,500 units in 20X9.

3 Regression analysis

The high-low method only takes account of two observations – the highest and the lowest. To take account of all observations a more advanced calculation is used known as **linear regression** which uses a formula to estimate the linear relationship between the two variables as follows:

The equation of a straight line is:

$$y = a + bx$$

where
- y = dependent variable
- a = intercept (on y-axis)
- b = gradient
- x = independent variable

and

$$b = \frac{n\Sigma xy - \Sigma x\Sigma y}{n\Sigma x^2 - (\Sigma x)^2}$$

where n = number of pairs of data

and $a = \bar{y} - b\bar{x}$

Note:

$\bar{x}$ is the arithmetic mean (or average) of x and is calculated as:

$$\bar{x} = \frac{\Sigma x}{n}$$

$\bar{y}$ is the arithmetic mean (or average) of y and is calculated as:

$$\bar{y} = \frac{\Sigma y}{n}$$

Whilst so far in your studies you have used the high-low method predominantly to split semi-variable costs into their fixed and variable elements, it is also important to recognise that this method can be extremely useful in forecasting.

With semi-variable costs, we determined that:

Total semi-variable cost = Fixed cost + (variable cost per unit × activity level)

If we look at the formula for the equation of a straight line above, we can see that this could also be written as:

y = a + bx

Where:
- y = total semi-variable cost
- a = fixed cost
- b = variable cost per unit
- x = number of units produced

Throughout the rest of this chapter we will examine how the equation of a straight line, and the use of the high-low method, can also be used within forecasting. It is important to recognise that the y and the x variables will not always be used to denote cost and activity levels as you may have previously seen; they can relate to any two variables which have a linear relationship, for example y=sales and x=time or y=sales and x=advertising spend.

Example 3

Marcus Aurelius is a small supermarket chain that has 6 shops. Each shop advertises in their local newspapers and the marketing director is interested in the relationship between the amount that they spend on advertising and the sales revenue that they achieve. They have collated the following information for the 6 shops for the previous year:

Shop	Advertising expenditure $000	Sales revenue $000
1	80	730
2	60	610
3	120	880
4	90	750
5	70	650
6	30	430

They have further performed some calculations for a linear regression calculation as follows:

- the sum of the advertising expenditure (x) column is 450

- the sum of the sales revenue (y) column is 4,050

- when the two columns are multiplied together and summed (xy) the total is 326,500

- when the advertising expenditure is squared (x^2) and summed, the total is 38,300, and

- when the sales revenue is squared (y^2) and summed, the total is 2,849,300.

Calculate the line of best fit using regression analysis.

Expandable Text

Advertising expenditure $000	Sales $000			
x	y	xy	x^2	y^2
80	730	58,400	6,400	532,900
60	610	36,600	3,600	372,100
120	880	105,600	14,400	774,400
90	750	67,500	8,100	562,500
70	650	45,500	4,900	422,500
30	430	12,900	900	184,900
450	4,050	326,500	38,300	2,849,300

Interpretation of the line

It can be seen from the solution that the regression equation is y = 300 + 5x, where a=$300,000 and b=$5.

Mathematical interpretation

If x = 0, then y = 300 and then each time x increases by 1 y increases by 5

Business interpretation

If no money is spent on advertising then sales would still be $300,000. Then for every additional $1 increase in advertising sales revenue would increase by $5.

Linear regression in budgeting

Linear regression analysis can be used to make forecasts or estimates whenever a linear relationship is assumed between two variables, and historical data is available for analysis.

Two such relationships are:

- **A time series and trend line.** Linear regression analysis is an alternative to calculating moving averages to establish a trend line from a time series. (Time series is explained later in this chapter)

  – The independent variable (x) in a time series is time.

  – The dependent variable (y) is sales, production volume or cost etc.

- **Total costs, where costs consist of a combination of fixed costs and variable costs** (for example, total overheads, or a semi-variable cost item). Linear regression analysis is an alternative to using the high-low method of cost behaviour analysis. It should be more accurate than the high-low method, because it is based on more items of historical data, not just a 'high' and a 'low' value.

  - The independent variable (x) in total cost analysis is the volume of activity.
  - The dependent variable (y) is total cost.
  - The value of a is the amount of fixed costs.
  - The value of b is the variable cost per unit of activity.

Regression analysis is concerned with establishing the relationship between a number of variables. We are only concerned here with linear relationships between 2 variables.

When a linear relationship is identified and quantified using linear regression analysis, values for a and b are obtained, and these can be used to make a forecast for the budget. For example:

- a sales budget or forecast can be prepared, or
- total costs (or total overhead costs) can be estimated, for the budgeted level of activity.

Forecasting

The regression equation can be used for predicting values of y from a given x value.

Example 3 – CONTINUED

Marcus Aurelius has just taken on 2 new stores in the same area and the predicted advertising expenditure is expected to be $150,000 for one store and $50,000 for the other.

(a) Calculate the predicted sales revenues.

(b) Explain the reliability of the forecasts.

Correlation

Regression analysis attempts to find the linear relationship between two variables. Correlation is concerned with establishing how strong the relationship is.

Two variables are said to be **correlated** if they are related to one another, or, more precisely, if changes in the value of one tend to accompany changes in the other.

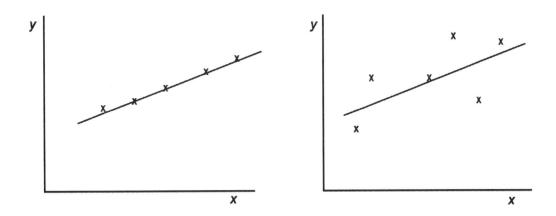

Clearly in the first diagram, the regression line would be a much more useful predictor than the regression line in the second diagram.

Degrees of correlation

Two variables might be:

(a)   perfectly correlated

(b)   partly correlated

(c)   uncorrelated.

Different types of correlation explained

Perfect correlation

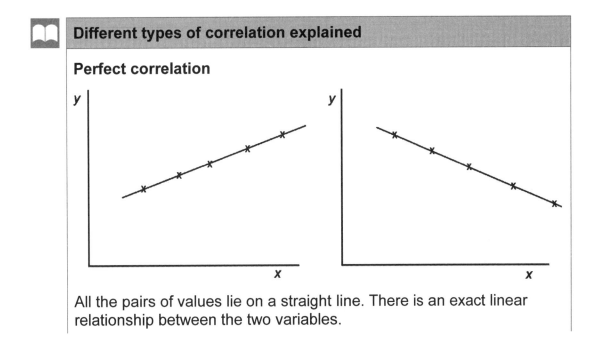

All the pairs of values lie on a straight line. There is an exact linear relationship between the two variables.

Partial correlation

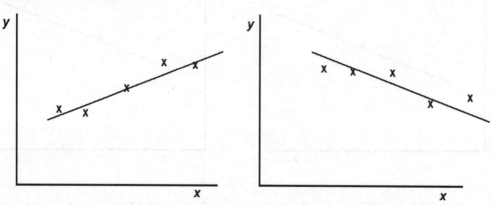

In the first diagram there is not an exact relationship, but low values of x tend to be associated with low values of y, and high values of x tend to be associated with high values of y.

In the second diagram again there is not an exact relationship, but low values of x tend to be associated with high values of y and vice versa.

No correlation

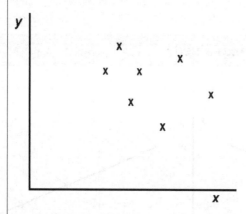

The values of the two variables seem to be completely unconnected.

Positive and negative correlation

Correlation can be positive or negative.

Positive correlation means that high values of one variable are associated with high values of the other and that low values of one are associated with low values of the other.

Negative correlation means that low values of one variable are associated with high values of the other and vice versa.

The correlation coefficient

The degree of correlation can be measured by the Pearsonian correlation coefficient, r (also known as the product moment correlation coefficient).

r must always be between –1 and +1.

If r = 1, there is perfect positive correlation

If r = 0, there is no correlation

If r = –1, there is perfect negative correlation

For other values of r, the meaning is not so clear. It is generally taken that if r > 0.8, then there is strong positive correlation and if r < –0.8, there is strong negative correlation, however more meaningful information can be gathered from calculating the coefficient of determination, r^2.

$$r = \frac{n\sum xy - \sum x \sum y}{\sqrt{\left(n\sum x^2 - (\sum x)^2\right)\left(n\sum y^2 - (\sum y)^2\right)}}$$

The coefficient of determination

This measures how good the estimated regression equation is, designated as r^2 (read as r-squared). The higher the r-squared, the more confidence one can have in the equation. Statistically, the coefficient of determination represents the proportion of the total variation in the y variable that is explained by the regression equation. It has the range of values between 0 and 1.

For example, if we read the following statement "factory overhead is a function of machine-hours with r^2 = 0.80," can be interpreted as "80% of the total variation of factory overhead is explained by the machine hours and the remaining 20% is accounted for by something other than machine-hours." The 20% is referred to as the error term.

Illustration 2 – correlation

Delivery Ltd runs a fleet of delivery vans. Management are investigating the degree of correlation between the costs of vehicle maintenance (y) and the vehicle running hours (x).

They have determined that the correlation coefficient, r = 0.97.

As this value is > 0.8 and is quite close to 1, this indicates a fairly high degree of positive correlation between vehicle maintenance costs and vehicle running hours.

More meaningful information can also be gathered by calculating the coefficient of determination, r^2

$r^2 = 0.97^2 = 0.9409$.

From this we can see that 94% of the variation in the value of y can be explained by a linear relationship with x. This leaves only 6% of variations to be accounted for by other factors. It is therefore likely that vehicle running hours could be used with a high degree of confidence to predict running costs during a period.

Limitations of simple linear regression

(1)   Assumes a linear relationship between the variables.

(2)   Only measures the relationship between two variables. In reality the dependent variable is affected by many independent variables.

(3)   Only interpolated forecasts tend to be reliable. The equation should not be used for extrapolation.

(4)   Regression assumes that the historical behaviour of the data continues into the foreseeable future.

(5)   Interpolated predictions are only reliable if there is a significant correlation between the data.

Interpolation and extrapolation

(1)   If the value of x is within the range of our original data, the prediction is known as Interpolation.

(2)   If the value of x is outside the range of our original data, the prediction is known as Extrapolation.

In general, interpolation is much safer than extrapolation.

4   Adjusting forecasts for inflation

The accuracy of forecasting is affected by the need to adjust historical data and future forecasts to allow for price or cost inflation.

- When historical data is used to calculate a trend line or line of best fit, it should ideally be adjusted to the same index level for prices or costs. If the actual cost or revenue data is used, without adjustments for inflation, the resulting line of best fit will include the inflationary differences.

- When a forecast is made from a line of best fit, an adjustment to the forecast should be made for anticipated inflation in the forecast period.

Illustration 3 – index numbers

The table below shows the sales performance of the Hot Wok Restaurant over the previous 4 years.

Year	Total Revenue $	Number of Customers	Price index
20X4	210,000	2,600	161
20X5	224,700	2,840	182
20X6	241,500	2,720	199
20X7	268,800	2,805	215

The initial revenue figures provided here will include increases due to inflationary rises over the years. By using the index values, the revenue figures can be restated at a common price level to reflect the volume changes underlying sales, i.e. strip out the extra revenue that is due to an increase in selling prices.

The general adjustment carried out to restate costs or revenues at a common price level is to multiply by:

<u>Index level to which costs/revenues will be adjusted</u>

Actual index level of costs/revenues

Where the base year is the year chosen as the common price level.

If revenue were restated at 20X7 prices, the revised revenue figures for Hot Wok Restaurant would be:

Year	Total Revenue $	Adjustment Factor	Revenue at 20X7 price level
20X4	210,000	× 215/161	280,435
20X5	224,700	× 215/182	265,442
20X6	241,500	× 215/199	260,917
20X7	268,800	× 215/215	268,800

This shows that volume fell considerably between 20X4 and 20X6 but improved again in 20X7.

Example 4

Production overhead costs at company BW are assumed to vary with the number of machine hours worked. A line of best fit will be calculated from the following historical data, with costs adjusted to allow for cost inflation over time.

Year	Total production overheads	Number of machine hours	Cost index
	$		
20X1	143,040	3,000	192
20X2	156,000	3,200	200
20X3	152,320	2,700	224
20X4	172,000	3,000	235

Required:

(a) Reconcile the cost data to a common price level, to remove differences caused by inflation.

(b) If the line of best fit, based on current (20X4) prices, is calculated as:

$y = 33,000 + 47x$

where y = total production overhead costs in $ and x = the number of machine hours:

Calculate the expected total overhead costs in 20X5 if expected production activity is 3,100 machine hours and the expected cost index is 250.

The high-low method with inflation

The high low method may be distorted in the presence of inflation. The best technique is to strip out the inflation, perform the technique as usual and then re-apply the inflation.

Illustration

A hotel cleaning department uses a combination of salaried staff (which are a fixed cost paid an annual fixed salary) supplemented at busy periods (such as at the weekend) with part-time staff (seen to be a variable cost). It has gathered the following information on wage cost over the last two months.

	Visitors	Total wages ($)
Month 1	260	7,600
Month 2	300	8,610

Month 2 corresponded with a wage review. At the start of that month all staff received a 5% pay rise.

The restaurant wants to determine the estimated wage cost for the next month when it is expected to have 340 visitors.

Solution

Firstly we should strip out the 5% inflation included in the Month 2 cost so that the uninflated wage cost would be $8,200 (i.e. $8,610/1.05).

Now we can apply the usual high-low technique:

Variable cost per visitor = [(8,200 – 7,600)/(300 – 260)] = $15

Monthly fixed costs = [$7,600 – (260 × $15)] = $3,700

Now we can inflate these estimates for the Month 2 pay rise:

Revised variable cost per visitor = $15 × 1.05 = $15.75

Revised total fixed cost = $3,700 × 1.05 = $3,885

The total estimated cost for 340 visitors will be:

= $3,885 + (340 × $15.75) = $9,240.

5 Time series analysis

A time series is a series of figures recorded over time, e.g. unemployment over the last 5 years, output over the last 12 months, etc.

A time series is often shown graphically as a histogram.

Examples of a time series

Examples of time series might include the following:

- quarterly sales revenue totals over a number of years
- annual overhead costs over a number of years
- daily production output over a month.

Where the item being measured is subject to 'seasonal' variations, time series measurements are usually taken for each season. For example, if sales volume varies in each quarter of the year, a time series should be for quarterly sales. Similarly, if the sales in a retail store vary according to the day of the week, a time series might measure daily sales.

A time series has 4 components:

(1) The trend (T)

(2) Seasonal variations (S)

(3) Cyclical variations (C)

(4) Residual variations (R)

We are primarily interested in the first two – the trend and the seasonal variation.

Time series analysis is a term used to describe techniques for analysing a time series, in order to:

- identify whether there is any **underlying historical trend** and if there is, measure it

- use this analysis of the historical trend to forecast the trend into the future

- identify whether there are any **seasonal variations** around the trend, and if there is measure them

- apply estimated seasonal variations to a trend line forecast in order to prepare a forecast season by season.

In other words, a trend over time, established from historical data, and adjusted for seasonal variations, can then be used to make predictions for the future.

The trend

Most series follow some sort of long term movement – upwards, downwards or sideways. In time series analysis the trend is measured.

Seasonal variations

Seasonal variations are short-term fluctuations in value due to different circumstances which occur at different times of the year, on different days of the week, different times of day, etc. Some examples might be:

- Ice cream sales are highest in summer

- Sales of groceries are highest on Saturdays

- Traffic is greatest in the morning and evening rush hours.

Illustration 4

A business might have a flat trend in sales, of $1 million each six months, but with sales $150,000 below trend in the first six months of the year and $150,000 above trend in the second six months. In this example, the sales would be $850,000 in the first six months of the year and $1,150,000 in the second six months.

- If there is a straight-line trend in the time series, seasonal variations must cancel each other out. The total of the seasonal variations over each cycle should be zero.

- Seasonal variations can be measured:

  - in units or in money values, or

  - as a percentage value or index value in relation to the underlying Trend

Cyclical and residual factors

Cyclical variations

Cyclical variations are medium-term to long term influences usually associated with the economy. These cycles are rarely of consistent length. A further problem is that we would need 6 or 7 full cycles of data to be sure that the cycle was there.

Residual or random factors

The residual is the difference between the actual value and the figure predicted using the trend, the cyclical variation and the seasonal variation, i.e. it is caused by irregular items, which could not be predicted.

Calculation of the trend

There are three main methods of finding the underlying trend of the data:

(1) Inspection. The trend line can be drawn by eye with the aim of plotting the line so that it lies in the middle of the data.

(2) Least squares regression analysis (and also high-low). The x axis represents time and the periods of time are numbers, e.g. January is 1, February is 2, March is 3, etc.

(3) Moving averages. This method attempts to remove seasonal or cyclical variations by a process of averaging.

Calculating a moving average

A moving average is in fact a series of averages, calculated from time series historical data.

- The first moving average value in the series is the average of the values for time period 1 to time period n. (So, if n = 4, the first moving average in the series would be the average of the historical values for time period 1 to time period 4.)

- The second moving average value in the series is the average of the values for time period 2 to time period (n + 1). (So, if n = 4, the second moving average in the series would be the average of the historical values for time period 2 to time period 5.)

- The third moving average value in the series is the average of the values for time period 3 to time period (n + 2). (So, if n = 4, the third moving average in the series would be the average of the historical values for time period 3 to time period 6.)

The moving average value is associated with the mid-point of the time periods used to calculate the average.

The moving average time period

When moving averages are used to estimate a trend line, an important issue is the choice of the number of time periods to use to calculate the moving average. How many time periods should a moving average be based on?

There is no definite or correct answer to this question. However, where there is a regular cycle of time periods, it would make sense to calculate the moving averages over a full cycle.

- When you are calculating a moving average of daily figures, it is probably appropriate to calculate a seven-day moving average.

- When you are calculating a moving average of quarterly figures, it is probably appropriate to calculate a four-quarter moving average.

- When you are calculating a moving average of monthly figures, it might be appropriate to calculate a 12-month moving average, although a shorter-period moving average might be preferred.

The seasonal variation

Once the trend has been found, the seasonal variation can be determined. A seasonal variation means that some periods are better than average (the trend) and some worse. Then the model can be used to predict future values.

Measuring seasonal variations

The technique for measuring seasonal variations differs between an additive model and a multiplicative model. The additive model method is described here.

- Seasonal variations can be estimated by comparing an actual time series with the trend line values calculated from the time series.

- For each 'season' (quarter, month, day etcetera), the seasonal variation is the difference between the trend line value and the actual historical value for the same period.

- A seasonal variation can be calculated for each period in the trend line. When the actual value is higher than the trend line value, the seasonal variation is positive. When the actual value is lower than the trend line value, the seasonal variation is negative.

- An average variation for each season is calculated.

- The sum of the seasonal variations has to be zero in the additive model. If they do not add up to zero, the seasonal variations should be adjusted so that they do add up to zero.

- The seasonal variations calculated in this way can be used in forecasting, by adding the seasonal variation to the trend line forecast if the seasonal variation is positive, or subtracting it from the trend line if it is negative.

When a multiplicative model is used to estimate seasonal variations, the seasonal variation for each period is calculated by expressing the actual sales for the period as a percentage value of the moving average figure for the same period.

The additive model

Here, the seasonal variation is expressed as an absolute amount to be added on the trend to find the actual result, e.g. ice-cream sales in summer are high and we would expect sales to be $200,000 above the trend.

Actual/Prediction = T + S + C + R

In exam questions we would not be required to calculate the cyclical variation, and the random variations are by nature random and cannot be predicted and also ignored. The equation simplifies to:

Prediction = T + S

Example of the calculation

A small business operating holiday homes in Scotland wishes to forecast next year's sales for the budget, using moving averages to establish a straight-line trend and seasonal variations. Next year is 20Y0. The accountant has assumed that sales are seasonal, with a summer season and a winter season each year. Seasonal sales for the past seven years have been as follows:

Sales

	Summer $000	Winter $000
20X4	124	70
20X5	230	180
20X6	310	270
20X7	440	360
20X8	520	470
20X9	650	

Required:

(a) Calculate a trend line based on a two-season moving average.

(b) Use the trend line to calculate the average increase in sales each season.

(c) Calculate the adjusted seasonal variations in sales.

(d) Use this data to prepare a sales forecast for each season in 20Y0.

Solution

(a)

Season and year	Actual sales	Two-season moving total	Seasonal moving average	Centred moving average (Trend)	Seasonal variation
	(A)			(B)	= (A) – (B)
	$000	$000	$000	$000	$000
Summer 20X4	124				
		194	97		
Winter 20X4	70			123.5	– 53.5
		300	150		
Summer 20X5	230			177.5	+ 52.5
		410	205		
Winter 20X5	180			225.0	– 45.0
		490	245		
Summer 20X6	310			267.5	+ 42.5
		580	290		
Winter 20X6	270			322.5	– 52.5
		710	355		
Summer 20X7	440			377.5	+ 62.5
		800	400		
Winter 20X7	360			420.0	– 60.0
		880	440		
Summer 20X8	520			467.5	+ 52.5
		990	495		
Winter 20X8	470			527.5	– 57.5
		1,120	560		
Summer 20X9	650				

The trend line is shown by the centred moving averages.

(b)   The average increase in sales each season in the trend line is:

($527,500 – $123,500)/8 seasons = $50,500 each season

(c)   Seasonal variations need to add up to zero in the additive model. The seasonal variations calculated so far are:

Year	Summer $000	Winter $000
20X4		– 53.5
20X5	+ 52.5	– 45.0
20X6	+ 42.5	– 52.5
20X7	+ 62.5	– 60.0
20X8	+ 52.5	– 57.5
Total variations	+ 210.0	– 268.5

	Summer	Winter	Total
Number of measurements	4	5	
Average seasonal variation	+ 52.5	– 53.7	– 1.2
Reduce to 0 (share equally)	+ 0.6	+ 0.6	+ 1.2
Adjusted seasonal variation	+ 53.1	– 53.1	0.0

The seasonal variations could be rounded to + $53,000 in summer and – $53,000 in winter.

(d) To predict the sales in 20Y0 we first need to extrapolate the trend line into 20Y0 and then adjust it for the expected seasonal variation

	Expected Trend (W1)	Adjusted seasonal variation	Forecast sales
Summer 20X9	578.0		
Winter 20X9	628.5		
Summer 20Y0	679.0	+ 53.0	732.0
Winter 20Y0	729.5	– 53.0	676.5

Workings

(W1)

If the actual trend in Winter 20X8 was 527.5, then we can expect the next trend figure to be 578 (527.5 plus the average increase in trend calculated in part (b) of 50.5). We can continue this process for each trend figure over the next few periods.

The multiplicative model

Here, the seasonal variation is expressed as a ratio/proportion/percentage to be multiplied by the trend to arrive at the actual figure, e.g. ice-cream sales in summer are high and we would expect sales to be 50% more than the trend.

Actual/Prediction = T × S × C × R

Again, this simplifies to:

Prediction = T × S

Illustration 5

Consider a business with the following actual results in a year:

Year	Quarter	Units sold
20X1	1	65
20X1	2	80
20X1	3	70
20X1	4	85

The trend is expected to increase by 10 units per month and has been calculated as 60 units for the first quarter. This provides the following table:

Year	Quarter	Units sold	Trend
20X1	1	65	60
20X1	2	80	70
20X1	3	70	80
20X1	4	85	90

Required:

How might might those figures be used to develop a time series model in order to forecast unit sales in each quarter of year 2, using:

(a) an additive modelling approach

(b) a multiplicative modelling approach

Solution

The point of departure is to take the actual unit sales and compare the trend figures with the actual figures for year 1 in order to determine the seasonal variation for each quarter. This variation can be expressed as either an absolute amount (the additive approach) or a proportion of the trend (the multiplicative approach).

Year	Quarter	Units sold	Trend	(a) variation	(b) variation %
20X1	1	65	60	+5	+8.33
20X1	2	80	70	+10	+14.29
20X1	3	70	80	-10	-12.50
20X1	4	85	90	-5	-5.56

Notes:

(1) The multiplicative model season variations may be expressed in several different ways. For example, the quarter 3 factor may be expressed as an indexation 87.5% or 0.875.

(2) In the multiplicative model the total seasonal variations should add up to zero (or 0%). In this scenario we are looking only at an abstract of a longer based trend and therefore it does not add to 0% here.

We can now apply these variation figures to trend projections in order to produce a quarterly forecast for unit sales in Year 2. The two modelling approaches produce two alternative forecasts under headings (a) and (b).

Year	Quarter	Trend	Additive (a)	Multiplicative (b)
20X2	1	100	105	108
20X2	2	110	120	126
20X2	3	120	110	105
20X2	4	130	125	123

Note that this is a basic example to explain the basis of the calculations. In particular, we are basing our analysis on only one set of observations (for 20X1 only). In practice, the seasonal variations would be based on an average of two or three sets of observations. The averaging process has the effect of 'ironing out' the impact of random variations over the past period you are considering.

Example 5

A company has identified the trend in its sales figures through the regression equation:

$y = 25,600 + 57.8x$

Where y is the sales revenue and x is the quarter number. (x=1 is year 20X0, quarter 1).The average seasonal variation for quarter 3 is -510.

Required:

Calculate the forecast sales revenue for quarter 3 in 20X2 using the additive model.

Advantages and disadvantages

The advantages of forecasting using time series analysis are that:

- forecasts are based on clearly-understood assumptions

- trend lines can be reviewed after each successive time period, when the most recent historical data is added to the analysis; consequently, the reliability of the forecasts can be assessed

- forecasting accuracy can possibly be improved with experience.

The disadvantages of forecasting with time series analysis are that:

- there is an assumption that what has happened in the past is a reliable guide to the future

- there is an assumption that a straight-line trend exists

- there is an assumption that seasonal variations are constant, either in actual values using the additive model (such as dollars of sales) or as a proportion of the trend line value using the multiplicative model.

None of these assumptions might be valid.

However, the reliability of a forecasting method can be established over time. If forecasts turn out to be inaccurate, management might decide that they are not worth producing, and that different methods of forecasting should be tried. On the other hand, if forecasts prove to be reasonably accurate, management are likely to continue with the same forecasting method.

6 Chapter summary

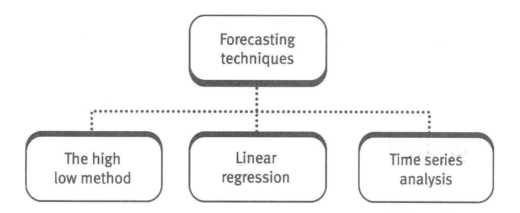

Forecasting techniques

The high low method
- The key is to use the highest and lowest output
- Calculate variable costs first
- Watch out for inflation and steps in fixed costs

Linear regression
- Assumes a linear relationship between two variables
- $y = a + bx$
- y = dependent variable (e.g. sales)
- x = independent variables (e.g. time)
- Variables must be correlated

Time series analysis
- Takes account of inflation
- The trend is calculated using a moving average
- Forecast trend needs to be adjusted for seasonal variations

7 Practice questions

Test your understanding 1

The following extract is taken from the production cost budget of S Limited:

Production (units)	2,000	3,000
Production cost ($)	11,100	12,900

The budget cost allowance for an activity level of 4,000 units would be

$ _14,700_

Test your understanding 2

The following data have been extracted from the budget working papers of BL Limited.

Production volume	1,000	2,000
	$/unit	$/unit
Direct materials	4.00	4.00
Direct labour	3.50	3.50
Production overhead – department 1	6.00	4.20
Production overhead – department 2	4.00	2.00

Identify the total fixed cost and variable cost per unit (circle the correct figure in each column)

Total fixed cost	Variable cost per unit
3,600	7.50
7,600	9.90

Test your understanding 3

A company will forecast its quarterly sales units for a new product by using a formula to predict the base sales units and then adjusting the figure by a seasonal index.

The formula is BU = 4,000 + 80Q

Where BU = Base sales units and Q is the quarterly period number.

The seasonal index values are:

Quarter 1	105%
Quarter 2	80%
Quarter 3	95%
Quarter 4	120%

Identify the forecast increase in sales units from Quarter 3 to Quarter 4:

A   25%

B   80 units

C   100 units

D   1,156 units ✓

Test your understanding 4

W plc is preparing its budgets for next year.

The following regression equation has been found to be a reliable estimate of W plc's deseasonalised sales in units:

$y = 10x + 420$

Where y is the total sales units and x refers to the accountancy period. Quarterly seasonal variations have been found to be:

Q1	Q2	Q3	Q4
+75	+188	−38	−225

In accounting period 33 (which is quarter 4) identify the forecast seasonally adjusted sales units:

A   525

B   589   ✓

C   750

D   975

Test your understanding 5

A company has achieved the following sales levels of its key product, article B, over the last four years:

Sales of article B ('000 units)

	Q1	Q2	Q3	Q4
20X3	24.8	36.3	38.1	47.5
20X4	31.2	42.0	43.4	55.9
20X5	40.0	48.8	54.0	69.1
20X6	54.7	57.8	60.3	68.9

Using linear regression numbering 20X3 Q1 as t = 1, through to 20X6 Q4 as t = 16, and letting x = t and y = T

The trend equation is:

$T = 28.54 + 2.3244t$

Required:

The forecast sales of B in Quarter 3 of 20X7 are 72.7% (in '000 units and rounded to one decimal place)

Test your understanding 6

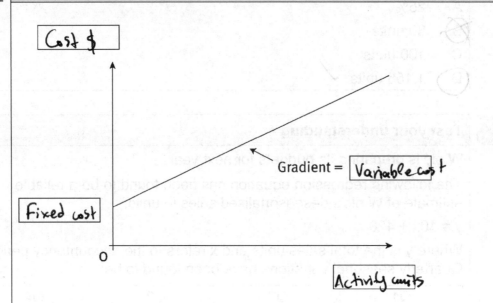

The above graph plots total cost against activity levels.

Place the following elements on to the correct place on the graph.

Cost $
Fixed cost
Variable cost
Activity units

Test your understanding 7

A car sales business is trying to understand the relationship between the level of car sales and the total salaries for the sales team. The management accountant has carried out some analysis investigating whether the level of salary had an impact on the volume of sales and has found that the coefficient of determination is 0.75.

Which of the following is correct?

A   For every $0.75 spent on salaries, $1.00 of sales will be generated.

B   For every $1.00 spent on salaries, $0.75 of sales will be generated.

C   75% of the variation in sales can be explained by the corresponding variation in salaries.

D   75% of the variation in salaries can be explained by the corresponding variation in sales.

Test your understanding 8

A company which manufactures paint is preparing its forecast purchases of pigment for next year.

Regression analysis has been carried out and the following trend equation has been derived:

$y = 3,115 + 22.61x$

Where y is the forecast kgs of pigment and x is the period number.

The purchase price per kg in month 8 was $34 when the cost index was 131. The cost index for month 15 is expected to be 167.

Required:

Calculate the purchase cost for month 15. $K9,715$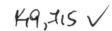

Test your understanding 9

A business is forecasting the value of their sales for the first quarter of the coming year. Current year values to date are as follows:

Month	Sales value $
June	851
July	771
August	916
September	935
October	855
November	1,000
December	1,019

Required:

Using a 3 point moving average, calculate the forecast sales values for January to March.

Test your understanding answers

Example 1

Step 1: Calculate the variable cost per unit

$$\text{Variable cost per unit} = \frac{\text{Increase in cost}}{\text{Increase in level of activity}}$$

$$= \frac{\$46{,}000 - \$26{,}000}{10{,}000 \text{ units} - 5{,}000 \text{ units}}$$

$$= \$4 \text{ per unit}$$

Step 2: Find the fixed cost

The fixed cost can be determined either at the high level or the low level.

	High level $	Low level $
Semi-variable cost	46,000	26,000
Variable costs		
$4 per unit × 10,000 units	40,000	
$4 per unit × 5,000 units		20,000
Fixed cost	6,000	6,000

Step 3: Calculate the expected cost

Therefore cost for 13,000 units = (13,000 units × $4 per unit) + $6,000
= $58,000

Example 2

Choose the highest and lowest activity levels where the fixed cost remains unchanged, i.e. at output below 1,700 units.

Highest activity = 1,500 units; Lowest activity = 900 units.

Step 1: Calculate the variable cost per unit

$$\text{Variable cost per unit} = \frac{\text{Increase in cost}}{\text{Increase in level of activity}}$$

$$= \frac{\$31{,}750 - \$29{,}050}{1{,}500 \text{ units} - 900 \text{ units}}$$

$$= \$4.50 \text{ per unit}$$

Step 2: Find the fixed cost

The fixed cost can be determined either at the high level or the low level.

	High level $	Low level $
Total semi-variable cost	31,750	29,050
Less variable costs		
$4.50 per unit × 1,500 units	(6,750)	
$4.50 per unit × 900 units		(4,050)
Fixed cost	25,000	25,000

Step 3: Calculate the expected cost of producing 2,500 units

Fixed costs will increase by 100%, as output is above 1,700 units.

Variable costs will increase by 10% in 20X9, which will be $4.50 × 1.1 = $4.95 per unit.

	2,500 units $
Fixed cost ($25,000 × 200%)	50,000
Variable cost ($4.95 × 2,500 units)	12,375
Total semi-variable cost	62,375

Example 3

$$b = \frac{n\Sigma xy - \Sigma x\Sigma y}{n\Sigma x^2 - (\Sigma x)^2}$$

$$= \frac{6 \times 326,500 - 450 \times 4,050}{6 \times 38,300 - 450^2}$$

$$= \frac{136,500}{27,300} \qquad = 5$$

$$a = \bar{y} - b\bar{x}$$

$$a = \frac{4,050}{6} - 5 \times \frac{450}{6} \qquad = 300$$

The regression equation is $\qquad y = 300 + 5x$

Workings:

$\bar{x} = (\Sigma x)/n = 450/6 = 75$

$\bar{y} = (\Sigma y)/n = 4,050/6 = 675$

Example 3 – CONTINUED

(a)

	$000
Sales revenue = $300k + (5 × $150k) =	1,050
Sales revenue = $300k + (5 × $50k) =	550

(b) The second prediction is the more reliable as it involves interpolation. The first prediction goes beyond the original data upon which the regression line was based and thus assumes that the relationship will continue on in the same way, which may not be true.

Example 4

(a) As the line of best fit is based on 20X4 prices, use this as the common price level. Costs should therefore be adjusted by a factor:

$$\frac{\text{Index level to which costs will be adjusted}}{\text{Actual index level of costs}}$$

Year	Actual overheads	Cost index	Adjustment factor	Costs at 20X4 price level
	$			$
20X1	143,040	192	× 235/192	175,075
20X2	156,000	200	× 235/200	183,300
20X3	152,320	224	× 235/224	159,800
20X4	172,000	235	× 235/235	172,000

(b) If the forecast number of machine hours is 3,100 and the cost index is 250:

Forecast overhead costs = [$33,000 + ($47 × 3,100 hours)] × (250/235)

= $178,700 × (250/235)

= $190,106

Example 5

y = 25,600 + 57.8x

If quarter 1 in 20X0 is x=1, then quarter 3 in 20X2 will be x=11.

y = 25,600 + (57.8 × 11) = 26,236 (Trend)

Forecast = trend + seasonal variation

= $26,236 – 510 = $25,726

Test your understanding 1

The high-low method

Step 1 Calculate the variable cost per unit

$$\text{Variable cost per unit} = \frac{\text{Increase in cost}}{\text{Increase in level of activity}}$$

$$= \frac{\$12,900 - \$11,100}{3,000 \text{ units} - 2,000 \text{ units}}$$

$$= \$1.80 \text{ per unit}$$

Step 2 Find the fixed cost

A semi-variable cost has only got 2 components – a fixed bit and a variable bit. We now know the variable part. The bit that's left must be the fixed cost. It can be determined either at the high level or the low level.

	High level $	Low level $
Semi-variable cost	12,900	11,100
Variable part		
$1.80/unit × 3,000 units	5,400	
$1.80/unit × 2,000 units		3,600
Fixed cost	7,500	7,500

Therefore cost for 4,000 units = 4,000 units × $1.80 per unit + $7,500 = **$14,700.** ✓

Test your understanding 2

We know the cost per unit. We need to multiply by the number of units so that we can find the total cost for 1,000 units and 2,000 units. Then we can apply the high-low method.

Production volume	1,000	2,000
	$/unit	$/unit
Direct materials	4.00	4.00
Direct labour	3.50	3.50
Production overhead – department 1	6.00	4.20
Production overhead – department 2	4.00	2.00
	___	___
	17.50	13.70
× No of units	× 1,000	× 2,000
	___	___
Total cost	17,500	27,400
	___	___

Now we can do the high-low method.

The high-low method

Step 1 Calculate the variable cost per unit

$$\text{Variable cost per unit} = \frac{\text{Increase in cost}}{\text{Increase in level of activity}}$$

$$= \frac{\$27,400 - \$17,500}{2,000 \text{ units} - 1,000 \text{ units}}$$

$$= \textbf{\$9.90 per unit}$$

Step 2 Find the fixed cost

A semi-variable cost has only got 2 components – a fixed bit and a variable bit. We now know the variable part. The bit that's left must be the fixed cost. It can be determined either at the high level or the low level.

	High level $	Low level $
Semi-variable cost	27,400	17,500
Variable part		
$9.90/unit × 2,000 units	19,800	
$9.90/unit × 1,000 units		9,900
Fixed cost	**7,600**	7,600

Test your understanding 3

D

Sales in quarter 3 (Q = 3)		
Base = 4,000 + (80 × 3)	=	4,240
Seasonal adjustment		95%
Actual sales	=	4,028
Sales in quarter 4 (Q = 4)		
Base = 4,000 + (80 × 4)	=	4,320
Seasonal adjustment		120%
Actual sales	=	5,184
Overall increase in sales	=	5,184 – 4,028 = 1,156 units

Test your understanding 4

A

y = 10x + 420

We are told that x refers to the accounting period, which is 33, therefore:

y = 420 + (33 × 10) = 750

This is the trend, however and we need to consider the seasonal variation too. Accounting period 33 is quarter 4. Quarter 4 is a bad quarter and the seasonal variation is –225, therefore the expected results for period 33 are 225 less than the trend.

Expected sales = 750 – 225 = 525 units

Test your understanding 5

72.7

In 20X7, t takes values 17 to 20. Quarter 3 will correspond to a t value of 19. The forecast sales will be:

Q3 t = 19 T = 28.54 + (2.3244 × 19) = 72.7036

Test your understanding 6

The completed diagram is:

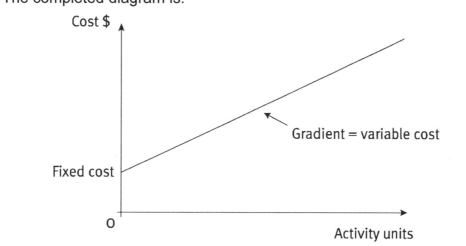

Test your understanding 7

C

The coefficient of determination gives the percentage of the variation in y (in this case, sales) which can be explained by the regression relationship with x (in this case, salary cost).

Test your understanding 8

For period 15, x = 15.

y = 3,115 + (22.61 × 15) = 3,454.15 kgs purchased.

Purchase cost = $34 × 3,454.15kg × 167/131 = $149,715

Test your understanding 9

Firstly calculate the trend:

Month	Actual Sales	Trend
June	851	
July	771	846
August	916	874
September	935	902
October	855	930
November	1,000	958
December	1,019	

Compare the trend to the actual sales values to calculate the seasonal variation. Remember that the variation is 'from the trend' so in the case of July the sales value of $771 is less than the trend of $846 hence the negative variation:

Month	Actual Sales $	Trend $	Seasonal variation $
June	851		
July	771	846	-75
August	916	874	42
September	935	902	33
October	855	930	-75
November	1,000	958	42
December	1,019		

We can see that the trend is increasing by $28 each month and so the trend for December to March will be as follows:

Month	Actual Sales $	Trend $	Seasonal variation $
June	851		
July	771	846	-75
August	916	874	42
September	935	902	33
October	855	930	-75
November	1,000	958	42
December	1,019	958+28=986	
January		986+28=1,014	
February		1,014+28=1,042	
March		1,042+28=1,070	

The final step is to apply the seasonal variation to the trend to calculate the forecast sales value. In this example the seasonal variation has a cyclical pattern so we repeat the variation until we have forecast the figures required:

Month	Actual Sales	Trend	Seasonal variation	Forecast Sales
	$	$	$	$
June	851			
July	771	846	-75	
August	916	874	42	
September	935	902	33	
October	855	930	-75	
November	1,000	958	42	
December	1,019	986	33	
January		1,014	**-75**	**939**
February		1,042	**42**	**1,084**
March		1,070	**33**	**1,103**

Budgetary control

Chapter learning objectives

Lead outcome	Component outcome
B3. Discuss budgetary control	(a) The concept of budgetary control
	(b) Human dimensions of budgeting

1 Session content diagram

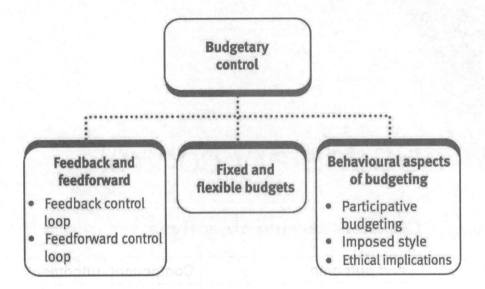

2 The meaning of budgetary control

Budgetary control is about assessing actual performance against budgeted performance and taking corrective action when necessary.

The control system is a systematic approach which tells managers whether or not they are achieving what they planned to achieve.

It focuses on total costs for a department or business unit, and responsibility for these total costs is allocated to an individual (this is known as responsibility accounting). If there are any differences between actual and budgeted performance (known as a variance), the responsible individual can act to either correct the budget or to take action to bring the cost back under control (whichever is most appropriate).

Effective budgetary control

Atrill and McLaney identify a number of characteristics that are common to businesses with effective budgetary control:

- a serious attitude is taken to the system
- clear demarcation between areas of managerial responsibility
- budget targets that are challenging yet achievable
- established data collection, analysis and reporting techniques
- reports aimed at individual managers
- fairly short reporting periods
- timely variance reports
- action being taken to get operations back under control if they are shown to be out of control.

3 Feedback and feedforward control

There are two main types of control system:

- **feedback control** – in this system the aim is to correct problems that have been discovered at the period end when the actual results are compared with the budget.

More details on feedback control

Feedback control is the comparison of actual results against expected results and if there is a significant difference, then it is investigated and if possible and desirable it is corrected.

It is defined as:

'Measurement of differences between planned outputs and actual outputs achieved, and **the modification of subsequent action** and/or plans to achieve future required results. Feedback control is an integral part of budgetary control and standard costing systems.' (CIMA Official Terminology)

Corrective action that brings actual performance closer to the target or plan is called negative feedback.

Corrective action that increases the difference between actual performance and the target or plan is called positive feedback.

Feedback control in budgeting

- An organisation prepares a budget, and commits resources to achieving the budget targets.

- The business uses its resources to make products or provide services. Private sector organisations sell their output.

- Outputs from the system are measured. In budgetary control, output measurements will be quantities of products made or services provided, costs incurred, revenues earned, and profits and return. Some non-financial performance measurements might also be taken.

- The measurements provide feedback information to management, who compare actual results with the budget.

- Where a need for control action is identified, the manager responsible takes suitable control action.

With negative feedback, the control action is intended to bring actual performance back into line with the budget. For example, if actual costs are higher than budget, control action might be taken to cut costs. Similarly, if actual sales volume is lower than budgeted sales, action might be taken to boost sales.

With positive feedback, control action would be intended to increase the differences between the budget and actual results. For example, if actual sales are higher than budget, control action might be taken to make this situation continue. Similarly, when actual costs are less than budget, measures might be taken to keep costs down.

The manner in which a feedback control loop might work in the context of a budgetary control system may be illustrated by the following diagram:

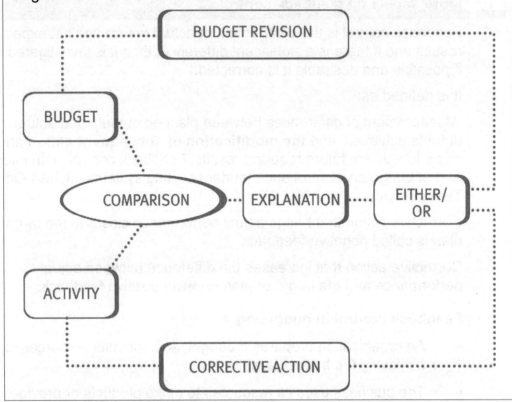

Budgetary control systems are typically feedback systems – an expenditure budget is set and then a comparison is made with actual expenditure at the end of the budget period. If this shows that actual expenditure exceeds budget then it is not possible to take control action to prevent this overspending as it has already been incurred. The information can, however, be used to avoid the situation happening again in the future.

- **feedforward control** – in this system the aim is to anticipate problems with the aim of preventing them from occurring. Feedforward control should be used in conjunction with feedback control.

More details on feedforward control

Feedforward

Feedforward is the comparison of the results that are currently expected in the light of the latest information and the desired results. If there is a difference, then it is investigated and corrected.

Feedback happens after the event and discovers that something **has** gone wrong (or right). It is obviously too late to affect the result that has just happened, but the idea is that if we can understand what went wrong in the previous period, then we can stop the problem from recurring.

Feedforward is more proactive and aims to **anticipate** problems and prevent them from occurring.

It is defined as the 'forecasting of differences between actual and planned outcomes and the implementation of actions before the event, to avoid such differences' (CIMA Official Terminology).

Whereas feedback is based on a comparison of historical actual results with the budget for the period to date, feedforward looks ahead and compares:

*   the target or objectives for the period, and

*   what actual results are now forecast.

An example of a feedforward control is cash budgeting (which we looked at in an earlier chapter) which will warn management if a major cash surplus or deficit is expected to arise at some date in the future so that management can take action now.

Advantages and problems with feedforward control

Feedforward control reporting offers the key advantage that it is forward-looking. It informs management what is likely to happen unless control measures are taken. Management can compare their targets for the period with current expectations.

In contrast, feedback control is backward-looking, and historical variances or differences from plan are not necessarily a guide to what will happen over the full budget period.

A problem with feedforward control is that control reports should be produced regularly, which means that forecasts must be updated regularly. To implement an efficient feed-forward control system, it is therefore necessary to have an efficient forecasting system. Forecasts might be prepared using computer models, with revisions to the forecast each month based on updated information about actual results to date, and where appropriate by making alterations to the basic assumptions in the model.

A departmental manager is responsible for the cash budget for the department for the year. The organisation uses feedforward control systems.

The cash budget at the start of the year stated that there would be a cash balance of $400,000 at the beginning of June and that a piece of capital equipment costing $320,000 was to be purchased in the month.

Two months earlier, in April, using the feedforward control systems in the organisation, the manager responsible for the budget realises that the cash budget was optimistic and that, because some credit customers are paying later than was expected, the expected cash balance will be only $220,000 at the start of June.

Feedforward control

Feedforward control has two elements here. Firstly, it has been used to identify a problem in advance (i.e. in April). The manager can see that the department will not have enough cash in June to purchase the machine as planned.

Secondly, having anticipated the potential problem if the machine is purchased, it allows the manager to take steps to eliminate the problem before it occurs:

- the department could simply delay the purchase of the machine for 1 or 2 months

- or it could negotiate with the supplier of the equipment to see if they would be willing to accept instalments

- or it could speak to the bank manager and obtain a temporary overdraft, etc.

Control reports

Feedback control reports and feedforward control reports might be presented at the same time but they will have a different layout, present different information and have different uses in that:

- the feedback control report will look backwards at the performance for the period and consider any difference from the planned performance for that period

- the feedforward control report will look forward and create expectations about expected future performance with the aim of identifying potential future issues for resolution.

Illustration 2

A sales manager receives monthly control reports about sales values. The budgeted sales for the year to 31 December are $600,000 in total. At the end of April the manager might receive the following feedback control report.

Feedback control report

Sales report for April

	Month			Cumulative		
	Budget	Actual	Variance	Budget	Actual	Variance
Product	$000	$000	$000	$000	$000	$000
P1	35	38	3 (F)	90	94	4 (F)
P2	20	14	6 (A)	50	39	11 (A)
P3	25	23	2 (A)	50	45	5 (A)
Total	80	75	5 (A)	190	178	12 (A)

The aim of this report is to assess performance in April. The sales manager can see that product P3 has had a poor month of sales and has achieved $2,000 less sales than expected. The manager can also see that product P3 is now $5,000 below where it should have been at this point in the year. The manager might want to take some corrective action at this point such as replacing some of the sales team for P3 or reducing performance related pay for that product.

Feedforward control report

Alternatively, the sales manager might be presented with a feedforward control report, as follows:

Sales report, April

Product	Budget $000	Current forecast $000	Variance $000
P1	240	250	10 (F)
P2	150	120	30 (A)
P3	210	194	16 (A)
Total	600	564	36 (A)

This report compares the expected year end totals for each product against the original budget for the year. For example, P2 was budgeted to achieve sales by the end of the year of $150,000, but a revised budget for the year now suggest that P2 will only achieve $120,000 of sales by the end of December.

The manager can react to this by seeking ways to make up the deficit in sales in P2 before the year end (for example, by improving the marketing of P2 or by motivating the sales staff to sell more of P2 before the year-end).

Example 1

Which of the following statement/(s) in relation to a feedback control system are correct:

(A) In a feedback control system actual results are compared with the budget to correct problems that have been discovered.

B In a feedback control system, problems are anticipated in advance to try and prevent them from occurring.

C Corrective action that brings actual performance closer to the target is called 'positive feedback'.

D A feedback control system requires an efficient forecasting system.

4 Fixed and flexible budgets

A **fixed** budget contains information on costs and revenues for one level of activity.

A **flexible** budget shows the same information, but for a number of different levels of activity. Flexible budgets are useful for both planning purposes and control purposes.

(1) When preparing a flexible budget, managers are forced to consider the different scenarios and their responses to them. Thus for a number of different situations, managers will have calculated their costs and revenues. If an unexpected event does occur, changing the level of activity, management will be better prepared.

(2) Budgetary control is the comparison of actual results against budget. Where the actual level of activity is different to that expected, comparisons of actual results against a fixed budget can give misleading results.

> In budgetary control systems managers should always compare performance against a flexed budget.

Illustration 3

A company manufactures a single product and the following data show the actual results for costs for the month of April compared with the budgeted figures.

Operating statement for April

	Budget	Actual	Variance
Units produced	1,200	1,000	(200)
	$	$	$
Direct material	19,200	16,490	2,710
Direct labour	13,200	12,380	820
Production overhead	24,000	24,120	(120)
Administration overhead	21,000	21,600	(600)
Selling overhead	16,400	16,200	200
Total	93,800	90,790	3,010

Note: Variances in brackets are adverse.

Looking at the costs incurred in April, a cost saving of $3,010 has been made compared with the budget. However, the number of units produced was 200 less than budget so some savings in expenditure might be expected. It is not possible to tell from this comparison how much of the saving is due to efficient cost control, and how much is the result of the reduction in activity.

The type of budget being used here is a **fixed budget.** A fixed budget is one which remains **unchanged regardless of the actual level of activity**. In situations where activity levels are likely to change, and there is a significant proportion of variable costs, it is difficult to control expenditure satisfactorily with a fixed budget.

If costs are mostly fixed, then changes in activity levels will not cause problems for cost comparisons with fixed budgets.

A **flexible budget** can help managers to make more valid comparisons.

It is designed to show the allowed expenditure for the actual number of units produced and sold. Comparing this flexible budget with the actual expenditure, it is possible to distinguish genuine efficiencies and inefficiencies.

Preparing a flexible budget

Before a flexible budget can be prepared, managers must identify the cost behaviour, i.e. which costs are fixed, which are variable and which are semi-variable. The allowed expenditure on variable costs can then be increased or decreased as the level of activity changes. You will recall that fixed costs are those costs which will not increase or decrease over the relevant range of activity. The allowance for these items will therefore remain constant. Semi-variable costs have both a fixed and a variable element.

We can now continue with the example.

Management has identified that the following budgeted costs are fixed:

	$
Direct labour	8,400
Production overhead	18,000
Administration overhead	21,000
Selling overhead	14,000

It is now possible to identify the expected variable cost per unit produced.

	Original budget	Fixed cost	Variable cost	Variable cost per unit
	(a)	(b)	(c) = (a) – (b)	(c) ÷ 1,200
Units produced	1,200			
	$	$	$	$
Direct material	19,200	–	19,200	16
Direct labour	13,200	8,400	4,800	4
Production overhead	24,000	18,000	6,000	5
Administration overhead	21,000	21,000	–	–
Selling overhead	16,400	14,000	2,400	2
	93,800	61,400	32,400	27

From this you can see that:

- administration overhead is fixed
- direct material is variable
- direct labour, production overhead and selling and distribution overheads are semi-variable.

Now that managers are aware of the fixed costs and the variable costs per unit it is possible to 'flex' the original budget to produce a budget cost allowance for the actual 1,000 units produced.

The budget cost allowance (or flexed budget) for each item is calculated as follows:

> Budget cost allowance = Budgeted fixed cost + (number of units produced × variable cost per unit)

The budget cost allowances can be calculated as follows:

Direct material = 0 + (1,000 × 16) = $16,000

Direct labour = 8,400 + (1,000 × 4) = $12,400

Production overhead = 18,000 + (1,000 × 5) = $23,000

Administration overhead = 21,000 + 0 = $21,000

Selling overhead = 14,000 + (1,000 × 2) = $16,000

A flexible budget statement can now be produced:

Flexible budget comparison for April

	Flexible budget $	Actual cost $	Variance $
Direct material	16,000	16,490	(480)
Direct labour	12,400	12,380	20
Production overhead	23,000	24,120	(1,120)
Administration overhead	21,000	21,600	(600)
Selling overhead	16,000	16,200	(200)
Total	88,400	90,790	(2,390)

Note: Variances in brackets are adverse.

This revised analysis shows that in fact the cost was $2,390 higher than would have been expected from a production volume of 1,000 units.

The cost variances in the flexible budget comparison are almost all adverse. These overspendings were not revealed when the fixed budget was used and managers may have been under the false impression that costs were being adequately controlled.

The total budget variance

If we now produce a statement showing the fixed budget, the flexible budget and the actual results together, it is possible to analyse the total variance between the original budget and the actual results

	Fixed budget $	Flexible budget $	Actual results $	Expenditure variances $
Direct material	19,200	16,000	16,490	(490)
Direct labour	13,200	12,400	12,380	20
Production overhead	24,000	23,000	24,120	(1,120)
Administration overhead	21,000	21,000	21,600	(600)
Selling and distribution overhead	16,400	16,000	16,200	(200)
	93,800	88,400	90,790	(2,390)

5,400
Volume variance

(2,390)
Expenditure variance

3,010
Total variance

The total variance is therefore made up of two parts:

(1) the volume variance of $5,400 favourable, which is the expected cost saving resulting from producing 200 units less than budgeted

(2) the expenditure variance of $2,390 adverse, which is the net total of the over- and under-expenditure on each of the costs for the actual output of 1,000 units.

Notice that the volume variance is the saving in standard variable cost: 200 units × $27 per unit = $5,400.

When you looked at standard costing, you learned how some of the expenditure variances can be analysed between their price and usage elements – for example, how much of the variance is caused by paying a different price per hour of labour (the labour rate variance), or per kilogram of material (the material price variance), and how much is caused by using a different quantity of material or labour (the usage and efficiency variances).

Using flexible budgets for planning

You should appreciate that while flexible budgets can be useful for control purposes they are not particularly useful for planning. The original budget must contain a single target level of activity so that managers can plan such factors as the resource requirements and the product pricing policy. This would not be possible if they were faced with a range of possible activity levels, although managers will of course consider a range of possible activity levels before they select the target budgeted activity level.

The budget can be designed so that the fixed costs are distinguished from the variable costs. This will facilitate the preparation of a budget cost allowance (flexed budget) for control purposes at the end of each period, when the actual activity is known.

Example 2

Smart Ltd manufactures scientific calculators. Production levels in the manufacturing department average at 20,000 units per month. The actual results for March are as follows:

	Budget *20,000 units* $	*Actual* *17,600 units* $
Direct labour	20,000	19,540
Direct expenses	800	1,000
Direct material	4,200	3,660
Depreciation	10,000	10,000
Semi-variable overheads	5,000	4,760
	40,000	38,960

Assume that at a level of production of 15,000 units, semi-variable overheads are forecast to be $4,500.

Required:

Produce a budgetary control statement showing the actual costs, flexed costs and variances produced.

Example 3

Mahogany Ltd manufactures specialist wooden tables. Their budgeted data for the year 20X8 is showing below:

	Output 12,000 units $000
Direct labour (6 hours per unit @ $45 per hour)	3,240
Direct materials (25kg @ $112 per kg)	33,600
Variable overheads ($20 per unit)	240
Fixed overheads ($25 per unit)	300
	37,380

There is a stepped increase in fixed overheads of $8,000 when production exceeds 15,000 units. Actual production for the year was 16,400 units.

Required:

What is the flexed budgeted cost for the year?

5 Responsibility accounting and controllability of costs

A key aspect of budgetary control is responsibility accounting – that is, making managers account for the costs (and/or revenues) for which they have responsibility. However this will only work effectively if managers are appraised only on the costs which they can control. The success of responsibility accounting relies on the ability of the organisation to correctly identify the costs that a manager can control.

Controllable **costs are costs which can be influenced by the budget holder and are generally** considered to be those which are:

- variable or
- directly attributable fixed costs.

Uncontrollable costs are costs that cannot be influenced (i.e. their value can neither be increased nor decreased) by management action.

Further details

Most variable costs within a department are thought to be controllable in the short term because a manager can influence the efficiency with which resources are used, even if they cannot do anything to raise or lower price levels. So costs such as direct labour costs and material costs in a manager's department are said to be controllable by that manager.

Many fixed costs are uncontrollable (or committed) in the short term (such as insurance etc.) and these are not normally treated as controllable costs. But some fixed costs are directly attributable to a department in that, although they are fixed (in the short term) within the relevant range of output, a drastic reduction in the department's output, or closure of the division entirely, would reduce or remove these costs. This might include costs such as supervisors' salaries, department rent etc.

A useful distinction can be made between **committed** fixed costs, which are costs that are uncontrollable in the short term, but are controllable over the longer term; and **discretionary** fixed costs, which are costs treated as fixed cost items that can nevertheless be controlled in the short term, because spending is subject to management discretion. Examples of discretionary fixed costs are advertising expenditure, and executive travel and subsistence costs, and these would normally be included as directly attributable fixed costs.

Example 4

The manager of the purchasing department is given responsibility for the total expenditure in their department for the year. In calculating the organisation's budgeted profit for the year, the accountant in the organisation included the following total costs for the purchasing department:

	Total $
Direct materials	1,165,000
Direct labour	28,000
Indirect fixed labour cost	80,000
Other fixed overheads	100,000
Share of central overheads	67,000
Total costs	1,440,000

It has been determined that the indirect fixed labour cost and 40% of the other fixed overheads are directly attributable to the department.

When assessing the total cost variance for the department, what total cost should be used as the budgeted controllable cost for the manager?

A $1,313,000

B $1,333,000

C $1,373,000

D $1,440,000

Recharging uncontrollable costs

Focusing solely on controllable costs, however, can bring in some further complications in that it may mean that uncontrollable costs are ignored by all managers. In order to rectify this, some organisations decide that even uncontrollable costs should be charged to departments

Illustration

A summarised report for the profit centres of an organisation might be

	Centre A $	Centre B $	Centre C $	Total $
Revenue	300,000	280,000	420,000	980,000
Variable costs	170,000	100,000	240,00	510,000
Directly attributable costs	70,000	120,000	80,000	270,000
Controllable costs	**240,000**	**220,000**	**320,000**	**780,000**
Attributable gross profit	60,000	40,000	100,000	200,000
Other overhead costs				**(180,000)**
Net profit				20,000

A criticism of the controllability accounting principle is that managers are not encouraged to think about costs for which they are not responsible. In the example above, there are $180,000 of costs not attributable to any profit centre. These might be head office costs, for example, or marketing overheads.

- Within a system of responsibility accounting, there should be cost centre managers accountable for these costs.

- Even so, these overhead costs might be caused to some extent by the demands placed on head office administration or marketing services by the profit centre managers.

- When these costs are high, a further problem is that profit centre profits need to be large enough to cover the general non-allocated overhead costs.

An argument could therefore be made that profit centre managers should be made accountable for a share of overhead costs that are not under their control, and a share of these costs should be charged to each profit centre. Profit reporting would therefore be as follows:

	Centre A $	Centre B $	Centre C $	Total $
Revenue	300,000	280,000	420,000	980,000
Variable costs	170,000	100,000	240,00	510,000
Directly attributable costs	70,000	120,000	80,000	270,000
Controllable costs	**240,000**	**220,000**	**320,000**	**780,000**
Attributable gross profit	60,000	40,000	100,000	200,000
Other overhead costs	(50,000)	(50,000)	(80,000)	**(180,000)**
Net profit	10,000	(10,000)	20,000	20,000

Pros and Cons

The advantages of this approach to responsibility accounting are

- business unit managers are made aware of the significance of other overhead costs

- business unit managers are made aware that they need to earn a sufficient profit to cover a fair share of other overhead costs.

The disadvantages of this approach are that:

- business unit managers are made accountable for a share of other overhead costs, but they can do nothing to control them

- the apportionment of other overhead costs between business units, like overhead apportionment generally, is usually a matter of judgement, lacking any economic or commercial justification.

6   The behavioural aspects of budgeting

Senior managers will often get less junior managers and other members of staff involved in creating budgets. This helps satisfy one of the purposes of budgeting in that it can aid motivation. But it can have a detrimental impact on the other purposes such as distorting the evaluation of actual performance if managers incorporate 'slack' into the budget in order to make it easier to achieve.

Distorting the purposes of budgeting

Involving managers in the completion of a budget can help achieve some of the purposes of budgets but may distort others.

Some of the purposes that are **enhanced** by manager involvement are:

- **Planning.** Planning is taking place at many levels, and should be more accurate than if it simply takes place at a high level, by individuals who are not familiar with the day to day needs of the business. More junior managers will have better information as they are 'closer to the action' and this should improve the quality of budgets overall.

- **Communication.** There should be more communication across all levels of management. It might also make it possible to communicate overall strategic goals to managers by explaining to them the purpose of the budget being prepared and how it fits in to overall budgets and organisational goals.

- **Motivation.** Managers often want to take on extra responsibilities and get further involved in the decision making process. Giving them the power to set budgets might achieve this goal. Managers might also take more personal ownership of achieving budget goals which they have set and be more motivated to achieve what they have promised in the budget.

Whilst the following purposes might be **distorted:**

- **Co-ordination.** This may become more complicated and slower. This is because, not only does there need to be co-ordination between departments but there also has to be co-ordination between the different levels of management within each department. Managers will have to co-ordinate with each other and it may be that inaccuracies occur in budgets if individual manager cannot see the overall ('big') picture or do not understand fully the organisation's goals for the budget period.

- **Evaluation.** In some instances managers might build 'slack' into a budget that they control. This means that they will make it more easily achievable by overstating target costs and/or understating target revenues (if these are included in their budget). This will make it easier for them to achieve the budget targets and associated rewards. But it will make the evaluation of budget performance less useful for senior managers. For example, the variance system might only generate favourable variances because the original plan or standard was understated.

- **Authorisation.** It may be harder to control the authorisation of budget items if there are no checks on the manager. It may also be that managers disagree over budget responsibility and try to allocate costs to other managers rather than take responsibility for themselves.

But this will not always be the case. Every manager and every company will react differently to a budgetary control system. For example, involvement of managers in one firm might lead to better motivation, but other managers may be reluctant to get involved and therefore become dissatisfied if they are asked to get involved in the process.

Conflicts between the goals of budgeting

These behavioural aspects help explain that many of the goals of budgeting are contradictory. One the one side we want to be able to fairly evaluate the performance of managers. But we also want to motivate managers and therefore, even if managers are not involved in the process, managers may find the budget too challenging and therefore reduce their effort. That in turn would distort any evaluation.

Likewise, we want budgets to act as a way of communicating organisational goals. But the budget themselves may distort the goals as they will be very short-term, be focused on cost reduction rather than, say, quality aspects, and they will solely focus on financial aspects of the organisation's goals. There is therefore a conflict between aiming to achieve financial control and communicating the organisation's goals.

Furthermore, the budget is designed to act as a plan for a manager or department. The manager may therefore follow this plan at the expense of other critical success factors that arise in the internal or external environment of the firm. For example, a production manager may continue to use the planned materials mix even if the sales department are indicating that customers would prefer a different product design and the purchasing department have adjusted their purchases accordingly. The production manager then has to choose between the plan and inter-departmental co-ordination.

Many of the conflicts arise due to the human nature of a budgetary control system. Managers do not always follow organisational goals, they do not always think long term, they may be wary of moving away from the plan etc. This provides a conflict between many of the goals of a budgetary control system which needs to be considered at a strategic level when implementing such a system.

Choosing the level of participation in budgeting

These behavioural aspects are influenced by the amount of participation that is given to managers in the preparation of the budget. It results in organisations choosing between two extremes of budgetary participation:

- **The imposed style.** In this style of budgeting the budget is set centrally with little involvement by the budget holder. This reduces the scope for slack in the budget, improves co-ordination and avoids some of the goal congruence issues identified with budgetary participation.

- **The participative style.** In this style the budget holder is involved in setting the budget. This should make the budget more accurate and better motivate the budget holder to achieve it.

 Further details

Imposed style

An imposed/top-down budget is defined in CIMA's Official Terminology as 'A budget allowance which is set without permitting the ultimate budget holder to have the opportunity to participate in the budgeting process'

Advantages of imposed style

There are a number of reasons why it might be preferable for managers not to be involved in setting their own budgets:

(1) Involving managers in the setting of budgets is more time consuming than if senior managers simply imposed the budgets.

(2) Managers may not have the skills or motivation to participate usefully in the budgeting process.

(3) Senior managers have the better overall view of the company and its resources and may be better-placed to create a budget which utilises those scarce resources to best effect.

(4) Senior managers also are aware of the longer term strategic objectives of the organisation and can prepare a budget which is in line with that strategy.

(5) Managers may build budgetary slack or bias into the budget in order to make the budget easy to achieve and themselves look good.

(6) Managers cannot use budgets to play games which disadvantage other budget holders.

(7) By having the budgets imposed by senior managers, i.e. someone outside the department, a more objective, fresher perspective may be gained.

(8) If the participation is only pseudo-participation and the budgets are frequently drastically changed by senior management, then this will cause dissatisfaction and the effect will be to demotivate staff.

Participative style

Participative/bottom up budgeting is a 'budgeting system in which all budget holders are given the opportunity to participate in setting their own budgets'. (CIMA Official Terminology)

Advantages of participative budgets

(1) The morale of the management is improved. Managers feel like their opinion is listened to, that their opinion is valuable.

(2) Managers are more likely to accept the plans contained within the budget and strive to achieve the targets if they had some say in setting the budget, rather than if the budget was imposed upon them. Failure to achieve the target that they themselves set is seen as a personal failure as well as an organisational failure.

(3) The lower level managers will have a more detailed knowledge of their particular part of the business than senior managers and thus will be able to produce more realistic budgets

Example 5

Involving managers in the budget setting process helps an organisation with the following: (select ALL that apply)

(A) Communication

B Co-ordination

(C) Planning

D Evaluation

> **Example 6**
>
> Identify whether the following would be consequences of an 'imposed' or a 'participative' budgeting styles:
>
> A   Managers feel that they 'own' the budget and will be more committed to the targets and committed to achieve them. **P**
>
> B   There would be slack in the budget. **P**
>
> C   Failure of goal congruence. **P**
>
> D   The budget preparation would be more timely. **I**
>
> E   The budget would be in line with the organisation's long term strategic objectives **I**

Budgets and motivation

Motivation is the drive or urge to achieve an end result. Motivation is a force operating within an individual which drives that individual on to attain some goals or objectives. The word motivation comes from the Latin word meaning to move – this shows the key idea involved. An individual is motivated if they are moving forward to achieving goals or objectives.

Motivation may affect many aspects of the life of an individual. You have to be motivated to pass your examinations and to gain a recognised accounting qualification. At work you are motivated to achieve promotion and to gain a position of greater authority and responsibility within the organisation.

In a business context, if employees and managers are not motivated, they will lack the drive or urge to improve their performance and to help the organisation to achieve its goals and move forward. This is the importance of motivation in a business.

Budgets as motivational targets

If a budget is to have any influence on performance:

*   The recipient must be aware of its existence and feel committed to achieving it

*   It must be set at the right level of difficulty to act as a motivator; both unrealistic and over-generous targets will be demotivational.

Care should be taken to reward success as well as penalising failure, in order that a benefit is perceived in bettering rather than just achieving the target.

Budgets become stronger motivators as they become tighter up to a point, but thereafter motivation declines. The optimal degree of tightness depends on both the situation and the personality of the individuals concerned.

Empirical evidence suggests that if a budget target is set that is too easy, then actual performance will be a little better than the budget but it will not be optimised. In other words, managers do not usually work to their full potential if they know that a lower level of performance will still meet the budget – human behaviour will tend to lead to individuals putting in the minimum possible effort to achieve a set target. If greater effort were applied, a higher target may be achieved.

On the other hand, if the budget is too difficult, because it is based on ideal levels of performance, managers become discouraged at what they regard as an unattainable standard. This may de-motivate and as a result, actual performance falls short of what might reasonably have been expected.

You can apply these points to your own position in the context of examinations. If the pass mark for an examination is very low – say 10% – you know you can pass with little effort and you will (perhaps) not work to your full potential. On the other hand, if the pass mark were 99% you would, probably, view that as impossible to achieve and decide not to try at all! The aim should therefore be to agree a budget that falls between these two extremes and therefore incorporates just the right degree of difficulty which will lead to the optimal level of performance. At this level the budget should be challenging enough to motivate a manager to optimise their performance without being too ambitious. Authors writing on this subject have used the phrase 'tough but attainable' for the targets to be set. The right level of difficulty is that which is acceptable to that individual manager. It is important to recognise that this level of acceptability will differ from manager to manager, and from business to business, as each individuals behave and react in a different ways in similar circumstances.

Other behavioural aspects of budgeting

Other aspects that managers may have to incorporate into a budgetary control system include:

- incorporating the achievement of personal goals in order to motivate the budget holder
- achieving goal congruence between the budget holder's goals and the organisation's goals
- avoiding budget holders seeing the budget as a pot of cash that must be spent
- negotiating budgets with the budget holder
- coping with conflicts with the accounting treatment of some costs
- allowing the budget holder to have some freedom and not to feel too constrained by the budget
- setting the correct level of 'difficulty' in a budget.

Further details

Achieving personal goals

To be fully effective, any system of financial control must provide for motivation and incentive. If this requirement is not satisfied, managers will approach their responsibilities in a very cautious and conservative manner.

Personal goals and ambitions are, in theory, strongly linked to organisational goals. These personal goals may include a desire for higher income and higher social standing. To simultaneously satisfy the goals of the organisation and the goals of the individual there must be 'goal congruence'. That is, the individual manager perceives that his or her own goals are achieved by his or her acting in a manner that allows the organisation to achieve its goals. The problem is that reliance on budgetary control systems does not always result in goal congruence.

The success of a budgetary control system depends on the people who operate and are affected by it. They must work within the system in an understanding and co-operative manner. This can only be achieved by individuals who have a total involvement at all stages in the budget process.

However, it is often found that

(1)   A budget is used simply as a pressure device. If the budget is perceived as 'a stick with which to beat people', then it will be sabotaged in all sorts of subtle ways.

(2)   The budgeting process and subsequent budgetary control exercises induce competition between individual departments and executives. Managers may be induced to do things in order to 'meet budget' that are not in the best interests of the business as a whole.

(3)   Adverse variances attract investigation and censure but there is no incentive to achieve favourable variances.

(4)   Failure to distinguish controllable from uncontrollable costs in budgetary control can alienate managers from the whole process.

Failure of goal congruence

It has been seen that an essential element in budgetary control is performance evaluation. Actual results are compared with budget or standard in order to determine whether performance is good or bad. What is being evaluated is not just the business operation but the managers responsible for it. The purpose of budgetary control is to induce managers to behave in a manner that is to the best advantage of the organisation. Compliance with budget is enforced by a variety of negative and positive sanctions.

When adverse variances are reported for operations then this implies poor performance by the managers of the operations. If they are unable to correct or explain away the adverse variances, then they may suffer negative sanctions. They may have forgo salary increases, or they may be demoted to a less prestigious post. Other more subtle negative sanctions are possible that anyone who has ever worked for a large organisation will be aware of.

Positive inducements may be offered to encourage managers to avoid adverse variances. A manager who meets budget may be granted a performance-related salary bonus, promotion, a new company car or use of the executive dining room.

Consequently, the manager has a considerable incentive to ensure that the department or operation he/she is responsible for achieves its budgeted level of performance. However, there are a variety of ways of doing this that might not be to the advantage of the organisation as a whole.

For example, the manager of a production line can cut costs and hence improve its reported performances by reducing quality controls. This may result in long-term problems concerning failure of products in service, loss of customer goodwill and rectification costs – but these are not the concern of the production line manager. This is a clear failure of goal congruence.

The control system is capable of distorting the process it is meant to serve – or 'the tail wags the dog'. The enforcement of a budgetary control system requires sensitivity if this is not to happen.

The budget as a pot of cash

In some environments managers may come to consider the budget as a sum of money that has to be spent. This arises particularly in service departments or public sector organisations, the performance of which is gauged mainly through comparison of actual and budget spending.

The manager of a local authority 'street cleaning' department may be given an annual budget of $120,000 to clean the streets. The manager knows that she will be punished if she spends more than $120,000 in the year. She also knows that if she spends less than $120,000 in the year then her budget will probably be reduced next year. Such a reduction will involve a personal loss of status in the organisation and will make her job more difficult in the next year.

In order to ensure that she does not overspend her annual budget in the current year the manager may spend at a rate of $9,000 per month for the first 11 months of the year. This can be achieved by reducing the frequency of street cleaning and using poor-quality materials. It allows a contingency fund to be accumulated in case of emergencies.

However, in the final month of the year the manager has to spend $21,000 if she wishes to ensure that her whole budget is fully used. She might achieve this by using extra labour and high-quality materials.

Does this behaviour make sense? Of course it does not. The whole pattern of behaviour is distorted by the control system. It means that local residents have a substandard service for 11 months of the year and money is wasted in the 12th month.

It is, however, a fact that suppliers to government departments and local councils often experience a surge in orders towards the end of the financial year. This surge is caused by managers placing orders at the last moment in order to ensure that their full budget for the year is committed.

Budget negotiation

Budgets are normally arrived at by a process of negotiation with the managers concerned. A budget may actually be initiated by departmental managers and then corrected as a result of negotiation with the budget officer.

Clearly, a manager has an incentive to negotiate a budget that is not difficult to achieve. This produces a phenomenon known as 'padding the budget' or 'budgetary slack'. A manager will exaggerate the costs required to achieve objectives. This has the following results:

(1) If the manager succeeds in padding his budget, then the whole control exercise is damaged. Comparison of actual with budget gives no meaningful measure of performance and the manager is able to include inefficiencies in his operation if he wishes.

(2) A successful manager becomes one who is a hard negotiator. The problem with this is that the negotiations in question are between colleagues and not with customers. 'Infighting' may become entrenched in the management process.

(3) A great deal of time and energy that could be directed to the actual management of the business is distracted by what are essentially administrative procedures.

These are all examples of a control system distorting the processes they are meant to serve.

Influence on accounting policies

Any management accountant who has been engaged in the preparation of financial control reports will be familiar with attempts by managers to influence the accounting policies that are used. For example, the apportionment of indirect costs between departments often contains subjective elements. Should security costs be apportioned on the basis of floor space or staff numbers?

The manner in which the indirect costs are apportioned can have a considerable impact on how the performance of individual departments is perceived. This position creates the scope and incentive for managers to argue over accounting policies.

If a manager perceives that her department's performance is falling below budget, then he/she may sift through the costs charged to his/her department and demand that some be reclassified and charged elsewhere. The time and energy that goes into this kind of exercise has to be diverted from that available for the regular management of the business.

Budget constrained management styles

When the performance of a manager is assessed by his ability to meet budget, then he is likely to adopt a conservative approach to new business opportunities that appear. The immediate impact of new business ventures is likely to be a rise in capital and operating costs – with an adverse impact on current period profit. The benefits of such ventures may only be felt in the long term. Hence, when a new opportunity appears, the manager evaluating it may only perceive that its acceptance will result in below-budget performance in the current period – and turn it down on this ground alone. Another consideration is that reliance on budgetary control is an approach to management that involves sitting in an office and reading financial reports. Such an approach (in conjunction with features such as executive dining rooms) may result in an unsatisfactory corporate culture based on hierarchies and social divisions. Large organisations that rely heavily on budgetary control systems often take on an 'ossified' character.

Yet another consideration is that a reliance on budgetary planning may induce managers to favour projects and developments that are most amenable to the construction of budgets. Projects that involve little uncertainty and few unknowns are easy to incorporate in budgets and hence managers may be more inclined to adopt such projects than the alternatives.

Projects that involve significant uncertainties may be attractive if they incorporate some combination of high expected returns and low cost interim exit routes – but a budget constrained manager may be disinclined to adopt such projects simply because they are difficult to incorporate in budgets. Some writers suggest that the budgetary approach may be particularly inappropriate in a dynamic and turbulent business environment.

The general conclusion concerning this and previous points is that good budgetary control can offer certain benefits. However, when budgetary control is enforced in a rigid or insensitive manner it may end up doing more harm than good.

Setting the difficulty level of targets

Much of the early academic work on budgets concerned the extent to which the 'tightness' or looseness' of a budget acted as an incentive or disincentive to management effort. This was the issue of 'budget stretch'.

The main thrust of the findings that emerged from these studies was:

(1) Loose budgets (i.e. ones easily attainable) are poor motivators

(2) As budgets are tightened, up to a point they become more motivational

(3) Beyond that point, a very tight budget ceases to be motivational.

The role of budget participation and the manner in which aspirations and objectives are stated was also explored in certain studies. It was suggested that the participation of managers in budget setting was a motivational factor – but see earlier discussion concerning budget padding and negotiation.

 ## Ethical aspects of budgeting

Budgeting creates a number of ethical dilemmas for organisations. We have already seen one of these dilemmas where the level of participation must be determined. If managers are allowed to have a high level of participation and a bottom-up approach is used this can have a number of ethical implications such as:

• Inclusion of slack. The manager may make the budget easier to achieve in order to protect financial rewards, improve performance appraisals, reduce their workload etc. Not only does this unethical practice create unwarranted rewards for the budget holder it can have knock-on implications elsewhere in the business. It could mean that resources are not allocated to other parts of the business that require them (thus impacting on financial rewards for the business as a whole), it may mean that production does not meet customer demand (so that sales and market share are lost) and could have implications for other budget holders (such as marketing and recruitment) who are aiming to co-ordinate their activities with the activities presented in this budget. The poor ethical practices of the budget holder, caused by the bottom-up approach to budgeting, can therefore fail in achieving many of the purposes of budgeting such as co-ordination, utilisation, motivation and evaluation.

- The manager puts personal goals ahead of organisational goals. The manager may be more concerned with, say, quality of the product or levels of staffing than is planned for in the overall organisational plan. This lack of goal congruence can mean that the organisation is likely to fail in meeting its strategic objectives. For example, in a competitive market an organisation might choose to pursue a strategy which aims to sell the product at a price which undercuts the selling price of rivals. This strategy will be difficult to achieve if a manager pursues a strategy of improving quality (and therefore increasing costs) which makes it more difficult to achieve a low selling price. Likewise, in a government funded health service there may be a goal to reduce repeat treatments for patients. But this would be frustrated if budget holders create a budget focused on reducing time per patient appointment in order to achieve reduced waiting times for patients.

- The manager might produce overly-optimistic budgets. The manager of a subsidiary, for example, may want potential performance to look as favourable as possible in order to protect the subsidiary from sell-off or closure or to improve their own chances of promotion. But this can lead to further unethical practices such as over-stating results or even fraudulently recording non-existing sales in order to then satisfy the overly-optimistic forecast. If these practices come to light there can be a very negative reaction from wider stakeholders such as the general public.

Moving to a top-down approach to budgeting does not offer a solution to the ethical dilemmas as this system can create its own dilemmas:

- The budget preparer may be putting undue pressure on the budget holder to achieve a desired result. Budget preparers often set challenging (or 'stretch' goals) in order to motivate the budget holder to achieve improved performance. This can cause stress for the budget holder as well as inducing the budget holder to employ unethical practices of their own in order to achieve the target.

- Likewise, budget preparers are often accused of 'pseudo' participation in the budget setting process which may in itself be unethical. The budget holder is allowed to feel that they have some input and participation in the budget but actual decisions are approved and controlled centrally. This can ultimately lead to poor motivation and job satisfaction for the budget holder with typical repercussions such as poor time keeping, absenteeism and even the loss of the employee altogether.

The level of participation considers the ethical issues with respect to the preparation of the budget. But there are further ethical issues in the budgetary control process:

- The budget holder may overstate results in order to appear to achieve a target that they did not actually meet (and this may even be achieved through fraudulent practices). This can result in undue rewards given to the budget holder but also to false information being provided to other key stakeholders. For example, higher dividends might be paid to shareholders or inaccurate information being provided to other providers of finance such as banks. In the long term this is likely to catch up with the organisations when these results are not maintainable and the associated cash from the positive performance is not built up within the organisation.

- The budget holder may make decisions which focus on short-term performance at the expense of the long term good health of the business. For example, staff training may be reduced in order to meet a cost target, thus harming staff development in career paths in the longer term.

- In order to meet targets the budget holder may employ unethical practices. For example, in order to achieve a high sales target in a competitive market a budget holder might use aggressive sales tactics on potential customers such as over-representing product features or putting pressure on customers to buy complementary products that they may not actually need.

- When reviewing the performance of the budget holder there is often a system of 'management by exception' in place. This means that budgets are only reviewed for unusual areas of performance where there is a substantial difference between the actual results and the budget. This means that managers who achieve a performance that is near to the original budgeted performance may feel that they receive no attention and consideration. The budget holder can feel undervalued and demotivated by this.

- If top-down budgeting is used there can be an unethical desire to broaden the area of responsibility for what is controllable by the budget holder. For example, a subsidiary may be made to bear the cost of parent company accounting costs even though it has no control over this activity. This can impact on the appraisal of the subsidiary's financial performance as removing budget holder trust in the entire budgeting process.

The budget process therefore needs to find an ethical balance which motivates improved and optimal performance without creating conflicts of interest and motivating dishonest accounting and the improper allocation of resources. Many of these problems are caused by focusing on a single financial measure of performance which is why many organisations are moving to approaches such as beyond budgeting approaches covered in the previous chapter.

7 Chapter summary

Budgetary control

Feedback & feedforward
- Feedback: aimed at correcting problems
- Feedforward: aimed at preventing problems

Fixed & flexible budgets
- Fixed budget information on costs and revenues for one level of activity
- Flexible budget shows the same information, but for a number of different levels of activity.

Behavioural aspects
- Responsibility accounting: making managers account for the costs for which they have responsibility and can control
- A choice needs to be made between an imposed or participative style of budgeting.
- budgets can have unintended ethical consequences for organisations

8 Practice questions

Test your understanding 1

The following fixed and flexible budgets have been prepared:

	Fixed budget 100% level	Flexible budget 90% level
	$	$
Sales	750,000	675,000
Direct variable costs	420,000	378,000
Overheads	230,000	216,800
Total costs	650,000	594,800
Profit	100,000	80,200

Actual sales for the period were $700,000 and there was an adverse sales price variance of $5,000 (A).

Required:

Prepare a flexible budget for the actual level of sales.

Test your understanding 2

An office manager uses the high-low method to establish the expected costs for office expenses, based on the following data for monthly expenses:

	Costs for 6,000 labour hours	Costs for 8,000 labour hours
	$	$
Heating and lighting	17,000	18,000
Telephones	7,200	8,400
Sundry expenses	29,400	33,400

Variable costs are assumed to vary with the number of labour hours worked in the office during the period.

In the most recent month, 7,700 labour hours were worked and actual costs were as follows:

	$
Heating and lighting	17,600
Telephones	8,750
Sundry expenses	32,600

Required:

Calculate the cost variances for the month.

Test your understanding 3

Extracts from the budgets of B Ltd are given below:

Sales and inventory budgets (units)

	Period 1	Period 2	Period 3	Period 4	Period 5
Opening inventory	4,000	2,500	3,300	2,500	3,000
Sales	15,000	20,000	16,500	21,000	18,000

Cost budgets ($000)

	Period 1	Period 2	Period 3
Direct materials	108.0	166.4	125.6
Direct labour	270.0	444.0	314.0
Production overheads (excluding depreciation)	117.5	154.0	128.5
Depreciation	40.0	40.0	40.0
Administration overhead	92.0	106.6	96.4
Selling overhead	60.0	65.0	61.5

The following information is also available:

(i) Production above 18,000 units incurs a bonus in addition to normal wages rates

(ii) Any variable costs contained in the selling overhead are assumed to vary with sales. All other variable costs are assumed to vary with production.

Required:

(a) Calculate the budgeted production for periods 1 to 4

(b) Prepare a suitable cost budget for period 4.

In period 4 the inventory and sales budgets were achieved and the following actual costs recorded:

	$000
Direct material	176
Direct labour	458
Production overhead	181
Depreciation	40
Administration overhead	128
Selling overhead	62
	1,045

Required:

(c) Show the budget variances from actual

(d) Criticise the assumptions on which the cost budgets have been prepared.

Test your understanding 4

A company has prepared an activity-based budget for its stores department. The budgeted costs are:

	Cost driver	Budgeted cost
Receiving goods	Number of deliveries	$80 per delivery
Issuing goods from store	Number of stores requisitions	$40 per requisition
Ordering	Number of orders	$25 per order
Counting inventory	Number of inventory counts	$1,000 per count

Keeping records – $24,000 each year

Supervision – $30,000 each year

Actual results for April were:

	Activity	Actual cost $
Receiving goods	45 orders delivered	3,450
Issuing goods	100 requisitions	4,400
Ordering	36 orders	960
Counting	2 inventory counts	1,750
Record keeping		1,900
Supervision		2,700
Total costs		15,160

Required:

Prepare a variance report for the month.

Test your understanding 5

Scenario

The materials purchasing manager is assessed on:

- total material expenditure for the organisation

- the cost of introducing safety measures, regarding the standard and the quality of materials, in accordance with revised government legislation

- a notional rental cost, allocated by head office, for the material storage area.

Task:

Discuss whether these costs are controllable by the manager and if they should be used to appraise the manager.

(Time allowed: 10 minutes)

Test your understanding 6

Explain whether a production manager should be accountable for direct labour and direct materials cost variances.

(Time allowed: 10 minutes)

Test your understanding 7

DRG Ltd operates a system of budgetary control using flexible budgets. The following figures were produced for last month:

	Budget $	Actual $
Sales (units)	30,000	27,500
Direct material costs	72,000	70,000
Contribution	51,000	48,300

Required:

Which of the following statements is correct?

A There is a favourable variance on material costs and contribution is lower than expected using the flexible budget.

B There is an adverse variance on material costs and contribution is lower than expected using the flexible budget.

C There is a favourable variance on material costs and contribution is higher than expected using the flexible budget.

D There is an adverse variance on material costs and contribution is higher than expected using the flexible budget.

Test your understanding 8

Responsibility accounting aims to (select ONE):

A   Allocate all costs to all areas of a business

B   Ensure that all managers are responsible for their fair share of head office costs

C   Ensure that costs become the responsibility of a specific manager

D   Reduce the costs that a department incurs

Test your understanding 9

Key motivational factors in budgeting do not include: (select ONE)

A   The setting of fair, achievable targets

B   Correct identification of the blame for below budget performance

C   Training in the budget process

D   The feedback of information

Test your understanding answers

Example 1

Correct solution A.

With a feedback system, actual results are compared with the budget, the aim of which is to correct problems that have been discovered in the past.

Option B refers to a feedforward control system, in which the aim is to anticipate problems that may arise in the future, to try and prevent them from occurring.

Option C is referring to negative feedback. Positive feedback, control action would be taken to increase the difference between the budget and the actual result.

Option D also refers to a feedforward control system. With feedforward control, control reports need to be produced regularly, and therefore there needs to be an efficient forecasting system.

Example 2

Identify the cost behaviours and calculate the cost per unit based on budget of 20,000 units:

	Behaviour	Cost per unit
Direct labour	Variable	$20,000/20,000 = $1
Direct expenses	Variable	$800/20,000 = $0.04
Direct material	Variable	$4,200/20,000 = $0.21
Depreciation	Fixed	n/a
Semi-variable overheads	Semi-variable	See working

Working for semi-variable overheads (high low method):

Variable cost = change in cost / change in activity

$$= (\$5000 - \$4,500) / (20,000 - 15,000)$$

$$= \$0.10 \text{ per unit}$$

Fixed cost = total cost – variable cost

$$= \$5,000 - (\$0.10 \times 20,000 \text{ units})$$

$$= \$3,000$$

Budget control statement:

	Actual 17,600 units		Flexed 17,600 units	Variance
	$		$	$
Direct labour	19,540	$1 × 17,600	17,600	1,940A
Direct expenses	1,000	$0.04 × 17,600	704	296A
Direct material	3,660	$0.21 × 17,600	3,696	36F
Depreciation	10,000		10,000	–
Semi-variable overheads	4,760	3,000 + ($0.10 × 17,600)	4,760	–
	38,960		36,760	2,200A

Example 3

Flexed budget:

	Output 16,400 units $000
Direct labour (6 hrs × $45 × 16,400 units)	4,428
Direct materials (25kg × $112/kg × 16,400 units)	45,920
Variable overheads ($20 × 16,400 units)	328
Fixed overheads ($300 + $8)	308
	50,984

Example 4

The correct answer is answer A.

The shared central overheads should not be included as a controllable cost as the manager cannot normally influence costs which are incurred elsewhere. All of the variable (direct) costs should be included as being controllable by the manager. In terms of the fixed costs, all of the indirect fixed labour cost and 40% of the other fixed overheads are directly attributable to the department and should be included as a controllable cost.

Therefore the total controllable costs are = $1,165,000 + $28,000 + $80,000 + (40% × $100,000) = $1,313,000.

Example 5

Correct solutions A, C

Manager involvement in the budget setting process should enhance communication across all levels of management.

Co-ordination may become more complicated or slower due to the need for co-ordination between departments and also between different levels of managers within each department.

Planning should be enhanced with manager involvement. More junior managers will have better information about the day to day needs of the business which should improve the quality of the information included in the budget.

Evaluation may become distorted as a result of manager involvement. Managers may build 'slack' into the budget that they control, making it more easy for them to achieve their targets. This makes evaluation of budget performance less useful for senior managers.

Example 6

A   Managers feel that they 'own' the budget and will be more committed to the targets and committed to achieve them. This is most likely to be true of a participative budget style.

B   There would be slack in the budget. This is more likely to be true of a participative budget style. Managers may include some budgetary slack to ensure that they are able to meet their own targets. They may deliberately set targets that they cannot fail to achieve, particularly if bonuses are awarded for meeting the budget.

C   Failure of goal congruence. This is more likely to be a consequence where participation is encouraged. The objectives of the managers and the objectives of the organisation as a whole may not be the same.

D   The budget preparation would be more timely. This is true of a participative budget style as each manager will prepare their own budget and then all individual budgets would need to be collated into a master budget.

E   The budget would be in line with the organisation's long term strategic objectives. This is true of an imposed budget style.

Test your understanding 1

(W1) Actual sales at budgeted prices

	$
Actual sales at actual prices	700,000
Sales price variance	5,000 (A)
Actual sales at budgeted prices	705,000

Actual sales are therefore at the (705/750) 94% activity level.

(W2) Fixed and variable overheads

	$
Overheads at 100% activity level	230,000
Overheads at 90% activity level	216,800
Variable overheads for 10% activity	13,200

	$
Total overheads at 100% activity level	230,000
Variable overheads at 100% activity level	132,000
Fixed overheads	98,000

Flexed budget 94% activity

	$	$
Sales		705,000
Direct variable costs (420,000 × 94%)		394,800
Variable overhead (13,200 × 94/10)		124,080
Fixed overhead		98,000
Total overheads		222,080
Total costs		616,880
Profit		88,120

Test your understanding 2

	Heating and lighting $	Telephones $	Sundry expenses $
Total cost for 8,000 hours	18,000	8,400	33,400
Total cost for 6,000 hours	17,000	7,200	29,400
Variable cost for 2,000 hours	1,000	1,200	4,000
Variable cost per hour	$0.50	$0.60	$2.00

	Heating and lighting $	Telephones $	Sundry expenses $
Total cost for 8,000 hours	18,000	8,400	33,400
Variable cost for 8,000 hours	4,000	4,800	16,000
Fixed costs	14,000	3,600	17,400

For 7,700 hours

	Heating and lighting $	Telephones $	Sundry expenses $
Expected fixed costs	14,000	3,600	17,400
Expected variable cost	3,850	4,620	15,400
Expected total cost	17,850	8,220	32,800
Actual cost	17,600	8,750	32,600
Cost variance	**250 (A)**	**530 (A)**	**200 (F)**

Test your understanding 3

(a)

	Period 1	Period 2	Period 3	Period 4	Period 5
Sales	15,000	20,000	16,500	21,000	18,000
Add: Closing inventory	2,500	3,300	2,500	3,000	
Less: Opening inventory	(4,000)	(2,500)	(3,300)	(2,500)	(3,000)
Production	13,500	20,800	15,700	21,500	–

(b) In Period 4, Production = 21,500 units

		$000
Direct materials	(W1)	172.0
Direct labour	(W2)	465.0
Production overhead	(W3)	157.5
Depreciation		40.0
Administration overhead	(W4)	108.0
Selling overhead	(W5)	66.0
		1,008.5

Working 1

$$\frac{\$108,000 \ (Period \ 1)}{13,500 \ units} = \$8 \times 21,500 = \$172,000$$

Working 2

$$Normal \ wage \ \frac{\$270,000}{13,500} = \$20 \ per \ unit$$

Bonus (Period 2) = $444,000 – (20,800 × $20) = $28,000 premium

$$Premium \ rate: \ \frac{\$28,000}{2,800 \ units \ above \ 18,000} = \$10 \ per \ unit$$

in Period 4, (21,500 × $20) + (3,500 × $10) = $465,000

Working 3

$$\text{Variable cost per unit} = \frac{154 - 117.5}{20.8 - 13.5} = \frac{36.5}{7.3} = \$5 \text{ per unit}$$

Working 4

$$\text{Variable cost per unit} = \frac{106.6 - 92.0}{20.8 - 13.5} = \frac{14.6}{7.3} = \$2 \text{ per unit}$$

Working 5

$$\text{Variable cost per unit} = \frac{65.0 - 60}{20.0 \text{ sales} - 15.0} = \$1 \text{ per unit}$$

Fixed cost = $60,000 − ($1 × 15,000) = $45,000

In Period 4, ($1 × 21,000) + $45,000 = $66,000

	P4 Budget $	P4 Actual $	Variance $	Adverse/ Favourable
Material	172.0	176.0	4.0	
Labour	465.0	458.0	7.0	Adverse
Production overhead	157.5	181.0	23.5	Favourable
Depreciation	40.0	40.0	0.0	–
Administration overhead	108.0	128.0	20.0	Adverse
Selling overhead	66.0	62.0	4.0	Favourable
	1,008.5	1,045.0	36.5	Adverse

(d)

- Linear costs
- No Incremental fixed costs
- Variable cost per unit is constant
- Volume the only factor to affect total costs.

Test your understanding 4

Activity	Expected cost $	Actual cost $	Variance $
Receiving goods 45 orders delivered	3,600	3,450	150 (F)
Issuing goods 100 requisitions	4,000	4,400	400 (A)
Ordering 36 orders	900	960	60 (A)
Counting 2 inventory counts	2,000	1,750	250 (F)
Record keeping	2,000	1,900	100 (F)
Supervision	2,500	2,700	200 (A)
	15,000	15,160	160 (A)

Test your understanding 5

The total material expenditure for the organisation will be dependent partly on the prices negotiated by the purchasing manager and partly by the requirements and performance of the production department. If it is included as a target for performance appraisal the manager may be tempted to purchase cheaper material which may have an adverse effect elsewhere in the organisation.

The requirement to introduce safety measures may be imposed but the manager should be able to ensure that implementation meets budget targets.

A notional rental cost is outside the control of the manager and should not be included in a target for performance appraisal purposes.

Test your understanding 6

- The production manager will be responsible for managing direct labour and direct material usage.
- However, the manager may not be able to influence:
  - the cost of the material
  - the quality of the material
  - the cost of labour
  - the quality of labour.
- Performance should be measured against the element of direct cost which the manager can control.

Test your understanding 7

Correct solution D

Flexible budget for production of 27,500 units:

	Flexible budget	Actual	Variance
	$	$	$
Direct material costs	66,000 (W1)	70,000	4,000A
Contribution	46,750 (W2)	48,300	1,550F

(W1) Budgeted direct material per unit = $72,000 / 30,000 units = $2.40 per unit.

Direct material cost for 27,500 units = $2.40 × 27,500 units = $66,000

(W2) Budgeted contribution per unit = $51,000 / 30,000 units = $1.70 per unit.

Budgeted contribution for 27,500 units = $1.70 × 27,500 units = $46,750.

Test your understanding 8

Correct solution C

In responsibility accounting, each manager should have a well-defined area of responsibility and the authority to make decisions within that area. Managers should account for the costs (and/or revenues) for which they have responsibility.

Test your understanding 9

Key motivational factors in budgeting do not include: (select ONE)

A   The setting of fair, achievable targets

B   Correct identification of the blame for below budget performance

C   Training in the budget process

D   The feedback of information

Relevant costs and decision making

Chapter learning objectives

Lead outcome	Component outcome
C1. Describe the main types of short-term decisions made by organisations	(a) Describe pricing and revenue maximisation decisions. (b) Describe product decisions.
C2. Explain the underlying concepts used for short-term decision making	(a) Explain the objectives of decision making. (b) Explain the underlying concepts of short-term decision making.
C3. Apply appropriate techniques to support short-term decisions	(a) Relevant cost analysis.

1 Session Content Diagram

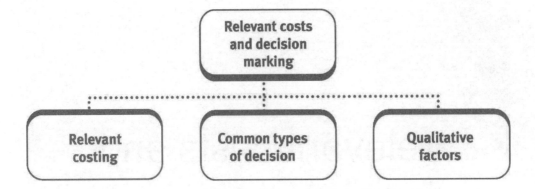

2 Introduction to relevant costs and revenues

Organisations face many decisions, and they usually must choose between two or more alternatives. Decisions will generally be based on taking the decision that maximises shareholder value, so all decisions will be taken using relevant costs and revenues. **Relevant costs and revenues are those costs and revenues that change as a direct result of a decision taken.**

Characteristics of relevant costs

In its Official Terminology, CIMA defines **'relevant costs'** and **'relevant revenues'** as the 'costs and revenues appropriate to a specific management decision; they are represented by future cash flows whose magnitude will vary depending upon the outcome of the management decision made(...)'.

Relevant costs and revenues have the following features:

(1) **They are future costs and revenues** – as it is not possible to change what has happened in the past, then relevant costs and revenues must be future costs and revenues.

(2) **They are incremental** or **differential** – relevant costs are incremental costs and it is the increase in costs and revenues that occurs as a direct result of a decision taken that is relevant. Common costs can be ignored for the purposes of decision making. Look out for costs detailed as differential, specific or avoidable.

CIMA defines 'avoidable costs' as 'the specific costs of an activity or sector of a business which would be avoided if that activity or sector did not exist.'

For example, if a company is considering shutting down a department, then the avoidable costs are those that would be saved as a result of the shutdown. Such costs might include the labour costs of those employed in the department and the rental cost of the space occupied by the department. The latter is an example of an **attributable** or **specific** fixed cost. Costs such as apportioned head office costs that would not be saved as a result of the shutdown are unavoidable costs. They are not relevant to the decision.

(3) **They are cash flows** – in addition, future costs and revenues must be cash flows arising as a direct consequence of the decision taken. Relevant costs do not include items which do not involve cash flows (depreciation and notional costs for example).

In an examination, unless told otherwise, assume that variable costs are relevant costs.

Non-relevant costs

A distinction must be made between **relevant** and **non-relevant** costs for the purposes of management decision-making.

This has many implications:

Sunk costs

A sunk cost has already been incurred and therefore will not be relevant to the investment decision.

Committed costs

Expenditure that will be incurred in the future, but as a result of decisions taken in the past that cannot now be changed. These are known as committed costs and are not treated as relevant costs for decision making.

Fixed costs

Should be treated as a whole, and only where relevant. This means that fixed overheads that are "absorbed"/"charged"/"allocated"/"apportioned" to a project should be ignored. Only extra/incremental changes in fixed overheads should be included in decisions.

Depreciation

Depreciation is not a cash flow, and so should **never** be included in decisions

Further details

Relevant costs are those which will be affected by the decision being taken. All relevant costs should be considered in management decision-making. If a cost will remain unaltered regardless of the decision being taken, then it is called a non-relevant cost or irrelevant cost.

Costs that are not usually relevant in management decisions include the following:

(a) Sunk or past costs. This is a 'cost that has been irreversibly incurred or committed and cannot therefore be considered relevant to a decision. Sunk costs may also be termed irrecoverable costs' (CIMA Official Terminology). An example of a sunk cost is expenditure that has been incurred in developing a new product. The money cannot be recovered even if a decision is taken to abandon further development of the new product. The cost is therefore not relevant to future decisions concerning the product.

(b) Expenditure that will be incurred in the future, but as a result of decisions taken in the past that cannot now be changed. These are known as committed costs. They can sometimes cause confusion because they are future costs. However, a committed cost will be incurred regardless of the decision being taken and therefore it is not relevant. An example of this type of cost could be expenditure on special packaging for a new product, where the packaging has been ordered and delivered but not yet paid for. The company is obliged to pay for the packaging even if they decide not to proceed with the product; therefore it is not a relevant cost.

(c) Absorbed fixed overheads that will not increase or decrease as a result of the decision being taken. The amount of overhead to be absorbed by a particular cost unit might alter because of the decision; however, this is a result of the company's cost accounting procedures for overheads. If the actual amount of overhead incurred by the company will not alter, then the overhead is not a relevant cost.

(d) Historical cost depreciation. Depreciation is an accounting adjustment but does not result in any future cash flows. They are merely the book entries that are designed to spread the original cost of an asset over its useful life.

(e) Notional costs such as notional rent and notional interest. These are only relevant if they represent an identified lost opportunity to use the premises or the finance for some alternative purpose.

In these circumstances, the notional costs would be opportunity costs. This explanation will become clearer when you learn more about opportunity costs later in this chapter.

> *Conclusion*
>
> It is essential to look to the future when deciding which costs are relevant to a decision. Costs that have already been incurred or that will not be altered in the future as a result of the decision being taken are not relevant costs.

Example 1

As part of a new product development a company has employed a building consultant to perform an initial survey. This initial survey has cost $40,000. But there will be an ongoing need for her services if the company decides to proceed with the project. This work will be charged at a fixed rate of $20,000 per annum.

What relevant cost should be included for the building consultants services in the first year when considering whether the project should proceed?

A $0

B $20,000

C $40,000

D $60,000

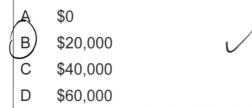

Opportunity cost

'Opportunity cost' is an important concept in decision making. It represents **the best alternative that is forgone in taking the decision**. The opportunity cost emphasises that decision making is concerned with alternatives and that a cost of taking one decision is the profit or contribution forgone by not taking the next best alternative.

If resources to be used on projects are scarce (e.g. labour, materials, machines), then consideration must be given to profits or contribution which could have been earned from alternative uses of the resources.

For example, the skilled labour which may be needed on a new project might have to be withdrawn from normal production. This withdrawal would cause a loss in contribution which is obviously relevant to the project appraisal.

The cash flows of a single department or division cannot be looked at in isolation. It is always the effects on cash flows of the whole organisation which must be considered.

Further details on opportunity costs

> An opportunity cost is a special type of relevant cost. It is defined in the CIMA Terminology as 'the value of the benefit sacrificed when one course of action is chosen, in preference to an alternative. The opportunity cost is represented by the forgone potential benefit from the best rejected course of action.'

With opportunity costs we are concerned with identifying the value of any benefit forgone as the result of choosing one course of action in preference to another.*Examples of opportunity costs*

The best way to demonstrate opportunity costs is to consider some examples.

(a) A company has some obsolete material in inventory that it is considering to use for a special contract. If the material is not used on the contract it can either be sold back to the supplier for $2 per tonne or it can be used on another contract in place of a different material that would usually cost $2.20 per tonne.

   The opportunity cost of using the material on the special contract is $2.20 per tonne. This is the value of the next best alternative use for the material, or the benefit forgone by not using it for the other contract.

(b) Chris is deciding whether or not to take a skiing holiday this year. The travel agent is quoting an all-inclusive holiday cost of $675 for a week. Chris will lose the chance to earn $200 for a part-time job during the week that the holiday would be taken.

   The relevant cost of taking the holiday is $875. This is made up of the out-of-pocket cost of $675, plus the $200 opportunity cost, that is the part-time wages forgone.

Notional costs and opportunity costs

Notional costs and opportunity costs are often similar. This is particularly noticeable in the case of notional rent. The notional rent could be the rental that the company is forgoing by occupying the premises itself, that is it could be an opportunity cost. However, it is only a true opportunity cost if the company can actually identify a forgone opportunity to rent the premises. If nobody is willing to pay the rent, then it is not an opportunity cost.

Avoidable, differential and incremental costs

There are two other types of relevant cost that you will need to know about: avoidable costs and differential/incremental costs.

Avoidable costs

CIMA defines avoidable costs as 'the specific costs of an activity or sector of a business which would be avoided if that activity or sector did not exist'.

For example, if a company is considering shutting down a department, then the avoidable costs are those that would be saved as a result of the shutdown. Such costs might include the labour costs of those employed in the department and the rental cost of the space occupied by the department. The latter is an example of an attributable or specific fixed cost. Costs such as apportioned head office costs that would not be saved as a result of the shutdown are unavoidable costs. They are not relevant to the decision.

Differential/incremental costs

CIMA defines a differential/incremental cost as 'the difference in total cost between alternatives. This is calculated to assist decision making'.

For example, if the relevant cost of contract X is $5,700 and the relevant cost of contract Y is $6,200, we would say that the differential or incremental cost is $500, that is the extra cost of contract Y is $500.

Using incremental costs

Incremental costs can be useful if the cost accountant wishes to highlight the consequences of taking sequential steps in a decision. For example, the accountant might be providing cost information for a decision about whether to increase the number of employees in a department.

Instead of quoting several different total-cost figures, it might be more useful to say 'the incremental cost per five employees will be $5,800 per month'.

Remember that only relevant costs should be used in the calculations.

Example 2

A company which manufactures and sells a single product is currently operating at 85% of full capacity, producing 102,000 units per month. The current total monthly costs of production amount to $330,000, of which $75,000 are fixed and are expected to remain unchanged for all levels of activity up to full capacity.

A new potential customer has expressed interest in taking regular monthly delivery of 12,000 units at a price of $2.80 per unit.

All existing production is sold each month at a price of $3.25 per unit. If the new business is accepted, existing sales are expected to fall by 2 units for every 15 units sold to the new customer.

What is the overall increase in monthly profit which would result from accepting the new business?

Incremental revenue

Just as incremental costs are the differences in cost between alternatives, so incremental revenues are the differences in revenues between the alternatives. Matching the incremental costs against the incremental revenues will produce a figure for the incremental gain or loss between the alternatives.

3 The relevant cost of variable costs and overheads

When we put the principles of relevant and non-relevant costs together, and then combine these with the complications brought in by opportunity costs, we have many things to consider in determining the relevant costs of areas such as materials, labour and overheads. This section looks at some of these costs in more detail in order to develop some criteria for determining the relevant cost.

The relevant cost of materials

The following flow chart should provide a useful reminder of the points that must be considered when ascertaining the relevant cost of materials:

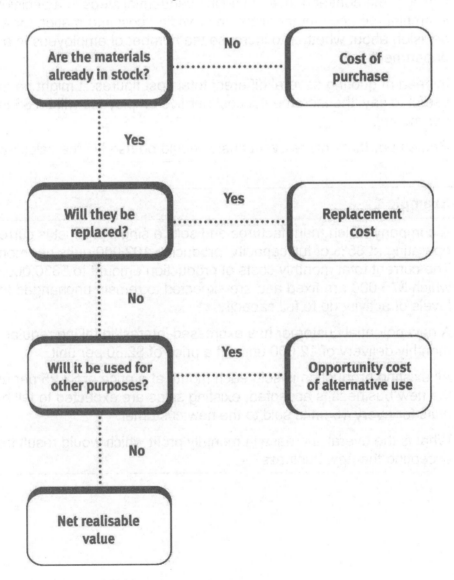

Example 3

A company is considering a short-term pricing decision for a contract that would utilise some material P that it has held in inventory for some time. The company does not foresee any other use for the material. The work would require 1,000 kgs of Material P.

There are 800 kgs of Material P in inventory, which were bought some time ago at a cost of $3 per kg. The material held in inventory could currently be sold for $3.50 per kg. The current purchase price of Material P is $4.50 per kg.

What is the relevant cost of Material P for the company to use when making its pricing decision for the contract closest to?

The relevant cost of labour

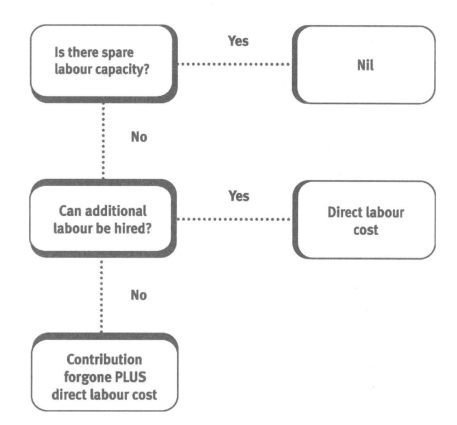

Example 4

100 hours of skilled labour are needed for a special contract. The staff are working at full capacity at the moment and the workers would have to be taken off production of a different product in order to work on the special contract. The details of the other product are shown below:

	$/unit
Selling price	60
Direct material	10
Direct labour 1 hour @ $10/hour	10
Variable overheads	15
Fixed overheads	15

The skilled workers' pay rate would not change, regardless of which product they worked on. What would be the relevant cost?

The relevant cost of overheads

In addition to calculating the relevant cost of materials and labour, you may also be required to calculate the relevant cost of overheads.

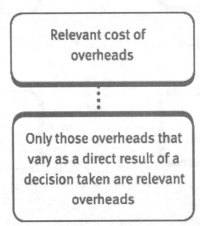

Example 5

JB absorbs overheads on a machine hour rate, currently $20/hour, of which $7 is for variable overheads and $13 for fixed overheads. The company is deciding whether to undertake a contract in the coming year. If the contract is undertaken, it is estimated that fixed costs will increase for the duration of the contract by $3,200. The contract would require 800 hours of machine time.

What is the relevant cost of overheads for the contract?

A $3,200

B $5,600

C $8,800

D $16,000

The relevant cost of non-current assets

The relevant costs associated with non-current assets, such as plant and machinery, are determined in a similar way to the relevant costs of materials.

- If plant and machinery is to be replaced at the end of its useful life, then the relevant cost is the current replacement cost.

- If plant and machinery is not to be replaced, then the relevant cost is the higher of the sale proceeds (if sold) and the net cash inflows arising from the use of the asset (if not sold).

Example 6

Equipment owned by a company has a net book value of $1,800 and has been idle for some months. It could now be used on a six months contract that is being considered. If not used on this contract, the equipment would be sold now for a net amount of $2,000. After use on the contract, the equipment would have no resale value and would be dismantled.

What is the total relevant cost of the equipment to the contract?

A $0

B $1,800   ✓

C $2,000

D $3,800

Example 7

The CS group is planning its annual marketing conference for its sales executives and has approached the VBJ Holiday company (VBJ) to obtain a quotation. VBJ has been trying to win the business of the CS group for some time and is keen to provide a quotation which the CS group will find acceptable in the hope that this will lead to future contracts.

The manager of VBJ has produced the following cost estimate for the conference:

	$
Coach running costs	2,000
Driver costs	3,000
Hotel costs	5,000
General overheads	2,000
Sub total	12,000
Profit 30%	3,600
Total	15,600

You have considered this cost estimate but you believe that it would be more appropriate to base the quotation on relevant costs. You have therefore obtained the following further information:

Coach running costs represent the fuel costs of $1,500 plus an apportionment of the annual fixed costs of operating the coach. No specific fixed costs would be incurred if the coach is used on this contract. If the contract did not go ahead, the coach would not be in use for eight out of the ten days of the conference. For the other two days a contract has already been accepted which contains a significant financial penalty clause. This contract earns a contribution of $250 per day. A replacement coach could be hired for $180 per day.

Driver costs represent the salary and related employment costs of one driver for 10 days. If the driver is used on this contract the company will need to replace the driver so that VBJ can complete its existing work. The replacement driver would be hired from a recruitment agency that charges $400 per day for a suitably qualified driver. Hotel costs are the expected costs of hiring the hotel for the conference.

General overheads are based upon the overhead absorption rate of VBJ and are set annually when the company prepares its budgets. The only general overhead cost that can be specifically identified with the conference is the time that has been spent in considering the costs of the conference and preparing the quotation. This amounted to $250.

Required:

Prepare a statement showing the total relevant cost of the contract. Explain clearly the reasons for each of the values in your quotation and for excluding any of the costs (if appropriate).

4 Decision making based on relevant costing principles

There are many decisions that an organisation might have to make which will either be to solve short term problems (such as a short term scarcity of resources) or that may only be one-off in nature (such as whether to close a particular division).

The types of decisions that you may be asked to deal with include and which are explored in the following sections are:

- Limiting factor decisions
- Make or buy decisions
- Shutdown decisions, including deleting a segment or temporary closure
- Accept or reject an order decisions
- Minimum pricing decisions
- Joint product and further processing decisions.

In all of these decisions it will be important to remember that only **relevant costs** should be used in the calculations.

Limiting factor decisions

A limiting factor refers to a resource which prevents a company from achieving the output and sales that it would like to achieve. Businesses often operate under short term restrictions on resources (for example, staff time may be limited during a strike). They therefore may not be able to produce all products that make a positive contribution and need to prioritise products and choose between them.

Single limiting factor

 If there is a just one limiting factor then the rule is to maximise the **contribution per unit of scarce resource.**

The contribution per unit of each product is calculated and divided by the amount of scarce resource each product uses. The higher the contribution per unit of scarce resource the greater the priority that should be given to the product.

 Once the priorities have been decided the scarce resource is allocated to the products in the order of the priorities until used up.

 Limiting factor analysis step-by-step technique

The usual objective in questions is to maximise profit. Given that fixed costs are unaffected by the production decision in the short run, the approach should be to maximise the contribution earned.

If there is one limiting factor, then the problem is best solved as follows:

Step 1: identify the limiting factor (also known as the bottleneck resource, scarce resource or principal budget factor).

Step 2: calculate the contribution per unit for each product.

Step 3: calculate the contribution per unit of the limiting factor for each product.

Step 4: rank the products in order of the contribution per unit of the limiting factor.

Step 5: allocate resources using this ranking and answer the question.

Barbeque Ltd manufactures two products for which the following details are available:

	Product X	Product Y
Selling price	$38	$38
Direct materials (8kg / 4 kg)	$8	$4
Direct labour (4 hours / 6 hours)	$8	$12
Variable overheads	$12	$9
Fixed overheads	$5	$7
Minimum demand	500 units	500 units
Maximum demand	2,500 units	2,000 units

Calculate the optimum production plan and the contribution earned if labour in the next period is limited to 16,000 hours.

Step 1: Identify the limiting factor:

This has been provided as being direct labour hours.

Step 2: Calculate the contribution per unit for each product:

	Product X	Product Y
Selling price	$38	$38
Direct materials	($8)	($4)
Direct labour	($8)	($12)
Variable overheads	($12)	($9)
Contribution per unit	$10	$13

Step 3: Calculate the contribution per unit of the limiting factor:

	Product X	Product Y
Contribution per unit	$10	$13
Units of limiting resource	4 hours	6 hours
Contribution per labour hour	$10 / 4 hours = $2.50	$13 / 6 hours = $2.17

Step 4: Rank the products:

Product X generates the highest contribution per labour hour and so would be produced first.

Step 5: Allocate resources:

First of all the minimum demand constraint must be met. This means producing 500 units of each product:

500 units of Product X requires 500 × 4 hours = 2,000 hours

500 units of Product Y requires 500 × 6 hours = 3,000 hours

This uses 5,000 hours of the available 16,000 hours, leaving 11,000 hours.

Next, allocate the labour hours to the production of Product X first of all as this has the highest contribution per labour hour.

Maximum demand for X is 2,500 units. We have already allocated resource for 500 units and so an additional 2,000 are to be made. This will require 2,000 × 4 hours = 8,000 labour hours.

This leaves 3,000 labour hours (16,000 total less 10,000 used for X and 3,000 for Y's minimum demand) with which to produce Product Y.

Each Y requires 6 labour hours, therefore in 3,000 hours Barbeque can produce 3,000 hours / 6 hours per unit = 500 units of Y.

Contribution earned:

Product X: $10 per unit × 2,500 units = $25,000

Product Y: $13 per unit × 1,000 units = $13,000

Total contribution = $38,000.

Example 8

A company produces three products, and is reviewing the production and sales budgets for the next accounting period. The following information is available for the three products:

	Product P		Product Q		Product R	
	$	$	$	$	$	$
Selling price		600		300		100
Labour ($20 per hour)	300		160		40	
Other variable costs	90		68		14	
	———		———		———	
		(390)		(228)		(54)
		———		———		———
Contribution/unit		210		72		46
		———		———		———
Maximum demand (units)		200		600		1,000

Labour hours are strictly limited to 7,800 hours in total.

Required:

(a) Calculate the optimum product mix and the maximum contribution.

(b) A special contract requires 2,995 labour hours. What is the relevant cost of obtaining these hours?

Contrasting TA with the limiting factor approach

Illustration

A company produces two products, A and B, the production costs of which are shown below:

	A $	B $
Direct materials	10	10
Direct labour	5	9
Variable overhead	5	9
Fixed overhead	5	9
	25	37

Fixed overhead is absorbed on the basis of direct labour cost.

The products pass through two processes, Y and Z, with associated labour cost of $10 per direct labour hour in each. The direct labour time taken associated with the two products for these processes is shown below:

Process	Product A	Product B
Y	10 mins	39 mins
Z	20 mins	15 mins

Selling prices are set by the market. The current market price for A is $65 and that for B, $52. At these prices, the market will absorb as many units of A and B as the company can produce. The ability of the company to produce A and B is limited by the capacity to process the products through Y and Z. The company operates a two-shift system, giving 16 working hours per day. Process Z is a single-process line and 2 hours in each shift will be downtime. Process Y can process two units simultaneously, although this doubles the requirement for direct labour. Process Y can operate for the full 16 working hours each day.

Required:

What production plan should the company follow in order to maximise profits?

Solution

In order to find the profit maximising solution in any problem, the constraints which prevent the profit from being infinite must be identified; the greater the number of constraints, the more difficult the problem is to solve. In the simplest case, where there is only one binding constraint, the profit maximising solution is found by maximising the contribution per unit of the scarce resource, that is binding constraint. Linear programming (covered in a later chapter) may be used to solve the problem where more than one constraint is binding for some, but not all, feasible solutions.

Where the number of products is limited to two, and such constraints are relatively few in number, the problem can easily be expressed graphically to reveal the profit maximising solution, and/or the problem can be expressed in the form of a set of simultaneous equations. As the number of potentially binding constraints increases, the use of a computer becomes the only feasible way to solve the necessary number of simultaneous equations.

In this question, the only constraint is the company's ability to process the product. The total daily processing time for processes Y and Z are:

- Maximum process time Y = 2 × 16 hours × 60 minutes = 1,920 minutes

- Maximum process time Z = 12 hours × 60 minutes = 720 minutes

So the maximum number that could be produced of each of the two products is:

	Product A		Product B	
	Maximum units		*Maximum units*	
Y	$\dfrac{1{,}920}{10}$	= 192	$\dfrac{1{,}920}{39}$	= 49.23
Z	$\dfrac{720}{20}$	= 36	$\dfrac{720}{15}$	= 48

In the case of both products, the maximum number of units which can be produced in Process Y exceeds the number that can be produced in Process Z, and thus the capacity of Process Y is not a binding constraint.

The problem therefore becomes one of deciding how to allocate the scarce production capacity of Process Z in such a way as to maximise profit.

Traditional approach – maximising the contribution per minute in Process Z

Contribution of A = $65 (selling price) – $20 (variable cost) = $45
Contribution of B = $52 (selling price) – $28 (variable cost) = $24

Contribution of A per minute in process Z = $45/20 = $2.25 Contribution of B per minute in process Z = $24/15 = $1.60

The profit maximising solution is therefore to produce the maximum possible number of units of A, 36, giving a contribution of $45 × 36 = $1,620.

Throughput approach – maximising throughput contribution per minute in bottleneck resource Z

Throughput of A = $65 (selling price) – $10 (material cost) = $55
Throughput of B = $52 (selling price) – $10 (material cost) = $42

Throughput contribution of A per minute in process Z = $55/20 = $2.75
Throughput contribution of B per minute in process Z = $42/15 = $2.80

The profit maximising solution is therefore to produce the maximum number of units of B, 48, giving a throughput contribution of $42 × 48 = $2,016.

It is clear that, given the different solutions, the two approaches cannot both lead to profit maximisation. Which technique is correct depends on the variability or otherwise of labour and variable overheads, which in turn depends on the time horizon of the decision. This type of profit maximisation technique is a short-term one and in today's world labour is likely to be fixed in the short term and so it can be argued that TA provides the more correct solution. Variable overheads would need to be analysed to assess their variability.

Marginal costing rose to popularity in the 1930s when labour costs were usually variable as the workforce was usually paid on a piece-rate basis. Since then textbooks, at least, have always assumed that labour is a variable cost in the short term. All that has happened with TA is that it tends to recognise the present reality, which is that most cost excluding materials are now fixed in the short term.

The marginal costing approach should of course be modified to accommodate this, as it requires only variable costs to be used to calculate contribution. If only material costs are variable, then only those costs should be used in the calculation of contribution. Thus there should be no difference between the two systems in this respect.

This technique is the appropriate approach for dealing with a situation where there is only one scarce resource. If there is more than one scarce resource then linear programming would have to be used. Linear programming is covered in a later chapter.

Make or buy decisions

This is an extension of the limiting factor problem. If it is possible to buy-in the product and therefore avoid the use of the limiting factor then the products need to be ranked differently:

 Products should be ranked (from highest to lowest) based on the **saving made** (the difference between the buy-in cost and the incremental cost of internal production) **per usage of the scarce resource.**

In the presence of a limiting factor, the following step-by-step approach could be adopted with a make vs. buy question:

(1)   The saving per unit of each product is calculated. Saving = Purchases price – VC to make.

(2)   Divide this by the amount of scarce resource (a.k.a. limiting factor) each product uses. This gives the saving per unit of limiting factor (LF).

(3)   Rank. The higher the saving per unit of limiting factor the greater the priority to make that should be given to the product.

(4)   Once the priorities have been decided, the scarce resource is allocated to the products in the order of the priorities until it is fully used up.

(5)   Any products with unsatisfied demand can be satisfied by buying from the external source.

 Further details

Businesses may be faced with the decision whether to make components for their own products themselves or to concentrate their resources on assembling the products, obtaining the components from outside suppliers instead of making them 'in house'.

If the resources are bought in, their purchase cost is wholly marginal (i.e. direct). However, if it is decided to manufacture the components internally, the comparative costs of doing so will be the direct materials and wages costs, plus the variable factory overhead. If the total variable costs of internally manufactured components is seen to be greater than the cost of obtaining similar components elsewhere, it is obviously uneconomic to produce these items internally.

Business therefore need to compare these two costs (the buy-in cost and the internal production cost). The techniques to determine the production plan is then based on the same techniques used in any other limiting factor decision.

Illustration 2

Tablet Ltd is a manufacturer of tablets. Until now the company has manufactured all tablets, including accessories, in-house. The company is expecting a shortage of experienced production staff in the next period and is considering whether to outsource production of any of the three of the main tablet components: battery, screen, earphones.

The following information has been provided:

	Battery	Screen	Earphones
Labour hours per unit	1.0	1.5	0.5
Machine hours per unit	0.5	0.75	0.25
Production cost (5,000 units):	$	$	$
Direct labour	$15.00	$22.50	$7.50
Direct materials	$12.00	$20.00	$7.50
Variable overhead	$7.50	$11.25	$3.75
Fixed overhead	$6.00	$8.50	$4.00
Purchase price from outside supplier	$40.00	$50.00	$22.75

Manufacturing requirements show that 4,000 units of each type of product will be required in the next month and that labour is expected to be limited to 3500 hours.

Required:

Calculate how many of each product should be made in-house and how many should be outsourced.

Solution:

(1) Calculate saving = purchase price – variable cost to make in-house.

	Battery	Screen	Earphones
	$	$	$
External purchase price	40.00	50.00	22.75
Variable costs to make (direct materials + direct labour + variable costs)	34.50	53.75	18.75
Saving	5.50	(3.75)	4.00

(2) Calculate the saving per unit of limiting factor:

As the internal cost of making the screens exceeds the external purchase price of buying, it would be beneficial to outsource their production entirely. Batteries and earphones will continue to be produced internally.

	Battery	Screen	Earphones
	$	$	$
Saving	5.50	–	4.00
Scarce resource (labour hours)	1.00	–	0.5
Saving per unit of scarce resource	5.50	–	8.00

(3) Rank:

Earphones generate $8.00 per labour hour and so priority should be given to that product. Batteries will be made after production has been satisfied for Earphones.

(4) Allocate the scarce resource:

Make all 4,000 Earphones, using 4,000 × 0.5 labour hours = 2,000 labour hours. This leaves 1,500 labour hours (3,500 – 2,000) in which to manufacture the Batteries.

Each Battery requires 1 labour hour. Therefore in the remaining 1,500 hours it will be possible to manufacture 1,500 Batteries.

(5) Unsatisfied demand = 4,000 Batteries – 1,500 Batteries made in-house. These will have to be bought externally.

Example 9

A company manufactures four components (L, M, N and P) which are incorporated into different products. All the components are manufactured using the same general purpose machinery. The following production cost and machine hour data are available, together with the purchase prices from an outside supplier.

	L	M	N	P
Production cost:	$	$	$	$
Direct material	12	18	15	8
Direct labour	25	15	10	8
Variable overhead	8	7	5	4
Fixed overhead	10	6	4	3
Total	55	46	34	23
Purchase price from outside supplier	$57	$55	$54	$50
	Hours	Hours	Hours	Hours
Machine hours per unit	3	5	4	6

Manufacturing requirements show a need for 1,500 units of each component per week. The maximum number of general purpose machinery hours available per week is 24,000.

Required:

Calculate the number of units which should be purchased from the outside supplier.

Accept or reject decisions

This might occur where a customer has placed a one-off order for a product or a service.

The selling price will already be known and if it is greater than the relevant costs the order should be accepted.

Example 10

A company manufactures two models of a pocket calculator: The basic model sells for $5.50, has a direct material cost of $1.25 and requires 0.25 hours of labour time to produce. The other model, the Scientist, sells for $7.50, has a direct material cost of $1.63 and takes 0.375 hours to produce.

Labour, which is paid at the rate of $6 per hour, is currently very scarce, while demand for the company's calculators is heavy. The company is currently producing 8,000 of the basic model and 4,000 of the Scientist model per month, while fixed costs are $24,000 per month.

An overseas customer has offered the company a contract, worth $35,000, for a number of calculators made to its requirements. The estimating department has ascertained the following facts in respect of the work:

- The labour time for the contract would be 1,200 hours.

- The material cost would be $9,000 plus the cost of a particular component not normally used in the company's models.

- These components could be purchased from a supplier for $2,500 or alternatively, they could be made internally for a material cost of $1,000 and an additional labour time of 150 hours.

Required:

Advise the management as to the action they should take.

Shutdown decisions

This type of decision may involve deleting (or shutting down) a segment of the business, a product line, a service, etc. In the normal everyday reporting system of the business, it is likely that absorption costing will be used. It may appear under this system that one or more of the business segments appears unprofitable. Closure decisions taken on the basis of full absorption costs statements may fail to consider the fact that certain fixed costs allotted to the segment to be discontinued are fixed and may continue if the segment is dropped. The focus for shutdown decisions should be whether the costs and revenues are avoidable.

Businesses need to therefore determine the difference between forgone revenue from the closure and the incremental cost savings from closure.

 Illustration 3

The management of MD Ltd is considering the closure of one of its operations, department 3, based on the information included within the following report:

	1	2	3	Total
Sales (units)	5,000	6,000	2,000	13,000
Sales ($)	150,000	240,000	24,000	414,000
Cost of sales ($):				
Direct material	75,000	150,000	8,000	233,000
Direct labour	25,000	30,000	8,000	63,000
Production overhead	5,769	6,923	2,308	15,000
	———	———	———	———
Gross profit ($)	44,231	53,077	5,692	103,000
Expenses ($)	15,384	18,461	6,155	40,000
	———	———	———	———
Net profit ($)	28,847	34,616	(463)	63,000

Additional information:

- Total production overheads have been apportioned to the three departments on the basis of sales volume. However, upon further investigation it has been determined that only 50% of the production overheads can be directly traced to the departments in the proportion 2:2:1.

- Total expenses are head office overheads, again apportioned to the departments on the basis of sales volume. It has since been determined that only 60% of these can be directly traced to the departments, in the ratio 3:3:2.

Required:

Restate the financial position in terms of the controllable profit made by each department and advise whether department 3 should be closed.

Solution:

First of all we must restate the figures so that they present the situation in its true light. Only relevant cash flows should be considered. This will enable each department to be readily evaluated on its locally controllable performance.

	1	2	3	Total
Sales (units)	5,000	6,000	2,000	13,000
Sales ($)	150,000	240,000	24,000	414,000
Cost of sales ($):				
Direct material	75,000	150,000	8,000	233,000
Direct labour	25,000	30,000	8,000	63,000
Production overhead (Note 1)	3,000	3,000	1,500	7,500
Expenses ($) (Note 2)	9,000	9,000	6,000	24,000
Controllable profit ($)	38,000	48,000	500	86,500
Other costs ($):				
Overhead (50%)				7,500
Expenses (40%)				16,000
Net profit ($)				63,000

Looking at the restated figures, department 3 should be kept open. The department is making a positive contribution towards the overall profit of the business. The apparent loss arises purely due to inappropriate apportionment of overheads and head office expenses.

(Note 1)

Only 50% of the existing production overhead charge should be included as only 50% is controllable.

50% of production overhead = $15,000 × 0.5 = $7,500.

Proportion 2:2:1 = $3,000:$3,000:$1,500

(Note 2)

60% of expenses = $40,000 × 0.6 = $24,000.

Proportion 3:3:2 = $9,000:$9,000:$6,000

Example 11

Wye plc makes and sells four products. The profit and loss statement for April is as follows:

	W $	X $	Y $	Z $	Total $
Sales	30,000	20,000	35,000	15,000	100,000
Cost of sales	16,000	8,000	22,000	10,000	56,000
Gross profit	14,000	12,000	13,000	5,000	44,000
Overhead cost:					
Selling	8,000	7,000	8,500	6,500	30,000
Administration	2,000	2,000	2,000	2,000	8,000
Net profit	4,000	3,000	2,500	(3,500)	6,000

The management team is concerned about the results, particularly those of product Z, and it has been suggested that Wye plc would be better off if it ceased production of product Z. The production manager has said that if product Z were discontinued the resources which would become available could be used to increase production of product Y by 40 per cent. You have analysed the cost structures of each of the products and discovered the following:

	W $	X $	Y $	Z $	Total $
Variable costs	4,800	1,600	13,200	5,000	24,600
Fixed costs	11,200	6,400	8,800	5,000	31,400
Cost of sales	16,000	8,000	22,000	10,000	56,000

The total fixed costs figure includes $20,000 which is not specific to any one product, and which has been apportioned to each product on the basis of sales values. If the quantity of any product increases by more than 25 per cent, then the specific fixed production costs of the product will increase by 30 per cent.

The selling overhead comprises a fixed cost of $5,000 per product plus a variable cost which varies in proportion to sales value. The fixed cost is not specific to any product but the sales director believes that it should be shared equally by the four products.

The administration cost is a fixed central overhead cost; it is not affected by the products made.

Required:

(a) Prepare a statement which shows clearly the results of continuing to produce products W, X, Y and Z at the same volumes as were achieved in April. Present your statement in a format suitable for management decision-making.

(b) (i) Prepare a statement showing clearly the results if product Z is discontinued, and the number of units of Y is increased in accordance with the production manager's statement. (Assume that no change in selling price per unit is necessary to sell the additional units.)

    (ii) Reconcile the profit calculated in (a) and (b) (i) above; advise the management team as to whether product Z should be discontinued.

(c) Explain briefly any non-financial factors which should be considered before discontinuing a product.

Minimum pricing decisions

The minimum pricing approach is a useful method in situations where there is a lot of intense competition, surplus production capacity, clearance of old inventories, getting special orders and/or improving market share of the product.

 The minimum price should be set at the incremental costs of manufacturing, plus opportunity costs (if any).

For this type of pricing, the selling price is the lowest price that a company may sell its product at – usually the price will be the total relevant costs of manufacturing.

Illustration 4

ABC Company has prepared a summary of its relevant costs for a special order:

		$
(i)	Material P	120
	Material Q	(280)
(ii)	Labour	–
(iii)	Variable overhead	600
(iv)	Rent forgone	210
	Total relevant cost	**$650**

This cost of $650 represents the minimum price that the company should charge for the order if they wish to make neither a profit nor a loss. As long as the customer pays $650 for the order, the company profits will not be affected.

Obviously, this represents the absolute minimum price that could be charged. It is unlikely that ABC would actually charge this amount. They would probably wish to add a profit margin to improve the company's profits. However, this absolute minimum value does give managers a starting point for their pricing decision. They know that the company will be worse off if the price is less than $650. If perhaps ABC is tendering for the order in competition with other suppliers, they may try to obtain some information on the likely prices to be tendered by their competitors. If these prices are less than or close to $650, then ABC knows that they will not be able to offer a competitive price.

On the other hand, if competitors are likely to tender a much higher price, then the managers know that they are able to price competitively.

Joint products and further processing decisions

Joint products were examined in a previous chapter where costs up until the split-off point were allocated to the products.

With many joint products it is possible to sell the product at the split-off point or to send it through a further process which will enhance its value. There are two rules to follow when ascertaining whether the further processing is worthwhile:

(1) Only the incremental costs and revenues of the further process are relevant

(2) The joint process costs are irrelevant – they are already 'sunk' at the point of separation.

📖 **Further details**

The main decisions involving joint products are:

*   To carry out the whole process or not. This decision is made by considering the total revenues and costs of the process. A decision cannot be taken to just process some of the products as all products are produced simultaneously. The basis of common cost apportionment is irrelevant but the common costs in total are relevant.

*   Whether or not to further process products. This decision is based on the incremental costs and incremental revenues of further processing. Revenue and cost at the split-off point are irrelevant to the decision as they will not change.

Example 12

A processing company operates a common process from which three different products emerge. Each of the three products can then either be sold in a market that has many buyers and sellers or further processed independently of each other in three other processes. After further processing, each of the products can be sold in the same market for a higher unit selling price.

Which of the following is required to determine whether or not any of the products should be further processed? (choose all that apply)

(i)   Total cost of the common process

(ii)   The basis of sharing the common process cost between the three products

(iii)   The cost of each of the three additional processes

(iv)   The unit selling price of each product after further processing

(v)   The unit selling price of each product before further processing

(vi)   The percentage normal loss of each further process

(vii)   The actual units of output of each product from the common process

Qualitative factors in decision making

In some decision-making situations, qualitative aspects are more important than immediate financial benefit from a decision. They will vary with different business circumstances and are those factors relevant to a decision that are difficult or impossible to measure in terms of money.

> CIMA's Official Terminology defines 'Qualitative factors' as 'factors that are relevant to a decision but are not expressed numerically'.

For an organisation faced with a decision, qualitative factors may include:

(1)   The state of the economy, and its levels of inflation

(2)   The availability of cash

(3)   Effect of a decision on employee morale, schedules and other internal elements

(4)   Effect of a decision on long-term future profitability

(5)   Effect of a decision on a company's public image and the reaction of customers

(6)   The likely reaction of competitors.

Conflicts with financial accounting

The decision making techniques described are more concerned with the impact on cash flow rather than the impact on profits. This is because cash flow is more objective and harder to manipulate than profits.

 Cash versus profit

In the short term, profits and cash flow are different. There are several reasons for this:

- Some items of cash spending and cash receipt do not affect profits at all. In particular capital receipts and capital payments do not affect profits. A business could earn a profit but spend large sums of money on capital expenditure, so that it makes a profit but has a negative cash flow.

- Profits are calculated after deducting depreciation charges on non-current assets. Depreciation is a notional charge, and does not affect cash flow at all. It is an accounting device for spreading the cost of a non-current asset over its useful life.

- Cash flow is affected by the need to invest in operational working capital. Operational working capital is defined as the working capital a business needs to carry on its day-to-day business operations. It consists of its inventory (inventories) plus its trade receivables minus its trade payables. Investing in working capital affects cash flow, and when the total amount of working capital of a business changes, the profits earned in the period will differ from the operational cash flows.

For accounting purposes, in preparing an income statement there are two possible systems that can be used:

- Cash accounting
- Accruals accounting

These systems will provide different profit figures for the period based on different assumptions about how revenues and costs are recorded in the income statement.

In a system of accruals accounting, revenues and costs are reported in the period where the sale occurs, even if the cash flows for the sale and costs of sale occur in different periods, whereas a system of cash accounting records cash payments and cash receipts as they occur within an accounting period. Cash accounting is an accounting method where receipts are recorded during the period they are received, and the expenses in the period in which they are actually paid. Basically, when the cash is received for a sale, it is recorded in the accounting books as a sale. Its focus is on determining the operational cash flow for the year.

However, cash accounting is not generally accepted as good accounting practice because businesses enter into transactions that are legally enforceable prior to the exchange of cash, but the use of cash accounting does not reflect any transactions which have taken place but are not yet paid for.

Accruals accounting is recognised by law, and businesses are required to use it to measure their profitability for the purpose of external financial reporting.

Therefore, the decisions that an organisation makes may have a different impact on cash flows than they have on profits. This may cause an issue for the business in that shareholders (and many other stakeholders) are not always provided with the cash impact of decisions. Instead the financial reporting that they do receive comes from financial statements that focus on profit rather than cash.

In the long term, the cash impact and the profit impact of a decision should be equal. However, in the short term there is likely to be a difference and shareholders are more likely to react to a change in profit than a change in cash.

There may also be a conflict between decision making and performance measurement. In making decisions managers are encouraged to only consider relevant costs. But they might then find that their performance is based on total costs, whether relevant or not.

Further details and illustration

Managers should make decisions on relevant costs. For example, consider a manager who is making a decision on whether to discontinue one of many products made by an organisation. The manager would ignore, for example, the cost already spent on acquiring survey data on future expected sales for the product as this would be deemed an historic cost.

Using numbers, imagine if the relevant benefit of discontinuing the product was $4,000 because the survey cost (which is sunk) was ignored. The survey cost was $7,000. The manager has made a good decision which will increase the organisation's future cash flows by $4,000.

But the manager's performance for the period will not be based on relevant costs. Instead it will be based on total controllable cost. The decision to carry out the sales survey would be seen as a controllable one and therefore the survey cost would therefore be deducted from the manager's profit for the year (which could impact on elements such as the manager's annual bonus.

> The manager's profit for the year, using the numbers above, would fall by $3,000 (the $4,000 net benefit minus the $7,000 controllable survey cost). The manager's performance would look worse in the year despite the manager making a good decision which will benefit the organisation overall.
>
> This type of conflict will be explored more in the CIMA P2 syllabus.

Therefore, decision makers need to consider this when making decisions. This could be one of the 'other factors' that may be relevant to decisions.

 ## 5 Ethical considerations in short-term decision making

This chapter has examined a range of decisions and suggested how decisions should be made from a financial view point. But this is only one aspect of decision making. There are many non-financial factors that an organisation should consider, including the ethical implications of its decisions.

Typically, acting ethically means making decisions that go beyond purely financial considerations and instead considers a much wider scope of stakeholder perspectives. Ethical organisations will not simply consider the impact on shareholder wealth but will also consider the impact on employees, customers and even wider society.

In this chapter we have considered the relevant costs and revenues in shut-down decisions. For example, a bank might look at the relevant financial cost or benefit of closing down a branch in a particular location. But if the decision was broadened to consider ethical issues then the organisation might consider issues such as:

- The impact on staff. If the branch is closed then staff will be made redundant if they cannot (or will not) be relocated elsewhere within the banks operations). The bank may consider how easy or difficult it might be for staff to find other employment or the impact on staff's career paths. Ethical decision makers may consider paying for staff to retrain for new careers or paying a higher redundancy figure than is required by law.

- There may be a knock-on impact on wider staff morale if staff in other locations fear that they too might lose their jobs. This could impact on staff absence and motivation and may lead to the loss of key staff and an inability to hire replacements. Even if staff in other locations do not fear for their job security they may be dissatisfied with the bank's lack of ethical focus and actively seek employment in an organisation that considers ethical impacts of decisions alongside financial ones.

- Customers may be left without a banking service in this location. For many customers a switch to mobile, computer and telephone banking can replace such services. But for many customers this may not be possible or wanted. For example, if the location is in a rural area with poor or little internet or mobile network coverage then customers may have to use physical branches in other locations. This may not be possible for many customers such as the elderly or those who have mobility issues.

- The local community (who may not even use this bank branch) may also be impacted if the closure results in an empty property that cannot be let out to another business or organisation. This may, for example, detract from the attractiveness of the location for new homes or for government investment. This can affect the quality of life for the local community as a whole.

- There may be a wider impact on the organisation's reputation if the bank is seen to be acting purely on financial interests rather than in the interests of its wider community.

Typical questions that an ethical decision maker might ask are:

- Does this decision make financial sense?

- What will be the impact on staff, customers and the wider community?

- Which decision generates the most benefit for the lowest adverse impact on wider stakeholders?

- Can a trade-off be found which creates the least amount of adverse impact on stakeholders?

- Should/have all stakeholders be/been consulted?

- Does the decision conform to organisational values?

- How can adverse impacts be mitigated?

Acting ethically means going beyond simple legal or financial impacts of business decision and instead considering a wider set of viewpoints in order to create and preserve organisational value. Considering ethical issues as part of business decisions can result in some options no longer being available to the organisation but it may also open up alternative options. It will also mean that decisions are more in line with organisational values and goals which will ultimately help the organisation in creating more value for stakeholders.

Apart from an ethical organisation being, perhaps, 'morally correct', there are more quantifiable business benefits from acting ethically such as:

- Acting ethically can lower business risk that, for example, should create more stable earnings and should make cheaper finance available. Ethics is not just a matter of being righteous: if an organisation has a reputation for making unethical decisions it will be perceived as being a high risk organisation that it might be better not to deal with.

- Acting ethically can make an organisation attractive to customers, collaborators and partners

- The organisation can also become more attractive to potential employees

- Less time and cost is spent dealing with investigations by regulatory bodies

- Less is spent on paying damages and fines.

On the other hand, acting ethically can bring the following problems:

- If the sole aim of acting ethically is to differentiate the organisation from rivals then, unfortunately, the strategy is easily copied by rivals and any advantages can be short-lived

- Acting ethically typically adds costs to activities

- Success often relies on trial and error

- International businesses may have to adopt different ethical approaches in different markets. What is considered good ethical practice in one country may not be considered ethical in another. This may give a lack of global consistency.

6 Chapter summary

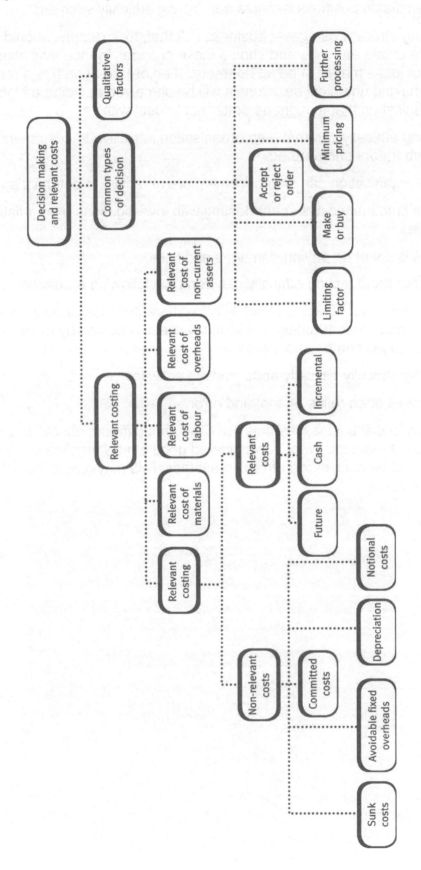

7 Practice Questions

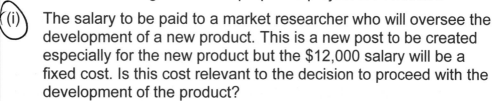

Test your understanding 1

Which of the following costs for a proposed project are relevant?

(i) The salary to be paid to a market researcher who will oversee the development of a new product. This is a new post to be created especially for the new product but the $12,000 salary will be a fixed cost. Is this cost relevant to the decision to proceed with the development of the product?

(ii) The $2,500 additional monthly running costs of a new machine to be purchased to manufacture an established product. Since the new machine will save on labour time, the fixed overhead to be absorbed by the product will reduce by $100 per month. Are these costs relevant to the decision to purchase the new machine?

(iii) Office cleaning expenses of $125 for next month. The office is cleaned by contractors and the contract can be cancelled by giving 1 months' notice. Is this cost relevant to a decision to close the office?

(iv) Expenses of $75 paid to the marketing manager. This was to reimburse the manager for the cost of travelling to meet a client with whom the company is currently negotiating a major contract. Is this cost relevant to the decision to continue negotiations?

(select all costs that are relevant)

Test your understanding 2

A company is considering a short-term pricing decision to utilise some spare capacity. The item to be manufactured and sold would use 1,500 kgs of raw material Q.

Material Q is in regular use by the company. It currently has 1,000 kgs in inventory, which was purchased last month at a cost of $4 per kg. The current replacement cost of material Q is $4.80 per kg and the current inventory could be sold for $4.30 per kg.

Calculate the relevant cost of material Q for the purposes of this decision

Test your understanding 3

A mining operation uses skilled labour costing $4 per hour, which generates a contribution, after deducting these labour costs, of $3 per hour.

A new project is now being considered that requires 5,000 hours of skilled labour. There is a shortage of the required labour. Any used on the new project must be transferred from normal working. Calculate the relevant cost of using the skilled labour on the project. Calculate the contribution cash flow that is lost if the labour is transferred from normal working.

Activity 2

Suppose the facts about labour are as above, but there is a surplus of skilled labour already employed (and paid) by the business which is sufficient to cope with the new project. The presently idle men are being paid full wages.

Calculate the contribution cash flow that is lost if the labour is transferred to the project from doing nothing.

Test your understanding 4

P Limited is considering whether to continue making a component or buy it from an outside supplier. It uses 12,000 of the components each year.

The internal manufacturing cost comprises:

	$/unit
Direct materials	3.00
Direct labour	4.00
Variable overhead	1.00
Specific fixed cost	2.50
Other fixed costs	2.00
	12.50

If the direct labour were not used to manufacture the component, it would be used to increase the production of another item for which there is unlimited demand. This other item has a contribution of $10.00 per unit but requires $8.00 of labour per unit.

The maximum price per component at which buying is preferable to internal manufacture is:

A $8.00

B $10.50

C $12.50

D $15.50

Test your understanding 5

Budgeted data relating to a single-product firm that is working to full capacity are as follows:

Production and sales for the year   20,000 units

Machine capacity available and fully utilised   40,000 hours

	$
Variable cost	8.20
Fixed cost	1.30
Total cost	9.50
Selling price	12.50
Net profit per unit	3.00

An order is received for 3,000 modified units which will use 6,600 hours of machine time and cost $1.00 per unit for additional materials.

At what price should the firm be indifferent between taking on, and rejecting, the order?

A $41,790

B $40,500

C $27,600

D $17,190

Test your understanding 6

Lauda operates a joint process from which four products arise. The products may be sold at the separation point of the process or can be refined further and be sold at a premium. Information regarding the products and the refining process can be found below:

Products	E	F	G	H
Selling prices per litre ($)				
At separation point	12	16	15	18
After refining	20	23	25	22
Costs ($)				
Joint process (per litre):	8	8	8	8
Refining process:				
Variable (per litre)	5	5	5	5
Specific fixed (in total)	1,000	2,000	3,000	4,000
Budgeted litres	2,000	500	5,000	6,000

481

The general fixed overheads in the refining process amount to $30,000.

Which products should be further processed?

A E, F and G only

B E and G only

C G only

D None of them

Test your understanding 7

Company A manufactures four products in two different locations. It operates under strict Just-In-Time principles and does not hold any inventory of either finished goods or raw materials.

Company A has a long-standing agreement to supply its main customer with 100 units of each of its products Product 1, Product 2, Product 3 and Product 4. No negotiation is possible and the contract must be fulfilled.

Details of the company's additional, non-contract related production on Site 1 are as follows:

	Product 1	Product 2	Product 3	Product 4
Selling price	$60	$70	$80	$90
Direct labour, at $8 per hour	$16	$8	$12	$16
Direct Material A, at $3 per litre	$4.50	$3.00	$0	$3.00
Direct Material B, at $5 per kg	$5.00	$0	$15	$10
Variable overhead, labour related (*)	$1.25	$0.63	$0.94	$1.25
Variable overhead, machine related (*)	$1.25	$2.00	$0.75	$1.00
Total variable cost	$28.00	$13.63	$28.69	$31.25
Machine hours per unit	5	8	3	4
Maximum demand per week	900 units	950 units	950 units	900 units

(*) An analysis of the variable overhead shows that some of it is caused by the number of labour hours and the remainder is caused by the number of machine hours.

All the above products use the same resources (materials A and B). Currently, the company also purchases a component, Component Alpha, from an external supplier in the US for $50. A single unit of this component is used in producing Product 5, the company's only other product, on Site 2. Product 5 yields a positive contribution and does not use any materials used by the other products.

Company A could manufacture Component Alpha on Site 1, but to do so would require 2 hours of direct labour, half an hour of machine time as well as 1.5 kilograms of Material B.

The purchasing director has recently advised you that the availability of Direct Materials A and B is to be restricted to 5,000 litres and 6,000 kilograms every week. This restriction is unlikely to change in the near future, but no restrictions are expected on any other materials.

Required:

(a) Calculate whether Company A should continue to purchase Component Alpha or whether it should manufacture it internally.

(b) Prepare a statement to show the optimum weekly usage of Site 1's available resources.

(c) Assuming no other changes, calculate the purchase price of Component Alpha at which your advice in (a) would change.

Test your understanding 8

Scenario

Z is one of a number of companies that produce three products for an external market. The three products, R, S and T may be bought or sold in this market. The common process account of Z for March 20X7 is shown below:

	Kg	$		Kg	$
Inputs					
Material A	1,000	3,500	Normal loss	500	0
Material B	2,000	2,000	Outputs:		
Material C	1,500	3,000	Product R	800	3,500
Direct labour		6,000	Product S	2,000	8,750
Variable overhead		2,000	Product T	1,200	5,250
Fixed cost		1,00			
Totals	**4,500**	**17,500**		**4,500**	**17,500**

Z can sell products R, S or T after this common process or they can be individually further processed and sold as RZ, SZ and TZ respectively. The market prices for the products at the intermediate stage and after further processing are (Market prices per kg):

	$
R	3.00
S	5.00
T	3.50
RZ	6.00
SZ	5.75
TZ	6.75

The specific costs of the three individual further processes are:

Process R to RZ – variable cost of $1.40 per kg, no fixed costs

Process S to SZ – variable cost of $0.90 per kg, no fixed costs

Process T to TZ – variable cost of $1.00 per kg, fixed cost of $600 per month

Tasks:

(a) Produce calculations to determine whether any of the intermediate products should be further processed before being sold. Clearly state your recommendations together with any relevant assumptions that you have made.

(b) Produce calculations to assess the viability of the common process:

(i) assuming that there is an external market for products R, S and T; and

(ii) assuming that there is not an external market for products R, S and T.

State clearly your recommendations.

Test your understanding answers

Example 1

The correct answer is **B.**

The initial $40,000 fee will be deemed to be a sunk cost – it has already been committed and won't be affected by any decision to proceed from this point.

The $20,000 is a future cost. Despite the fact that it is called a fixed cost it will only be incurred if the project proceeds. It is therefore and extra or incremental cost of the project and should be included in any future decision making.

Example 2

100% capacity = 102,000 ÷ 0.85 = 120,000 units

Spare capacity amounts to 18,000 units. So there is sufficient slack to meet the new order

Variable costs = $330,000 less $75,000 = $255,000

Variable cost per unit = $255,000 ÷ 102,000 = $2.50

Contribution per unit from existing product = $3.25 – $2.50 = $0.75

Contribution per unit from new product = $2.80 – $2.50 = $0.30

	$
Increase in contribution from new product: $0.30 × 12,000 units	3,600
Fall in contribution from existing product: $0.75 × (12,000 ÷ 15) × 2 = $0.75 × 1,600	(1,200)
Net gain in contribution	**2,400**

Example 3

1,000 kgs of P:

	$
Purchase 200 kgs; Current replacement price $4.50/Kg	900
Use 800 kgs from inventory (800 × $3.50)	2,800
Total	**$3,700**

Example 4

Existing product earns a contribution per hour of $60 – $10 – $10 – $15 = $25

Relevant cost	= Contribution forgone PLUS direct labour cost
	= $25 + $10
	= $35 per hour
Total cost	= $35 × 100 hours = $3,500

Example 5

- The variable cost per hour of overhead is relevant since this cost would be avoidable if the contract were not undertaken. The relevant cost of variable overheads is therefore $7 per machine hour.

- The fixed cost per hour is an absorption rate. Actual fixed costs would not increase by $13 per hour, but by $3,200 in total. The incremental relevant cost of fixed overheads is therefore $3,200.

- This would make the total cost = (800 hours of machine time for variable overheads @ $7 per hour) + $3,200 or fixed overheads = $8,800.

- The correct answer is therefore Answer C.

Example 6

Opportunity cost now = **$2,000** (Answer C)

Example 7

	Note	$
Relevant costs		
Fuel costs	1	1,500
Replacement coach	2	360
Replacement driver	3	800
Hotel costs	4	5,000
Total		7,660

Notes:

(1) The fuel cost is directly traceable to the contract and is therefore relevant. The apportionment of annual fixed costs for operating the coach are not relevant. The total fixed cost would remain the same whether the contract were accepted or not.

(2) The company should hire a replacement coach for two days @ $180 per day. This will ensure that the contribution of $250 per day continues to be earned from the other contract.

(3) The company's employed driver will be paid whether VBJ wins the contract or not. As a consequence of winning the contract, it would become necessary to hire a replacement driver for two days @ $400 per day to cover the existing work. This incremental cost is relevant.

(4) The hotel cost is directly attributable to the contract and is therefore relevant.

(5) The general overhead that has been traced to the contract ($250) should be ignored as this cost is sunk.

(6) The profit is not a relevant cost.

Example 8

(a)

	Product		
	P	Q	R
Contribution per unit	$210	$72	$46
Hours per unit	15	8	2
Contribution per hour	$14	$9	$23
Rank	2nd	3rd	1st

Product	Units	Hrs/per unit	Total hours	Contribution per hour	Total contribution
R	1,000	2	2,000	$23	$46,000
P	200	15	3,000	$14	$42,000
Q	350	8	2,800	$9	$25,200
			7,800		$113,200

(b)   The special contract requires 2,995 SCARCE labour hours.

Relevant cost = Direct cost + Opportunity cost

Direct cost	2,995 hrs × $20	$59,900
Opportunity cost	2,800 hrs × $9	$25,200
	195 hrs × $14	$2,730
Relevant cost		**$87,830**

Example 9

Technique

The following method could be adopted in this example:

(1)   The saving per unit of each product is calculated. Saving = Purchases price – VC to make.

(2)   Divide this by the amount of scarce resource (a.k.a. limiting factor) each product uses. This gives the saving per unit of limiting factor (LF).

(3)   Rank. The higher the saving per unit of LF the greater the priority to make that should be given to the product.

(4)   Once the priorities have been decided, the scarce resource is allocated to the products in the order of the priorities until it is fully used up.

(5)   Any products with unsatisfied demand can be satisfied by buying from the external source.

This can be applied as follows:

(1)   Calculate saving = Purchases price – VC to make:

	L	M	N	P
External purchase price	$57	$55	$54	$50
Variable costs to make	$45	$40	$30	$20
Saving	$12	$15	$24	$30

(2)   Calculate the saving per unit of limiting factor/scarce resource:

	L	M	N	P
Saving	$12	$15	$24	$30
Scarce resource (machine hours) per unit	3 hours	5 hours	4 hours	6 hours
Saving per unit of the scarce resource	$4	$3	$6	$5

(3) Rank

	L	M	N	P
Saving per unit of the scarce resource	$4	$3	$6	$5
Rank : product to make in priority	3	4	1	2

(4) Allocate scarce resource of 24,000 machine hours to production

Make all Ns (1,500 units). This will use up 1,500 × 4 hours = 6,000 hours.

Then, make all Ps (1,500 units). This will use up 1,500 × 6 hours = 9,000 hours. The cumulative total is 6,000 + 9,000 = 15,000 hours.

Then, make all Ls (1,500 units). This will use up 1,500 × 3 hours = 4,500 hours. The cumulative total is 15,000 + 4,500 = 19,500 hours.

This leaves (24,000 − 19,500) = 4,500 hours, in which to make

$$\frac{4,500}{5} = 900 \text{ units of Products M}$$

(5) Unsatisfied demand = 1,500 Ms − 900 Ms = 600 Ms. These will have to be bought externally.

	L	M	N	P
Variable production cost	$45	$40	$30	$20
External cost	$57	$55	$54	$50
Incremental cost	**$12**	**$15**	**$24**	**$30**
Hours per unit	÷ 3	÷ 5	÷ 4	÷ 6
Incremental cost per hour	**$4**	**$3**	**$6**	**$5**
Cheapest per hour	2nd	1st	4th	3rd

The analysis shows that it is actually cheaper to try and make ALL the components within the factory.

Hours required to make 1,500 units of each component:

(1,500 × 3) + (1,500 × 5) + (1,500 × 4) + (1,500 × 6) = 27,000 hours

The company only has 24,000 hours available. So, 3,000 hours of work must be sub-contracted. The CHEAPEST component per hour must be bought externally. This is component M.

3,000 hours of time on M equates to 3,000 ÷ 5 = **600 units of M.**

Example 10

In view of its scarcity, labour is taken as the limiting factor.

The decision on whether to make or buy the component has to be made before it can be decided whether or not to accept the contract. In order to do this the contribution per labour hour for normal production must first be calculated, as the contract will replace some normal production.

Normal products	Basic		Scientist	
	$	$	$	$
Selling price		5.50		7.50
Materials	1.25		1.63	
Labour	1.50		2.25	
		2.75		3.88
Contribution		2.75		3.62
Contribution per direct labour hour (@0.25/0.375 hours per unit)		11.00		9.64

Therefore, if the company is to make the component it would be better to reduce production of the 'Scientist' model, in order to accommodate the special order.

The company should now compare the costs of making or buying the component.

An opportunity cost arises due to the lost contribution on the scientist model:

Special contract	Manufacture of component
	$
Materials	1,000
Labour ($6 × 150 hours)	900
Opportunity cost (150 hours × $9.6533)	1,448
	3,348

Since this is higher than the bought-in price of $2,500 the company would be advised to buy the component from the supplier if they accept the contract.

The contract can now be evaluated:

	Contract contribution	
	$	$
Sales revenue		35,000
Material cost	9,000	
Component	2,500	
Labour ($6 × 1,200)	7,200	
	———	
		18,700
		———
Contribution		16,300
		———

Contribution per direct labour hour (for 1,200 labour hours) $13.58

Since the contribution is higher than either of the existing products, the company should accept the contract assuming this would not prejudice the market for existing products.

Because the contribution is higher for the 'Basic' model, it would be wise to reduce production of the Scientist model. However, the hours spent on producing the Scientist model per month are (4,000 units × 0.375 hours =) 1,500, and so the contract would displace 80% of the production time of the scientist model. The recommendation assumes that this can be done without harming long-term sales of the scientist model (the scenario suggests that the demand for the product is high and therefore there would be no lost sales of the product in the long term).

As the customer is overseas, this seems a reasonable assumption. However, if this were not the case then the opportunity cost from the lost sales of scientific calculators should be deducted from the contribution calculated above

Before finalising the decision there are many other factors that should be considered such as:

- whether all costs have been considered (for example, extra delivery costs for the overseas customer)

- the potential impact of any foreign exchange rate movements

- whether this will be a one-off contract or whether it will open the door for more profitable work with this customer

- the value of the experience and impact on overseas reputation of beginning to export the product

- the level of competition for the contract

- the extra administration involved in dealing with a foreign customer (such as dealing in a foreign language and performing reasonable credit checks etc.

- the potential impact on existing customers who buy packages of basic and scientific models

Example 11

(a)

	W $	X $	Y $	Z $	Total $
Sales	30,000	20,000	35,000	15,000	
Variable cost of sales	4,800	1,600	13,200	5,000	
Variable selling overhead (*)	3,000	2,000	3,500	1,500	
Contribution	22,200	16,400	18,300	8,500	
Specific fixed costs (W1)	5,200	2,400	1,800	2,000	
Net benefit	17,000	14,000	16,500	6,500	54,000
Non-specific fixed cost of sales					(20,000)
Fixed selling overhead (W2)					(20,000)
Administration costs					(8,000)
Net profit					6,000

(*) Total overhead less $5,000 fixed cost.

Workings

(1)

	W $	X $	Y $	Z $	Total $
Fixed costs	11,200	6,400	8,800	5,000	31,400
Non-specific fixed costs (*)	6,000	4,000	7,000	3,000	20,000
Specific fixed costs	5,200	2,400	1,800	2,000	11,400

(*) Given as $20,000 apportioned on the basis of sales value (3:2:3.5:1.5).

(2) $5,000 per product × 4 = $20,000

(b) (i) **Z discontinued**

	$
Contribution from 40% additional sales of Y ($18,300 × 0.4)	7,320
Additional specific fixed costs	(540)
Loss of net benefit from Z	(6,500)
Net gain	280

(ii) **Profit reconciliation**

	$
Existing profit	6,000
Discontinuation of Z	(6,500)
Additional contribution from Y	7,320
Additional specific fixed costs	(540)
Profit if Z is discontinued and Y substituted in	6,280

(c) Non-financial factors to consider include:

(1) Possible redundancies among the workforce

(2) Signals which it may give to competitors, who may perceive the company as being unwilling to support its products

(3) The reaction of customers, particularly those who may recently have purchased the product.

Sometimes, even when management has made the decision to discontinue a product or activity, there is still a further decision to be made: when to discontinue it. The following exercise shows how such a decision could be made.

Example 12

The following costs are relevant:

(iii) The total cost of each of the three additional processes – this represents the incremental total cost

(iv) The unit selling price of each product after further processing – this is required to calculate incremental revenue

(v) The unit selling price of each product before further processing – this is required to calculate incremental revenue

(vi) The percentage normal loss of each further process – this will be required to calculate total output per product after further processing

(vii) The actual units of output of each product from the common process – this will be required to calculate total output per product after further processing

The following costs are not relevant:

(i) Total cost of the common process – this is related to the common cost

(ii) The basis of sharing the common process cost between the three products – this is related to the common cost

---

Test your understanding 1

(i) The salary is a relevant cost of $12,000. Do not be fooled by the fact that it is a fixed cost. The cost may be fixed in total but it is definitely a cost that is relevant to the decision to proceed with the future development of the new product. This is an example of a directly attributable fixed cost. A directly attributable fixed cost may also be called product-specific fixed cost.

(ii) The $2,500 additional running costs are relevant to the decision to purchase the new machine. The saving in overhead absorption is not relevant since we are not told that the total overhead expenditure will be altered. The saving in labour cost would be relevant but we shall assume that this has been accounted for in determining the additional monthly running costs.

(iii) This is not a relevant cost for next month since it will be incurred even if the contract is cancelled today. If a decision is being made to close the office, this cost cannot be included as a saving to be made next month. However, it will be saved in the months after that so it will become a relevant cost saving from month 2 onwards.

(iv) This is not a relevant cost of the decision to continue with the contract. The $75 is sunk and cannot be recovered even if the company does not proceed with the negotiations.

Test your understanding 2

In regular use, so relevant cost = replacement cost

Replacement cost for Q = 1,500 kgs × $4.80

$$= \$7,200$$

Test your understanding 3

	$
Contribution per hour lost from normal working	3
Add back: labour cost per hour that is not saved	4
	7

The contract should be charged with 5,000 × $7 = $35,000

Activity 2

Nothing. The relevant cost is zero.

Test your understanding 4

D

The relevant cost of making the product is the variable cost of $3, $4 and $1 AND the specific fixed cost of $2.50. In addition there is another cost – an opportunity cost – every unit of the component that we make uses $4 of labour. If $8 of labour were used on the other product contribution would increase by $10. So therefore there is an extra opportunity cost of $5 per $4 of labour.

Test your understanding 5

A

The 6,600 hours of machine time for the special order would have produced 3,300 units (2 hours each).

Existing contribution = 3,300 × $4.30

= $14,190

The firm will be indifferent to the new order if the 3,000 modified units also give $14,190 contribution.

Variable cost per unit of special order = $9.20

Total variable costs	= 3,000 × $9.20
	= $27,600
Therefore required selling price	= $27,600 + $14,190
	= $41,790

Test your understanding 6

D

Any product with negative additional contribution should not be further refined

	E	F	G	H
Incremental revenue per litre	8	7	10	4
Variable cost of refining	(5)	(5)	(5)	(5)
Additional contribution from refining	3	2	5	(1)
Decision:				Sell at split-off

Now take account of the further processing costs. Any profit which does not make a an additional profit should not be further refined:

	E	F	G
Units	2,000	500	5,000
Additional total contribution($)	6,000	1,000	25,000
Specific fixed costs	(1,000)	(2,000)	(3,000)
Additional profit from refining	5,000	(1,000)	22,000
Decision:	Refine	Sell at split-off	Refine

Finally, the overall profit or loss on the remaining products should be determined:

Total relevant profit from refining ($5,000 + $22,000)	27,000
General fixed costs of refining	30,000
Total loss from refining	$(3,000)

None of the products should be further processed.

Test your understanding 7

(a) The Internal Manufacturing cost of Component Alpha is as follows

	Component Alpha
2 hours of direct labour, at $8 per hour	$16.00
1.5 kg direct Material B, at $5 per kg	$7.50
Variable overhead, labour related 2 hours	$1.25
Variable overhead, machine related, 0.5 hours	$0.125
Total variable cost	**$24.875**

The buying price of the component is **$50** per unit. So, if resources are readily available, the company should manufacture the component, because it is cheaper than buying it. However, due to the scarcity of resources in the near future, the contribution earned from the component needs to be compared with the contribution that can be earned from the other products.

Using Product 1 (though any product could be used) the variable overhead rates per hour can be calculated:

Labour related variable overhead per unit = $1.25

Direct labour hours per unit = $16/$8 = 2 hours

Labour related variable overhead per hour = $1.25/2 hours = $0.625 per hour

Machine related variable overhead per unit = $1.25

Machine related variable overhead per hour = $1.25/5 hours = $0.25 per hour

Both material A and material B are limited in supply, but calculations are required to determine whether this scarcity affects our production plans. The resources required for the maximum demand must be compared with the resources available to determine whether either of the materials is a binding constraint.

	Product 1	Product 2	Product 3	Product 4	Total
Existing Contract	100 units	100 units	100 units	100 units	
Direct Material A	150 litres	100 litres	0 litres	100 litres	**350 litres**
Direct Material B	100 kgs	0 kgs	300 kgs	200 kgs	**600 kgs**

We can now determine whether Material A or Material B is a limiting factor:

	Maximum Availability	Post-contract availability	Needed for total production
Direct Material A	5,000 litres	4,650 litres	3,200 litres
Direct Material B	6,000 kgs	5,400 kgs	5,550 kgs

The scarcity of **material B** is a binding constraint and therefore the contributions of each product and the component per kg of material B must be compared. (At this point, Product 2 can be ignored because it does not use material B):

	Product 1	Product 3	Product 4	Component Alpha
Contribution	$32	$51.325	$58.75	
Direct Material B	1 kg	3 kgs	2 kgs	
Contribution per kg of Material B	$32.00	$17.10	$29.38	$16.75 **(W1)**
Rank	1	3	2	4

Since Component Alpha has the lowest ranked contribution per usage of material B, **the company should continue to purchase the component** so that the available resources can be used to manufacture Product 1, Product 4 and Product 3.

We can now determine whether Material A or Material B is a limiting factor:

(W1) Component Alpha – Contribution per kg of B

	$
Buying cost of component Alpha	50.00
Variable production cost	(24.875)
Contribution per component	$25.125

Contribution per kg of Material B = $25.125/1.5 kgs of B = **$16.75**

(b) Direct material B at $5/kg available: 5,400 kgs

First, we make Product 1: 900 units @ 1 kgs per unit = 900 kgs.

This leaves 4,500 kgs available for the next best-ranking product, Product 4. That is enough for (4,500 kgs/2 kgs per unit) = 2,250 units of Product 4. We only need 900 units of Product 4 though i.e. 1,800 kgs, which leaves (4,500 – 1,800 kgs = 2,700 kgs) available for the next product, Product 3.

Each unit of Product 3 uses 3 kgs of Material B, we can therefore make 900 units of Product 3.

Summary

	Product 1	Product 2	Product 3	Product 4
Contractual units	100 units	100 units	100 units	100 units
Non-contractual units	900 units	950 units	900 units	900 units
Total	1,000 units	1,050 units	1,000 units	1,000 units

(c)   The decision concerning the purchase of the component would change if the contribution from its manufacture were equal to the least best contribution from the products using material B. Apart from the minimum demand constraint the least best usage is derived from product 3 which has a contribution per kg of $17.10 which is $0.35 per kg higher than that from component Alpha.

Since each unit of Alpha requires 1.5 kgs of B then the buying price would have to be 1.5 × $0.35 = $0.525 per component higher than at present before it would have the same rank as product 3. Thus the buying price at which the decision would change = $50 + $0.525 = $50.525.

Test your understanding 8

(a)   On financial grounds, further processing is worthwhile if the further processing cost is less than the incremental revenue.

Evaluation of further processing, based on March 20X7 output and assuming no losses in the further process:

Product	Incremental revenue $	Incremental cost $	Increase /(decrease) in profit
RZ	800 × (6.00 − 3.00) = 2,400	800 × $1.40 = 1,120	1,280
SZ	2,000 × (5.75 − 5.00) = 1,500	2,000 × 0.90 = 1,800	(300)
TZ	1,200 × (6.75 − 3.50) = 3,900	1,200 × 1.00 + 600 = 1,800	2,100

Taking each product individually, it can be seen that products R and T should be converted as the incremental revenue exceeds the incremental cost of further processing. In the case of T, this assumes that the March 20X7 output is representative of other months and that the quantity produced is sufficient to ensure that the incremental revenue covers both the fixed and variable costs. However, as TZ can be sold for a relatively high price, volumes would have to drop considerably for this to become an issue.

This is not true of S. Considered in isolation product S should not be converted. However there may be other reasons for producing all three products, in particular marketing considerations such as whether the company needs to supply all three products in order to sell the two profitable products, RZ and TZ.

(b) (i) If there is a market for R, S and T, and assuming that all March 20X7 output can be sold at the prices given:

Product	Selling price per kg in $	Output in kgs	Sales value in $
R	$3.00	800	2,400
S	$5.00	2,000	10,000
T	$3.50	1,200	4,200
			$16,600

Total cost of common process in March 20X7 = $17,500

Loss in March 20X7 = $900 and therefore the common process is not financially viable.

(ii) If there is not an external market for R, S and T:

Revenue from selling RZ, SZ, TZ:		$	$
RZ	800 × $6.00	4,800	
SZ	2000 × $5.75	11,500	
TZ	1,200 × $6.75	8,100	24,400
Common costs			(17,500)
Further costs:			
R –> RZ	800 × $1.40	1,120	
S–>SZ	2,000 × $0.90	1,800	
T–>TZ	1,200 × $1.00 + ($600 fixed)	1,800	(4,720)
Net benefit			**$2,180**

Based on this analysis the common process is financially viable.

Break-even analysis

Chapter learning objectives

Lead outcome	Component outcome
C3. Apply appropriate techniques to support short-term decisions	(b) Break-even analysis

1   Session Content Diagram

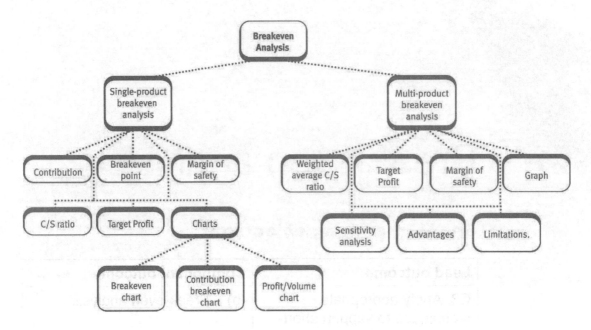

2   Introduction

One of the most important decisions that needs to be made before any business even starts, or a new product or service is launched, is 'how much do we need to sell in order to break even?' By 'break-even' we mean simply covering all our costs without making a profit. This type of analysis is more formally known as Cost-Volume-Profit Analysis (CVP Analysis).

CVP definition

Cost – Volume – Profit analysis is defined in CIMA's Official Terminology as 'the study of the effects on future profit of changes in fixed cost, variable cost, sales price, quantity and mix.'

CVP analysis is a particular example of 'what if?' analysis. A business sets a budget based upon various assumptions about revenues, costs, product mixes and overall volumes. CVP analysis considers the impact on the budgeted profit of changes in these various factors.

Cost-Volume-Profit (CVP) analysis

CVP analysis makes use of the contribution concept in order to assess the following measures for a single product:

*   contribution to sales (C/S) ratio

*   breakeven point

*   margin of safety.

The contribution concept

We have previously determined that variable costs are those that vary with the level of activity. If we can identify the variable costs associated with producing and selling a product or service we can highlight a very important measure: **contribution**.

Contribution = sales value LESS variable cost

Variable costs are sometimes referred to as **marginal costs**. The two terms are often used interchangeably.

Contribution is so called because it 'contributes' towards fixed costs and profit. Once the fixed costs have been fully covered, then any extra contribution contributes towards the profit of the organisation.

Illustration

Consider a product with a variable cost per unit of $26 and selling price of $42. Fixed costs for the period are $12,000.

(a) What is the contribution per unit for the product?

(b) If 1,000 units are sold, what is the total contribution?

(c) What is the total profit and the profit per unit at this level of sales?

(d) Calculate the total profit for the following levels of sales:

- 500

- 1,000

- 1,200

(e) Calculate the contribution per unit and profit per unit for each level of sales.

Solution:

(a) Contribution per unit = sales – variable cost
$42 – $26 = $16

(b) Total contribution = contribution per unit × number of units
$16 × 1,000 = $16,000

(c) Total profit = total contribution – fixed costs
$16,000 – $12,000 = $4,000

Profit per unit = total profit/number of units
$4,000/1,000 = $4

(d) It is easier to use a table for these calculations:

Units	500	1,000	1,200
	$	$	$
Sales	21,000	42,000	50,400
Variable cost	13,000	28,000	31,200
Total contribution	8,000	16,000	19,200
Fixed costs	12,000	12,000	12,000
Total Profit/(Loss)	(4,000)	4,000	7,200

(e)

Contribution per unit	$16	$16	$16
Profit/(loss) per unit	($8)	$4.00	$6

You can see from this that the contribution per unit does not change, but that the profit per unit can change significantly as the volume changes.

This makes contribution much more useful than profit in many decisions.

In the above example, it would have been quicker to start with contribution when working out the profit, as shown below. This saves some unnecessary calculations:

	$	$	$
Contribution per unit	16	16	16
× units	500	1,000	1,200
Total contribution	8,000	16,000	19,200
Fixed costs	12,000	12,000	12,000
Total Profit/(Loss)	(4,000)	4,000	7,200

C/S ratio

The contribution to sales ratio is a useful calculation in CVP analysis. It is usually expressed as a percentage. It can be calculated as follows.

$$\text{C/S ratio} = \frac{\text{Contribution per unit}}{\text{Selling price per unit}} \quad \text{or} \quad \frac{\text{Total contribution}}{\text{Total sales revenue}}$$

 The C/S ratio is sometimes referred to as the P/V (Profit/Volume) ratio.

Explanation of the contribution sales ratio

The C/S ratio of a product is the proportion of the selling price that contributes to fixed overheads and profits. It is comparable to the gross profit margin.

A higher contribution to sales ratio means that contribution grows more quickly as sales levels increase. Once the breakeven point has been passed, profits will accumulate more quickly than for a product with a lower contribution to sales ratio.

Breakeven point

The breakeven point is the point at which neither a profit nor a loss is made.

- At the breakeven point the following situations occur.

   Total sales revenue = Total costs, i.e. Profit = 0

   or

   Total contribution = Fixed costs, i.e. Profit = 0

- It can be calculated in terms of numbers of units sold.

$$\text{Breakeven point (in terms of numbers of units sold)} = \frac{\text{Fixed costs}}{\text{Contribution per unit}}$$

- It is also possible to calculated in terms of sales revenue using the C/S ratio

$$\text{Breakeven point (in terms of sales revenue)} = \frac{\text{Fixed costs}}{\text{C/S ratio}}$$

Where a certain level of profit is required, the breakeven formulae can also be used to calculate the level of activity that is required to generate that profit, as follows:

$$\text{Level of activity required to earn a required profit} = \frac{\text{Fixed costs + required profit}}{\text{Contribution per unit}}$$

$$\text{Sales revenue required to earn a required profit} = \frac{\text{Fixed costs + required profit}}{\text{C/S ratio}}$$

Margin of safety

The margin of safety is the amount by which anticipated sales (in units) can fall below budget before a business makes a loss. It can be calculated in terms of numbers of units or as a percentage of budgeted sales.

The following formulae are used to calculate the margin of safety:

Margin of safety calculation:

in units = **Budgeted sales – Breakeven point sales**

as a % of budgeted sales = $\dfrac{\text{Budgeted sales – Breakeven sales}}{\text{Budgeted sales}}$ × 100%

Example 1

A company manufactures and sells a single product that has the following cost and selling price structure:

	$/unit
Selling price	28
Variable costs	(20)
Fixed overhead	(2)
Profit per unit	5

The fixed overhead absorption rate is based on the normal capacity of 3,000 units per month. Assume that the same amount is spent each month on fixed overheads.

Budgeted sales for next month are 3,100 units.

Required:

(i)   the breakeven point, in sales units per month

(ii) the margin of safety for next month

(iii) the budgeted profit for next month

(iv) the sales required to achieve a profit of $20,000 in a month

(v) the contribution to sales ratio

(vi) the breakeven revenue that must be generated in order to break even

Using the margin of safety to calculate the expected profit

As a short cut to determining the expected profit for an organisation, the margin of safety can be used as follows:

Expected profit = Margin of safety (in units) × contribution per unit

This can be best explained through the use of an illustration.

Illustration

RT organisation manufactures one product. The product sells for $250, and has variable costs per unit of $120. Fixed costs for the month were $780,000. The monthly projected sales for the product were 8,000. The margin of safety can be calculated as:

First calculate the breakeven sales: 780,000/(250 – 120) = 6,000

Margin of safety in units = projected sales – breakeven sales

$$= 8,000 – 6,000 = 2,000$$

Margin of safety % = (projected sales – breakeven sales)/projected sales

$$= (8,000 – 6,000)/8,000 = 25\%$$

The margin of safety can also be used as one route to a profit calculation. We have seen that the contribution goes towards fixed costs and profit. Once breakeven point is reached the fixed costs have been covered. After the breakeven point there are no more fixed costs to be covered and all of the contribution goes towards making profits grow.

In this illustration, the monthly profit from projected sales of 8,000 would be $260,000.

This can be calculated the normal way:

Contribution per unit	$130
Total contribution ($130 × 8,000)	$1,040,000
Fixed costs	$ 780,000
Profit	$ 260,000

Or using margin of safety:

Margin of safety	= 2,000 units per month
Monthly profit	= 2,000 × contribution per unit
	= 2,000 × $130
	= $260,000

3   Break even charts

The information from CVP analysis can be represented diagramatically using a break even chart.

For example, if we were using the following data in our calculations

Selling price	$50 per unit
Variable cost	$30 per unit
Fixed costs	$20,000 per month
Forecast sales	1,700 units per month

the results of our analysis could be illustrated on a diagram as follows:

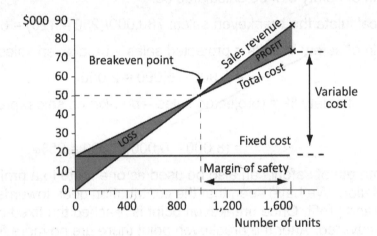

 Interpretation of a break even chart

An interpretation of the diagram would tell us many things:

* Fixed costs are $20,000 – this is the point at which the total cost line cuts the vertical axis.

* The break-even point occurs at 1,000 units – this is the point at which the line for total revenue crosses the line for total costs.

* At the break-even point, costs and revenues total $50,000 each – this can be found by reading across to the vertical axis at this point.

* We can see by reading along the horizontal axis that the margin of safety is 700 units.

* Budgeted sales are 1,700 units – this is determined by adding the margin of safety to the break-even point.

Example 2

Choose from the following list all the information than can be easily determined from a break even chart (choose all that apply):

- the break-even point (in units)
- the break-even point (in terms of total revenue)
- selling price per unit
- total fixed costs
- total costs
- variable cost per unit
- margin of safety

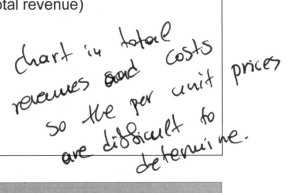

chart in total revenues and costs so the per unit prices are difficult to determine.

Drawing a break even chart

> Although you will not be required to do so in your exam, learning to draw a chart to scale will provide a firm foundation for your understanding of breakeven charts. To give yourself some practice, it would be a good idea to follow the step-by-step guide which follows to produce your own chart on a piece of graph paper

A basic breakeven chart records costs and revenues on the vertical axis (y) and the level of activity on the horizontal axis (x). Lines are drawn on the chart to represent costs and sales revenue. The breakeven point can be read off where the sales revenue line cuts the total cost line.

Let's look at constructing the diagram that has just been illustrated.

- *Step 1.* Select appropriate scales for the axes and draw and label them. Your graph should fill as much of the page as possible. This will make it clearer and easier to read. You can make sure that you do this by putting the extremes of the axes right at the end of the available space.

  The furthest point on the vertical axis will be the monthly sales revenue, that is:

    1,700 units × $50 = $ 85,000

    The furthest point on the horizontal axis will be monthly sales volume of 1,700 units.

  Make sure that you do not need to read data for volumes higher than 1,700 units before you set these extremes for your scales.

- *Step 2.* Draw the fixed cost line and label it. This will be a straight line parallel to the horizontal axis at the $20,000 level.

  The $20,000 fixed costs are incurred in the short term even with zero activity.

- *Step 3*. Draw the total cost line and label it. The best way to do this is to calculate the total costs for the maximum sales level, which is 1,700 units in our example. Mark this point on the graph and join it to the cost incurred at zero activity, that is, $20,000.

	$
Variable costs for 1,700 units (1,700 × $30)	51,000
Fixed costs	20,000
Total cost for 1,700 units	71,000

- *Step 4*. Draw the revenue line and label it. Once again, the best way is to plot the extreme points. The revenue at maximum activity in our example is 1,700 × $50 = $85,000. This point can be joined to the origin, since at zero activity there will be no sales revenue.

- *Step 5*. Mark any required information on the chart and read off solutions as required. You can check that your chart is accurate by reading off the breakeven point and then check this against the calculation for breakeven:

  The margin of safety can be seen as the area to the right of the breakeven point up to the forecast sales level of 1,700.

  = 20,000/(50 − 30) = **1,000 units.**

  $$\text{Breakeven point in units} = \frac{\text{Fixed costs}}{\text{Contribution per unit}}$$

  = 20,000/(50 − 30) = **1,000 units.**

The margin of safety can be seen as the area to the right of the breakeven point up to the forecast sales level of 1,700.

The contribution breakeven chart

One of the problems with the conventional or basic breakeven chart is that it is not possible to read contribution directly from the chart. A contribution breakeven chart is based on the same principles but it shows the variable cost line instead of the fixed cost line. The same lines for total cost and sales revenue are shown so the breakeven point and profit can be read off in the same way as with a conventional chart. However, it is also possible also to read the contribution for any level of activity.

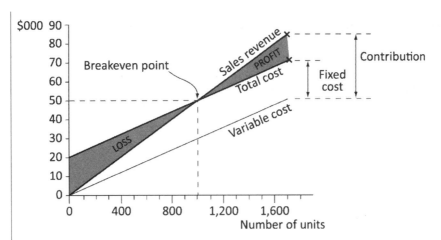

Using the same basic example as for the conventional chart, the total variable cost for an output of 1,700 units is 1,700 × $30 = $51,000. This point can be joined to the origin since the variable cost is nil at zero activity.

The contribution can be read as the difference between the sales revenue line and the variable cost line.

The form of presentation might be used when it is desirable to highlight the importance of contribution and to focus attention on the variable costs.

Ensure you are familiar with these charts and that you are able to identify all the component parts.

However, it can be difficult in this diagram to see how much profit (or loss) is made at each level of activity. For this we would need a profit-volume chart.

4 The profit–volume chart

The profit volume chart

Another form of breakeven chart is the profit–volume chart. This chart plots a single line depicting the profit or loss at each level of activity.

A profit–volume graph for our example is shown below.

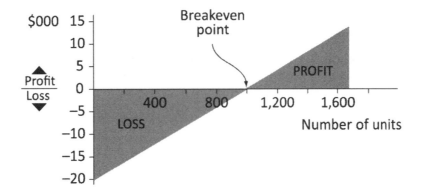

Drawing and interpreting a profit-volume chart

Drawing a profit-volume chart

The vertical axis shows profits and losses and the horizontal axis is drawn at zero profit or loss.

In order to plot the profit line only two points are required and a line is plotted through these:

- Firstly, at zero activity the loss is equal to $20,000, that is, the amount of fixed costs.

- Secondly, the line needs to cross the horizontal axis at the calculated breakeven point (1,000 units).

Note: the profit–volume chart may also be called a profit graph or a contribution–volume graph.

Interpretation

An analysis of this profit volume chart would highlight the following:

- The break-even point occurs where the line crosses the horizontal axis.

- This would appear to be at 1,000 units.

- A user of the chart could quickly see the expected profit or loss for any expected level of activity. For example, if sales were to be 1,400 units then a profit of around $8,000 would be expected.

The main advantage of the profit–volume chart is that it is capable of depicting clearly the effect on profit and breakeven point of any changes in the variables.

 Example 3

An organisation is considering launching a new product, but it has yet to determine final production design. This decision will affect the costs and quality of the product, as well as its ultimate selling price.

Two situations are being considered:

- In situation (a), a lower product specification will be used, resulting in a lower selling price and production cost per unit.

- In situation (b), a higher product specification will be used, resulting in a higher selling price and a higher production cost per unit.

A profit volume chart has been prepared illustrating the impact of each situation as follows:

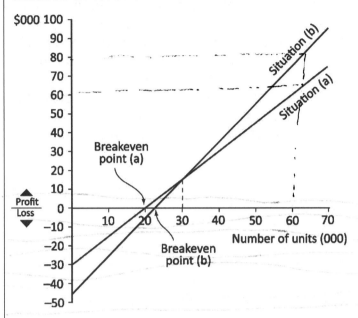

Answer the following questions based on this profit-volume chart:

The situation which results in the higher contribution per unit is situation _b_ ?

This is because....

A   Situation (a) has a lower production cost per unit

B   Situation (b) has a higher selling price

C   Situation (a) has a lower break-even point

D   The graph for situation (b) has a steeper slope

At what level of sales would the organisation be indifferent between the two options?

A   20,000 units

B   22,500 units

C   30,000 units

D   70,000 units

The impact of cost structures on the breakeven point

Different organisations will have different cost structures. This will often be heavily influenced by the industry in which they operate. For example, a service company, such as a firm of accountants, will find that most of their costs are fixed costs such as salaries and rent. On the other hand, a retailer such as a supermarket is likely to find that most of its costs are variable (such as the purchasing costs of the items it is selling). Other factors such as the level of computerisation and mechanisation will also impact on the cost structure.

Operational gearing

The proportion of costs which are fixed is referred to as operational gearing. There are many different ways to measure operational gearing such as taking fixed costs as a percentage of total costs or by simply examining an organisation's contribution to sales ratio. A firm of accountants is likely to have a high proportion of fixed costs relative to total costs, it is also likely to have a high contribution to sales ratio. The firm would then be said to have a high level of operational gearing.

An organisation with a low operating gearing will have a small proportion of fixed costs relative to total costs and it will have a low contribution to sales ratio.

Changing operational gearing

Organisations can influence and change their operational gearing if they choose. For example, a company giving training company is likely to have a high level of operational gearing as it will have to pay fixed cost salaries to its lecturers. The company may be concerned that, if the economy moves towards a recession, the company will suffer a reduction in revenue but still have to pay these fixed salaries. It will therefore see its high level of operational gearing as a problem.

The problem can be alleviated by converting some of the fixed costs into variable costs. It could, for example, move lecturers onto daily rates rather than fixed annual salaries. Therefore, if there are no courses running because of a lack of demand then no costs are incurred on staff salaries. This reduction in operational gearing reduces the potential negative impact from a fall in sales.

This should highlight that, whilst much of the operational gearing of a business is determined by its industry, operational gearing can also be influenced by the decisions of an organisation's management. Therefore, even organisations who operate in the same industry can have very different levels of operational gearing.

The impact of operational gearing on the break-even point and profits

Organisations with high operational gearing will have a higher break-even point than organisations with low operational gearing. More contribution will have to be earned in order to cover the high levels of fixed costs. Because of the high contribution to sales ratio, these organisations will also find that small changes in revenue will have a large impact on profit. Therefore, as sales increase beyond the break-even point, profits and will increase greatly.

The opposite will be true for organisations with a low operating gearing. However, organisations with low operating gearing will perform better as sales fall (for example, in a recession) as they will be able to cut back on costs. For example, in a recession a supermarket can reduce its costs by purchasing fewer items, but an accountancy practice must still pay its salaries and rent.

Operational gearing and the profit volume chart

Organisations with high operational gearing are likely to have a steeper profit volume chart. For example, consider the following diagram for two similar sized companies operating in the same industry:

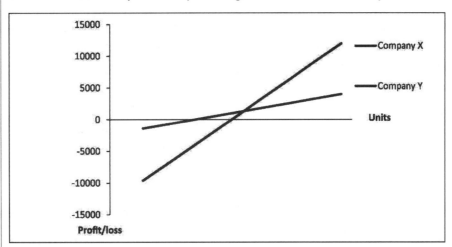

Company X has high operational gearing. As a consequence it has a higher break-even point. It can be seen that it has the potential to make higher profits at higher sales levels but it will suffer higher losses as sales fall (for example, if the economy moves into a recession).

Company Y has lower operational gearing (it has converted some fixed costs to variable costs). As a consequence it has a lower break-even point and doesn't suffer such high losses as sales fall. But, likewise, it won't make as much profit if sales units rise to high levels beyond the break-even point.

5 Multi-product break-even analysis

Where an organisation produces and sells more than one product, a weighted average C/S ratio is calculated by using the formula:

$$\text{Weighted average C/S ratio} = \frac{\text{Total contribution}}{\text{Total revenue}}$$

The breakeven point in sales revenue is then calculated as:

$$\text{Breakeven revenue} = \frac{\text{Fixed costs}}{\text{Weighted average C/S ratio}}$$

Explanation of the weighted average calculation

The basic breakeven model can be used satisfactorily for a business that produces and sells only one product. However, most companies sell a range of different products, and the model has to be adapted when one is considering a business operation with several products.

If a company sells multiple products, break even analysis is somewhat more complex. The reason is that the different products will have different selling prices, different costs, and different contribution margins. Consequently, the break-even point will depend on the mix in which the various products are sold.

In order to cope with this, CVP analysis assumes that a **pre-determined sales mix will remain constant** for all volumes of activity. For example, if product A makes up 20% of production and sales and product B makes up 80%, CVP analysis assumes that these proportions will continue into the future.

This allows for the calculation of a **weighted average contribution margin** or a **weighted average contribution sales ratio** which can be used in the breakeven calculations. The weightings used in the calculations are those from the predetermined sales mix.

Illustration 1

Motor Ltd produces and sells three products, A, B and C, in the ratio 2:4:4. Fixed overheads total $80,000 each year.

	A	B	C
Selling price	$20	$11	$30
Variable costs	$12	$2	$18
Budgeted sales (units)	4,800	9,600	9,600

Calculate the weighted average contribution margin.

To find the weighted average contribution, we take the individual contributions for each product and apply the pre-determined sales mix proportions, as follows:

Product	Sales mix	Contribution per unit (W1)	Weighted average contribution
A	20%	$8	$1.60
B	40%	$9	$3.60
C	40%	$12	$4.80
Total			**$10.00**

Calculate the breakeven point in units:

$$\text{Breakeven point in units} = \frac{\text{Fixed costs}}{\text{Weighted average contribution}}$$

$$\text{Breakeven point in units} = \frac{\$80,000}{\$10} = 8,000 \text{ units}$$

The assumption would be that these sales are made in the pre-determined sales mix proportion, 2:4:4.

Calculate the breakeven point in revenue:

$$\text{Breakeven point in revenue} = \frac{\text{Fixed costs}}{\text{Weighted average C/S ratio}}$$

$$\text{Breakeven point in revenue} = \frac{\$80,000}{49.02\% \text{ (W2)}}$$

$$\text{Breakeven point in revenue} = \$163,200$$

Alternative method:

If we had not been provided with the information about budgeted sales volumes in this question, we could have arrived at the breakeven point in revenue using an alternative method.

We are able to calculate the breakeven number of units at 8,000 units. If these are sold in the proportion 2:4:4 then this gives us sales of:

Product A = 8,000 units × 2/10 = 1,600 units

Product B = 8,000 units × 4/10 = 3,200 units

Product C = 8,000 units × 4/10 = 3,200 units

If we then multiply these sales by the sales revenue per unit, this gives:

Product A = 1,600 units × $20 = $32,000

Product B = 3,200 units × $11 = $35,200

Product C = 3,200 units × $30 = $96,000

Total revenue = $163,200, as with the previous method.

(W1) Contribution:

	A	B	C
Selling price	$20	$11	$30
Variable costs	($12)	($2)	($18)
Contribution per unit	$8	$9	$12

(W2) Weighted average C/S ratio:

$$\text{Weighted average C/S ratio} = \frac{\text{Total contribution}}{\text{Total revenue}}$$

$$\text{Weighted average C/S ratio} = \frac{(\$8 \times 4{,}800) + (\$9 \times 9{,}600) + (\$12 \times 9{,}600)}{(\$20 \times 4{,}800) + (\$11 \times 9{,}600) + (\$30 \times 9{,}600)}$$

$$\text{Weighted average C/S ratio} = \frac{\$240{,}000}{\$489{,}600}$$

Weighted average C/S ratio = 0.4902 or 49.02%

Example 4

Company A produces Product X and Product Y. Fixed overhead costs amount to $200,000 every year. The following budgeted information is available for both products for next year:

	Product X	Product Y
Sales price	$50	$60
Variable cost	$30	$45
Budgeted sales (in units)	20,000	10,000

To the nearest $000, what is the breakeven sales revenue?

A $500,000

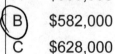
B $582,000

C $628,000

D $800,000

Margin of safety calculations

The basic breakeven model for calculating the margin of safety can be adapted to multi-product environments. Three alternative approaches are considered in the example below.

A business operation produces three products, the X, the Y and the Z. Relevant details are:

	Product X	Product Y	Product Z
Budgeted sales	400	400	200
Selling price per unit	$9	$7	$5
Variable cost per unit	$6	$5	$1
Contribution per unit	$3	$2	$4
Forecast unit sales	400	400	200

Fixed costs are $2,000 per period, not attributable to individual products. A budget for the forecast is as follows:

	Product X	Product Y	Product Z	Total
Sales revenue	$3,600	$2,800	$1,000	$7,400
Variable cost	$2,400	$2,000	$200	$4,600
Contribution	$1,200	$800	$800	$2,800
Fixed costs				$2,000
Profit				$800

The margin of safety

The contribution ratio is 37.84% (i.e. $2,800/$7,400). The breakeven point, in terms of sales revenue, can be determined by dividing the total fixed costs ($2,000) by this contribution ratio = $2,000/37.84% = $5,285

The margin of safety is the difference between forecast sales and this break even sales revenue = $7,400 forecast sales – $5,285 = $2,115. It may also be expressed as a percentage of forecast sales = $2,115/ $7,400 = 28.58%.

6 Establishing a target profit for multiple products

The approach is the same as in single product situations, but the weighted average contribution to sales ratio is now used so that:

$$\text{Revenue required to generate a target profit} = \frac{\text{Fixed costs + required profit}}{\text{Weighted average C/S ratio}}$$

Example 5

Referring to the previous example, what is the target revenue required (to the nearest $000) to achieve a profit of $300,000?

A $873,000

B $882,000

C $1,384,000

D $1,455,000

7   The multi-product profit-volume graph

In a multi-product environment, two lines must be shown on the profit-volume graph: one straight line, where a constant mix between the products is assumed; and one bow shaped line, where it is assumed that the company sells its most profitable product first and then its next most profitable product and so on.

Example:

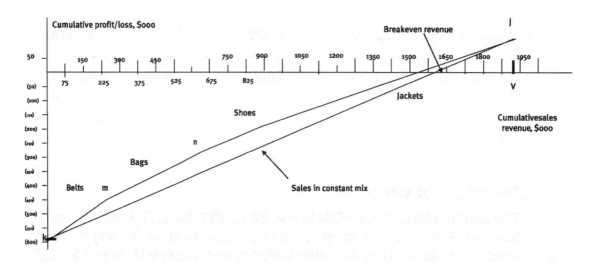

In this example, a ranking of the c/s ratio of each product would put belts first, bags next, shoes thirds and jackets last. This can be seen from the diagram as it is the order in which the products appear on the upper of the two lines.

The diagram illustrates two potential break even points:

- the lower line indicates the breakeven point if the products are sold in the standard product mix.

- the upper line indicates the break-even point if the products are sold in order of the c/s ratio ranking.

Drawing and interpreting a multi-product PV graph

Tutorial note: you will not be required to draw a graph in your examination, however learning to draw a chart to scale will provide a firm foundation for your understanding. We will use the following example to illustrate a step-by-step approach:

	Sales units	Selling price per unit	Variable cost per unit
Bags	1,000	$400	$210
Belts	2,000	$125	$65
Shoes	1,500	$150	$95
Jackets	3,500	$300	$215

Fixed costs amount to $580,000.

STEP 1: Calculate the contribution to sales (C/S) ratio of each product being sold, and rank the products in order of profitability.

	C/S ratio	Rank
Bags	0.475	2
Belts	0.480	1
Shoes	0.367	3
Jackets	0.283	4

STEP 2: Assuming that the products are sold in order of their C/S ratio, determine cumulative revenue and profit/loss as each product is sold.

In our example:

Sales	Cumulative revenue	Individual product contribution	Cumulative profit or loss
None	$0	$0	$(580,000)
Belts	$250,000	$120,000	$(460,000)
Bags	$650,000	$190,000	$(270,000)
Shoes	$875,000	$82,500	$(187,500)
Jackets	$1,925,000	$297,500	$110,000

STEP 3: Draw a graph, showing cumulative sales revenue on the x-axis and the initial cumulative profit or loss on the vertical axis.

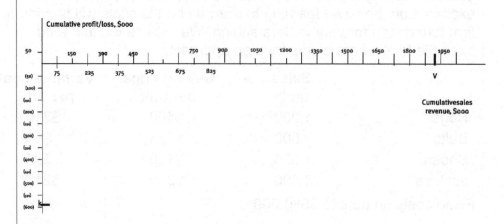

Point K on the graph (on the vertical axis) represents the profit or loss when revenue is zero. This will always be the total of the fixed costs.

Point V on the graph represents the total cumulative revenue (in this case, $1,925,000).

STEP 4: Starting from point k, plot the first point of cumulative revenue.

This represents the revenue from the product with the highest C/S ratio (in this case, belts). The slope of the line is determined by the C/S ratio achieved on sales of that product. We can see that it goes to the point of $250,000 on the revenue axis and −$460,000 on the profit/loss axis.

These points can be read from the table created in Step 2.

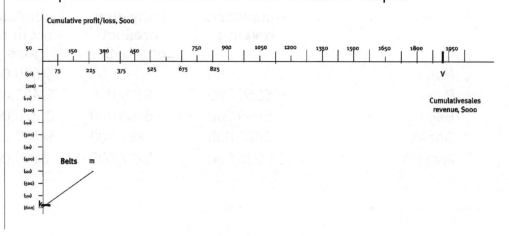

STEP 5: Plot each subsequent point from the table in Step 2 and join the points together with a line.

In our example, 'Bags' is ranked at 2nd and 'Shoes' at 3rd. The lines could be drawn as follows:

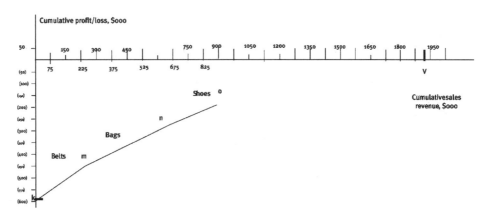

Note how the lines become flatter (or less steep) as they are drawn in turn. This reflects the lower C/S ratio of each product.

STEP 6: Draw a final line between the starting point (k) and the finishing point.

The final point will be the final figure from the table in Step 2, where cumulative revenue is $1,925,000 (the co-ordinates for the horizontal axis) and cumulative profit or loss of $110,000 (the co-ordinates for the vertical axis).

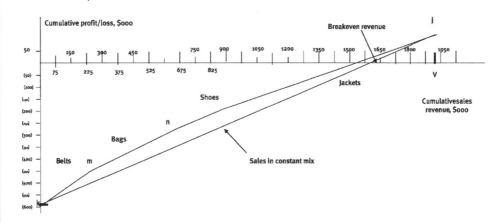

It can be seen that the resulting diagram provides two potential break even points (i.e. the horizontal axis is crossed twice – indicating that there are two points at which profits will be zero).

The first point that is crossed (the lower value of revenue) represents the break-even point if products are sold in the order of highest to lowest C/S ratio.

The higher break-even point would be achieved if products are sold in a constant standard mix.

Example 6

BJS produces and sells the following three products:

Product	X	Y	Z
Selling price per unit	$16	$20	$10
Variable cost per unit	$5	$15	$7
Contribution per unit	$11	$5	$3
Budgeted sales volume	50,000 units	10,000 units	100,000 units

The company expects the fixed costs to be $300,000 for the coming year. Assume that sales arise throughout the year in a constant mix.

Required:

(a) Calculate the weighted average C/S ratio for the products.

(b) Calculate the break-even sales revenue required.

(c) Calculate the amount of sales revenue required to generate a profit of $600,000.

(d) A multi-product profit-volume chart (assuming the budget is achieved) for the products is provided as follows.

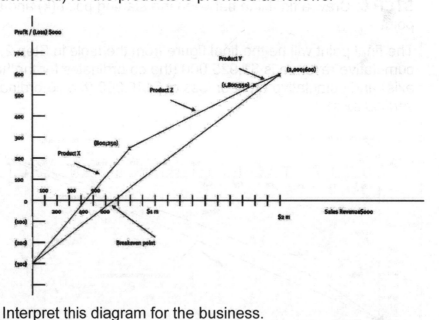

Interpret this diagram for the business.

8 Sensitivity analysis

Sensitivity (or 'What-if?') analysis involves determining the effects of various types of changes in the CVP model. These effects can be determined by simply changing the constants in the CVP model, i.e., prices, variable cost per unit, sales mix ratios etc. For example, it answers questions such as 'What will be the impact on our revenue if variable cost per unit increases by 30%?'

The sensitivity of revenue to various possible outcomes broadens the perspective of management regarding what might actually occur before making cost commitments. This would be fairly easy with spreadsheets, or other software developed to handle these calculations.

Illustration 2

RM Ltd sells three products, X, Y and Z. Budgeted costs and revenues for the next year are as follows:

	X	Y	Z	Total
Sales revenue	$350,000	$400,000	$450,000	$1,200,000
Variable costs	$210,000	$240,000	$270,000	$720,000
Contribution	$140,000	$160,000	$180,000	$480,000

Total budgeted fixed costs next year are expected to be $400,000.

The directors of RM Ltd are concerned that, due to a change in consumer preferences, demand for their products may fall next year.

By what percentage can sales revenue fall before RM Ltd begins to make a loss?

First of all we need to calculate the breakeven revenue based on the current budget:

$$\text{Breakeven point in revenue} = \frac{\text{Fixed costs}}{\text{Weighted average C/S ratio}}$$

$$\text{Breakeven point in revenue} = \frac{\$400,000}{0.4 \text{ (W1)}}$$

$$\text{Breakeven point in revenue} = \$1,000,000$$

Now that we know the breakeven revenue, we can calculate the margin of safety (as this is the amount that sales revenue can fall before the company begins to make a loss):

$$\text{Margin of safety (as \% of budgeted sales)} = \frac{\text{Budgeted sales - breakeven sales}}{\text{Budgeted sales}} \times 100$$

$$\text{Margin of safety (as \% of budgeted sales)} = \frac{1,200,000 - 1,000,000}{1,200,000} \times 100 = 16.67\%$$

This tells us that for the company to fall into a loss making position its sales revenue next year would have to fall by more than 16.67% from its current position.

(W1)

$$\text{Weighted average C/S ratio} = \frac{\text{Total contribution}}{\text{Total sales}}$$

$$\text{Weighted average C/S ratio} = \frac{\$480,000}{\$1,200,000} = 0.4$$

Example 7

Vivaldi manufactures and sells four types of products under the brand name Summer, Autumn, Winter and Spring. The Sales Mix in value comprises the following:

Brand name	Percentage
Summer	33.33%
Autumn	41.67%
Winter	16.67%
Spring	8.33%
	100%

Total Budgeted sales are set to reach $600,000 per month.

Variable costs are as follows:

Brand name	
Summer	60% of selling price
Autumn	68% of selling price
Winter	80% of selling price
Spring	40% of selling price

Fixed costs amount to $159,000 per month.

Required:

(a) Calculate the breakeven point for the products on an overall basis.

(b) It has been proposed to change the sales mix as follows, with the sales per month remaining at $600,000:

Brand name	Percentage
Summer	25%
Autumn	40%
Winter	30%
Spring	5%
	100%

Assuming that the above proposal is implemented, calculate the new breakeven point.

9 Advantages and disadvantages of CVP analysis

Advantages	Disadvantages
• Provides a target volume	• Profits can be affected by other factors besides volume
• Helps the understanding of costs and revenues and the relationship between them	• A small change in the assumptions could have a large change in the outcome

More details

Advantages of CVP analysis

The major benefit of using breakeven analysis is that it indicates the lowest amount of activity necessary to prevent losses.

Breakeven analysis aids Decision Making as it explains the relationship between cost, production volume and returns. It can be extended to show how changes in fixed costs – variable costs relationships or in revenues will affect profit levels and breakeven points.

CVP disadvantages

Any CVP analysis is based on assumptions about the behaviour of revenue, costs and volume. A change in expected behaviour will alter the break-even point; in other words, profits are affected by changes in other factors besides volume. Other factors include unit prices of input, efficiency, changes in production technology, wars, strikes, legislation, and so forth.

A CVP chart must be interpreted in the light of the limitations imposed by its underlying assumptions. The following underlying assumptions will limit the precision and reliability of a given cost-volume-profit analysis.

(1) The behaviour of total cost and total revenue has been reliably determined and is linear over the relevant range.

(2) All costs can be divided into fixed and variable elements.

(3) Total fixed costs remain constant over the relevant volume range of the CVP analysis.

(4) Total variable costs are directly proportional to volume over the relevant range.

(5) Selling prices are to be unchanged.

(6) Prices of the factors of production are to be unchanged (for example, material, prices, wage rates).

(7) Efficiency and productivity are to be unchanged.

(8) The analysis either covers a single product or assumes that a given sales mix will be maintained as total volume changes.

(9)   Revenue and costs are being compared on a single activity basis (for example, units produced and sold or sales value of production).

(10)   Perhaps the most basic assumption of all is that volume is the only relevant factor affecting cost. Of course, other factors also affect costs and sales. Ordinary cost-volume-profit analysis is a crude oversimplification when these factors are unjustifiably ignored.

(11)   The volume of production equals the volume of sales, or changes in beginning and ending inventory levels are insignificant in amount.

In multi-product situations, CVP analysis is further hampered by the assumption that the sales mix will remain constant. This is unlikely and it also ignores the situation in some organisations where products may be inter-related – an increase in sales for one product might result in a decrease in sales for another. For example, a theatre might find that as adult ticket sales rise (for example, if stage shows are more attractive to this age group) then there is a corresponding fall in sales to children. A multi-product CVP analysis would ignore this and assume that the ratio of adult to child tickets remains constant.

Also, in multi-product situations, the presence of two potential break even points is both confusing and misleading. It confuses because it is difficult for managers to understand (and it is based on a very unlikely assumption). But it is also misleading in that as more of each product is introduced into the mix (i.e. rather than selling each product in turn in order of its C/S ratio) then the break even point will start to increase and there will in fact be multiple break even points.

10   Chapter summary

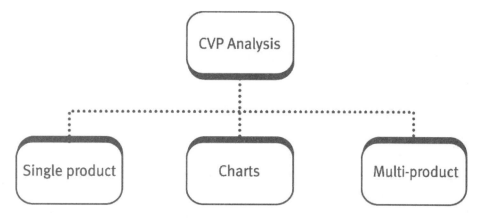

Single product

- Break-even point

$$= \frac{\text{Fixed costs}}{\text{Contribution per unit}}$$

- Margin of safety
  = Budgeted sales –
  break even sales

Charts

- A profit-volume chart plots a single line depicting the profit or loss at each level of activity
- In multi-product situations products are plotted in order of their c/s ratio
- Multi-product charts provide two possible break even points

Multi-product

- Similar to single product situations but uses a weighed average contribution per uni
- Weighted Average C/S ratio

$$= \frac{\text{Total contribution}}{\text{Total Revenue}}$$

11 Practice Questions

Test your understanding 1

The following information relates to Product Alpha.

Selling price per unit	$100
Variable cost per unit	$56
Fixed costs	$220,000

Budgeted sales are 7,500 units.

Required:

(a) Calculate the breakeven point in terms of units sold and overall sales revenue.

(b) Calculate the margin of safety (expressed as a percentage of budgeted sales).

Test your understanding 2

A company manufactures and sells a single product which has the following cost and selling price structure.

	$/unit	$/unit
Selling price		120
Direct material	22	
Direct labour	36	
Variable overhead	14	
Fixed overhead	12	
		84
Profit per unit		36

The fixed overhead absorption rate is based on the normal capacity of 2,000 units per month. Assume that the same amount is spent each month on fixed overheads.

Budgeted sales for next month are 2,200 units.

You are required to calculate:

(i) the breakeven point, in sales units per month

(ii) the margin of safety for next month

(iii) the budgeted profit for next month

(iv) the sales required to achieve a profit of $96,000 in a month

(v) the contribution to sales ratio

(vi) the breakeven revenue that must be generated in order to break even.

Test your understanding 3

A break-down of KP's profit in the last accounting period showed the following:

	$000
Sales	450
Variable costs	(220)
Fixed costs	(160)
Profit	70

Due to a downturn in market conditions the company is worried that next year may result in losses and would like to know the change in sales that would make this happen.

Required:

The percentage fall in sales that would be necessary before the company would begin to incur losses is 30.44 % (work to two decimal places).

Test your understanding 4

OT Ltd plans to produce and sell 4,000 units of product C each month, at a selling price of $18 per unit. The unit cost of product C is as follows

	$ per unit
Variable cost	8
Fixed cost	4
Profit	12

To the nearest whole number, the monthly margin of safety, as a percentage of planned sales is _____%.

Test your understanding 5

A company's summary budgeted operating statement is as follows:

	$
Revenue	60,000
Variable costs	24,000
Fixed costs	25,000
Profit	11,000

Assuming that the sales mix does not change, identify the percentage increase in sales revenue that would be needed to increase the profit to $35,000 (to the nearest percentage):

A   31%

B   40%

C   67%

D   69%

Test your understanding 6

Scenario

A company manufactures five products in one factory. The company's budgeted fixed costs for the next year are $300,000. The table below summarises the budgeted sales and contribution details for the five products for the next year.

Product	A	B	C	D	E
Unit selling price	$40	$15	$40	$30	$20
Total sales ($000)	400	180	1,400	900	200
Contribution to sales ratio	45%	30%	25%	20%	(10%)

The following diagram has been prepared to summarise the above budget figures:

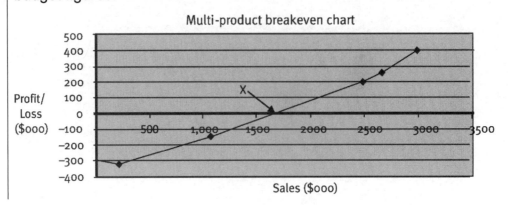

Multi-product breakeven chart

Tasks:

(a)   Explain the meaning of point X on the chart.

(b)   Calculate the breakeven revenue for the next year using the budgeted sales mix.

(Time allowed: 10 minutes)

Test your understanding 7

Scenario

JK has prepared a budget for the next 12 months when it intends to make and sell four products, details of which are shown below:

Product	Sales in units (thousands)	Selling price per unit $	Variable cost per unit $
J	10	20	14.00
K	10	40	8.00
L	50	4	4.20
M	20	10	7.00

Budgeted fixed costs are $240,000 per annum and total assets employed are $570,000.

Tasks:

(a)   Calculate the total contribution earned by each product and their combined total contributions.

The accountant at JK has produced the following profit-revenue graph for the products:

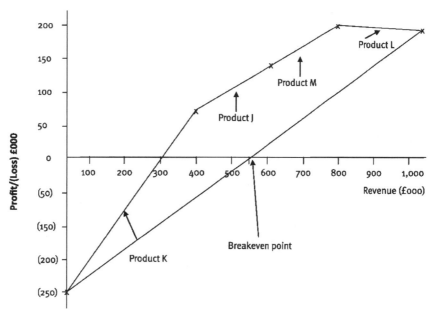

(b) Explain this graph to management, comment on the results shown and state the break-even point.

(c) Describe briefly three ways in which the overall contribution to sales ratio could be improved.

(Time allowed: 30 minutes)

Test your understanding 8

Scenario

A summary of a manufacturing company's budgeted profit statement for its next financial year, when it expects to be operating at 75% capacity, is given below.

	$	$
Sales 9,000 units at $32		288,000
Less:		
direct materials	54,000	
direct wages	72,000	
production overhead – fixed	42,000	
– variable	18,000	
		188,000
Gross profit		102,000
Less: admin., selling and distribution costs		
– fixed	36,000	
– varying with sales volume	27,000	
		63,000
Net profit		39,000

It has been estimated that:

(i) if the selling price per unit were reduced to $28, the increased demand would utilise 90 per cent of the company's capacity without any additional advertising expenditure

(ii) to attract sufficient demand to utilise full capacity would require a 15 per cent reduction in the current selling price and a $5,000 special advertising campaign.

Tasks:

(a) Calculate the breakeven point in units, based on the original budget.

(b) Calculate the profits and breakeven points which would result from each of the two alternatives and compare them with the original budget.

(c) The manufacturing company decided to proceed with the original budget and has asked you to calculate how many units must be sold to achieve a profit of $45,500.

(Time allowed: 30 minutes)

Test your understanding 9

A company makes and sells three products, R, S and T. Extracts from the weekly profit statements are as follows:

	R	S	T	Total
	$	$	$	$
Sales revenue	10,000	15,000	20,000	45,000
Variable cost of sales	4,000	9,000	10,000	23,000
Fixed costs (*)	3,000	3,000	3,000	9,000
Profit	3,000	3,000	7,000	13,000

(*) General fixed costs absorbed using a unit absorption rate.

If the sales revenue mix of products produced and sold were to be changed to: R 20%, S 50% and T 30%, the new average contribution to sales ratio would be _lower_. (choose from higher, lower, or remain unchanged)?

Test your understanding 10

MC manufactures one product only, and for the last accounting period has produced the simplified profit and loss statement below:

	$	$
Sales		300,000
Direct costs		
Direct materials	60,000	
Direct wages	40,000	
	———	
Prime cost	100,000	
Variable production overhead	10,000	
Fixed production overhead	40,000	
Fixed administration overhead	60,000	
Variable selling overhead	40,000	
Fixed selling overhead	20,000	
	———	
		270,000
		———
		30,000
		———

The organisation has created the following profit–volume graph from this information as follows:

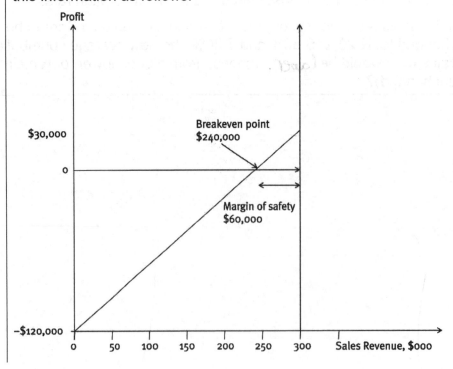

Examine the following diagrams:

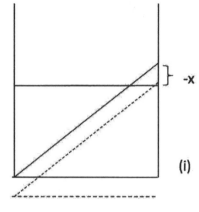

(i)

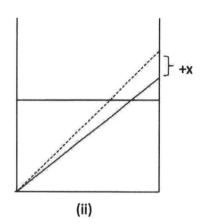

(ii)

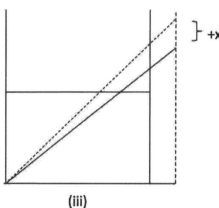

(iii)

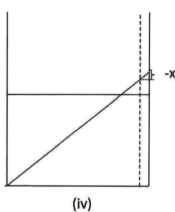

(iv)

These graphs show increase or decrease in profit by +x or −x.

Match each diagram to each of the following potential changes to the business' assumptions:

- a decrease in variable cost (i) (ii)
- a decrease in sales volume (iv) ✓
- an increase in fixed cost (ii) (i)
- an increase in sales price (iii) ✓

Test your understanding 11

A company provides three different holiday packages to a popular destination. Details on the profits made from the packages are as follows:

	Standard $	Premium $	Superior $
Retail price	450	600	800
Variable costs	70	90	120
Fixed costs	180	200	240
Profit per package	200	310	440

The total annual fixed costs are budgeted to be $200,000 and, whilst none of these costs are specific to any particular package, they are charged to packages on the basis of average numbers of service staff per package.

The company expects to sell the packages in the following proportion:

- Standard 50%

- Premium 30%

- Superior 20%

The annual revenue that needs to be generated in order to break even is closest to:

A $200,000

B $236,000 ✓

C $237,000

D $402,000

Test your understanding 12

A provider of language courses has three courses with the following information:

Product	Introductory	Intermediate	Advanced
Contribution to sales ratio	40%	80%	60%
Expected sales mix	60%	30%	10%

Total fixed costs are budgeted to be $120,000.

To the nearest $, the total break-even revenue is $_____

Test your understanding 13

A retailer has taken a decision to decrease its operational gearing by outsourcing its home delivery service. Its total costs at the existing budgeted volume will remain the same.

Which two of the following statements will be true?

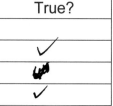

	True?
Its fixed costs will increase	
Its fixed costs will decrease	✓
Its contribution to sales ratio will increase	~~✓~~
Its contribution to sales ratio will decrease	✓

Test your understanding 14

Two profit making organisations in the same industry have identical levels of volume, selling price and total costs. But Company 1 has a higher level of operational gearing than Company 2.

Which of the following statements are true?

A Company 2 has a higher level of fixed costs as a proportion of total costs

(B) Company 1 will have a higher break-even point than Company 2 ✓

C Company 2 will have a higher contribution to sales ratio than Company 1

D Both companies will break-even at the same number of units sold

Test your understanding 15

A business has budgeted to produce and sell 400 units in the next month and created the following budgeted profit statement:

	$
Sales	8,000
Total variable costs	2,000
Total fixed costs	4,500
Profit	1,500

If the business was to convert 20% of its fixed costs into variable costs, what would happen to its break-even revenue?

A Increase by 20%

B Increase by 6%

~~C~~ Decrease by 20%

(D) Decrease by 6%

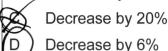

Test your understanding answers

Example 1

(i) Break-even point

The key to calculating the breakeven point is to determine the contribution per unit.

Contribution per unit = 28 – 20 = $8

$$\text{Breakeven point (in terms of number of units sold)} = \frac{\text{Fixed costs}}{\text{Contribution per unit}}$$

$$\text{Breakeven point} = \frac{\$2 \times 3,000 \text{ units}}{\$8}$$

Breakeven point = 750 units

(ii) Margin of safety

Margin of safety = Budgeted sales – Breakeven point sales

Margin of safety = 3,100 – 750

Margin of safety = 2,350 units (or 76% of budgeted sales)

(iii) Budgeted profit

Once breakeven point has been reached, all of the contribution goes towards profits because all of the fixed costs have been covered.

Budgeted profit = 2,350 units (margin of safety) × $8

Budgeted profit = $18,800

(iv) Target profit

To achieve the desired level of profit, sufficient units must be sold to earn a contribution that covers the fixed costs and leaves the desired profit for the month.

$$\text{Unit sales required} = \frac{\text{Fixed overhead + desired profit}}{\text{Contribution per unit}}$$

$$\text{Unit sales required} = \frac{\$6,000 + \$20,000}{\$8}$$

Unit sales required = 3,250 units

(v) Contribution to sales ratio

$$\text{C/S ratio} = \frac{\text{Contribution}}{\text{Sales}}$$

$$\text{C/S ratio} = \frac{\$8}{\$28}$$

$$\text{C/S ratio} = 28.57\%$$

(iv) Breakeven revenue

$$\text{Breakeven revenue} = \frac{\text{Fixed costs}}{\text{C/S ratio}}$$

$$\text{Breakeven revenue} = \frac{\$6,000}{(8/28)}$$

$$\text{Breakeven revenue} = \$21,000$$

Example 2

It would be possible to determine the following information:

- the break-even point (in units) – this can be seen from reading down from where total revenue cuts the total cost line and reading along the horizontal axis

- the break-even point (in terms of total revenue) – this can be seen from reading along from where total revenue cuts the total cost line and reading up the vertical axis

- total fixed costs – this is the point at which the total costs line cuts the vertical axis

- total costs – this is a line used in the construction of the chart

- margin of safety – this is usually indicated on the chart.

However, it would not be possible to easily determine the following:

- selling price per unit

- variable cost per unit.

The chart deals in total revenue and total costs and individual revenue and cost per unit values are difficult to determine.

Example 3

Note: the profit–volume graph is the clearest way of presenting information like the one presented in this scenario. If we were to attempt to draw two conventional breakeven charts on one set of axes the result would be a jumble, which is very difficult to interpret.

The profit-volume chart is easier for analysts to interpret. The graph depicts clearly the larger profits available from option (b). It also shows that the breakeven point increases from 20,000 units to 22,500 units but that this is not a large increase when viewed in the context of the projected sales volume. It is also possible to see that for sales volumes above 30,000 units the profit achieved will be higher with option (b). For sales volumes below 30,000 units option (a) will yield higher profits (or lower losses).

In answer to the specific questions:

- Scenario (b) has the higher contribution.

- This cannot be deduced from the difference in selling price or costs. For example, having a higher selling price would normally lead to a higher contribution, but only if the costs remain the same. If selling price and costs change then it is difficult to determine what will happen to contribution. This rules out options A and B in the next question.

- It also cannot be deduced from the different break even points as this is influenced by the level of fixed costs for each option.

- But the fact that situation (b) has a steeper slope indicates that as volume increases profit is increasing at a higher rate. This would indicate that situation (b) has a higher contribution per unit (answer D).

- For the final question, the point of indifference between the two situations would occur when the profit from each situation is the same. This occurs where their profit lines cross, at 30,000 units (answer C).

Example 4

The breakeven revenue can be calculated as:

$$\text{Breakdown revenue} = \frac{\text{Fixed costs}}{\text{Weighted average C/S ratio}}$$

We know that the fixed costs are $200,000. We need the weighted average C/S ratio as follows:

$$\text{Weighted average C/S ratio} = \frac{\text{Total contribution}}{\text{Total revenue}}$$

$$\text{Weighted average C/S ratio} = \frac{(20,000 \times \$20) + (10,000 \times \$15)}{(20,000 \times \$50) + (10,000 \times \$60)}$$

Weighted average C/S ratio = 34.375%

This indicates that for every $1 of revenue generated, the company will earn $0.34 in contribution.

The breakeven revenue can now be calculated this way for company A:

$$\text{Breakdown revenue} = \frac{\text{Fixed costs}}{\text{Weighted average C/S ratio}}$$

$$\text{Breakdown revenue} = \frac{\$200,000}{0.34375}$$

Breakeven revenue = $581,819

Answer B is therefore the correct answer.

Calculations in the illustration above provide only estimated information because they assume that products X and Y are sold in a constant mix of 2X to 1Y. In reality, this constant mix is unlikely to exist and, at times, more Y may be sold than X. Such changes in the mix throughout a period, even if the overall mix for the period is 2:1, will lead to the actual breakeven point being different than anticipated.

Alternative solution

An alternative (though potentially more complex solution) to this question would be to use the weighted average contribution per unit in the calculations (rather than the C/S ratio). In an exam, you would only use this method if there is not enough information available to calculate the weighted average contribution sales ratio.

The weighted average contribution per unit can be calculated as follows:

$$\text{Weighted average contribution per unit} = \frac{(20,000 \times \$20) + (10,000 \times \$15)}{(20,000 + 10,000)}$$

Weighted average contribution per unit = $18.33 per unit

The break-even point can then be calculated as follows:

$$\text{Breakdown units} = \frac{\text{Fixed costs}}{\text{Weighted average contribution per unit}}$$

$$\text{Breakdown units} = \frac{\$200,000}{\$18.33}$$

Breakeven units = 10,911 units

This represents the total number of units that must be sold in order to break even. If we assume that the pre-determined sales mix still applies (i.e. that the company plans to sell twice as many Product X and Product Y) then this can be split between the products so that Product X needs to sell two thirds of 10,911 units (i.e. 7,274 units) and Product X needs to sell one third of 10,911 (i.e. 3,637 units).

This would give a target revenue of:

	Product X	Product Y
Sales price	$50	$60
Break even sales (in units)	7,274	3,637
Break even revenue	$363,700	$218,220

The total break even revenue would then be ($363,700 + $218,220) $581,920.

There is a little bit of a rounding difference but we could still conclude that Answer B is the correct answer.

Example 5

To achieve a target profit of $300,000 in Company A:

$$\text{Sales revenue required for profit of } \$300,000 = \frac{(\text{Fixed costs + required profit})}{\text{Weighted average C/S ratio}}$$

$$\text{Sales revenue required for profit of } \$300,000 = \frac{\$200,000 + \$300,000}{0.34375}$$

Sales revenue required for profit of $300,000 = $1,454,545

The correct answer is Answer D.

Example 6

(a)

Product	Contribution	Sales revenue	C/S ratio
	$000	$000	
X	550	800	0.6875
Y	50	200	0.2500
Z	300	1,000	0.3000
Total	900	2,000	

$$\text{Breakdown revenue} = \frac{\text{Total contribution}}{\text{Total sales}}$$

$$\frac{\$900,000}{\$2,000,000}$$

$$= 0.45 \text{ or } 45\%$$

(b)

$$\text{Breakdown sales revenue required} = \frac{\text{Fixed costs}}{\text{C/S ratio}}$$

$$\frac{\$300,000}{45\%}$$

$$= \$666,667$$

(c)

$$\text{Sales revenue required} = \frac{\text{Fixed costs + required profit}}{\text{C/S ratio}}$$

$$\frac{\$300,000 + \$600,000}{0.45}$$

$$= \$2,000,000$$

(d)

The chart is, essentially, a profit/volume chart. Cumulative profit is plotted against cumulative sales revenue.

Like P/V charts for single products the line drawn starts at the fixed costs below the line. It can therefore be determined that the fixed costs for the business are $300,000.

The product lines are then drawn in order of the ranking of their contribution/sales ratio. From the diagram we can therefore determine that the c/s ratio of product X must be the highest of the three products and that product Y must be the lowest of the three products.

The highest point on the diagram represents the highest potential revenue ($2m) and profits for the business ($600,000).

Assuming that the products are sold in the standard sales mix then the break-even point is the point at which the lower line crosses the horizontal axis. This is at around $650,000.

If, however, the products were sold in order of their c/s ratios, then the higher line shows a potentially lower break-even point. The higher line indicates that this would be achieved at around $440,000.

Note: the table below provides the workings which enabled the chart to be drawn.

Product	Contribution $000	Cumulative Profit/Loss $000	Revenue $000	Cumulative revenue $000
		(300)		0
X	550	250	800	800
Z	300	550	1,000	1,800
Y	50	600	200	2,000

Example 7

(a) To calculate the overall breakeven point (expressed in sales value terms), we need to calculate a weighted average contribution to sales ratio. To this end, we will need a total sales revenue, as well as a total contribution in $:

	Summer	Autumn	Winter	Spring	Total
Sales mix	33.33%	41.67%	16.67%	8.33%	100%
Sales in $	200,000	250,000	100,000	50,000	600,000
Less: Variable costs in $	120,000	170,000	80,000	20,000	390,000
Contribution	80,000	80,000	20,000	30,000	210,000

Weighted average C/S ratio = ($210,000/$600,000)

Weighted average C/S ratio = 35%

$$\text{Breakeven point (sales value)} = \frac{\text{Fixed costs}}{\text{Weighted average C/S ratio}}$$

Breakeven point (sales value) = **$454,286**

(b) After the change in sales mix, contribution can be calculated as follows:

	Summer	Autumn	Winter	Spring	Total
Sales mix	25%	40%	30%	5%	100%
Sales in $	150,000	240,000	180,000	30,000	600,000
Less: Variable costs in $	90,000	163,200	144,000	12,000	409,200
Contribution	60,000	78,800	36,000	18,000	190,800

Weighted average C/S ratio = ($190,800/$600,000)

Weighted average C/S ratio = 31.8%

$$\text{Breakeven point (sales value)} = \frac{\text{Fixed costs}}{\text{Weighted average C/S ratio}}$$

Breakeven point (sales value) = **$500,000.**

Test your understanding 1

(a) **Break-even point**

Contribution per unit = $(100 – 56) = $44

$$\text{C/S ratio} = \frac{\text{Contribution per unit}}{\text{Selling price per unit}} = \frac{\$44}{\$100} = 0.44$$

Breakeven point in terms numbers of units sold

$$= \frac{\text{Fixed costs}}{\text{Contribution per unit}}$$

$$= \frac{\$220,000}{\$44} = 5,000 \text{ units}$$

Breakeven point in terms of sales revenue

$$= \frac{\text{Fixed costs}}{\text{C/S ratio}}$$

$$= \frac{\$220,000}{0.44} = \$500,000$$

(Proof: breakeven units × selling price per unit = 5,000 × $100 = $500,000)

(b) **Margin of safety**

(as a % of Budgeted sales)

$$= \frac{\text{Budgeted sales} - \text{Break-even sales}}{\text{Budgeted sales}} \times 100\%$$

$$= \frac{7,500 - 5,000}{7,500} \times 100\%$$

$$= 33.33\%$$

Test your understanding 2

(i)   The key to calculating the breakeven point is to determine the contribution per unit.

Contribution point = $120 – ($22 + $36 + $14) = $48

$$\text{Breakeven point} = \frac{\text{Fixed overhead}}{\text{Contribution per unit}}$$

$$= \frac{\$12 \times 2{,}000}{\$48} = 500 \text{ units}$$

(ii)   Margin of safety   = budgeted sales – breakeven point

= 2,200 – 500

= **1,700 units** (or 1,700/2,200 × 100 %)

= **77 %**

(iii)   Once breakeven point has been reached, all of the contribution goes towards profits because all of the fixed costs have been covered.

Budgeted   = 1,700 units margin of safety × $48 contribution
per   profit unit

= **$81,600**

(iv)   To achieve the desired level of profit, sufficient units must be sold to earn a contribution which covers the fixed costs and leaves the desired profit for the month.

$$\text{Number of sales units required} = \frac{\text{Fixed overhead + desired profit}}{\text{Contribution per unit}}$$

$$= \frac{(\$12 \times 2{,}000) + \$96{,}000}{\$48}$$

$$= 2{,}500 \text{ units}$$

(v) Contribution per unit is calculated as $120 – $72 sum of variable costs = $48

$$\text{Contribution to sales ratio} = \frac{\text{Contribution per unit}}{\text{Sales revenue per unit}}$$

$$= \frac{\$48}{\$120}$$

$$= 40\%$$

(iv) Breakeven revenue can be calculated in two ways

$$\text{Break even revenue} = \frac{\text{Monthly fixed costs}}{\text{Contribution to sales ratio}}$$

$$= \frac{\$12 \times 2{,}000 \text{ units}}{40\%}$$

$$= \mathbf{\$60{,}000}$$

This could also have been calculated as Breakeven Point 500 units × Selling price $120

$$= \mathbf{\$60{,}000}$$

Test your understanding 3

Firstly we need to calculate the breakeven sales revenue.

Because we haven't been given any information on units, we must have to use the contribution sales revenue technique:

$$\text{C/S ratio} = \frac{\text{Fixed contribution}}{\text{Total sales revenue}} = \frac{(450 - 220)}{450}$$

$$= 0.511 \text{ (or 51.1\%)}$$

$$\text{Breakeven point (in terms of sales revenue)} = \frac{\text{Fixed costs}}{\text{C/S ratio}}$$

$$\text{Breakeven point (in terms of sales revenue)} = \frac{\$160{,}000}{0.511}$$

$$\text{Breakeven point (in terms of sales revenue)} = \$313{,}000$$

Now that we know the break-even position we can calculate the margin of safety (this is what is required in the second element of the question).

$$\text{Margin of safety (as a \% of budgeted sales)} = \frac{\text{Budgeted sales} - \text{Breakeven sales}}{\text{Budgeted sales}} \times 100\%$$

$$\text{Margin of safety (as a \% of budgeted sales)} = \frac{450 - 313}{450} \times 100\%$$

$$= 0.3044 \text{ (or } 30.44\%)$$

This tells us that for the company to fall into a loss making position its sales next year would have to fall by over 30.44% from their current position.

Test your understanding 4

Monthly fixed costs = 4,000 units × $4 = $16,000.

First calculate the breakeven sales: 16,000/(18 − 8) = 1,600

Margin of safety % = (projected sales − breakeven sales)/projected sales

$$= (4,000 - 1,600)/4,000 = 60\%$$

Test your understanding 5

C

$$\text{Contribution margin} = \frac{36,000}{60,000} = 60\%$$

We need an additional $24,000 of contribution. The revenue to achieve this will therefore be $24,000/0.60 = $40,000.

Target revenue = 60,000 + 40,000 = 100,000

$$\% \text{ Increase in revenue} = \frac{100,000 - 60,000}{60,000} = 0.67 \text{ or } 67\%$$

Test your understanding 6

(a) Point X on the chart shows the highest value of sales at which break-even will occur, assuming that the budgeted sales value is the maximum achievable for each of the products. It looks like that breakeven point is achieved when all of E, all of D and some of Cs are sold.

Note that it is not meaningful here, because it is unlikely that in reality, all of D and Es products will be sold whilst none of As or Bs will.

(b)

$$\text{Breakeven revenue} = \frac{\text{Fixed costs}}{\text{Weighted average contribution to sales ratio}}$$

$$\text{Breakeven revenue} = \frac{\$300,000}{24.16\% \text{ (working 1)}}$$

$$= \$1,241,935$$

Working 1 – Weighted average contribution to sales ratio:

Product	A	B	C	D	E	Total
Unit selling price	$40	$15	$40	$30	$20	
Total sales ($000)	400	180	1,400	900	200	3,080
Contribution to sales ratio	45%	30%	25%	20%	(10%)	
Contribution ($000)	180	54	350	180	(20)	744

$$\text{Weighted average C/S ratio} = \frac{\text{Total contribution } \$744,000}{\text{Total sales } \$3,080,000}$$

$$= 0.2416 \text{ or } 24.16\%$$

Test your understanding 7

(a)

Product	Revenue $000	Variable costs $000	Contribution $000	C/S ratio
J	200	140	60	0.30
K	400	80	320	0.80
L	200	210	(10)	(0.05)
M	200	140	60	0.30
	1,000	**570**	**430**	

(b) The products are plotted in the order of their C/S ratios. The fixed costs of the company are $240,000. The chart reveals that if only product K is produced, the company will generate a profit of $80,000. The profit of the company is maximised at $200,000. This is achieved by producing Products K, J and M only.

If all four products are produced then JK Ltd can expect a profit of $190,000 from sales revenue of $1,000,000. If all four products are sold in the budget sales mix then the company will break even when revenue reaches $558,140. This point has been indicated on the graph. This point can also be calculated. Thus:

Average contribution/ = 430/1,000 = 43% sales ratio

$$\text{Breakeven point} = \frac{\text{Fixed costs}}{\text{Average C/S ratio}}$$

$$= \frac{\$240,000}{0.43} = \$558,140$$

Note: the diagram was constructed using the following product information:

Product	Contribution $000	Cumulative Profit/(Loss) $000	Revenue $000	Cumulative revenue $000
		(240)		0
K	320	80	400	400
J	60	140	200	600
M	60	200	200	800
L	(10)	190	200	1,000

(c) The overall C/S ratio could be improved by:

– Changing the product mix in favour of products with above-average C/S ratios. In this example that would mean increasing production of Product K.

– Increasing sales prices or cutting production costs.

– Deleting product L.

Test your understanding 8

(a) First calculate the current contribution per unit.

	$000	$000
Sales revenue		288
Direct materials	54	
Direct wages	72	
Variable production overhead	18	
Variable administration etc.	27	
	171	
Contribution		117
Contribution per unit ($117,000/9,000 units)		$13

Now you can use the formula to calculate the breakeven point.

Breakeven point =

$$\frac{\text{Fixed costs}}{\text{Contribution per unit}} = \frac{\$42,000 + \$36,000}{\$13} = 6,000 \text{ units}$$

(b) *Alternative (i)*

Budgeted contribution per unit	$13
Reduction in selling price ($32 – $28)	$4
Revised contribution per unit	$8

Revised breakeven point = $78,000/$9	8,667	Units
Revised sales volume = 9,000 × (90/75)	10,800	Units
Revised contribution = 10,800 × $9	$97,200	
Less fixed costs	$78,000	
Revised profit	$19,200	

Alternative (ii)

Budgeted contribution per unit	$13.00
Reduction in selling price (15% × $32)	$4.80
Revised contribution per unit	$8.20

$$\text{Revised breakeven point} = \frac{\$78,000 + \$5,000}{\$8.20} \qquad 10,122 \quad \text{Units}$$

Revised sales volume = 9,000 units × (100/75)   12,000   Units
Revised contribution = 12,000 × $8.20 $98,400
Less fixed costs $83,000
                                                        ─────────
Revised profit $15,400
                                                        ─────────

Neither of the two alternative proposals is worthwhile. They both result in lower forecast profits. In addition, they will both increase the breakeven point and will therefore increase the risk associated with the company's operations.

(c) This exercise has shown you how an understanding of cost behaviour patterns and the manipulation of contribution can enable the rapid evaluation of the financial effects of a proposal. We can now expand it to demonstrate another aspect of the application of CVP analysis to short-term decision-making.

Once again, the key is the required contribution. This time the contribution must be sufficient to cover both the fixed costs and the required profit. If we then divide this amount by the contribution earned from each unit, we can determine the required sales volume

$$\text{Required sales} = \frac{\text{Fixed costs} + \text{required profit}}{\text{Contribution per unit}}$$

$$= \frac{(\$42,000 + \$36,000 + \$45,500)}{\$13} = \textbf{9,500 units}$$

Test your understanding 9

Answer: lower

	R	S	T	Total
	$	$	$	$
Sales revenue	10,000	15,000	20,000	45,000
Contribution	6,000	6,000	10,000	22,000
C/S ratio	0.6	0.4	0.5	0.489
New weightings	20%	50%	30%	
New weighted C/S ratio	0.12	0.2	0.15	0.47

So the new C/S ratio is lower.

Test your understanding 10

(i) An increase in fixed costs

(ii) A decrease in variable costs

(iii) An increase in sales price

(iv) A decrease in sales volume

Test your understanding 11

The correct answer is option **B**.

Package	Volume	Contribution per package	Total contribution	Selling price per package	Total revenue
		$	$	$	$
Standard	50	380	19,000	450	22,500
Premium	30	510	15,300	600	18,000
Superior	20	680	13,600	800	16,000
			47,900		56,500

Average C/S ratio = 47,900/56,500 = 0.8478

Breakeven point = $200,000/0.8478 = $235,908

Test your understanding 12

To the nearest $, the total break-even revenue is **$222,222**

The weighted average contribution margin is:

= [(40% × 60%) + (80% × 30%) + (60% × 10%)] = [24% + 24% + 6%] = 54%

The break-even point = $120,000/54% = $222,222.

Test your understanding 13

	True?
Its fixed costs will increase	
Its fixed costs will decrease	Correct
Its contribution to sales ratio will increase	
Its contribution to sales ratio will decrease	Correct

Reducing operational gearing means converting some fixed costs into variable costs. This will reduce the level of fixed costs and increase the level of variable costs. Increasing variable costs will decrease the contribution per unit and the contribution to sales ratio.

Test your understanding 14

Correct answer: B

Organisations with a higher level of operational gearing will have a higher break-even point than identical organisations with lower operational gearing. Statement B is true.

Organisations with a lower operational gearing will have a lower break-even point, a lower contribution to sales ratio and lower levels of fixed costs. The other statements are false.

Test your understanding 15

Correct answer: D

Existing contribution to sales ratio = ($8,000 – $2,000)/$8,000 = 75%
Existing break-even revenue = $4,500/75% = $6,000

Revised contribution to sales ratio = ($8,000 – $2,000 – $900)/$8,000 = 63.75%

Revised fixed costs = $3,600

Revised break-even revenue = $3,600/63.75% = $5,647

Fall in break-even revenue = $353 = 5.89% (approximately 6%)

Linear programming

Chapter learning objectives

Lead outcome	Component outcome
C3. Apply appropriate techniques to support short-term decision making	(c) Product mix decisions with constraints. (d) Data and technology.

1 Session Content Diagram

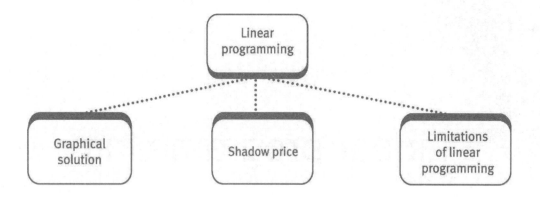

2 Introduction

We saw in an earlier chapter that when faced with one limiting factor, we calculate the contribution per unit of the limiting factor and rank the products, allocating the scarce resource to the best product and then the next best product and so on until the resource is fully utilised.

If faced with two or more limiting factors, then the situation is more complicated and linear programming techniques must be used (and the limiting factors are now called **constraints**).

Further details

In the previous chapter, you saw how to use basic limiting factor analysis to determine the profit-maximising sales mix for a company with a single resource constraint. The decision rule was to allocate the resource to products according to the **contribution earned per unit of scarce resource**, subject to any other constraints such as maximum or minimum demands for the individual products.

This technique cannot be applied when there is more than one limiting factor. In this situation a **linear programming** technique is used.

Linear programming is the name given to a collection of tools that are among the most widely used in management science. It is essentially a technique that encompasses the problem of allocating scarce resources between competing activities so as to maximise or minimise some numerical quantity, such as contribution or cost. In business it can be applied to areas such as planning production to maximise profit, mixing ingredients to minimise costs, selecting a portfolio of investments to maximise worth, transporting goods to minimise distance, assigning people to maximise efficiency and scheduling jobs to minimise time.

Linear programming involves the construction of a mathematical model to represent the decision problem. The model is then solved by an appropriate method or by the use of a computer package to obtain the optimal values for the activities.

The technique employed will require a basic level of mathematics that you should have obtained from previous studies

Algebra revision

In this chapter you will need to be familiar with some algebraic mathematical techniques. This part of the text provides a revision of the ones that are most commonly used in linear programming.

Understanding inequalities

Inequalities are treated in almost exactly the same way as equations. In fact an inequality says much the same thing as an equation, except that one side will be

- less than the other (<)

- greater than the other, (>)

- less than or equal to the other, ($\leq$), or

- greater than or equal to the other. ($\geq$)

Inequalities can be manipulated in the same way as equations, except that when multiplying or dividing by a negative number it is necessary to **reverse** the inequality sign.

For example,

$5 - 2x < 25$

$-2x < 20$ (deduct 5 from each side)

$-x < 10$ (divide each side by 2)

$x > -10$ (divide each side by -1, so reverse direction of inequality)

Using simultaneous equations

Simultaneous equations are where you have two equations that must both be satisfied at the same time, of the type:

$3X + 4Y = 18$ (i)

$5X + 2Y = 16$ (ii)

which must both be satisfied by the solutions X and Y.

Provided you multiply both sides of an equation by the same amount, it continues to be true. In the solution of these equations, one or both of the equations are multiplied by numbers chosen so that either the X or the Y terms in the two equations become numerically identical.

We have labelled the equations (i) and (ii) for clarity. Suppose we were to multiply (i) by 5 and (ii) by 3. Both equations would contain a 15X-term that we could eliminate by subtraction, it being the case that you can add or subtract two equations and the result remains true.

In this case, however, the simplest method is to multiply equation (ii) by 2, so that both equations will contain 4Y and we can subtract to eliminate Y. The full solution is shown below.

$3X + 4Y = 18$ (i)

$5X + 2Y = 16$ (ii)

Multiply (ii) by 2:

$10X + 4Y = 32$ (iii)

Subtract (iii) – (i):

$7X + 0 = 14$

$X = 14 \div 7 = 2$

Substitute X = 2 into (i)

$6 + 4Y = 18$

$4Y = 18 - 6 = 12 \quad Y = 12 \div 4 = 3$

Check the results in (ii):

$5 \times 2 + 2 \times 3 = 16$

The solution is X = 2, Y = 3.

Had we chosen to substitute X = 2 into equation (ii) it would not have affected the result but we would then have checked in the other equation (i).

Solving simultaneous linear equations using graphs

Each equation represents a straight line and solving simultaneous equations is the same as identifying the point at which the two lines cross.

This is the graphical interpretation of the solution of simultaneous linear equations, and a graphical method could be used instead of an algebraic method (provided that the scale was big enough to give the required accuracy).

Example 1

Solve the equations:

$10x + 20y = 140$

$6x + 8y = 72$

3   Step-by-step technique

The technique requires the translation of a decision problem into a system of variables, equations and inequalities.

For examination purposes a five-step procedure is used to construct the mathematical model. Any of these steps might be examined.

Product X and Product Y

A company produces two products in three departments. Details are shown below regarding the time per unit required in each department, the available hours in each department and the contribution per unit of each product:

	Product X Hours per unit	Product Y Hours per unit	Available hours
Department A	8	10	11,000
Department B	4	10	9,000
Department C	12	6	12,000
Contribution per unit ($)	4	8	

Required:

Following the procedure for the graphical solution, define the optimum production plan.

Step 1 – Define the variables

The first step is to simplify the equations by using abbreviations for the products or variables.

Step 1 – Product X and Product Y

Let x = number of units of Product X produced.

Let y = number of units of Product Y produced.

Step 2 – State the objective function

The objective function expresses the **total contribution** that will be made from the production of the two products

Step 2 – Product X and Product Y

The objective of the business is usually to maximise profit, and as fixed costs are fixed this would mean the objective function is to **maximise contribution.**

The objective function is stated in terms of the defined variables.

Note however that in some questions the objective function might be to minimise costs. If that was the case then we would create an equation for the total cost line.

In our illustration the objective function is to maximise contribution (we should always make this assumption unless told specifically otherwise). The contribution on each unit of X is $4 and on each unit of Y, $8. The objective function 'Z' is to be maximised is as follows:

Contribution (Z) = 4x + 8y

It is important that the **contribution** per unit of each product is used in the construction of this formula, rather than, say, the selling price per unit.

Step 3 – State the constraints

Each constraint under which the organisation operates should be expressed as an equation. This involves illustrating that the total for that resource must be less than or equal to the total of that resource that is available.

Step 3 – Product X and Product Y

In our illustration, we can see that available hours are limited in Departments A, B and C and we therefore can illustrate that the total hours in each department must be less than or equal to the total hours available.

There are limited hours in Department A (11,000). Within that department each unit X takes 8 hours and each unit Y takes 10 hours. So the total hours in department A will be 8 hours for every Product X (i.e. 8x when expressed in our formula), and 10 hours for every Product Y (i.e. 10y when expressed in our formula). Because of the limitation on hours in Department A we know that these total hours must be less than or equal to 11,000 hours, and this then allows us to express a formula for the total hours equation in Department A as follows:

$$8x + 10y \leq 11,000$$

A similar equation can be created for Department B as follows:

$$4x + 10y \leq 9,000$$

Likewise, there are limited hours in Department C and its equation would be as follows:

$$12x + 6y \leq 12{,}000$$

Finally, we have to remember that we cannot make negative numbers of products, and, therefore, for completeness we should state that the values for x and y cannot be negative (this is known as the non-negativity constraint) as follows:

$$x, y \geq 0$$

Step 4 – Draw the graph

The constraints lines can then be plotted on a graph.

To draw the constraint lines, you need to find two points on each line and join them together. These are commonly the intersects on the x and y axis.

In our illustration one of the constraints is $8x + 10y \leq 11{,}000$. To see where this crosses the y axis, we need to substitute x=0 into the equation:

$$(8 \times 0) + 10y = 11{,}000$$

$$10y = 11{,}000$$

$$y = 1100$$

The first coordinate of our line is therefore (x,y) = (0, 1100).

Next we see where this crosses the x axis, we need to substitute y=0 into the equation:

$$8x + (10 \times 0) = 11{,}000$$

$$8x = 11{,}000$$

$$x = 1{,}375$$

The second coordinate of our line is therefore (x,y) = (1375, 0).

Step 4 – Product X and Y

The graph of the constraints in our illustration would appear as follows:

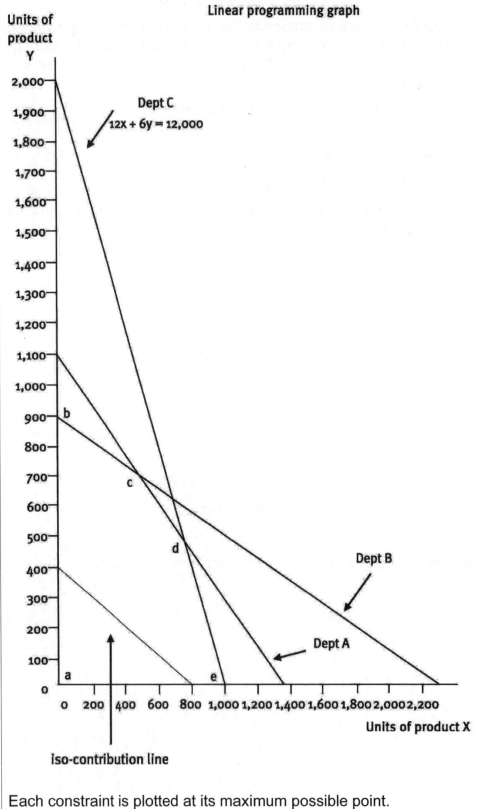

Linear programming graph

Each constraint is plotted at its maximum possible point.

You will not be asked to construct a graph in the examination. But you may be given a graph and asked to choose which line represents a particular constraint.

This should allow for the identification of the **feasible region** of production values.

The feasible region shows those combinations of the variables which are possible given the resource constraints.

In the example for Product X and Y, the original constraints were '≤' types, so the feasible region is shown by the shaded area formed by the points a, b, c, d and e. Production can be any combination of x and y that fall within this area or on the outlining boundaries of this area.

The lines drawn on the graph represent equations where the left hand side equals the right hand side. However, the original constraint was either '≤' or '≥'.

Where there is a '≤' constraint, this means that all the equation is satisfied by all points either on the line, or in the area underneath the line. The feasible region will therefore fall below the line.

Where there is a '≥' constraint, this means that all the equation is satisfied by all points either on the line, or in the area above the line.

Make sure that you pay attention to the direction of the inequality, as this will determine on which side of the line your feasible region will fall.

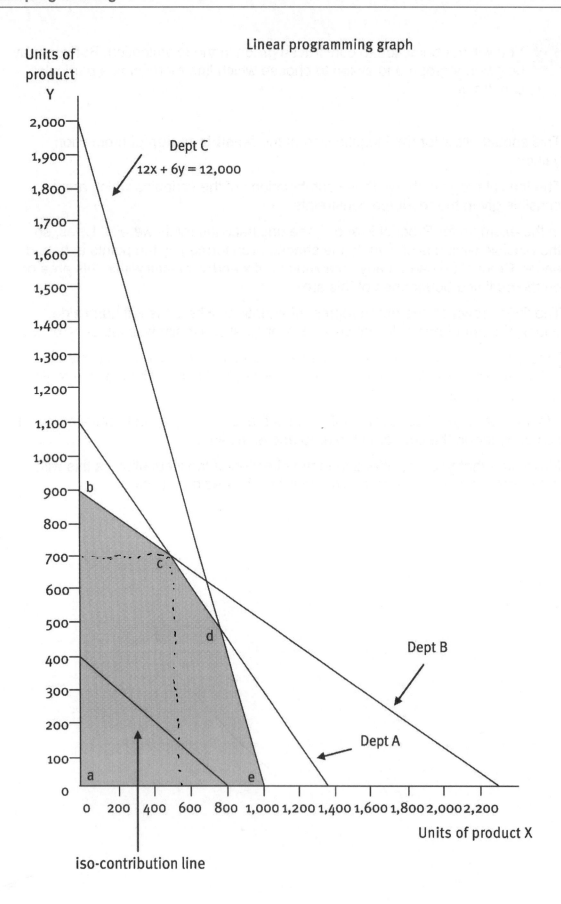

Linear programming graph

The feasible region

The **feasible region** represents all the possible production combinations that the company may undertake.

> CIMA's Official Terminology defines a feasible area as 'an area contained within all of the constraint lines shown on a graphical depiction of a linear programming problem. All feasible combinations of output are contained within, or located on, the boundaries of the feasible region'

If such an area does not exist, then the model has no solution

Step 5 – Find the optimum solution

Having found the feasible region the problem now is to find the optimal solution within this feasible region.

An **iso-contribution line** can then be used to determine the outer most point of the feasible region. This will be the optimal point of production.

The iso-contribution line

In this step, consider how the objective can be achieved. The graph is used to determine the optimum production plan. There are two methods that may be used to determine the optimum point on the graph:

Method 1: Using simultaneous equations

In this method we calculate the coordinates of each vertex (furthest points) on the feasible region. Then calculate the contribution (using the objective function) at each vertex.

Method 2: Using an iso-contribution line

We do not know the maximum value of the objective function; however, we can draw an iso-contribution line that shows all the combinations of x and y that provide the **same total value for the objective function.**

- If, for example, we need to maximise contribution $4x + $8y, we can draw a line on a graph that shows combinations of values for x and y that give the same total contribution, when x has a contribution of $4 and y has a contribution of $8. Any total contribution figure can be picked, but a multiple of $4 and $8 is easiest.

- For example, assume 4x + 8y = 4,000. This iso-contribution line could be found by joining the points on the graph x = 0, y = 500 and x = 1,000 and y = 0.

- Instead, we might select a total contribution value of $4x + 8y = \$8,000$. This iso-contribution line could be found by joining the points on the graph $x = 0$, $y = 1,000$ and $x = 2,000$ and $y = 0$.

- When drawing both of these iso-contribution lines on a graph, we find that the two lines are parallel and the line with the higher total contribution value for values x and y ($\$8,000$) is further away from the origin of the graph (point 0).

- This can be used to identify the solution to a linear programming problem. We draw the iso-contribution line showing combinations of values for x and y that give the same total value for the objective function.

- Look at the slope of the iso-contribution line and visualise the line 'moving' across the page, towards the top right of the page and away from the origin, maintaining the same gradient at all times. As it moves, the line will pass over the corners of the feasible region. The optimal point will be at the final vertex which the iso-contribution line passes before it leaves the feasible region completely. The coordinates of x and y at this vertex provide the solution to the linear programming problem. Some students find it helps to hold a ruler along the iso-contribution line, and then to 'slide' this across the page.

Given the difficulty in applying Method 2 in a computer-based exam, it is more likely that you would have to apply Method 1 in an exam. However, you may not be asked to check all points on the feasible region – the examiner may tell you which constraints form the optimal point so that you only have one point of intersection to calculate.

Step 5 – Product X and Product Y

Method 1

In our example, the co-ordinates of some of the points can easily be determined from the diagram and we can quickly calculate the level of contribution made at each of these points

Potential optimal point	Production of X (units) $	Production of Y (units) $	Total contribution $
a	0	0	0
b	0	900	7,200
e	1,000	0	4,000

But for the remaining points (c and d) we must use simultaneous equations to determine their coordinates.

Point c occurs where the constraints for Dept A and Dept B intersect. Because the point is at the furthest point of each of the lines we know that all of the constraint is being used and the less than or equal to sign in the equations can be converted to an equal sign:

Dept A: $8x + 10y = 11{,}000$

Dept B: $4x + 10y = 9{,}000$

We need to use simultaneous equations to solve this problem and find the coordinates of x and y where they intersect:

$8x + 10y = 11{,}000$ (call this equation 1)

$4x + 10y = 9{,}000$ (call this equation 2)

As we have 10y in both of these equations, we can subtract equation 2 from equation 1, to leave us with:

$(8x - 4x) + (10y - 10y) = (11{,}000 - 9{,}000)$

$4x = 2{,}000$

$x = 2{,}000/4 = 500$

We can now substitute this value of x back into either of the two equations (let's use equation 1), to find the value for y:

$8x + 10y = 11{,}000$

$(8 \times 500) + 10y = 11{,}000$

$4{,}000 + 10y = 11{,}000$

$10y = 11{,}000 - 4{,}000 = 7{,}000$

$y = 7{,}000/10 = 700$

Point d occurs where the constraints for Dept A and Dept C intersect. Because the point is at the furthest point of each of the lines we know that all of the constraint is being used and the less than or equal to sign in the equations can be converted to an equal sign:

Dept A: $8x + 10y = 11{,}000$

Dept C: $12x + 6y = 12{,}000$

Again, we need to use simultaneous equations to solve this problem provides the coordinates:

$8x + 10y = 11{,}000$ (call this equation 1)

$12x + 6y = 12{,}000$ (call this equation 2)

As we need to have 'matching' values for either x or y in both equations, we can multiply equation 1 by 1.5, so that we have 12x in both equations, as follows:

$(8x \times 1.5) + (10y \times 1.5) = (11{,}000 \times 1.5)$

$12x + 15y = 16{,}500$ (call this equation 3)

Now we can subtract equation 2 from equation 3, to get:

$(12x - 12x) + (15y - 6y) = (16,500 - 12,000)$

$9y = 4,500$

$y = 4,500/9 = 500$

Substituting y=500 back into equation 1 gives us:

$8x + 10y = 11,000$

$8x + (10 \times 500) = 11,000$

$8x + 5,000 = 11,000$

$8x = 11,000 - 5,000 = 6,000$

$x = 6,000/8 = 750$

We have now got the coordinates for all 5 points at the vertex of the feasible region and can determine the total contribution at each point:

Potential optimal point	Production of X (units) $	Production of Y (units) $	Total contribution $
a	0	0	0
b	0	900	7,200
c	500	700	7,600
d	750	500	7,000
e	1,000	0	4,000

The optimal production plan occurs at the point at which contribution is maximised (as that was our objective in Step 2). This occurs at point c, where 500 units of Product X are produced, 700 units of Product Y are produced and the total contribution is $7,600.

Ensure that you answer the question that has been asked by the examiner.

If asked for the optimal production plan then you need to state how much of each product should be manufactured (i.e. the co-ordinates for the optimal point on the diagram).

If instead you are asked for the optimal contribution then you must go further and calculate the contribution at the optimal point.

Step 5 – Product X and Product Y

Method 2

The line plotted from point 400 on the y axis to point 800 on the x axis is the iso-contribution line. If you were to put a ruler along this line and move it outwards in parallel to that line, the last point that you would meet in the feasible region would be point C. This tells us that the optimal point in the feasible region in our illustration is at point C.

We would then use simultaneous equations as in Method 1 to determine that the co-ordinates for this point are x = 500 and y = 700.

The optimum production plan is therefore to produce 500 units of Product X and 700 units of Product Y.

Contribution at this point = (500 × \$4) + (700 × \$8) = \$7,600.

Illustration 1 – Linear programming in practice

The airline industry uses **linear programming** to optimise profits and minimise expenses in their business.

The products

Airlines decided to charge different fares for different seats and promoted different prices depending on how early you bought your ticket. This required some linear programming.

Different prices brought different levels of contribution. These therefore became the airlines 'products' for the linear programming calculations. Through linear programming, airlines were able to find the optimal breakdown of how many tickets to sell at which price, including various prices in between.

The constraints

Airlines also need to consider plane routes, pilot schedules, direct and in-direct flights, and layovers. There are certain standards that require pilots to sleep for so many hours and to have so many days rest before flying (so available flying time became a constraint). Airlines want to maximise the amount of time that their pilots are in the air, as well. Pilots have certain specialisations, as not all pilots are able to fly the same planes, so the number of pilots available becomes a constraint. The most controllable factor an airline has is its pilot's salary, so it is important that airlines use their optimisation teams to keep this expense as low as possible. Because all of these constraints must be considered when making economic decisions about the airline, linear programming becomes a crucial job.

Because there is more than one scarce resource, computers were used to create solutions to the problem for airlines.

Example 2

A coffee shop makes two types of cheesecake, the Regular and the Premium. For a single batch of Regular cheesecakes they require 3kg of butter and 7kg of cream cheese, while for a single batch of the Premium cheesecakes they require 11kg of butter and 13kg of cream cheese. The coffee shop makes $65 profit on a batch of Regular cheesecakes and $90 profit on a batch of Premium cheesecakes. This week, the coffee shop has access to 700kg of butter and 1150kg of cream cheese.

Let x = number of batches of Regular cheesecake produced

Let y = number of batches of Premium cheesecake produced

Required:

(i)   state the objective function

(ii) state the constraints

(iii) determine how many batches of the Regular and Premium cheesecakes that the coffee shop should make this week in order to maximise profits

4   Minimisation problems

Linear programming enables organisations to find optimal solutions to economic decisions. Generally, this means maximising but it could aim to minimise costs instead; so, rather than finding a contribution line touching the feasible polygon at a tangent as far away from the origin as possible, the aim is to find a total cost line touching the feasible polygon at a tangent **as close to the origin as possible**.

5   The slack

At the optimal production point it is unlikely that all of the scarce resources will have been used up. If one of the constraints has remaining resources at this point this is known as slack.

Slack and surplus

Slack

This is the amount of a resource that is under-utilised when the optimum plan is implemented. The actual utilisation is below a maximum specification. In other terms, slack will occur when the optimum does not fall on a given resource line.

Slack is important, because unused resources can be put to another use, for example, they could be hired out to another manufacturer. A constraint that has a slack of zero is known as a **scarce resource.** Scarce resources are fully utilised resources.

> CIMA's Official Terminology defines slack variables as 'the amount of each resource which will be unused if a specific linear programming solution is implemented.'

Surplus

This is utilisation of a resource over and above a minimum. Surpluses tend to arise in minimisation of cost problems. For example, a constraint may state that it is necessary to produce a minimum of 400 widgets. If the optimum plan then recommends producing 450 widgets, the surplus in this case would be 50 widgets.

At the optimal production point, there will be no slack in the constraints lines that make up the optimal point. These are known as **binding constraints.**

The only slack in the system will come from the other constraint lines on the graph. These are **non-binding constraints.**

Slack – Product X and Product Y

Slack in Department A, Department B and Department C can be calculated based on the optimum solution where x = 500 and y = 700, and production plan slacks are:

Department A = (500 units of Product X × 8 hours) + (700 units of Product Y × 10 hours) = 11,000 hours.

This uses all available hours in Department A. **No slack in A => The constraint is binding.**

Department B = (500 units of Product X × 4 hours) + (700 units of Product Y × 10 hours) = 9,000 hours.

This uses all available hours in Department B. **No slack in B => The constraint is binding.**

Department C = (500 units of Product X × 12 hours) + (700 units of Product Y × 6 hours) = 10,200 hours.

There are 12,000 hours available in Department C. Therefore, the slack is 12,000 – 10,200 hours = 1,800 hours. There is **slack in C => The constraint is non-binding.**

Example 3

A company produces two products, X and Y, both of which require skilled and semi-skilled labour. Both grades of labour are expected to be limited in the following month and managers have formulated a linear programming model with the below information:

Objective function	$= 50x + 40y$
Skilled labour hours	$10x + 10y \le 2{,}000$
Semi-skilled labour hours	$5x + 25y \le 2{,}500$
x	≤ 150
y	≤ 80
x, y	≥ 0

The optimal solution has been identified as the intersection of the skilled labour hours constraint and the demand constraint for product X.

Required:

Which of the following resources will have slack at the optimal production level?

A   Skilled labour

B   Semi-skilled labour

C   Skilled labour hours and semi-skilled labour

Neither skilled nor semi-skilled labour

6   The shadow price

It may be that the problem of the scarce resources can be alleviated by, say, buying in the scarce resource at a premium price. The extra resource would allow the organisation to make more products and create more contribution.

The maximum premium on price that the organisation would pay for the extra resource is known as the **shadow price**.

More details on the shadow price

After finding an optimum solution to a graphical linear programming problem, it should be possible to provide further information by interpreting the graph more fully, to see what would happen if certain values in the scenario were to change.

It is **the premium (over and above the normal price) it would be worth paying to obtain one more unit of the scarce resource.**

> *CIMA's Official Terminology defines a shadow price as 'the increase in value which would be created by having available one additional unit of a limiting resource at its original cost. This represents the opportunity cost of not having the use of the one extra unit. This information is routinely produced when mathematical programming (especially linear programming) is used to model activity.'*

The shadow price of a scarce resource is the extra contribution that would arise if one more unit of that scarce resource became available, or it is the drop in contribution that would result from having one fewer unit of that scarce resource.

Non-binding constraints have no shadow price as slack exists already.

The simplest way to calculate shadow prices for a critical constraint is as follows:

Step 1: Take the equations of the lines that intersect at the optimal point. Add one unit (i.e. one more kg, one more hour etc.) to the constraint concerned, while leaving the other critical constraint unchanged.

Step 2: Use simultaneous equations to derive a new optimal solution.

Step 3: Calculate the revised optimal contribution and compare to the original contribution calculated. The increase is the shadow price.

Shadow prices – Product X and Product Y

Shadow prices in Department A:

Step 1:

We need to calculate the impact if one extra hour of Department A time was made available, so that 11,001 hours were available.

Step 2:

The new optimum product mix would be at the intersection of the two constraint lines:

(i) $8x + 10y = 11,001$ hours

(ii) $4x + 10y = 9,000$ hours

With (i) – (ii), $4x = 2,001$ and therefore $x = 500.25$ units.

Step 3:

When substituting x with '500.25' in (i) or (ii) we get y = 699.9 and new total contribution is calculated as follows:

	Units	Contribution per unit	Total contribution $
X	500.25	$4	2,001.00
Y	699.9	$8	5,599.20
			$7,600.20

The original contribution was equal to (500 units of X × $4) + (700 units of Y × $8) = **$7,600.**

Therefore, the increase in contribution from one extra hour in Department A is $0.20. In other words, the shadow price of an extra hour in Department A is $0.20. The company should be prepared to pay up to $0.20 extra per hour.

Shadow prices in Department B:

Step 1:

We need to calculate the impact if one extra hour of Department B time was made available, so that 9,001 hours were available.

Step 2:

The new optimum product mix would be at the intersection of the two constraint lines:

(i)   8x + 10y = 11,000 hours

(ii)   4x + 10y = 9,001 hours

With (i) – (ii), 4x = 1,999 and therefore x = 499.75 units.

Step 3:

When substituting x with '499.75' in (i) or (ii) we get y = 700.2 and new total contribution is calculated as follows:

	Units	Contribution per unit	Total contribution $
X	499.75	$4	1,999.00
Y	700.20	$8	5,601.60
			$7,600.60

The original contribution was equal to (500 units of X × $4) + (700 units of:

Y × $8) = **$7,600.**

Therefore, the increase in contribution from one extra hour in Department B is $0.60. In other words, the shadow price of an extra hour in Department B is $0.60. The company should be prepared to pay up to $0.60 extra per hour.

Shadow prices in Department C:

The shadow price of an extra hour in Department C is 0, as there is slack in Department C (1,800 hours are still available.)

Example 4

Referring back to the information in Example 3. Suppose that it was possible to pay overtime to the skilled labourers in order to increase production levels.

Required:

Calculate the maximum overtime premium that the company would be willing to pay per hour.

7 LP and Decision Making: minimum contractual requirements

When, in the question, information is given regarding a customer order the business has to meet, it is necessary to take this order into account **before** formulating the Linear Programming problem.

Example 5

ND Ltd produces two products, the Alpha and the Beta. For the next quarter, the following information is relevant:

Material A: 1,200 kgs are available.

 Per unit of Alpha: 2 kgs

 Per unit of Beta: 3 kgs

Material B: 1,500 kgs are available.

 Per unit of Alpha: 5 kgs

 Per unit of Beta: 2 kgs

Labour: 2,000 hours are available.

 Per unit of Alpha: 7 hours

 Per unit of Beta: 5 hours.

Each unit of Alpha and Beta make a contribution of $8 each.

> ND Ltd has already agreed a contract to supply 20 Alphas and 20 Betas with a key customer. This order, if cancelled, would incur a significant financial penalty.
>
> **Required:**
>
> Formulate the Linear Programming problem.

8   Limitations of linear programming

There are a number of assumptions and limitations to this technique.

- Linear relationships must exist.

- Only suitable when there is one clearly defined objective function.

- When there are a number of variables, it becomes too complex to solve manually and a computer is required.

- It is assumed that the variables are completely divisible.

- Single value estimates are used for the uncertain variables.

- It is assumed that the situation remains static in all other respects.

9   Using data and technology in linear programming

The method seen in this chapter can be a long and complex task for many decision makers. It is also limited to the use of only two products. Therefore, decision makers are turning to technology to help speed up and ease the burden of such product mix decisions.

Many widely available spreadsheet packages such as Microsoft excel have built in tools for performing such tasks. For example, Excel has a solver tool for linear programming scenarios:

It even has tools which can help in both decision making and budgeting such as a 'What-if analysis' tool:

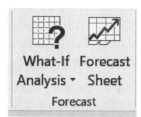

This can be supplemented with other software which can provide diagrams and pictures to help better visualise problems and solutions. This can make the decisions on the optimal product mix a less challenging task for decision makers.

Using such technology can bring many advantages to decision makers such as:

- More complex scenarios with more data can be worked with.

- Tasks become quicker and more efficient.

- Using visualisations can make problems and solutions easier for decision makers to understand.

- Formulae and look up tables can be used so that if any figure is amended, all the figures will be immediately recalculated. This is very useful for carrying out sensitivity analysis.

- The results can be printed out or distributed to other users electronically quickly and easily.

However, there are some issues with software that users need to be aware of:

- Simple, off-the-shelf programmes may not have the full capabilities to solve all problem scenarios. More advanced (and expensive) software programmes may be required. This may only have an overall benefit for organisations who expect to make decisions on the optimal product mix more often.

- The output from technology will only be as good as the input. If errors are made at the input stage (such as, for example, an incorrect total for a constraint) then the output will not provide the correct solution to the organisation's problem.

- Using visualisations and graphics can give a simpler and quickly understood picture of information but it can hide much of the detail and subtleties in the raw data. Decision makers should not make decisions based on such simple sources.

Non-financial data in product mix decisions

As with all decisions you must be aware that the decisions we have explored on optimal product mix have focused on solely the financial implications of the decision. There are many more non-financial factors that an organisation should consider when making decisions (as seen in an earlier chapter).

Gathering this non-financial information can be done in much the same way as gathering data for the purposes of budgeting – such as consulting staff or customers or using available big data. It will also experience similar advantages and disadvantages.

The type of non-financial data that will be relevant to choosing the optimal product mix might be:

- Customer value placed on a product.

- Competitor plans for competing products.

- The length of time that a particular resource will be scarce.

- Opportunities to use alternative resources through product redesign.

- Expected demand for a product.

- The ethical impacts of removing a product.

These non-financial considerations should feed in decision maker plans as much as financial impacts.

10 Chapter summary

```
        ┌─────────────────┐
        │     Linear      │
        │  Programming    │
        └─────────────────┘
```

Graphical method

- Step 1: Define the variables
- Step 2: State the objective function
- Step 3: State the constraints
- Step 4: Draw the graph
- Step 5: Find the optimum solution

Shadow prices

- The shadow price is maximum premium on price for one extra unit of a scarce resource
- Non-binding constraints have no shadow price

11   Practice questions

Test your understanding 1

Solve the equations:

2X + 3Y = 190 (i)

7X + 4Y = 340 (ii)

Test your understanding 2

A company is using linear programming to decide how many units of each of its two products to make each week. Weekly production will be x units of Product X and y units of Product Y. At least 50 units of X must be produced each week, and at least twice as many units of Y as of X must be produced each week. Each unit of X requires 30 minutes of labour, and each unit of Y requires two hours of labour. There are 5,000 hours of labour available each week.

Which of the following is the correct set of constraints?

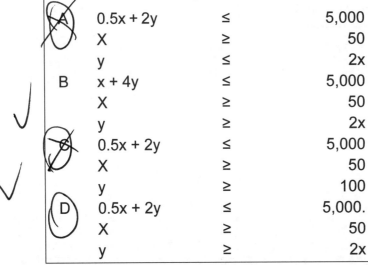

A	0.5x + 2y	≤	5,000
	X	≥	50
	y	≤	2x
B	x + 4y	≤	5,000
	X	≥	50
	y	≥	2x
C	0.5x + 2y	≤	5,000
	X	≥	50
	y	≥	100
D	0.5x + 2y	≤	5,000.
	X	≥	50
	y	≥	2x

Test your understanding 3

An office manager wishes to minimise the cost of telephone calls made. 40% of calls in peak hours cost $1 each and the remainder of such calls cost $1.50 each. 30% of calls at other times cost 80c each, 50% of them cost 90c each, and 20% of them cost $1 each. These proportions cannot be varied, though the total numbers of calls made in peak hours and of calls made at other times can be.

If x equals the number of calls made each day in peak hours, and y equals the number of calls made at other times, write the manager's objective function into the following box:

Test your understanding 4

The shadow price of a binding constraint is:

A The decrease in contribution which occurs when increasing the constraint limit by one unit

B The premium (over and above the normal price) that the company would be willing to pay to suppliers for supplying one more unit of the binding constraint

C The contribution gained from being able to produce one more unit of the most profitable product

D The cost of acquiring one more unit of the binding constraint from suppliers

Test your understanding 5

Direct labour is currently paid at a rate of $40 per hour. Direct labour is a scarce resource however the workforce has agreed to work additional hours but the rate is currently in negotiation. Each unit will require 2 hours of labour.

The shadow price of labour is $12 per hour.

What is the maximum amount per hour that the organisation would pay for the extra hours?

A $12

B $40

C $52

D $64

Test your understanding 6

QT manufactures two products, X and Y. It has created a linear programme problem and formulated the objective function as follows:

Maximise contribution = 20x + 5y

Where

X = Number of product X produced

Y = Number of product Y produced

QT has determined that two materials, A and B, form the binding constraints. The constraints have been represented by the following formulae:

(A) 5x + 2y = 11,000 kgs

(B) 10x + 5y = 25,000 kgs

The solution to the linear programme formulation provided a contribution of $35,000. However, a new market supplier for material A has been found and, although the supplier is more expensive than existing suppliers, this may alleviate the material A constraint.

The shadow price for material A is $ _10_

Test your understanding 7

Scenario

HJK is a light engineering company which produces a range of components, machine tools and electronic devices for the motor and aircraft industry. It employs about 1,000 people in 12 main divisions, one of which is the alarm systems division.

Alarm systems division

HJK produces two types of alarm system, one for offices and homes (X) and the other for motor vehicles (Y), on the same equipment. For financial reasons, it is important to minimise the costs of production. To match the current inventory and demand position, at least 100 alarm systems in total are required each week, but the quantity of one type must not exceed twice that of the other. The inputs necessary for the manufacture of one alarm system are given below, together with the availability of resources each week:

Type	Plating	Circuitry	Assembly
X	3 feet	4 units	20 mins
Y	2 feet	8 units	8 mins
Totals available each week	420 feet	800 units	34 hours

The management accountant estimates that the unit costs of production are $100 for X and $80 for Y. Past experience suggests that all alarms can be sold. At present, 75 of each alarm system are produced each week.

Tasks:

(a) State the objective function and the constraints for the production of alarm systems AND use a graphical method to find the optimal product mix.

(b) Explain briefly any points of significance for management.

(Time Allowed: 30 minutes)

Test your understanding answers

Example 1

We need to use simultaneous equations to solve the equations:

$10x + 20y = 140$ (call this equation 1)

$6x + 8y = 72$ (call this equation 2)

As we need to have 'matching' values for either x or y in both equations, we can multiply equation 1 by 6 to and equation 2 by 10 as this will give 60x in each equation, as follows:

$(10x \times 6) + (20y \times 6) = (140 \times 6)$

$(6x \times 10) + (8y \times 10) = (72 \times 10)$

$60x + 120y = 840$ (call this equation 3)

$60x + 80y = 720$ (call this equation 4)

Now we can subtract equation 4 from equation 3, to get:

$(60x - 60x) + (120y - 80y) = (840 - 720)$

$40y = 120$

$y = 120/40 = 3$

We now just substitute the y value into either of the original equations to find x. Let's substitute into equation 1:

$10x + 20y = 140$

$10x + (20 \times 3) = 140$

$10x + 60 = 140$ (subtract 60 from both sides)

$10x = 80$

$x = 80/10 = 8$

We can check whether these values of x and y are correct by substituting back into either of the original equations to see if the equations is satisfied:

$10x + 20y = 140$

$(10 \times 8) + (20 \times 3) = 140$

Example 2

(i) State the objective function

The objective is to maximise profits. Each batch of Regular cheesecake (x) generates profit of $65 and each batch of Premium cheesecake (y) generates profit of $90. The objective function is therefore:

$Z = 65x + 90y$

(ii) State the constraints

Production is limited by the availability of butter and cream cheese.

Each batch of Regular cheesecakes requires 3kg of butter and each Premium requires 11kg of butter. Butter is limited to 700kg. This constraint is therefore:

$3x + 11y \leq 700$

Each batch of Regular cheesecakes requires 7kg of cream cheese and each Premium requires 13kg. Cream cheese is limited to 1150kg. This constraint is therefore:

$7x + 13y \leq 1150$

Non-negativity constraint: $x, y \geq 0$

(iii) Production plan to maximise profits

If you sketch the graph of the feasible region you can see that it is the area between the origin and points a, b and c on the graph below.

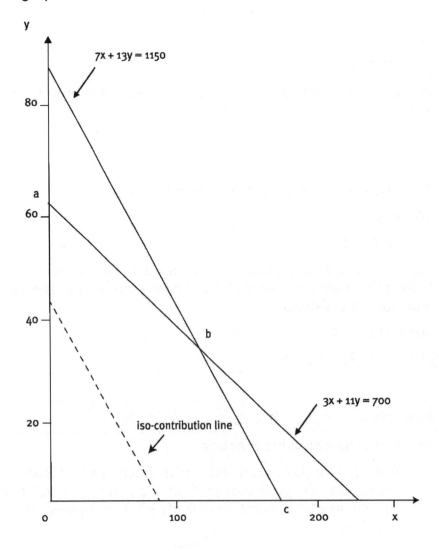

The optimal solution lies at one of the vertices. We can solve this by using the profit/iso-contribution line. If this is moved away from the origin, the final point on the feasible region that the line will touch will be point c. This is where the line 7x + 13y = 1150 crosses the x axis. On the x axis, the value for y is zero. We therefore substitute y=0 into the constraint to find the corresponding value for x:

7x + 13y = 1150

7x = 1150

x = 1150/7 = 164.3

We need to round this down to 164, as we cannot make part-batches.

The optimal solution is therefore to make zero batches of the Premium cheesecake and 164 batches of the Regular cheesecake.

Example 3

Correct solution is B, semi-skilled labour.

The optimal solution will typically occur where two critical (binding) constraint lines cross. There will be no slack for these resources as they will be fully utilised.

For other constraint lines, the fact that the optimal solution does not lie on these lines means that the resources are not fully utilised, so there will be slack.

Proof:

It is possible to prove this using the information in the question.

If the optimal solution lies at the intersect of 10x + 10y = 2000 and x=150, then we know that production for x must be 150. If we substitute x=150 into the constraint line for skilled labour, we can find the value of y at this point:

10x + 10y = 2000

(10 × 150) + 10y = 2000

1500 + 10y = 2000

10y = 500

y = 50

Our optimal production plan is therefore 150 units of x and 50 units of y.

If we substitute these values into the skilled labour constraint line, we can see that this level of production uses all of the available 2000 hours:

10x + 10y = (10 × 150) + (10 × 50) = 2000.

There is therefore no slack in skilled labour.

If we now substitute the production into the semi-skilled labour constraint we can see that this uses:

$5x + 25y = (5 \times 150) + (25 \times 50) = 2000$.

As the availability of semi-skilled labour is 2,500 hours, then there is slack in semi-skilled labour.

Example 4

Step 1: Add one more unit to the constraint line:

$10x + 10y = 2001$

Step 2: Derive a new optimal solution:

Optimal solution is where the skilled labour constraint intersects with the demand line for x, x=150. Substitute x=150 into the new equation from step 1:

$10x + 10y = 2001$

$(10 \times 150) + 10y = 2001$

$10y = 501$

$y = 50.1$

Revised optimal production is x = 150, y = 50.1

Step 3: Calculate shadow price

Substitute the solution from step 2 into the objective function equation:

Objective function = $50x + 40y$

Revised contribution = $(50 \times 150) + (40 \times 50.1) = 9504$

Original contribution = $(50 \times 150) + (40 \times 50) = 9500$

The shadow price is therefore the increase in contribution, which is $4. This means that the company should be willing to pay an extra $4 per hour as overtime. Anything above $4 would result in a lower contribution and so would not be beneficial.

Example 5

	Available	Required for order	Remaining
Material A	1,200	100	1,100
Material B	1,500	140	1,360
Labour	2,000	240	1,760

Required for order:

Material A: (20*2) + (20*3) = 100

Material B: (20*5) + (20*2) = 140

Labour: (20*7) + (20*5) = 240

(1) Define variables

Let A be the number of Alphas made **after** the customer order

Let B be the number of Betas made after the customer order.

(2) Objective function

The objective is to maximise contribution C, with C = $8A + $8B

(3) Constraints

Material A: 2A + 3B <1,100

Material B: 5A + 2B <1,360

Labour: 7A + 5B <1,760 and A,B ≥ 0

Test Your Understanding 1

Multiply (i) by 4 and (ii) by 3:

8X + 12Y = 760 (iii)

21X + 12Y = 1020 (iv)

Take equation (iii) away from equation (iv):

13X = 260

X = 260 ÷ 13 = 20

Substitute X = 20 in (ii):

140 + 4Y = 340

4Y = 340 – 140 = 200

Y = 200 ÷ 4 = 50

Check in (i):

(2 × 20) + (3 × 50) = 40 + 150 = 190

The solution is X = 20, Y = 50

Test Your Understanding 2

D

Test Your Understanding 3

Calculate the weighted average cost per call:

Peak hours ($1 × 0.40) + ($1.50 × 0.60) = $1.30

Other times ($0.80 × 0.30) + ($0.90 × 0.50) + ($1 × 0.20) = $0.89

Hence the objective is to

minimise 130x + 89y

Test Your Understanding 4

B

Option A is incorrect because a shadow price would represent the increase in contribution that could be earned from having more of the scarce resource.

Option C is incorrect because linear programming only works if product units are divisible. Contribution is likely to be stated per unit rather than per resource used. For example, labour would have a shadow price per hour rather than per unit.

Option D is incorrect because the shadow price may be very different from the price that is quoted by suppliers. The shadow price would allow the company to make a decision as to whether the purchase of extra supplies is a good decision.

Option B is the correct definition of a shadow price.

Test Your Understanding 5

C

The shadow price represents the highest acceptable premium (over and above the normal wage rate) that the organisation would be willing to pay.

The maximum overall rate that it would pay would therefore be the normal rate of $40 per hour plus the shadow price of $12 = $52 per hour.

Test Your Understanding 6

The shadow price for material A is **$10**

To calculate the shadow price of material A we add one more unit of material A to the constraint formula so that the two constraint formulae become:

(A)   5x + 2y = 11,001 kgs

(B)   10x + 5y = 25,000 kgs

Multiplying the first constraint by 5 and the second constraint by 2 in order to solve these simultaneous equations gives us:

(A)   25x + 10y = 55,005 kgs

(B)   20x + 10y = 50,000 kgs

Solving this provides the optimal quantity of each product:

x = 1,001 units

y = 2,998 units

The new total contribution is calculated as follows:

	Units	*Contribution per unit*	*Total contribution* $
x	1,001	$20	20,020
y	2,988	$5	14,990
Total			$35,010

The original contribution was $35,000.

Therefore, the increase in contribution from one kilogramme of material A is $10 – this is its shadow price. The company should be prepared to pay up to $10 extra per kilogramme to the new supplier.

Test Your Understanding 7

(a) Let x = number of alarm systems for offices and home

Let y = number of alarm systems for motor vehicles

Objective function:

Minimise cost = 100x + 80y

Subject to:

Minimum production	x + y	≥	100
	X	≤	2y
	y	≤	2x
Plating	3x + 2y	≤	420
Circuitry	4x + 8y	≤	800
Assembly	20x + 8y	≤	2,040
Non-negativity	x,y	≥	0

Workings for the graph

We are going to be drawing a number of straight lines. We need two points to define a straight line. The simplest thing to do in most cases is to make x = 0 and calculate what y must be to fit the equation and then make y = 0 and calculate what x must be.

x + y = 100		x = 2y		y = 2x	
X	y	X	y	X	y
0	100	0	0	0	0
100	0	200	100	100	200

3 x + 2y = 420		4x + 8y = 800		20x + 8y = 2040	
X	y	X	y	X	y
0	210	0	100	0	255
140	0	200	0	102	0

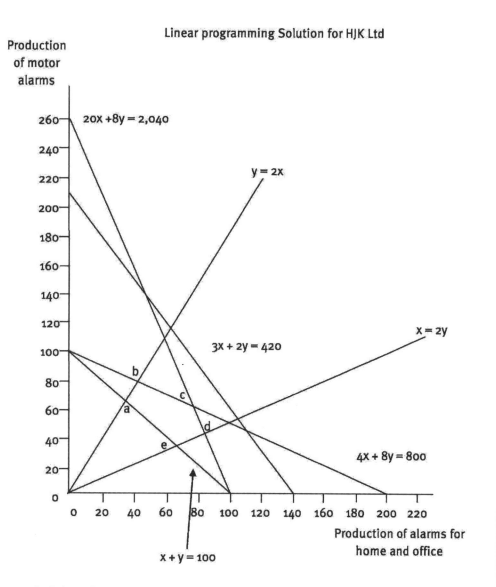

Linear programming Solution for HJK Ltd

Production of motor alarms

20x +8y = 2,040

y = 2x

x = 2y

3x + 2y = 420

4x + 8y = 800

x + y = 100

Production of alarms for home and office

Solving the graph

We are trying to minimise cost, So we want to produce as little x as possible, i.e. we want to be as far to the left as possible and we want to produce as little y as possible, i.e. we want to be as far down on the graph as possible.

We can therefore eliminate some of the possible solutions. The optimum solution has to be on a corner, i.e. has to be on an intersection of two lines, so the possible solutions are either nodes

(a), (b), (c), (d) or (e) (on the graph over the page), We can see, however, that node (b) is not as good as node (a) because node (a) is both lower down the graph and to the left of node (b) and therefore represents less x and less y and less cost.

Similarly, node (c) is not as good as node (e). (Node (e) is lower down the graph and to the left of node (c) and therefore represents less x and less y and therefore less cost.) Finally node (d) is not as good as node (e) for the same reasons.

So, the optimum solution is either node (a) or (node (e).

Node (a) lies on two lines:

$x + y = 100$

$y = 2x$

This gives a solution of 33.33 units of x and 66.67 units of y.

Cost = $(33.33 \times \$100) + (66.67 \times \$80) = \$8,667$

Node (e) lies on 2 lines:

$x + y = 100$

$x = 2y$

This gives a solution of 66.67 units of x and 33.33 units of y.

Cost = $(66.67 \times \$100) + (33.33 \times \$80) = \$9,333$

Therefore the optimum solution is to produce 33.33 units of X and 66.67 units of Y. This minimises cost at $8,667.

(b)   Management should question why HJK is trying to minimise cost. HJK Ltd is a commercial organisation and therefore its objective should be to maximise profit, not minimise cost.

The second most interesting point is that the current production plan is not feasible. It breaks the constraint for circuitry, i.e. 75 home and office alarms need 4 units each = 300 units in total and 75 motor vehicle alarms need 8 units each = 600 in total and 900 units as a grand total. This exceeds the available amount of 800.

13

Risk and uncertainty in the short-term

Chapter learning objectives

Lead outcome	Component outcome
D1: Apply basic risk management tools in the short term	(a) Explain nature of risk and uncertainty in the short term.
	(b) Apply basic sensitivity analysis to budgeting and short term decision making.

1 Chapter overview diagram

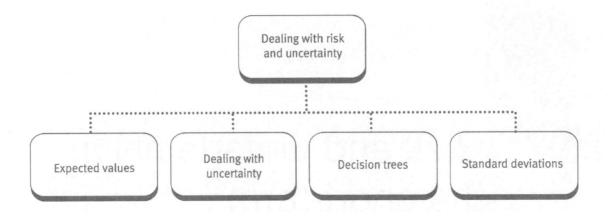

📖 Topic overview

Many business decisions will involve an element of risk and uncertainty. This chapter looks at how risk and uncertainty can be built into the decision making process. This is often achieved by building in probabilities for expected outcomes and using expected values and decision trees to assess the problem.

Forecasting and decision making often include an element of risk or uncertainty. Because they look to the future they often involve estimates of future costs and benefits. In this chapter we look at how these risks and uncertainty can be built into the decision making process.

Decision making involves making decisions now about what will happen in the future. Events in the future can be predicted, but managers can rarely be 100% confident that these predicted future events will actually arise. As actual results emerge managers are likely to discover that they have achieved better or worse results than those predicted originally.

There are several ways of dealing with this variability of outcomes. In this session we will consider several different possible outcomes that may arise. It is common in practice to consider three possible outcomes; the most likely outcome, the pessimistic (worst possible) outcome and the optimistic (best possible) outcome. Analysts may consider more than these three possibilities, but more information will become more complicated and cumbersome to analyse and understand.

Examination questions will generally provide all the different possible outcomes that may arise, together with the associated chance (probability) of the outcome occurring. It is our task to analyse the information given, recommend an appropriate strategy for management to follow and finally to highlight the potential risk involved in the various choices.

---

2 Risk and uncertainty

The difference between risk and uncertainty

 When making decisions, a decision maker will aim to account for risk but may struggle to account for uncertainty.

- **risk** – quantifiable – possible outcomes have associated probabilities, thus allowing the use of mathematical techniques

- **uncertainty** – unquantifiable – outcomes cannot be mathematically modelled.

Illustration on risk and uncertainty

Risk: there are a number of possible outcomes and the probability of each outcome is known.

For example, based on past experience of digging for oil in a particular area, an oil company may estimate that they have a 60% chance of finding oil and a 40% chance of not finding oil.

Uncertainty: there are a number of possible outcomes but the probability of each outcome is not known.

For example, the same oil company may dig for oil in a previously unexplored area. The company knows that it is possible for them to either find or not find oil but it does not know the probabilities of each of these outcomes.

One possible approach to dealing with risk is to deploy sophisticated modelling techniques in an attempt to improve the reliability of business forecasts. The use of trend analysis, encountered earlier in this text, is one possibility. Within this chapter we will look at how a simpler expected value technique may be of use.

3 Probabilities and expected values

One way to account for risk is to determine an expected value based on the range of possible outcomes.

 An expected value condenses all the different possible outcomes into one overall average result by calculating a single weighted average.

The expected value is not the most likely result. It may not even be a possible result, but instead it finds the average outcome if the same event was to take place thousands of times.

Expected value formula

$$EV = \Sigma px$$ **LEARN**

where x represents the future outcome

and p represents the probability of the outcome occurring

Example 1

A company has identified four possible outcomes from a new marketing strategy as follows:

Outcome	Profit / (loss) ($)	Probability
A	100,000	0.10
B	70,000	0.40
C	50,000	0.30
D	(20,000)	0.20

Calculate the expected outcome of this strategy.

Histograms

Probability data may be presented diagrammatically in the form of a histogram. The information given in the example immediately above might be presented as follows:

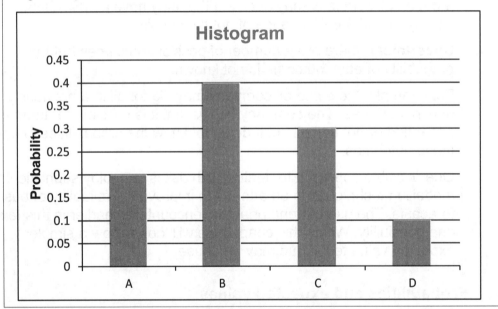

Advantages and disadvantages of EVs

The single figure of the expected value of revenue can hide a wide range of possible actual results It is important to recognise that the expected value is simply an average of all the possible outcomes. It does not represent the most likely outcome and may not even represent a possible outcome.

Illustration 1

An organisation is considering launching a new product. It will do so if the expected value of the total revenue is in excess of $1,000. It is decided to set the selling price at $10. After some investigation a number of probabilities for different levels of sales revenue are predicted; these are shown in the following table:

Units sold	Revenue $	Probability	Pay-off $
80	800	0.15	120
100	1,000	0.50	500
120	1,200	0.35	420
		1.00	EV = 1,040

The expected sales revenue at a selling price of $10 per unit is $1,040, that is [800 × 0.15] + [1,000 × 0.50] + [1,200 × 0.35]. In preparing forecasts and making decisions management may proceed on the assumption that it can expect sales revenue of $1,040 if it sets a selling price of $10 per unit. The actual outcome of adopting this selling price may be sales revenue that is higher or lower than $1,040. And $1,040 is not even the most likely outcome; the most likely outcome is $1,000, since this has the highest probability.

Another of the limitations of using expected value techniques is that it assumes that the decision maker is risk neutral.

There are three main types of decision-maker.

- **Risk neutral** decision-makers consider all possible outcomes and will select the strategy that maximises the expected value or benefit. These decision makers will focus attention on the expected value.

- **Risk seekers** are likely to select the strategy with the best possible outcomes, regardless of the likelihood that they will occur. These decision makers will ignore the expected value.

- **Risk averse** decision-makers try to avoid risk. They would rather select a lower, but certain, outcome than risk going for a higher pay-off which is less certain to occur.

Using an expected value technique assumes that the investor is risk neutral. But decision makers will not normally be risk neutral and they therefore may pay no attention at all to the expected value.

Illustration 2

Illustration 1 looked at determining the expected revenue based on predicted units sold and their associated expected values.

Let's consider the position if the expected outcomes had been very different. They might have been as follows:

Units sold	Revenue $	Probability	Pay-off $
40	400	0.15	60.00
100	1,000	0.50	500.00
137	1,370	0.35	479.50

The expected value of these pay offs is again approximately $1,040 which means that both situations give rise to the same expected sales revenue.

But the two situations are not the same. The second involves a wider dispersal of possible outcomes; hence it involves higher risk.

If the decision-makers are risk averse they will judge the range of possible outcomes described in the second situation to be worse than the first. If the decision-makers are risk seekers they may prefer the second situation, because of the higher outcome in the best possible situation. However, in this case, the dire downside of $400 may put them off.

Whatever the case it can be seen that the evaluation of the options solely on the basis of their expected value may not always be appropriate.

Utility theory

Utility is another important aspect of risk and uncertainty. The basis of the theory is that an individual's attitude to certain risk profiles will depend on the amount of money involved.

For example, most people would accept a bet on the toss of a coin, if the outcome were that they would win $6 if it came down heads and if it came down tails they would pay $4. The average person would be happy to play secure in the knowledge that they would win if the game were repeated over a long enough period; if not it would still be a good bet.

But if the stakes were raised so that the win was $6,000 on a single toss coming down heads and a loss of $4,000 if it came down tails, the average person might think twice and reject the bet as being too risky. Utility theory attaches weights to the sums of money involved; these are tailor-made to the individual's attitude towards winning and losing certain sums of money.

Overall, the advantages and disadvantages of expected values are summarised in the following table:

Advantages	Disadvantages
• takes account of risk • easy decision rule • simple	• subjective • not useful for one-offs • ignores attitudes to risk • answer may not be possible • ignores the spread of outcomes

Further explanation

Advantages:

- Takes risk into account by considering the probability of each possible outcome and using this information to calculate an expected value.

- The information is reduced to a single number resulting in easier decisions.

- Calculations are relatively simple.

Disadvantages:

- The probabilities used are usually very subjective and difficult to determine.

- The EV is merely a weighted average and therefore has little meaning for a one-off project.

- It assumes that the decision maker is risk neutral and ignores other attitudes to risk and uncertainty.

- The EV may not correspond to any of the actual possible outcomes.

- The EV gives no indication of the dispersion of possible outcomes about the EV, i.e. the risk, so that utility theory is not considered.

4 Pay off tables

When evaluating alternative courses of action, management's decision will often depend upon their attitude towards the risk. To consider the risk borne by each alternative it is necessary to consider ALL the different possible profits/losses that may arise. A pay off table is simply a table that illustrates all possible profits/losses.

Two way data tables

Two way data tables are used to represent inter-related data in an easy to understand manner.

For example, consider a company who are unsure about both selling price and variable cost. They believe that selling price may be either $40 or $50 depending on differing market conditions, and that variable production cost will be either $20 or $30 depending on wage negotiations currently taking place.

The company has therefore got a number of potential contributions per unit that could be represented in a two way table as follows:

	Selling price	
	$40	$50
Variable production cost		
$20	$20	$30
$30	$10	$20

A user can interpret the table quickly and easy. It can be seen, for example, that if selling price is $40 and variable production costs are $30, then the contribution per unit will be $10.

Two way data tables can be expanded to calculate expected contribution from different volume levels. This will be explored further in the following illustration.

Illustration 3

Geoffrey Ramsbottom runs a kitchen that provides food for various canteens throughout a large organisation. A particular salad is sold to the canteen for $10 and costs $8 to prepare. Therefore, the contribution per salad is $2.

Based upon past demands, it is expected that, during the 250-day working year, the canteens will require the following daily quantities:

On 25 days of the year	40 salads
On 50 days of the year	50 salads
On 100 days of the year	60 salads
On 75 days	70 salads

Total 250 days

The kitchen must prepare the salad in batches of 10 meals and it has to decide how many it will supply for each day of the forthcoming year.

Required:

Construct a pay-off table for this data and calculate the best number of salads to supply each Day.

Solution:

The pay-off table would be constructed as follows:

- If 40 salads will be required on 25 days of a 250-day year, the probability that demand = 40 salads is:

P(Demand of 40) = 25 days ÷ 250 days

P(Demand of 40) = 0.1

- Likewise, P(Demand of 50) = 0 .20; P(Demand of 60 = 0.4) and P (Demand of 70 = 0.30).

- Now let's look at the different values of profit or losses depending on how many salads are supplied and sold. For example, if we supply 40 salads and all are sold, our profits amount to 40 × $2 = 80.

- If however we supply 50 salads but only 40 are sold, our profits will amount to 40 × $2 – (10 unsold salads × $8 unit cost) = 0.

- Note too that there is an upper limit to the potential profit in some instances. If demand reaches 70 salads we can still only sell 60 salads and therefore the maximum profit we can make from supplying 60 salads is $120.

The payoff table would appear as follows:

Daily Demand (salads)	Probability	Daily Supply			
		40 salads	50 salads	60 salads	70 salads
40	0.10	$80	$0	($80)	($160)
50	0.20	$80	$100	$20	($60)
60	0.40	$80	$100	$120	$40
70	0.30	$80	$100	$120	$140

This could then be used to determine the expected value from each daily supply level:

EV (of supplying 40 salads) = 0.10(80) + 0.20(80) + 0.40(80) + 0.30 (80) = 80

EV (50 salads) = 0.10(0) + 0.20(100) + 0.40(100) + 0.30(100) = 90

EV (60 salads) = 0.10(–80) + 0.20(20) + 0.40(120) + 0.30(120) = 80

EV (70 salads) = 0.10(–160) + 0.20(–60) + 0.40(40) + 0.30(140) = 30

On the basis of expected values, the best strategy would be to supply 50 salads and gain an EV of 90.

Example 2

- Hofgarten Newsagents stocks a weekly magazine which advertises local second-hand goods. Marie, the owner, can:

    – buy the magazines for 15c each

    – sell them at the retail price of 25c.

- At the end of each week unsold magazines are obsolete and have no value.

- Marie estimates a probability distribution for weekly demand which looks like this

Weekly demand in units	Probability
10	0.20
15	0.55
20	0.25
	────
	1.00
	────

Required:

(i) Calculate the expected value of demand?

(ii) If Marie is to order a fixed quantity of magazines per week, calculate how many should be ordered each week, Assume no seasonal variations in demand.

5 Dealing with uncertainty in decision making

When probabilities are not available, there are still tools available for incorporating uncertainty into decision making.

Maximax

The maximax rule involves selecting the alternative that maximises the maximum pay-off achievable.

This approach would be suitable for an optimist who seeks to achieve the best results if the best happens.

Illustration 4 – The 'Maximax' rule

Let's apply the maximax rule to the previous illustration on Geoffrey Ramsbottom. Geoffrey Ramsbottom's table looks as follows:

Daily Demand (salads)	Probability	Daily Supply			
		40 salads	50 salads	60 salads	70 salads
40	0.10	$80	$0	($80)	($160)
50	0.20	$80	$100	$20	($60)
60	0.40	$80	$100	$120	$40
70	0.30	$80	$100	$120	$140

The manager who employs the maximax criterion is assuming that whatever action is taken, the best will happen; he/she is an optimist.

Here, the highest maximum possible pay-off is $140. Geoffrey should therefore decide to supply 70 salads a day.

Example 3

A company is choosing which of three new products to make (A, B or C) and has calculated likely pay-offs under three possible scenarios (I, II or III), giving the following pay-off table.

Profit (loss)	Product chosen		
Scenario	A	B	C
I	20	80	10
II	40	70	100
III	50	(10)	40

Required:

Using maximax, which product would be chosen?

Maximin

The maximin rule involves selecting the alternative that maximises the minimum pay-off achievable.

This approach would be appropriate for a pessimist who seeks to achieve the best results if the worst happens

Illustration 5 – The 'Maximin' rule

Geoffrey Ramsbottom's table looks as follows:

Daily Demand (salads)	Probability	Daily Supply			
		40 salads	50 salads	60 salads	70 salads
40	0.10	$80	$0	($80)	($160)
50	0.20	$80	$100	$20	($60)
60	0.40	$80	$100	$120	$40
70	0.30	$80	$100	$120	$140

If we decide to supply 40 salads, the minimum pay-off is $80.

If we decide to supply 50 salads, the minimum pay-off is $0.

If we decide to supply 60 salads, the minimum pay-off is ($80).

If we decide to supply 70 salads, the minimum pay-off is ($160).

The highest minimum payoff arises from supplying 40 salads.

Example 3 continued

Required:

Using the information from Example 3, apply the maximin rule to decide which product should be made.

The minimax regret rule

The minimax regret strategy is the one that minimises the maximum regret. It is useful when probabilities for outcomes are not available or where the investor wants to avoid making a bad decision. Essentially, this is the technique for a 'sore loser' who does not wish to make the wrong decision.

'Regret' in this context is defined as the opportunity loss through having made the wrong decision.

Illustration 6 – The 'Minimax Regret' rule

If the minimax regret rule is applied to Geofrrey Ramsbottom to decide how many salads should be made each day, we need to calculate the 'regrets'. This means we need to find the biggest pay-off for each demand row, then subtract all other numbers in this row from the largest number.

For example, if the demand is 40 salads, we will make a maximum profit of $80 if they all sell. If we had decided to supply 50 salads, we would achieve a nil profit. The difference, or 'regret' between that nil profit and the maximum of $80 achievable for that row is $80

Regrets can be tabulated as follows

	Daily Supply			
Daily Demand (salads)	40 salads	50 salads	60 salads	70 salads
40	$0	$80	$160	$240
50	$20	$0	$80	$160
60	$40	$20	$0	$80
70	$60	$40	$20	$0

Conclusion

If we decide to supply 40 salads, the maximum regret is $60. If we decide to supply 50 salads, the maximum regret is $80. For 60 salads, the maximum regret is $160, and $240 for 70 salads. A manager employing the minimax regret criterion would want to minimise that maximum regret, and therefore supply 40 salads only.

Example 3 continued

Required:

Using the information from Example 3, apply the minimax regret rule to decide which product should be made.

Perfect and imperfect information

In many questions the decision makers receive a forecast of a future outcome (for example a market research group may predict the forthcoming demand for a product). This forecast may turn out to be correct or incorrect. The question often requires the candidate to calculate the value of the forecast.

Perfect information The forecast of the future outcome is always a correct prediction. If a firm can obtain a 100% accurate prediction they will always be able to undertake the most beneficial course of action for that prediction.

Imperfect Information The forecast is usually correct, but can be incorrect. Imperfect information is not as valuable as perfect information. Imperfect information may be examined in conjunction with Decision Trees (see later in this chapter).

The value of information (either perfect or imperfect) may be calculated as follows:

Expected profit (outcome) WITH the information

minus

Expected profit (outcome) WITHOUT the information

Illustration 7 – The value of information

A new ordering system is being considered, whereby customers must order their salad online the day before. With this new system Mr Ramsbottom will know for certain the daily demand 24 hours in advance. He can adjust production levels on a daily basis. How much is this new system worth to Mr Ramsbottom?

Supply = demand	**X** Pay off	**P** Probability	px
40	$80	0.1	8
50	$100	0.2	20
60	$120	0.4	48
70	$140	0.3	42
			———
			118

E.V. with perfect information = $118

E.V. without perfect information (from the original EV calculation) = $90

———

Value of perfect information $28 per day

———

Example 3 continued

Following on from the data provided in Example 3, the company has made an estimate of the probability of each scenario occurring as follows:

Scenario	Probability
I	20%
II	50%
III	30%

However, an external consultant has some information about each likely scenario and can say with certainty which scenario will arise.

Calculate the value of the external consultant's information.

Example 4

Robotricks Lts have recently developed a new educational robot, known as 'The Core'. The core went into production in February using spare production capacity in the existing factory.

In April, the current supplier of one of the chemicals used in production of The Core unexpectedly increased the price of the chemical. The purchasing manager has therefore been sourcing an alternative supplier.

One potential supplier is offering a six month contract, where the price and quantity has to be agreed in advance. The new supplier has offered three alternatives, which have been used to create the below payoff table, which shows the total costs under each scenario.

	Options		
Expected demand	Quantity 1	Quantity 2	Quantity 3
Low	16,096	18,528	22,176
Medium	18,520	18,288	21,936
High	22,720	21,600	21,500

Required:

(a) Applying the maximax criteria, what quantity should be purchased?

(b) Applying the minimax criteria, what quantity should be purchased?

(c) Apply the minimax regret rule, what quantity should be purchased?

6 Decision trees and multi-stage decision problems

 A decision tree is a diagrammatic representation of a decision problem, where all possible courses of action are represented, and every possible outcome of each course of action is shown.

Decision trees should be used where a problem involves a series of decisions being made and several outcomes arise during the decision-making process. In some instances it may involve the use of joint probabilities – where the outcome of one event depends of the outcome of a preceding event.

 Joint probabilities

An important element in calculations involving decision trees will be in dealing with joint probabilities.

So far only a very small number of alternatives have been considered in the examples. In practice a greater number of alternative courses of action may exist, uncertainty may be associated with more than one variable and the values of variables may be interdependent, giving rise to many different outcomes.

The following exercise looks at the expected value of a manufacturing decision, where there are three alternative sales volumes, two alternative contributions, and three alternative levels of fixed cost. The number of possible outcomes will be 3 × 2 × 3 = 18.

Example

A company is assessing the desirability of producing a souvenir to celebrate a royal jubilee. The marketing life of the souvenir will be 6 months only. Uncertainty surrounds the likely sales volume and contribution, as well as the fixed costs of the venture. Estimated outcomes and probabilities are:

Units sold	Probability	Cont'n per Unit	Probability	Fixed cost	Probability
		$		$	
100,000	0.3	7	0.5	400,000	0.2
80,000	0.6	5	0.5	450,000	0.5
60,000	0.1			500,000	0.3
	___		___		___
	1.0		1.0		1.0
	___		___		___

A table can be constructed to represent all the possible outcomes from this new venture. For example the first possible payoff is that sales are 100,000 units (30% chance), the contribution per unit is $7 (50% chance) and the fixed costs are $400,000 (20% chance). This has a joint probability of 30% × 50% × 20% = 3% (or 0.03)

All the possibilities are represented in the following table:

Units sold	Cont'n per unit $	Total Cont'n $ a	Fixed Cost $ b	Probability	Joint Prob. c	EV of net cont. $ (a-b) x c
100,000	7	700,000	400,000	0.3×0.5×0.2=	0.030	9,000
	7	700,000	450,000	0.3×0.5×0.5=	0.075	18,750
	7	700,000	500,000	0.3×0.5×0.3=	0.045	9,000
	5	500,000	400,000	0.3×0.5×0.2=	0.030	3,000
	5	500,000	450,000	0.3×0.5×0.5=	0.075	3,750
	5	500,000	500,000	0.3×0.5×0.3=	0.045	0
80,000	7	560,000	400,000	0.6×0.5×0.2=	0.060	9,600
	7	560,000	450,000	0.6×0.5×0.5=	0.150	16,500
	7	560,000	500,000	0.6×0.5×0.3=	0.090	5,400
	5	400,000	400,000	0.6×0.5×0.2=	0.060	0
	5	400,000	450,000	0.6×0.5×0.5=	0.150	−7,500
	5	400,000	500,000	0.6×0.5×0.3=	0.090	−9,000
60,000	7	420,000	400,000	0.1×0.5×0.2=	0.010	200
	7	420,000	450,000	0.1×0.5×0.5=	0.025	−750
	7	420,000	500,000	0.1×0.5×0.3=	0.015	−1,200
	5	300,000	400,000	0.1×0.5×0.2=	0.010	−1,000
	5	300,000	450,000	0.1×0.5×0.5=	0.025	−3,750
	5	300,000	500,000	0.1×0.5×0.3=	0.015	−3,000
Total expected value			1.0		1.0	49,000

The joint probabilities can be used to summarise potential outcomes. For example, totalling up the joint probabilities for each set of sales shows the project has a 55.5 per cent chance of making a positive contribution, a 33 per cent chance of making a loss, and a 10.5 per cent chance of making neither a net contribution nor a loss. (For example, to calculate the probability of making a loss: we can see from the next table that a loss will arise in 7 situations. So if we add the overall probability of this happening we add up the joint probabilities associated with each of these outcomes – 0.150 + 0.090 + 0.025 + 0.015 + 0.010 + 0.025 + 0.015 = 0.33).Decisions like this can be quite hard to visualise and it may be more useful to use a decision tree to express the situation.

Example 5

A company has estimated that, depending on market conditions, contribution from sales will be $150,000, $112,500 or $90,000 in the next year. They have estimated the following probabilities:

Contribution	Probability
$150,000	20%
$112,500	65%
$90,000	15%

The company rents a factory and is currently negotiating the annual rental charge. There is uncertainty surrounding the rent figure. There is a 40% probability that it will be $70,000 and a 60% probability that it will be $50,000.

Required:

Calculate the expected profit value for the next year.

In an examination you will not be asked to create a decision tree, but you may want to use one as an aid to answering more complex risk questions. You may also be asked to interpret or use decision trees in examination questions and understanding how they are created should make this easier.

Drawing decision trees

Step 1: Draw the tree from **left to right** showing appropriate decisions and events/outcomes.

Symbols to use:

☐ A square is used to represent a decision point. At a decision point the decision maker has a choice of which course of action he wishes to undertake.

◯ A circle is used at a chance outcome point. The branches from here are always subject to probabilities.

Label the tree and relevant cash inflow/outflows and probabilities associated with outcomes.

Step 2: Evaluate the tree from **right to left** carrying out these two actions:

Calculate an EV at each outcome point.

Choose the best option at each decision point.

Step 3: Recommend a course of action to management.

Example 6

A business is considering launching a product that will have development costs of $6m. There is a 60% chance that the development of the product will be successful. If the launch is not successful then the product will be abandoned and the development costs will be lost.

If the development is a success then the company will continue on to marketing the product. There is a 70% chance that the marketing will be successful and make a profit of $20m. If the marketing campaign is unsuccessful a profit of only $1m is expected. Both profit figures are stated after taking account of marketing costs but before development costs.

The expected value of the development and marketing plan is $____m (round to two decimal places)

More on decision trees

Decision trees force the decision maker to consider the logical sequence of events. A complex problem is broken down into smaller, easier-to-handle sections. The financial outcomes and probabilities are shown separately, and the decision tree is 'rolled back' by calculating expected values and making decisions. In the examination ensure that only relevant costs and revenues are considered.

Consider the following example:

A company is planning on drilling for oil. It can either drill immediately (at a cost of $50m) or carry out some preliminary tests (cost ($10m). Alternatively, the company could sell the rights to the site to another company for $40m.

If it decides to drill now there is a 55% chance that it will find oil and extract it (with a value of $150m).

If further tests are carried out first there is a 70% chance that they will indicate the presence of oil. The sales rights would then be worth $65m. Alternatively, the company could drill for oil itself at a cost of $50m. There is then an 80% chance that oil extraction (worth $150m) is successful.

If further tests are carried out and indicate that no oil is present the value of any sales rights would fall to $15m. The company could still decide to drill for oil itself- but there is only a 20% chance that it would successfully find and extract oil at that point.

A decision tree for this problem would look as follows:

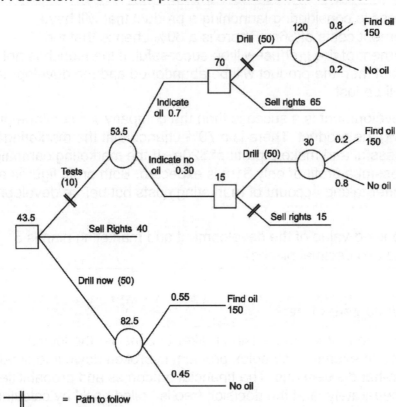

┼┼   = Path to follow

Explanation

It is easier to start at the bottom of the tree. The first box shows the first decision to be made – to test, to drill or to sell the rights. If we follow the 'drill' line/branch, we come a 'chance' point (represented by a circle). This shows that if we drill there are two possible outcomes – there is a 55% that we find oil and make a positive net return of $150m. There is also a 45% that no oil is found and that no return is made. The figure on the circle of $82.5m is the expected value calculated from these two outcomes. However, the drill line has a cost of $50m so that the overall net expected return would be $32.5m – and it is this figure that should be used to compare the drill option against the other options.

The middle branch of the tree shows the expected value from selling the rights – $40m.

The top branch shows the analysis of the testing decision. It can be seen that there are many more possible outcomes and also further decisions to made based on whether or not the tests indicate the presence of oil. Lines that have a double cross marking on them show the best choice to be made based on expected values.

Advice

The company should undertake geological tests. If the tests indicate that oil is present then a drilling programme should be carried out. However, if the tests indicate that there is no oil then the company should sell the drilling rights.

This strategy will maximise expected returns at £43.5m.

Benefits and problems in using decision trees

The main value of a decision tree is that it maps out clearly all the decisions and uncertain events and exactly how they are interrelated. They are especially beneficial where the outcome of one decision affects another decision. For example in the above, the probability of eventual success changes depending on the test outcomes. The analysis is made clearer by annotating the tree with probabilities, cash flows, and expected values so that the optimum decisions (based on expected values) can be clearly seen.

However, drawing a tree diagram is only one way of undertaking a decision. It is based on the concept of expected value and as such suffers from the limitations of this technique. For example, in this example, if the test drilling proves positive, the tree indicated the company should drill, as opposed to selling the rights. But if it does there is a 20% chance of it losing £50 million. A risk-averse company may well decide to accept the safer option and sell the rights and settle for £65 million.

A number of other factors should be taken into account when considering decision tree-type problems:

- *Assumes risk neutrality.* As mentioned under probability, some decision-makers do not choose options which give the greatest expected value, because they are either risk seekers or risk averse.

- *Sensitivity analysis.* The analysis depends very much on the values of the probabilities in the tree. The values are usually the subjective estimates of the decision-makers, and, no matter how experienced the people involved are, the values must be open to question. Sensitivity analysis can be used to consider 'break-even' positions for each variable – i.e. the value for a variable (such as probability) at which the decision would change. Sensitivity analysis is covered later in this chapter.

- *Oversimplification.* In order to make the tree manageable, the situation has often to be greatly simplified. This makes it appear far more discrete than it really is. In practice, it is much more likely that the outcomes would form a near continuous range of inflows and outflows. This cannot be shown on a decision tree, and so any decision tree usually represents a simplified situation.

7 Standard deviations and normal distributions

Standard deviations and normal distributions are ways of measuring risk and estimating probabilities for possible outcomes.

They are mathematical techniques that were first introduced at the CIMA Certificate level.

Standard deviations

In order to measure the risk associated with a particular project, it is helpful to find out how wide ranging the possible outcomes are. The conventional measure is the standard deviation.

 The standard deviation compares all the actual outcomes with the expected value (or mean outcome). It then calculates how far on average the outcomes deviate from the mean. It is calculated using a formula.

The basic idea is that the standard deviation is a measure of volatility: the more that actual outcomes vary from the average outcome, the more volatile the returns and therefore the more risk involved in the investment/decision.

 Calculating a standard deviation

The standard deviation is calculated using the following formula:

$$\sigma = \sqrt{\frac{\Sigma(x - \bar{x})^2}{n}}$$

σ = standard deviation

Σ = sum of

x = each value in the data set

$\bar{x}$ = mean of all values in the data set

n = number of value in the data set

However, the calculation can become a little more complex when probabilities need to be taken account of. Let's examine how standard deviations are calculated and used by considering the following illustration.

Illustration 8

A company is considering whether to make Product X or Product Y. They cannot make both products. The estimated sales demand for each product is uncertain and the following probability distribution of the expected profits for each product has been identified.

Product X

Profit ($)	Probability	Expected value ($)
3,000	0.10	300
3,500	0.20	700
4,000	0.40	1,600
4,500	0.20	900
5,000	0.10	500
	1.00	4,000

Product Y

Profit ($)	Probability	Expected value ($)
2,000	0.05	100
3,000	0.10	300
4,000	0.40	1,600
5,000	0.25	1,250
6,000	0.20	1,200
	1.00	4,450

The expected value for each product gives us an average value based upon the probability associated with each possible profit outcome. If profit is used for decision-making, then on that basis Product Y would be produced as it yields the highest return.

However, let's consider the standard deviation calculations for each product:

Product X

Profit Deviation from Expected value	Squared deviation	Probability	Weighted amount ($)
3,000 – 4,000 = –1,000	1,000,000	0.10	100,000
3,500 – 4,000 = –500	250,000	0.20	50,000
4,000 – 4,000 = 0	0	0.40	0
4,500 – 4,000 = 500	250,000	0.20	50,000
5,000 – 4,000 = 1,000	1,000,000	0.10	100,000

Sum of weighted squared deviation	300,000
Standard deviation (the square root of the total above)	547.72
Expected value	4,000

The standard deviation is calculated by taking the square root of the sum of the weighted squared deviation.

Product Y

Profit Deviation from Expected value	Squared deviation	Probability	Weighted amount ($)
2,000 – 4,450 = –2,450	6,002,500	0.05	300,125
3,000 – 4,450 = –1,450	2,102,500	0.10	210,250
4,000 – 4,450 = –450	202,500	0.40	81,000
5,000 – 4,450 = 550	302,500	0.25	75,625
6,000 – 4,450 = 1,550	2,402,500	0.20	480,500

Sum of weighted squared deviation	1,147,500
Standard deviation	1,071.21
Expected value	4,450

Summary:

Product	Expected value	Standard deviation
X	4,000	547.72
Y	4,450	1071.21

Using an expected value approach the company's decision would be to produce product Y. However, the profit for each product does not indicate the range of profits that may result. Examining the standard deviation, this allows us to evaluate the likely volatility of the profit for each product. Product Y has a higher standard deviation than Product X and is therefore more risky.

There is not a significant difference in profit for each of the products. However, Product X is less risky than Product Y and therefore the final selection will depend on the risk attitude of the company.

The coefficient of variation

In the above example, where the expected values were very close but the standard deviations are very different, it was easy to state that Product Y is much riskier than Product X. However, If we have two probability distributions with very different expected values their standard deviations are not as easily compared and it is much more difficult to state which is more risky.

We can overcome this problem by using the coefficient of variation which measures the relative size of the risk for projects that have very different standard deviations.

The variable with the smaller coefficient of variation is less dispersed than the variable with the larger coefficient of variation and is therefore less risky.

Example calculation

Consider a set of data observations where the results are 2, 7 and 9. The mean for this data is 6 {(2 + 7 + 9)/3}. The standard deviation is calculated by taking the squares of the three deviations from the mean (16 + 1 + 9 = 26) and then calculating the square root of their average ($\sqrt{26/3}$) = 2.94.

The coefficient of variation is the standard deviation of the series divided by its mean (2.94/6) which is 0.49 in this case. This is usually expressed as a percentage (i.e. 49% in this case). The lower this figure the lower the risk (when comparing this to other sets of data).

Example 7

A company is considering whether to make Product A or Product B. They cannot make both products. Summarised information is provided below:

Product	Expected value of return per unit	Standard deviation
A	$120	55 ✓
B	$90	50

If the company adopts a risk averse approach to decision making, which product should they produce?

Using normal distributions to determine probabilities

In the exam CIMA provides a table of the normal distribution. These are based on the principles of the normal distribution curve.

The normal distribution curve

Normal distributions were introduced in subject BA2 at the Certificate level. We will recap on this briefly here. We typically assume in this paper that data is normally distributed.

A normal distribution is often drawn as a "bell shaped" curve, with its peak at the mean in the centre, as shown:

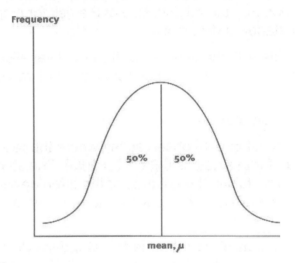

Characteristics of the normal distribution curve

- Normal distribution is a continuous probability distribution.

- Probabilities are represented by areas under the curve (50% of values lie below the mean and 50% of values lie above the mean).

- The total area under the curve is 1.

- The curve is symmetrical and bell shaped.

- The width of the curve (i.e. how far the values are spread out from the mean) is measured in terms of standard deviation.

- The mean, median and mode are at the centre of the curve.

In general 68% of values are within one standard deviation (between –1 and 1), 95% of values are within two standard deviations (between –2 and 2) and 99.7% of values are within three standard deviations (between –3 and 3) from the mean. Therefore, if we look at a set of data which fits a normal distribution the majority of values will occur closer to the mean, with fewer and fewer occurring the further from the mean we move.

Using normal distributions in decision making

If we know the mean and the standard deviation for a distribution we can work out the percentage chance (probability) of a certain value occurring. For example, a light bulb manufacturer may want to know how many bulbs will fail after a certain amount of time, or a chocolate bar manufacturer may want to know how many chocolate bars will weigh less than the minimum weight shown on the packaging.

As the curve is symmetrical, the values on the positive side will be exactly the same as the values on the negative side. In this way we can calculate either and assume it will be the same for the other side, for example if the chocolate bar manufacturer found that 0.05% of bars were lower that the acceptable weight, then 0.05% bars will also be higher than the acceptable weight.

The percentage figures can be obtained using normal distribution tables, which are given in your exam.

Note: The tables only show the positive values.

To use the tables we must first convert our normal distribution to a standard normal distribution

A standard normal distribution has:

- a mean of 0

- a standard deviation of 1.

This special distribution is denoted by the z and can be calculated with the following formula:

$$z = \frac{x - \mu}{\sigma}$$

Where x = variable, μ = mean, σ = standard deviation.

 The z score allows us to calculate the proportion of the distribution meeting certain criteria for any normal distribution.

It therefore allows us to determine probabilities.

Illustration 9

Crinkle Ltd is a manufacturer of crisps. The weights of the bags of crisps are normally distributed with a mean weight of 70g and a standard deviation of 5g.

Crinkle Ltd want to calculate the probability that a bag selected at random would be of an acceptable weight.

Required:

(i) Calculate the probability that a bag selected at random weighs less than 60g.

First, calculate the z score:

$$z = \frac{x - \mu}{\sigma}$$

$$z = \frac{60 - 70}{5} = -2$$

We want the probability that z is less than -2 standard deviations away from the mean. As the table only gives positive values for z, and we know that it is symmetrical, then this is the same area as the area above z=2, as can be seen in the following diagram:

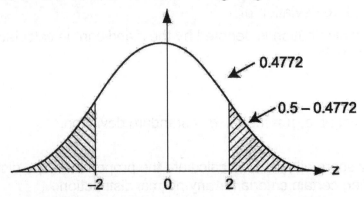

If we look in the tables for z=2, this gives a value of 0.4772. This is the area between the line z=2 and the mean value (0). As we are looking to find the probability of a value being MORE than 2 (the shaded area) then we need to subtract the area that we don't want from the area under that half of the curve.

Therefore, the probability that a bag selected at random weighs less than 60g = 0.5 – 0.4772 = 0.0228 or 2.3%.

Example 8

Monthly sales for a company are normally distributed and have a mean of $175,000 and a standard deviation of $5,000.

Required:

Calculate the probability that sales will be below $168,000.

8 Stress testing: sensitivity analysis

Stress testing and its importance was considered in the budgeting chapter. Stress testing can also be applied to decision making via the use of sensitivity analysis.

 Sensitivity analysis takes each uncertain factor in turn, and calculates the change that would be necessary in that factor before the original decision is reversed.

By using this technique it is possible to establish which estimates (variables) are more critical than others in affecting a decision.

The process

The process is as follows:

- Best estimates for variables are made and a decision arrived at For example, using expected values a profit calculation may indicate accepting a project.

- Each of the variables is then analysed in turn to see how much the original estimate can change before the original decision is reversed. For example, it may be that the estimated selling price can fall by 5% before the profit becomes negative and the project would be rejected.

- Estimates for each variable can then be reconsidered to assess the likelihood of the decision being wrong. For example, what is the chance of the selling price falling by more than 5%?

Illustration 10

A manager is considering a make v buy decision based on the following estimates:

	If made in-house $	If buy in and re-badge $
Variable production costs	10	2
External purchase costs	–	6
Ultimate selling price	15	14

Identify the sensitivity of the decision to the external purchase price.

Step 1: What is the original decision?

Comparing contribution figures, the product should be bought in and re-badged:

	If made in-house $	If buy in and re-badge $
Contribution	5	6

Step 2: Calculate the sensitivity (to the external purchase price)

For indifference, the contribution from outsourcing needs to fall to $5 per unit. Thus the external purchase price only needs to increase by $1 per unit (or $1/$6 = 17%).

If the external purchase price rose by more than 17% the original decision would be reversed.

Example 9

A manager has identified the following two possible outcomes for a process

Outcome	Probability	Financial implications ($000s)
Poor	0.4	Loss of 20
Good	0.6	Profit of 40

The expected value has been calculated as EV = (0.4 × –20) + (0.6 × 40) = +16. This would suggest that the opportunity should be accepted.

Required:

(a) Suppose the likely loss if results are poor has been underestimated. What level of loss would change the decision? In effect we want a break-even estimate.

(b) Suppose the probability of a loss has been underestimated. What is the break-even probability?

Strengths and weaknesses

Strengths of sensitivity analysis

- Information will be presented to management in a form which facilitates subjective judgement to decide the likelihood of the various possible outcomes considered.

- It identifies areas which are crucial to the success of the project. If the project is chosen, those areas can be carefully monitored.

Weaknesses of sensitivity analysis

- It assumes that changes to variables can be made independently, e.g. material prices will change independently of other variables. Simulation allows us to change more than one variable at a time.

- It only identifies how far a variable needs to change; it does not look at the probability of such a change.

- It provides information on the basis of which decisions can be made but it does not point to the correct decision directly.

9   Chapter summary

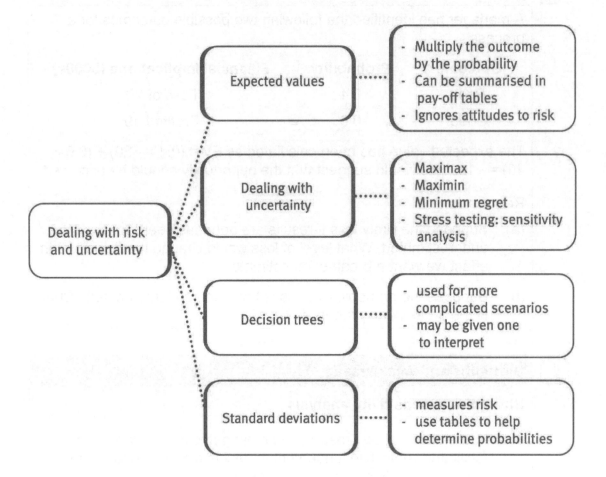

Dealing with risk and uncertainty

Expected values
- Multiply the outcome by the probability
- Can be summarised in pay-off tables
- Ignores attitudes to risk

Dealing with uncertainty
- Maximax
- Maximin
- Minimum regret
- Stress testing: sensitivity analysis

Decision trees
- used for more complicated scenarios
- may be given one to interpret

Standard deviations
- measures risk
- use tables to help determine probabilities

10 Practice questions

Test your understanding 1

A business is considering investing in a new product that will be impacted by whether the business can launch the product before rivals. Expected returns have been forecasted as follows:

	Launch before rivals	Launch after rivals
Total product profits	$20m	$2m

There is a 40% that the business will be able to launch the product before rivals.

The total expected profits from the product are $ 9.2 m (fill in the number to the nearest one decimal place)

Test your understanding 2

A company is considering investing in one of the following projects.

Project	Expected value	Standard deviation
	$000	$000
A	850	500
B	1,200	480
C	150	200
D	660	640

0.78
0.4
1.3
0.96

If the company wishes to select the project with the lowest risk factor (coefficient of variation) it select will select Project C (Enter the letter of the preferred project)

B ⇒ the lowest coefficient of variation, the lower the risk.

Test your understanding 3

PT has $8m of debt, on which it pays annual interest of 4%. The company's operating cash inflow in the coming year is forecast to be $600,000, and currently the company has $80,000 cash on deposit. The company has no other lines of credit available.

Required:

Given that the annual volatility (standard deviation) of the company's cash flows (measured over the last 5 years) has been 40%, the probability that Villa Co will default on its interest payment within the next year is _____% (fill in the number to the nearest 1 decimal place)

Test your understanding 4

An investor is an optimist in their attitude to uncertainty. The investor is considering making one of four possible investments, each of which is affected by whether the government provide financial assistance in the form of a grant. Details on the investments are as follows:

	Grant not awarded	Grant awarded
Probability	70%	30%
Investment A profits ($000)	40	90
Investment B profits ($000)	60	70
Investment C profits ($000)	20	140
Investment D profits ($000)	50	30

Which investment will the investor choose?

A   Investment A

B   Investment B

C   Investment C

D   Investment D

Test your understanding 5

A newspaper seller has prepared the following payoff table based on expected levels of demand each day and the number of newspapers purchased:

	Newspapers purchased			
	140	160	180	200
Probability	25%	25%	30%	20%
Demand				
140	$42	$28	$14	$0
160	$42	$48	$34	$20
180	$42	$48	$54	$40
200	$42	$48	$54	$60

Unsold newspapers are destroyed at the end of each day.

Using a maximin criteria, the number of newspapers that should be purchased each day is __140__

Test your understanding 6

A business has produced a profit table showing the profit earned depending on a combination of units produced and units demanded:

		Daily demand		
		2,000	3,000	4,000
	2,000	$40,000	$40,000	$40,000
Production	3,000	($40,000)	$60,000	$60,000
	4,000	($120,000)	($20,000)	$80,000

Minimax regret matrix

		Daily demand		
		2,000	3,000	4,000
	2,000	0	A	D
Production	3,000	B	0	A
	4,000	C	B	0

Match the values for A, B, C and D which should be used in the minimax regret table.

Position	Possibilities
A	$20,000
B	$40,000
C	$80,000
D	$160,000

Test your understanding 7

An organisation is making a decision on which of two products to launch. Future profit outcomes for each product will either be high or low.

It has created the following decision tree to summarise the problem:

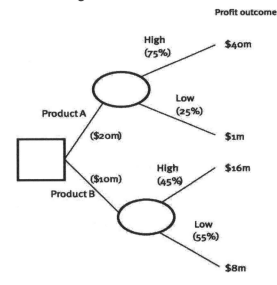

The expected value from the optimal decision is:

A $1.6m

(B) $10.25m

C $11.6m

D $30.25m

Test your understanding 8

An organisation is considering launching one of two new products and has created the following decision tree to represent its decision:

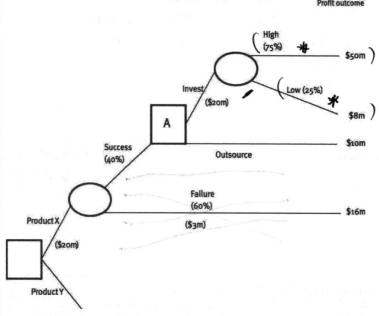

The maximum expected value of profit at decision point A is $ 19.5

Test your understanding 9

A company can make either of two new products, X and Y, but not both. The profitability of each product depends on the state of the market, as follows:

Market state	Profit from product		Probability of market state
	X $	Y $	
Good	20,000 4K	17,000 3.4K	0.2
Fair	15,000 7.5K	16,000 8K	0.5
Poor	6,000 1.8K	7,000 2.1K	0.3

13,30   13,50

7,400
15,500
3,900

The expected value of perfect information as to the state of the market is _____ 600 _____ (insert the correct figure)

Test your understanding 10

Scenario

The Venus Department Store operates a customer loan facility. If one of its new customers requests a loan then Venus either refuses it, gives a high loan limit, or gives a low loan limit. From a number of years past experience the probability that a new customer makes a full repayment of a loan is known to be 0.95, whilst the probability of non-repayment is 0.05 (these probabilities being independent of the size of loan limit). The average profit in $, per customer made by Venus is given by the following table.

	Loan Limit	
	High	**Low**
Full-repayment	50	20
Non-repayment	−200	−30

The junior accountant at the store has created a decision tree to summarise the store's position on providing credit to customers:

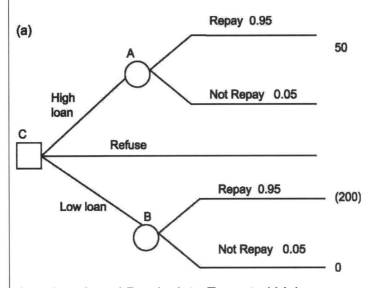

At points A and B calculate Expected Values:

At A   EV = (0.95 × 50) + (0.05 × (200))   = 37.5

At B   EV = (0.95 × 20) + (0.05 × (30))   = 17.5

Task:

Explain the decision tree to the store's management and recommend whether or not credit should be offered to customers.

(Time allowed: 10 minutes)

The junior accountant has also prepared the following information regarding the use of a credit agency who would assess customers before any decision was taken. Analysis of the last 1,000 customer ratings by this agency have been used in the construction of the following decision tree:

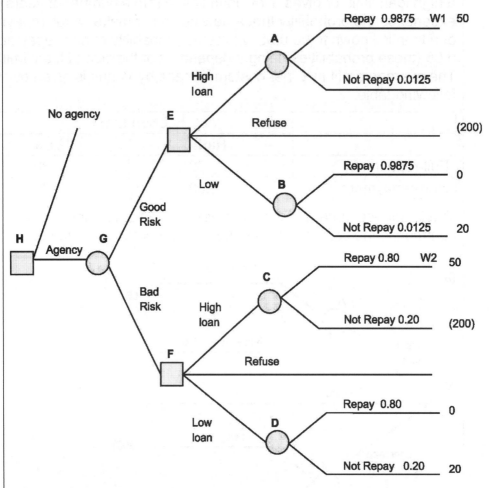

Workings:

(W1) A sample of 800 customers have been assessed by the agency as being a good risk. Of these 790 did repay the loan. This represents 98.75% (790 ÷ 800) of the good risk customers.

Hence, the remaining 1.25% of the good risk customers did not repay the loan. (10 ÷ 800).

(W2) In a similar way to (W1), 160 out of the 200 bad risk customers did repay the loan, i.e. 80%.

40 out of the 200 bad risk customers did not repay the loan, i.e. 20%.

Expected values

At A	(0.9875 × 50) + (0.0125 × (200))	=	$46.875
At B	(0.9875 × 20) + (0.0125 × (30))	=	$19.375
At C	(0.8 × 50) + (0.2 × (200))	=	0
At D	(0.8 × 20) + (0.2 × (30))	=	$10.00
At G	(0.8 × 46.875) + (0.2 × 10.00)	=	$39.50

Expected return with perfect information = $47.50

Tasks:

- Explain the difference between imperfect and perfect information.

- Explain how this applies to the department store's decision and recommend whether a credit agency should be used by the store.

(Time allowed: 20 minutes)

Test your understanding answers

Example 1

Outcome	Profit ($)	Probability	Profit x Probability ($)
A	100,000	0.10	10,000
B	70,000	0.40	28,000
C	50,000	0.30	15,000
D	(20,000)	0.20	(4,000)
Expected value			49,000

Expected profit is $49,000.

Example 2

(i)   EV of demand = $(10 \times 0.20) + (15 \times 0.55) + (20 \times 0.25) = 15.25$ units per week.

(ii) The first step is to set up a decision matrix of possible strategies (numbers bought) and possible demand, as follows:

Outcome (number demanded)	Strategy (number bought)		
	10	15	20
10			
15			
20			

The 'pay-off' from each combination of action and outcome is then computed:

No sale: cost of 15c per magazine.

Sale: profit of 25c – 15c = 10c per magazine.

Pay-offs are shown for each combination of strategy and outcome.

Probability	Outcome (number demanded)	Strategy (number bought)		
		10	15	20
0.20	10	100	25	(50)
0.55	15	100	150	75
0.25	20	100	150	200
1.00		100c	125c	81.25c

Conclusion: The strategy which gives the highest expected value is to stock 15 magazines each week.

Workings

(i) If 10 magazines are bought, then 10 are sold no matter how many are demanded and the payoff is always 10 × 10c = 100c.

(ii) If 15 magazines are bought and 10 are demanded, then 10 are sold at a profit of 10 × 10c = 100c, and 5 are scrapped at a loss of 5 × 15c = 75c, making a net profit of 25c.

(iii) The other contributions are similarly calculated.

Example 3

Using maximax, an optimist would consider the best possible outcome for each product and pick the product with the greatest potential.

Here C would be chosen with a maximum possible gain of 100.

Example 3 continued

- Using maximin, a pessimist would consider the poorest possible outcome for each product and would ensure that the maximum pay-off is achieved if the worst result were to happen.

- Therefore, product A would be chosen resulting in a minimum pay- off of 20 compared to a minimum pay-off of (10) for product B and 10 for product C.

Example 3 continued

In the pay-off matrix above, if the market state had been scenario I:

The correct decision would have been:	B (net income $80)
If A had been chosen instead:	The company would have been out of pocket by $60 (i.e. 80 – 20)
If C had been chosen:	It would have been out of pocket by $70 (i.e. 80 – 10)

- The opportunity loss associated with each product is: A = $60, B = $0, C = $70.

Scenario II and III can be considered in the same way and the results can be summarised in a regret table.

The completed opportunity loss ('regret') table is thus as follows.

State	Decision		
	A	**B**	**C**
I	60	0	70
II	60	30	0
III	0	60	10
Maximum regret	60	60	70

The maximum regret value for:

A = $60

B = $60

C = $70

The minimum value of these is $60, hence the minimax regret strategy would be either A or B.

B would probably be adopted because its second-highest regret outcome ($30) is lower than the second-highest for A ($60).

Example 3 continued

Firstly, we have to calculate the expected value without the information.

EV (A) = 0.2(20) + 0.5(40) + 0.3(50) = 39

EV (B) = 0.2(80) + 0.5(70) + 0.3(−10) = 48

EV (C) = 0.2(10) + 0.5(100) + 0.3(40) = 64

So the company would choose project C, with an expected pay-off of 64.

If the company had perfect information it would act as follows:

Scenario indicated by perfect information	Company's decision*	Pay-off
I	Invest in product B	80
II	Invest in product C	100
III	Invest in product A	50

* this will be based on the highest expected pay-off in that scenario. For example, if scenario I is predicted the company will face a pay-off of 20 from product A, 80 from product B, and 10 from product C. It will therefore decide to invest in product B.

The expected value from these decisions would be:

EV (C) = 0.2(80) + 0.5(100) + 0.3(50) = 81

This is 17 higher than the expected value (64) when the company had no information. Therefore the information has a value of 17.

Example 4

(a) Maximax:

A decision maker that uses the maximax criterion is an optimist because they will choose the option that maximises the maximum pay-off available out of all the various options available.

Because this decision is based on cost, this criterion will be to select the option which gives the lowest total cost for the chemical (as the lowest cost will lead to the highest profits).

Therefore, under this criterion, the lowest cost under each option would be:

Quantity 1 – $16,096

Quantity 2 – $18,288

Quantity 3 – $21,500

Robotrick would therefore choose to purchase Quantity 1, as this gives the lowest possible cost of $16,096.

(b) Maximin:

A decision maker that uses the maximin criterion is a pessimist because they will choose the option which maximises the minimum pay-off available – the best of the 'worse-case' scenarios.

Again, because this decision is based on cost, this criterion will be to select the option which gives the lowest of the highest costs under each option, in other words, the minimum of the maximum costs. The highest costs under each Option are as follows:

Quantity 1 – $22,720

Quantity 2 – $21,600

Quantity 3 – $22,176

Therefore, under this criterion, we would choose Quantity 2 because this gives the lowest of the maximum costs of $21,600.

(c) Minimax regret:

A decision maker that uses the minimax regret criterion is often referred to as a 'bad loser' because they are concerned about making the wrong decision. Regret represents the cost of getting the decision wrong. We therefore need to create a regret table:

	Options		
Expected demand	*Quantity 1*	*Quantity 2*	*Quantity 3*
Low	0	2,432	6,080
Medium	232	0	3,648
High	1,220	100	0

Regret workings for demand being 'Low':

If demand turns out to be low, then the 'right' decision would have been to purchase Quantity 1, as this gave the lowest cost (and hence results in the highest profit). The regret is therefore nil under Quantity 1. If Quantity 2 had been chosen, then the cost would have been $18,528. This is $2,432 ($18,528 – $16,096) more than the right decision. This is the regret under Quantity 2. Similarly, if Quantity 3 had been chosen, then the total cost would have been $22,176. This is $6,080 ($22,176 – $16,096) more than the right decision. This is the regret under Quantity 3.

Regret workings for demand being 'Medium':

We can calculate the regret for demand being 'Medium' in the same way. The 'right' decision with medium demand would be to purchase Quantity 2, as this results in the lowest of the three possible costs, at $18,288. The regret for Quantity 2 is therefore nil. If Quantity 1 had instead been purchased, then the total cost would have been $18,520 and regret would be $232 ($18,520 – $18,288). If Quantity 3 had been purchased then the regret would be $21,936 – $18,288 = $3,648.

Next we need to calculate the minimax regret. To do this, we look at the maximum regret under each scenario, and choose the option which minimises that maximum value. The maximum regrets are as follows:

Quantity 1 – $1,220

Quantity 2 – $2,432

Quantity 3 – $6,080

To minimise the maximum regret we would therefore choose Quantity 1.

Example 5

In this example we have two independent variables; the contribution and the rental cost. To work out the joint probabilities we have to multiply the probabilities together as can be seen in the table below:

Contribution $	Rent $	Profit/ (loss)	Joint probability	EV $
150,000	70,000	80,000	0.2 × 0.4 = 0.08	6,400
150,000	50,000	100,000	0.2 × 0.6 = 0.12	12,000
112,500	70,000	42,500	0.65 × 0.4 = 0.26	11,050
112,500	50,000	62,500	0.65 × 0.6 = 0.39	24,375
90,000	70,000	20,000	0.15 × 0.4 = 0.06	1,200
90,000	50,000	40,000	0.15 × 0.6 = 0.09	3,600
				———
				58,625

Note: always check that the total of the joint probabilities sums to 1.

Example 6

The situation can be summarised in a decision tree as follows:

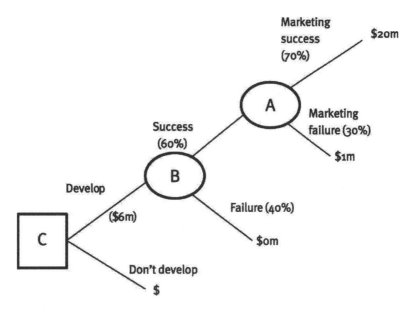

The expected value at point A = (0.7 × $20m) + (0.3 × $1m) = $14.3m

The expected value at point B = (0.6 × $14.3m) + (0.4 × $0k) = $8.58m

The value of the development (point C) = $8.58m – $6m = $2.58m

When compared to the $0 returns from not developing it is better to develop the product

The expected value of the development and marketing plan is **$2.58** m.

Example 7

Correct solution is Product A.

By simply looking at the two standard deviation figures, we might be tempted to say that Product A has the highest standard deviation and as such has the higher variability of returns and is the most risky. Therefore the company should invest in Product B.

However, as the expected value for Product A is higher than for Product B, then it stands to reason that the deviations from the mean and thus the standard deviation will tend to be higher. Therefore, to be able to make a like for like comparison, we need to calculate the coefficient of variation. This measures the relative size of the risk.

These will be as follows:

Product	Expected value of return per unit	Standard deviation	Coefficient of variation
A	$120	55	45.8%
B	$90	50	55.6%

This shows us that it is actually Product A which has the smaller coefficient of variation and is therefore less risky.

Example 8

The mean is $175,000. $168,000 is $7,000 away from the mean.

This represents $7k/$5k = 1.40 standard deviations. This is the z score.

From tables, on the left hand column, look up the z score to one decimal place, i.e. 1.4. Look along this row until it meets the column with the 2nd decimal place (0.00). The table gives us 0.4192. The normal distribution table used has a maximum value of 0.5. We want to determine the probability that sales are MORE than 1.4 standard deviations away from the mean and this is therefore calculated as 0.5 – 0.4192 = 0.0808. This can then be converted into a percentage by multiplying by 100 = 8.08%

Hence, the probability of sales being below $168,000 is 8.08% (approximately 8%).

Example 9

(a) The EV would have to decrease by $16,000 before the original decision is reversed, i.e. this is the break-even point.

– Let the loss be L

Currently, EV = (0.4 × L) + (0.6 × 40)

If EV falls to zero:

EV of 0 = (0.4 × L) + (0.6 × 40)

0 = 0.4L + 24

– 24 = 0.4L

– 24/0.4 = L

L = – 60

– The loss would have to increase from $20,000 to $60,000 before the decision is reversed. This is a 200% increase in the loss.

(b) The EV would have to decrease by $16,000 before the original decision is reversed, i.e. this is the break-even point.

- Let the probability of a loss be P and the probability of a profit be 1 – P.

Currently, EV = (P × –20) + (1 – p × 40)

If EV falls to zero:

EV of 0 = (P × –20) + (1 – p × 40)

0 = –20P + 40 –40P

60P = 40

P = 40/60

P = 0.67

- The probability of a loss would have to increase to 0.67 from 0.4 before the decision is reversed.

Test your understanding 1

$9.2m

If there is a 40% chance of launching before rivals there must be a 60% chance of launching after rivals.

The overall expected value = ($20m × 0.4) + ($2m × 0.6) = $9.2m

Test your understanding 2

If the company wishes to select the project with the lowest risk factor (coefficient of variation) it select will select Project **B**

Project	Expected value	Standard deviation	Coefficient Of variation
	$000	$000	
A	850	500	0.59
B	1,200	480	0.40
C	150	200	1.33
D	660	640	0.97

Test your understanding 3

PT will have expected cash of $600,000 + $80,000 = $680,000. It has an interest commitment (outgoing) of $320,000 (= 4% on $8m). If receipts fall by $360,000 ($680,000 – $320,000) the organisation will default on its interest commitment. So we need to calculate the probability that the cash available will fall by $360,000 over the next year.

Assuming that the annual cash flow is normally distributed, a volatility (standard deviation) of 40% on a cash flow of $600,000 represents a standard deviation of 0.40 × $600,000 = $240,000. Thus, our fall of $360,000 represents 360,000/240,000 = 1.50 standard deviations.

From the normal distribution tables, the area between the mean and 1.50 standard deviations = 0.4332. Hence, there must be a 0.5 – 0.4332 = 0.0668 chance of the cashflow being insufficient to meet the interest payment i.e. the probability of default is approximately **6.7**%.

Test your understanding 4

C

If the investor is an optimist it is likely to follow a maximax strategy. This aims to give the best result in the best case scenario (in the case, the best case scenario is that the grant is awarded). The best result for the investor in that scenario will be to have gone for Investment C which gives the highest pay out from all the possible outcomes available.

Test your understanding 5

140

The maximin criteria chooses this best possible return in the worst possible outcome. The worst possible outcome in this scenario is that demand is only for 140 newspapers per day, in which case it would provide the highest returns if only 140 newspapers were purchased each day.

Test your understanding 6

Position		Value
A		$20,000
B		$80,000
C		$160,000
D		$40,000

A regret table shows the shortfall from the maximum contribution that could be earned at each demand level

The completed regret table is as follows:

Daily demand

		2,000	3,000	4,000
	2,000	0	$20,000	$40,000
Production	3,000	$80,000	0	$20,000
	4,000	$160,000	$80,000	0

Test your understanding 7

The expected value from each product is:

Product A: ($40m × 0.75) + ($1m × 0.25) – $20m = $10.25m

Product B: ($16m × 0.45) + ($8m × 0.55) – $10m = $1.6m

So Product A would be selected, and the expected value would be $10.25m (**Option B**).

Test your understanding 8

Decision point A appears to represent a decision between the following two outcomes

		Value
Outsource		$10m
Invest	($50m × 0.75) + ($8m × 0.25) – $20m	$19.5m

The option to invest would appear to be the optimal decision at point A as it has the highest expected value.

The maximum expected value of profit at decision point A is **$19.5m**

Test your understanding 9

Without information, the expected profits are:

Product X: $20,000 × 0.2 + $15,000 × 0.5 + $6,000 × 0.3 = $13,300

Product Y: $17,000 × 0.2 + $16,000 × 0.5 + $7,000 × 0.3 = $13,500

So without information, product Y would be selected.

With perfect information, product X would be selected if the market was good, and product Y in the other two cases. The expected value would then be:

$20,000 × 0.2 + $16,000 × 0.5 + $7,000 × 0.3 = $14,100

The expected value of perfect information is therefore $14,100 – $13,500

= **$600**

Test your understanding 10

First decision tree

The decision tree provides information on the three possible decisions available to the business:

- the upper most line shows the returns from offering customers a high loan limit. It shows that there is a 95% chance of repayment and a respective return of $50. There is also a 5% chance of default with a loss of $200. The expected value calculated at point A illustrates that this would have an average overall value to the business of $37.50.

- the lowest line provides similar information on the returns from offering a low loan limit. The expected value at point B shows that this would have an average overall value to the business of $17.50.

- the middle line shows that if a loan limit is refused to the customer then the expected return is $0.

The three values can be compared at point C and the highest expected return ($37.50) comes from offering customers a high loan limit. This therefore instructs the store as to its optimal decision policy – if a new customer asks for credit, he/she should be offered a high loan limit.

Second decision tree

There are two types of information presented in the junior accountant's analysis:

Perfect information This assumes that the credit agency's prediction on whether a customer is a good or bad risk is always 100% accurate. In reality, this is unlikely to be achievable.

Imperfect information This recognises that the credit agency will not always get their prediction correct. Sometimes good risk customers will be classed as bad risk customers (and vice versa). This becomes a more complex problem and the decision tree summarises the information used to come to a decision on the value of this information.

- The uppermost line shows the decision making process if the credit agency indicates that a new customer will be a good credit risk (i.e. they are more than likely to repay the loan). This takes the store to decision point E where it must decide between offering a high loan limit (the expected value (EV) shows at point A that this would generate an average profit of $46.875), refusing credit (the EV is $0) and offering a low loan limit (EV = $19.375). So at point E, the best decision would be to offer a high loan limit if the agency indicates that the new customer is a good credit risk and this would have an EV of $46.875.

- The line stretching towards decision point F illustrates a similar analysis would take place if the agency indicated that the new customer was a bad credit risk. The optimal policy would be to follow along path D where the EV is $10. So if the agency indicates a bad credit risk for a new customer a low credit loan should be offered with an EV of $10.

- To bring all of this analysis together, points E and F are then compared at point G. This takes account of the probability of the agency indicating either good risk or bad risk and builds in the presence of imperfect information. The EV at point G ($39.50) indicates the overall profit to the business in the presence of this imperfect information

The business is therefore left with three important pieces of information:

- in the absence of any information, the store can expect to make a profit of $37.50

- in the presence of imperfect information from the agency, the store can expect to make a profit of $39.50

- if perfect information could be achieved, the store can expect to make a profit of $47.50.

So the value of the information has a maximum value of $10 ($47.50 – $37.50). The value of the agency's information is $2 ($39.50 – $37.50). The store should therefore use the credit scoring agency provided that they charge less than $2 for each credit assessment.

647

Applying knowledge to case study questions

Chapter learning objectives

To understand how to apply technical P1 areas to the relevant Operational Case Study tasks

1 Understanding the Operational Case Study

1.1 Overview

The case study combines the content covered in all three pillar subjects (P1, E1 and F1) into a single assessment. Its aim is the "undoing" of the pillar and subject divisions of the syllabus and the application of knowledge, skills and techniques to the type of problems that you might encounter in the workplace in a role matched to the appropriate level of the qualification.

Examination tasks will be practical and applied, not theoretical or academic. To be successful, you will have to perform these core activities in the same way and to the same standards that would be valid and valued in the workplace.

You will not be expected (and no marks are available) to perform any calculations. All Marks are for explaining / using / applying knowledge to the case study context. However, wherever relevant you can use the numbers to explain ideas – i.e. you will not be penalised for using the numbers and often using the numbers make an explanation easier and clearer.

1.2 Core Activities

In some respects one could argue that everything covered in E1, F1 and P1 was still relevant for the Case Study Examination. However, to make the task more accessible and clear, the blueprint defines the following core activities:

	Core Activity	Weighting
A	Prepare costing information for different purposes to meet the needs of management.	12–18%
B	Prepare budget information and assess its use for planning and control purposes.	17–25%
C	Analyse performance using financial and non-financial information.	17–25%
D	Apply relevant financial reporting standards and corporate governance, ethical and tax principles.	12–18%
E	Prepare information to support short-term decision-making.	17–25%
F	Prepare information to manage working capital.	7–13%

It should be evident from this that P1 topics are a significant driver of core activities A, B, C and E. The overall weighting of P1 subjects has increased in the 2019 syllabus. A strong understanding of P1 is thus vital for passing the Operational Case Study!

All core activities will be assessed in each form of the examination in line with these weightings.

1.3 Assessment Outcomes

Assessment outcomes translate core activities into a range of "I can" statements. The full list is as follows, with P1 tasks highlighted:

	Core Activities	Assessment outcomes
A	Prepare costing information for different purposes to meet the needs of management.	I can use appropriate technologies to gather data for costing purposes, from digital and other sources.
		I can apply different costing methods to produce costing information suitable for managers' needs.
		I can explain costing information to operational and senior management using appropriate formats and media.
		I can compare different costing methods and systems to determine the most suitable for use by the organisation for different purposes.
		I can identify the cost information required for digital cost objects.
B	Prepare budget information and assess its use for planning and control purposes.	I can use appropriate technologies to gather data from digital and other sources to co-ordinate budget preparation.
		I can explain and use different forecasting methods to assist in budget preparation.
		I can use different approaches to produce information for use by managers when preparing budgets.
		I can explain budget information to managers using appropriate formats and media.
		I can apply various techniques to determine the effect on budgets of changes to variables.
		I can explain to functional managers how budgets are used for planning and control purposes.
		I can discuss the behavioural implications of budgetary planning and control.
		I can compare alternative approaches to budgeting to determine their suitability for the organisation and for different purposes.

C	Analyse performance using financial and non-financial information.	I can identify information that can enable managers to review performance. **I can interpret variances to review functional and organisational performance.** I can identify appropriate KPIs for different functions of the organisation. I can explain company performance using KPIs. **I can prepare performance reports for use by different functions and for different purposes in appropriate formats and media.**
D	Apply relevant financial reporting standards and corporate governance, ethical and tax principles.	I can apply relevant IFRS in a given context, to facilitate the preparation of financial statements. I can apply the principles of corporate governance and ethics. I can identify the impact of tax regulation on transactions, decisions and profits.
E	Prepare information to support short-term decision-making.	**I can identify relevant costs and benefits.** **I can apply appropriate techniques that support short-term decision-making.** **I can prepare information to support operational decisions.** **I can explain factors that could influence short-term decisions.** **I can apply appropriate techniques to deal with situations where there is risk and uncertainty.**
F	Prepare information to manage working capital.	I can identify appropriate sources of short-term finance and methods of short-term investments. I can explain how to manage and control working capital. I can explain working capital ratios in comparison to prior periods or to other organisations. I can identify the impact of changing working capital policies.

2 Examples from previous cases

2.1 Introduction

As stated above P1 forms a critical part of the Operational level integrated Case Study. There are many skills which you must exhibit in the operational case study (OCS) such as presentation. The examiner's report from the May 17 exam, for example, stated:

> "It was pleasing to see that the majority of answers were well structured with headings and clearly spaced paragraphs. Whilst there are not specific marks for formatting, there are a number of advantages to setting out answers in this way, not least that it helps the marker to identify the points that are being made. In addition, having a clear structure should help candidates to ensure that they have addressed all the points that they want to. There were a few scripts where candidates wrote a plan and then wrote their answer out in full underneath, repeating what they had in the plan. Given that this exam is typed, this sort of approach wastes time, although it is good to see that planning is happening!"

This chapter will however focus on another key skill: the application of your P1 knowledge. The examiners regularly state that this can be a key differentiator between pass and fail in the OCS. The examiner's report from the May 17 exam, for example, stated:

> "As is consistent with other exam sessions, .. applying knowledge from P1 … to demonstrate technical skills appeared to be … challenging."

This section will use the May 17 exam to illustrate how this skill can be exhibited in exam answers.

2.2 Pre-seen material

The exam is based on:

- pre-seen material issued in advance of the exam day, supplemented by

- additional, previously unseen material given to you in the exam room.

From the May 2020 sitting onwards, one pre-seen will be used over two exam windows, giving candidates the opportunity to resit using the same pre-seen. The pre-seen will be shared as follows:

- May / August

- November / February

CIMA releases the pre-seen material approximately seven weeks before the first examination. This is posted on the student area of the CIMA website (www.cimaglobal.com) and it is your responsibility to download it and to print off a copy.

The pre-seen material is an introductory scenario to set the scene for the case study, together with accounting and financial information, and is usually around twenty pages long, consisting of approximately ten exhibits giving information about a business organisation.

The May 17 OCS provided students with pre-seen material regarding a company called Ashworth Lea ("Ashworth"), which makes and sells high quality luxury sports cars. Some of the key details about the company follow:

- The company is based in the country of Mayland and has shareholders as follows: the founding families 40%, DOM 15%, INV group 45%.

- Ashworth sells via over 100 dealership locations in over 40 countries around the world. It is felt that the brand sells itself, so marketing focusses on customer satisfaction and repeat purchases.

- 30 years ago the business nearly failed and was saved by DOM, who took a 60% stake (since reduced to 15%), invested in new production facilities, new designs, new engines and marketing.

- In many respects Ashworth Lea is facing a similar challenge today – sales of the Regent model are disappointing, the company is barely profitable and new investment is required to meet major changes in the industry.

- In particular, customers are becoming less brand-loyal and want more advanced technological features as standard. There is an industry-wide drive towards 'connected cars' and 'intelligent cars' and increasing pressure to improve fuel economy and reduce the environmental impact of cars, such as through the use of alternative fuel systems and electric cars.

- Against such challenges, Ashworth Lea has not significantly changed either its production methods or supply chain for many years. On the positive side, DOM is committed to supporting the development of self-drive vehicles and Ashworth Lea has a new model being released in 2017.

- Similarly the INV group is keen to see change, is helping support the self-driving cars and is looking to develop an electric car based on hydrogen fuel cell technology.

- Richard Ashworth, the recently appointed Managing Director will thus be under pressure to rectify any complacency, initiate change and try to ensure that the company is ready to face the considerable risks and uncertainty in the industry.

Now let's look at some of the key skills required in order to score well in the case study exam.

To do this we examine tasks that were set for students – focusing on the P1 elements and how these required the application of your P1 knowledge.

2.3 Focusing on the requirement

Scenario

Task 3 of Variant 3 of the case study exam (there are 3 variants in total, each with 4 tasks broken down into a number of sub-tasks) focused on a discussion of budgets based on forecasts.

Students were presented with a brief scenario whereby:

- Ashworth were planning to introduce a fleet management service for some large customers.

- This would involve providing vehicles, insuring them, maintaining them and selling them again in the future.

- This new service would require an IT system.

- A budget was required for the new service and the finance director suggested that a zero based budget would be the best approach to do this.

The task

The requirement asked students to explain how a zero based budgeting approach could be used to prepare a new budget for the service.

In the real exam you will told how to split your time between sub-tasks, effectively telling you how many marks each element is worth. In total there were 8 marks for this requirement.

The suggested approach

There will always be some marks for knowledge in the exam and you should therefore start by briefly explaining what zero based budgeting (ZBB) is.

"Using ZBB, every activity has to be justified (in comparison to incremental budgeting where the figures from last year are used as a base). ZBB is applicable for discretionary costs, where any expenditure or the amount of the expenditure is at the discretion of management."

However, it is vital that you make this answer relevant to the case scenario that you are considering. The easiest way to do this is to consider whether your definition is met in this situation. The next sentence could be:

"In the case of the new fleet management service there is clearly discretion over how much we spend although this will be partly determined by the contractual agreements with the customers."

It is then important to focus on the requirement and what has been asked by the examiner. The examiner has, for example, not asked whether ZBB is a good or bad idea or how it differs from other budgeting systems. Therefore the following approaches would not score marks:

- Explaining the benefits of ZBB

- Explaining the problems of ZBB

- Comparing ZBB to other budgeting approaches

- Advantages and disadvantages of other budgeting approaches

Taking any of these approaches would illustrate more of your knowledge but would show little application to the question that you have been asked. Unfortunately, many students adopted some or all of these approaches, but none of these would have scored any credit.

The question here is about HOW zero based budgeting would be used. You therefore need to explain:

- the steps that would be needed to create a ZBB

- how these steps would apply in Ashworth

So, for example, the official answer suggests that the first step is to determine what activities need to be performed:

> "The new manager will need to determine which activities need to be undertaken. The manager will need to consider what services we have agreed to provide to each customer and the activities that will need to be undertaken to provide the service. He will also need to estimate how much of the activity should be done. The level of each activity will depend on the projected volume both in terms of number of customers and number of vehicles. The standard of service to be provided will also need to be considered. For example, when maintaining the vehicles will we also provide a valet service?"

Notice the use of words such as services, vehicles, customers etc. This makes the answer much more relevant to the scenario and will be the best approach to maximising your marks.

 Official answer to the task

Zero based budgeting (ZBB) for fleet management service

Using ZBB, every activity has to be justified (in comparison to incremental budgeting where the figures from last year are used as a base). ZBB is applicable for discretionary costs, where any expenditure or the amount of the expenditure is at the discretion of management.

In the case of the new fleet management service there is clearly discretion over how much we spend although this will be partly determined by the contractual agreements with the customers.

The new manager will need to determine which activities need to be undertaken. The manager will need to consider what services we have agreed to provide to each customer and the activities that will need to be undertaken to provide the service. He will also need to estimate how much of the activity should be done. The level of each activity will depend on the projected volume both in terms of number of customers and number of vehicles. The standard of service to be provided will also need to be considered. For example, when maintaining the vehicles will we also provide a valet service?

The manager should determine a base package (which would be a minimum spend). The base package would be considered essential. He would need to determine what the base package can achieve and how the benefits can be measured and evaluated.

The next step is to prepare a number of alternative decision packages. He will need to consider how each activity should be done and how much each alternative would cost. ZBB encourages managers to consider different ways of achieving the same objectives. It will also be important to consider whether the additional costs can be passed on to the customer and the potential benefits in terms of reputation and customer loyalty.

The evaluated packages would then be presented to the budget committee for a final decision about how we will actually operate the new service.

In making this decision, the budget committee will take a wider view over the whole organisation. This will include resource constraints (not the least of which will be cash) and the conflicting calls upon these constrained resources. The budget committee would review each of the decision packages and decide the resources that should be allocated to the fleet management service depending on the combination of activities that are approved.

ZBB can result in significant cost savings, as all activities and costs are budgeted from scratch.

© Copyright CIMA – 2015 CIMA Professional Qualification Operational Level P1 Management Accounting Case Study Exam May 2017

2.4 Applying knowledge to the scenario

Scenario

Task 3 of Variant 2 of the case study exam required students to discuss time series analysis.

Students were presented with a brief scenario whereby:

- Ashworth would launch a new small car model, the Cub
- It would sell for M$60,000
- Initially, it would only be sold in Mayland

Students were also presented with some published market statistics as follows

New car registrations in Mayland

Segment	2014	2015	2016
Small compact	80,377	84,237	70,263
Compact	813,092	884,892	926,241
Lower medium	588,402	647,438	715,604
Upper medium	208,462	228,656	249,347
Executive	119,745	120,147	127,666
Luxury	8,346	9,766	9,061
Specialist sport	47,544	42,817	49,118
Dual purpose	248,003	292,347	355,118
MPV	150,766	166,135	131,085
Total	2,264,737	2,476,435	2,633,503

The task

The first part of the requirement asked students to explain how Ashworth could apply time series analysis to the figures in the schedule, to forecast sales of the Cub for each quarter of the first year stating what other information we would require to carry out the analysis.

The suggested approach

There will be a small amount of marks for explaining what time series analysis is.

However, the majority of marks here are for examining the data provided and explaining whether or not this would be useful to Ashworth in attempting to employ time series analysis. This does not mean brining in general problems from the text concerning the use of time series analysis.

Instead you need to highlight specific, relevant points from the data provided such as:

- It only has three years' worth of data

- It isn't broken down by quarter

- There is no way to calculate seasonality from the data provided (Note: remember that you would not be expected to do the calculations, even if it were possible)

There may be problems in using this method over and above the limitations in the data provided in that it may be difficult to determine where the Cub fits within the table ('small compact' or 'compact') and Ashworth has no internal data to rely on.

Notice how these issues are not derived from the text. Instead they come from the scenario. This illustrates what the examiner means when explaining to students that they need to APPLY knowledge from P1 in order to illustrate their technical skills.

It is best to:

- use examples from the scenario and knowledge of the pre-seen to support your answer,

- give examples that are relevant to the business you are discussing

- think about implications for this type of business

- use the scenario and related data rather than rely on just your study text

- make your knowledge relevant to the scenario rather than simply regurgitate it.

What not to do

As with the previous example on ZBB, this questions should not be seen an as opportunity for you to tell the examiner everything you know about time series analysis. Therefore, you will not score marks for covering areas such as:

- the limitations of time series analysis

- the benefits of time series analysis

- comparing time series analysis to other forecasting methods

Official answer to the task

Time series analysis

A time series is a series of figures recorded over a period of time. In this case, we have new car registrations in Mayland over the past three years.

'Time series analysis' is a term used to describe techniques for analysing the time series to determine whether there is any underlying historical trend and if there is, to use this analysis to forecast the trend into the future.

As this is a completely new market that we are entering and have no company historic data, the use of industry statistics would an appropriate substitute.

We can also identify whether there are any seasonal variations around the trend and if there are, we can measure the seasonal variation and apply these to a trend line forecast in order to forecast season by season. We would need to access more detailed statistics that break the annual registrations down into monthly or quarterly registrations. Again, it is unlikely that the information we have available on monthly sales of our current models would be useful as the markets are so dissimilar.

To apply time series analysis to the figures given, we need to firstly classify the Cub into one of the segments. It is most likely to fall into the segment of either a 'small compact' car or a 'compact' car. We can compare our small car with the cars models within each of the segments and then decide which segment is the best category for our small car.

Once we have established the segment we then need to identify the trend line for that segment. This can be done either through inspection (where the trend line is drawn by eye), using least squares regression analysis or using moving averages.

We then need to establish any cyclical variations which are medium term or long term influences usually associated with the economy. In order to do this, we would need data going back a few more years than the three years we have available.

If we were able to obtain data split between quarters or months we could use this to calculate the seasonal variations. Seasonal variations can be estimated by comparing an actual time series with the trend line calculated from the time series. For each 'season' the seasonal variation is the difference between the trend line value and the actual historical value for the same period. The seasonal variations can be used to forecast future sales by adding or subtracting it from the trend line forecast.

Using the trend line and the seasonal variations we can forecast the sales in units for the industry for the following year. We would then have to decide what percentage market share we would expect the Cub to capture and apply this percentage to our figures for the total market.

© Copyright CIMA – 2015 CIMA Professional Qualification Operational Level P1 Management Accounting Case Study Exam May 2017

2.5 Full syllabus coverage

It is important to recognise that the case study can examine every part of the P1 syllabus.

Scenario

Task 3 of Variant 2 of the case study exam (discussed in the previous section) also required students to discuss sensitivity analysis.

The task

- Explain how sensitivity analysis could be applied

- Give its advantages and limitations

- Explain how it could be improved by using probabilities

The suggested approach

Sensitivity analysis does not appear to be a large part of chapter 11. But this question illustrates that the exam team can choose any part of the syllabus and make it part of the OCS. You therefore need to avoid question spotting and ensure that you have fully covered the syllabus in order to be best prepared for the OCS.

The examiner's comments stated:

> "In the second element of this task, it was obvious that most candidates had not studied sensitivity analysis in preparation for this exam. Marks were often not awarded because answers were irrelevant or simply wrong. It was noted by the marking team that a lack of knowledge of the subject did not deter candidates from writing reams. Future candidates should note that even the most confidently stated, illustrated and fully explained points will be awarded no marks if they are not factually correct or pertinent to the question asked."

You then must apply the other techniques that we have illustrated in this chapter such as ensuring you focus on the question asked, covering all aspects of the requirement, making your answer relevant etc.

 Official answer to the task

Sensitivity analysis

Sensitivity analysis involves revising the budget on the basis of a series of varied assumptions. One assumption can be changed at a time to determine the impact on the budget overall. In this case, we can change our assumptions about the volume of sales of the Cub to determine the impact on the budgeted profit and cash flow. We will also be able to determine by how much our estimate of sales volume can change before we make a loss. Alternatively, we could look at the impact on profit of changing the selling price of the Cub.

Advantages and limitations of sensitivity analysis

Sensitivity analysis provides us with more information about the sensitivities of the project for the new car and allows us to make a decision about whether we are prepared to accept the risks involved. It will also allow us to decide whether it is worth spending time and money on further investigation of the market for the small car. We may decide, for example, that it would be worthwhile paying to obtain more detailed statistical information or market intelligence on the market segment for 'small compact' or 'compact' cars. We can also make contingency plans for the eventuality that the sales volume turns out to be much lower than expected.

> Sensitivity analysis, however, is limited as it assumes that changes to variables can be made independently however many variables are interdependent; for example, the sales volume of the Cub is likely to be very dependent on the selling price set for the Cub.
>
> We can establish from the analysis how far the sales volume needs to change before we make a loss but it does not tell us the probability of that change happening. We could apply probabilities for different sales volumes and then calculate an expected value for the sales volume and profit. However, the accuracy of the probabilities will be limited by our knowledge of what is a new market for us.
>
> Alternatively, we could determine the budget using the estimated volumes as the 'expected' case but also produce a 'worst-case' budget and a 'best-case' budget. This will give us a range of possible outcomes and allow us to make decisions accordingly.
>
> © Copyright CIMA – 2015 CIMA Professional Qualification Operational Level P1 Management Accounting Case Study Exam May 2017

2.6 Explaining graphs

Scenario

Task 4 of Variant 2 of the case study exam gave students a linear programming graph to discuss.

Students had to explain the optimal production plan in a choice between two models (products), the Regal and the Royale. Students were also given:

- Information on three constraining resources – including usage for each of two products and overall total availability

- Maximum demand for the two products under consideration

The task

The requirement asked students to

- Explain the axes, lines, points and areas in the graph

- Explain how the graph could be used to help make decisions

The suggested approach

Start by explaining the elements of the graph:

- There were nine lines on the graph – each donated by a separate letter. This would provide you with 9 items to explain.

- The data provided could be used to determine which constraint line was which

- The feasible area was shaded

- Only one point on the feasible region was indicated – this must have been the optimal production point

- Axes and other lines should have been easy to explain, but it was important to not forget to do this part of the requirement

Then explain what the graph tells us and how it can be useful:

- Explain what the optimal point means and where it is

- Consider whether this position is a good idea (what other factors might come into play)

- Briefly consider the problems in using such graphs

This question concerned linear programming but other graphs such as profit-volume charts have been examined in the past. You should still apply the same approach – start by explaining what the points/lines etc. are on the graph, then examine the usefulness of the graph itself.

Official answer to the task

Linear programming graph

X represents the quantity of model Regal to be produced and sold

Y represents the quantity of model Royale to be produced and sold

Line A – represents the machine hour constraint

Line B – represents the labour hour constraint

Line C – represents the special component constraint

Line D & E – represents the ISO – contribution line

Line F – represents the demand for the Regal model

Line G – represents the demand for the Royale model

Point H – represents the point at which profit will be maximised

Area J – represents the feasible area i.e. the area containing all the possible solutions that satisfy all the constraints

Identifying the profit-maximising production plan and other factors to be considered

From the graph, we can see that at Point H, the binding constraints are machine hours and labour hours. Area J is the feasible region and the ISO- contribution line indicates that the further point within this area is Point H and this is the point that will maximise contribution. The production plan can be read from the graph as 2,000 units of X and 1,200 units of Y.

The optimum production plan given by the graph may not be the most appropriate solution. The graph is based on Stephen's recommendation to produce the two newer models and produce none of the older model. This may not be a good decision; it may be appropriate to produce a small number of all three models. Our dealers and end customers may feel that a choice of only two models is restrictive.

Whilst the graph shows us the maximum contribution based on the supply of only two models, it may not be the overall profit maximising production mix. The graphical method only allows two products to be considered. If we wanted to include all three specialist car models and the new small car model, we would need to use the simplex method.

The production capacity required for the Cub is uncertain and dependent on our estimates of demand. The estimate of demand for the Regal model is also important since, although it is not a binding constraint, a variation from the estimate of more than 300 units will result in the production plan no longer being optimal.

© Copyright CIMA – 2015 CIMA Professional Qualification Operational Level P1 Management Accounting Case Study Exam May 2017

These sections have aimed at illustrating how to apply your P1 knowledge in the OCS. Be aware, however, that many other skills are needed in order to score well in any case study exam (such as time management, writing skills and planning skills). These are explored in more detail in official material aimed at preparing you for the OCS.

2.7 Other sample tasks

The following TYU's contain some other tasks that were covered in the May 17 OCS which are relevant to P1 areas. These are not the only tasks that covered P1 areas, but they should give you further evidence of the nature of the tasks in the case study. You could attempt these tasks for yourself – but be aware that we have only provided a limited amount of pre-seen material so there may be occasions when the official answer refers to material that is not presented in this chapter.

Test your understanding 1

Activity based costing – Variant 5, Task 2

Scenario

Students were presented with a brief scenario whereby:

- Ashworth had now been acquired by a larger group, the Naas Motor Company Group

- Naas used activity based costing in its systems

- Naas had asked Ashworth to consider employing an activity based costing system

- An existing department was to be used as an example – the paint shop

- This department currently employs a direct labour absorption rate

- A table of activities and drivers for the department were given as follows:

Activity	Description of activity
Cleansing	The vehicle bodies have be pre-treated before the paint can be applied. One part of the pre-treatment is cleansing which is intended to remove contaminants, which may have been in the body shop, from the product. This is performed over a series of water and cleansing solution rinses. Each of the vehicles receives the same number of rinses
Sealing	Prior to the coating of the vehicle body with primers and paint, the seams of the body are sealed to protect against weather effects on the body. A sealant compound is applied along the length of each seam on the car's body. The sealant is then baked onto the seam.
Cavity wax application	To proof the vehicles as much as possible against corrosion – a water-borne, cold-applied, cavity wax is injected into body sections and panel inners of the vehicles. Infra-red lights heat the bonnet, boot lid or hatch to warm the cold wax to encourage it to flow into corners and points where water might go

The task

- Explain how Ashworth could use ABC

- Provide suggestions and explanations for appropriate cost drivers for each of the activities in the schedule

Test your understanding 2

Attitudes to risk – Variant 5, Task 4

Scenario

Students were presented with a brief scenario whereby:

- Ashworth was considering 3 marketing packages

- The results of each were impacted by customer reactions

- Contribution from each was given based on whether customer reaction was strong moderate or weak as follows:

	Marketing package		
	Package A	Package B	Package C
Customer reaction:			
Strong	M$450,000	M$400,000	M$425,000
Moderate	M$350,000	M$340,000	M$360,000
Weak	M$275,000	M$300,000	M$250,000

© Copyright CIMA – 2015 CIMA Professional Qualification Operational Level P1 Management Accounting Case Study Exam May 2017

The task

The requirement had 2 parts:

- An explanation of three decision criteria used under conditions of uncertainty and how these would be used to select a matching package

- How Ashworth could use probabilities to improve the decision making process and what are the limitations of the expected value approach to decision making.

Test your understanding 3

Variance analysis – Variant 4, Task 4

Scenario

Students were presented with a variance report for self-drive cars for the first quarter of the year:

	M$	M$
Budgeted contribution		300,000
Sales volume contribution planning variance	60,000 A	
Sales volume contribution operational variance	90,000 A	
Standard contribution on actual sales volume		150,000
Planning variances:		
Material price variance	23,000 A	
Revised standard contribution		127,000
Operational variances:		
Sales price variance	30,000 A	
Material usage variance	15,000 F	
Labour efficiency variance	18,000 F	
Actual contribution		130,000

Some additional information was provided:

- The finance director was concerned by the performance shown in the variance report

- Ashworth's new competitor was due to release a new self-drive model in November 2016 – this wasn't accounted for in the budget

- The operations and production director made a change to the standard specification which impacted on material costs as higher quality materials were used – this wasn't accounted for in the original budget

- There were problems in the public perception of the cars following a fatal car crash in early February which arose as a result of quality failures with the vehicle

The task

Produce a report explaining each of the variances, giving suggested reasons why they may have arisen.

Test your understanding answers

Test your understanding 1

Activity based costing

In order to apply activity-based costing (ABC) to our products we would need to identify the activities that are carried out within the company. In each of our operational areas there will be a number of activities carried out. The activities chosen should be at a reasonable level of aggregation based on cost versus benefit. For example, rather than identifying the paint shop as a single activity we have disaggregated it into a number of separate activities which have different cost drivers.

After the activities have been established, the cost of resources consumed over a period must be assigned to each activity in a separate 'cost pool'.

In order to assign the activity costs to a product, the cost drivers that cause a change to the cost of activities are identified. For example in the paint shop operation the cost drivers could be as follows:

Cleansing:

The cost driver could be number of vehicles. As each of the vehicles receive the same number of rinses, the cost of the activity will depend on the number of vehicles. The higher the number of vehicles the more water, energy and cleansing solution will be used.

Sealing:

The cost driver could be the length of seams (in metres). The length of seams on the vehicles will determine the amount of sealant used and therefore the amount of time spent in the process applying and 'baking' the sealant.

Cavity wax application:

The cost driver could be litres of cavity wax applied. The size of the vehicle will determine the quantity of cavity wax that will be applied and therefore the time taken to heat the wax and ensure it flows into the cavities.

The final stage is to apply the cost drivers to the product. A pre-determined cost driver rate is calculated based on the total costs of the activity and the total number of cost drivers for the period. The activity costs would then be charged to the product groups dependent on their usage of the cost drivers.

© Copyright CIMA – 2015 CIMA Professional Qualification Operational Level P1 Management Accounting Case Study Exam May 2017

Test your understanding 2

Maximax criterion

The maximax criterion is where the decision maker takes an optimistic approach. In this approach, the alternative that maximises the maximum pay-off achievable under each alternative will be selected.

The maximum pay-off under each alternative is as follows:

If we choose Package A = M$450,000

If we choose Package B = M$400,000

If we choose Package C = M$425,000

We would therefore choose Package A.

Maximin criterion

Under the maximin criteria we would select the alternative that maximises the minimum pay-off achievable under each alternative. This is where a pessimistic approach is taken.

The minimum pay-offs are as follows:

If we choose Package A = M$275,000

If we choose Package B = M$300,000

If we choose Package C = M$250,000

We would therefore choose Package B

Minimax regret criterion

Under this criterion the alternative that minimises the maximum regret under each alternative is selected. This is generally used where we want to avoid making a bad decision. 'Regret' refers to the opportunity loss through having made the wrong decision. This is also where a pessimistic approach is taken to the decision.

We can produce a regret matrix which shows the regret depending on the customer reaction to the product and which marketing package we choose. For example, if the customer reaction is strong we would have no regret if we had chosen Package A. The regret for each of the other two selling prices would be the difference between a contribution of M$450,000 and the contribution for each of the marketing packages.

Having calculated the regret for each different customer reaction, we can then establish the maximum regret for each marketing package. We then choose the marketing package with the minimum of the maximum regrets.

Use of probabilities

Probabilities could be used to calculate the expected value of the total contribution. The marketing package that gives the highest expected value would then be chosen. Expected value is seen as a risk neutral approach to decision making.

Expected value is calculated by weighting each of the possible outcomes by their associated probability. The expected value is therefore the weighted average of the possible outcomes based on estimates of their probability.

Expected value has a number of limitations as follows:

- The analysis is very dependent on the estimate of the probabilities which are very subjective and dependent on knowledge of the market.

- The expected value is merely a weighted average if the decision is repeated several times. In business, there are few decisions that would be repeated many times. In this case, this is a major one-off decision so reliance solely on expected value would not be appropriate.

- The expected value gives no indication of the dispersion of possible outcomes around the expected value i.e. the risk. For example, Marketing Package B has a relatively narrow range of possible outcomes whereas both Marketing Package A and C have a much wider dispersion.

- The expected value may not correspond to any of the actual possible outcomes as it is an average.

Calculating the standard deviation of the data will give us a clearer indication of the risk. The standard deviation is the square root of the sum of the squared deviations of each outcome from the expected value taking account of the associated probabilities. The higher the standard deviation, the more widely dispersed is the distribution and therefore the greater the inherent risk. The standard deviation can be considered in respect of how comfortable the directors are with the situation in light of their attitude to risk.

© Copyright CIMA – 2015 CIMA Professional Qualification Operational Level P1 Management Accounting Case Study Exam May 2017

Test your understanding 3

Analysis of variances

The overall performance as you suggested is significantly worse than budget. The budgeted contribution for the period was M$300,000 but the actual contribution was M$170,000 lower at M$130,000.

Looking at the individual variances we can get some indication of the reason for the poor performance.

Total sales volume variance

From the pre-seen material, we can see that the budget for self-drive cars for the first half of 2017 was to sell 20 units and make a contribution of M$600,000. This has obviously been split evenly between the two quarters. The total variance of M$150,000 means that only 5 vehicles were sold compared to the budget of 10 vehicles.

Note: the part of this answer that refers to the number of vehicles is not possible to achieve in this exercise given the limited pre-seen information presented in this chapter. However it is provided as an illustration of the type of information from the pre-seen material that can be used in an answer.

Sales volume contribution planning variance

The sales volume planning variance measures the difference between the sales volume in the original budget and the sales volume in the revised budget multiplied by the standard contribution. The planning variance is adverse and has arisen as the original sales volume budget was set too high. The fact that the competitor was planning to launch a new self-drive vehicle should have been taken into account in the original budget and a lower sales volume budget set, hence this is a planning variance.

Sales volume contribution operational variance

This variance is adverse therefore actual volume was lower than the revised budgeted volume. The lower sales volume may be at least partly due to the effect that the car crash has had on public perception of self-drive cars. The car crash arose as a result of an operational failure and, particularly as the report is directed at the board, this would be reported as an operational variance. A sales variance report directed at the Sales Manager for self-drive cars may classify the part of the volume variance arising as a result of the car crash as a planning variance due to the principle of controllability – the variance arose as a consequence of production failures which were not controllable by the Sales Manager. An alternative, and perhaps better, approach would be to split the variance between its controllable and uncontrollable elements. The amount specifically relating to the car crash may however be difficult to determine since there will be many other factors that may have led to reduced sales volumes.

Material price planning variance

The material price planning variance measures the difference between the standard purchase price of material in the original budget and the standard purchase price of material in the revised budget multiplied by the standard material quantity for the actual production volume. It relates to the change in the standard specification which should have been reflected in the original budget. The higher quality material would have been more expensive thus resulting in an adverse variance.

Sales price operational variance

This variance measures the difference in budgeted selling price and actual selling price for the actual volume sold. The difficulties that were being experience with sales volumes may have resulted in higher than average discounts being given to customers and hence the adverse variance.

Material usage operational variance

This variance measures the difference in standard quantity of material for the actual production volume and the actual material used. The variance is favourable, which may be related to the use of higher quality material. If so, this could be argued to be a planning variance as it should have been recognised in the original budget that the higher quality material would potentially result in less wastage and therefore lower usage.

Labour efficiency operational variance

This variance measures the difference in standard labour hours for the actual production volume and the actual labour hours. This variance is also favourable and may also be related to the change in material specification since the workers may have found it easier to work with the new higher quality material.